The African Studies Companion:
A Resource Guide & Directory

Second revised edition

The African Studies Companion:
A Resource Guide & Directory

HANS M. ZELL & CECILE LOMER

Second revised edition

HANS ZELL PUBLISHERS

London • Melbourne • Munich • New Providence • 1997

960.07
251 a 2

First edition 1989
Second edition 1997
© Hans M. Zell 1989
© Bowker-Saur 1997

British Library Cataloguing in Publication Data
Zell, Hans M. (Hans Martin), 1940-
    The African studies companion: a resource guide and directory. - 2nd rev. ed.
    1. Africa - Bibliography 2. Africa - Study and teaching - Handbooks, manuals, etc.
    I. Title II. Lomer, Cécile
    960'.07
    ISBN 1-873836-41-4

Library of Congress Cataloging-in-Publication Data
Zell, Hans M.
    The African studies companion: a resource guide and directory /
    Hans M. Zell & Cécile Lomer. -- 2nd rev. ed.
    292 pp. 22 cm.
    Includes bibliographical references and index.
    ISBN 1-873836-41-4
    1. Africa --Study and teaching -- Handbooks, manuals, etc.
    I. Lomer, Cécile II. Title
    DT19.8.Z45   1997   97-5671
    960'.07--DC21   CIP

Published by Hans Zell Publishers, an imprint of Bowker-Saur, a division of Reed Elsevier (UK) Limited, Maypole House, Maypole Road, East Grinstead, West Sussex RH19 1HU, United Kingdom
Tel: +44(0)1342 330100 Fax: +44(0)1342 330191
Email: lis@bowker-saur.co.uk WWW: http://www.bowker-saur.co.uk/service
Bowker-Saur is a part of REED BUSINESS INFORMATION.

Cover design by Robin Caira
Printed on acid-free paper.
Printed and bound in Great Britain
by Antony Rowe Ltd., Chippenham, Wiltshire.

Contents

Preface to the second edition

The aims of this new edition of the *African Studies Companion* remain essentially the same as that of the previous edition published in 1989, namely to provide within the covers of a single, compact volume, quick and easy access to a wide range of information in the African studies field. It is intended as a desktop companion and working tool for African studies scholars, teachers and students, and as a first, time-saving source of relevant information for anyone involved in any aspect of African studies. We hope that it will also prove valuable for Africana librarians, for reference collections in academic and public libraries which touch in any way on Africa, or for collection development librarians who wish to expand their African studies holdings.

As almost ten years have elapsed since the publication of the first edition, revisions and updates for the new edition have been quite substantial. In addition to thorough revisions for all sections contained in the book, we have now added complete international dialling codes for all telephone and fax numbers. The latter were still sparse in 1989, but are now included for most entries in the directory sections, as are Email addresses where available, Websites, and, for the section on major libraries, details of on-line public access catalogues available through the Internet. Most sections have been expanded to provide extra details, and although we have been constrained by space restrictions, we have aimed to pack in as much information as possible, and have endeavoured to ensure that this information is as up-to-date as possible.

The total number of entries has grown from 667 in the first edition to 935 in this new second edition.

For sections I & II - the annotated listing of reference resources, and the major current bibliographies and continuing sources for African studies - we have dropped a total of 40 titles from the first edition, but have added 114 new titles or new editions. We have *not* however included reference sources which in our opinion contain major shortcomings in terms of factual accuracy, or which we believe to be seriously flawed in other respects. Section I has been reorganized, with entries appearing under fifteen sub-headings. Most entries are books, but a small number of bibliographic or other listings published in periodicals or in edited collections are now also included. Guides to materials for children and young adults, or resources for elementary and secondary school teachers, have been dropped, as other useful guides to such material already exist.

Information contained in sections III, IV, V, VIII, IX, and X are all now part of a new database and have been updated through mailings of printouts and questionnaire forms. Whereas the response was not 100%, and a number of organizations, institutions, journals or publishers, etc. failed to update and verify information despite follow-up reminders (and are flagged accordingly) the overall response - after some dogged determination to get replies! - was generally satisfactory.

Acknowledgements

For revisions to section I, and as a source for new titles, the annual listings "Africana Reference Works: An Annotated List of [1989, and up to 1995] Titles", which have appeared in the second issue of each volume of *The African Book Publishing Record* since 1986, have been most valuable. The lists were edited by Joe Lauer until 1988, by Yvette Scheven from 1989-1992, and by Phyllis Bischof from 1993-1996, with the active assistance of several Africana librarians.

We know that completing questionnaires can be a tedious and time-consuming business, and we are indebted to all those librarians, journal editors, publishers, donor agency representatives, and others who verified and updated printouts sent to them, or who completed and returned our questionnaires, thus ensuring accurate and up-to-date information. It is our hope that, for subsequent editions of this resource guide, those who failed to respond on this occasion can be persuaded to do so in future.

Proof-reading this volume has also been a time-consuming business, and we are very grateful to Kenneth G. Kelly for helping us in this task.

Accuracy

Whereas we have taken great care to ensure accuracy in our listings, the Publishers cannot of course accept responsibility for accidental omissions or errors. It has not always been easy to decipher frequently hand-written information for telephone and fax numbers, Email addresses and Websites (especially when information was submitted by fax), and we would be grateful if any errors in this edition could be brought to our attention.

Oxford,
February 1997   Hans M. Zell & Cécile Lomer

Introduction

The African Studies Companion seeks to bring together a wide range of sources of information in the African studies field. It includes annotated listings of the major reference tools, current bibliographies and continuing sources; journals and magazines; major libraries; publishers with African studies lists; dealers and distributors of African studies materials; the major regional and international organizations; and it also identifies donor agencies and foundations active in Africa, and/or supporting research on Africa. Other sections include a listing of African studies associations and societies, academic and literary awards in the African studies/African literature field, and the final section is a listing some of the most commonly used abbreviations and acronyms in African studies.

Scope and definitions

Although we have widened the scope slightly for this new edition - especially for the section on journals, where we have included a number of literary, cultural, as well as business journals - the majority of listings identify *general* and *current* sources of information, and for the most part those in English. Section I provides an annotated listing of the major general reference resources in African studies, but does *not* include monographs or any other material not of a reference book nature. Most of the material has been personally examined by the compilers. A number of forthcoming 1997 titles have been included, but have not been examined.

For this edition we have dropped a number of titles that are now considered to be too dated to be of significant use as a reference source, but some of the older titles published during the 1980s (and a few before 1980) have been retained as they are still of value for reference and research.

For more specialist reference resources, for example those in the field of the arts and literature, or in agriculture, economics, politics, sociology, women's studies, etc, readers will need to consult other sources, and in the introductory note to section one we have drawn attention to a number of other reference works which provide access to more specialist bibliographies and reference tools.

Before using information in any parts of the *African Studies Companion*, readers are also advised to consult the introductory paragraphs and list of abbreviations for each section, which provide more details about scope and the data gathering process.

Entries and annotations/Prices

Most of the entries are extensively annotated, thus providing a whole array of specifics. In Section I the annotations, for the most part, are descriptive rather than critical, intending to place, not judge, the material listed, although we have drawn attention to a number of particularly important or outstanding reference resources.

Entries are consecutively numbered throughout. Fairly extensive cross-referencing forms an integral part of the book, thus enabling users to move from one entry to others of relevance.

We have aimed to provide full bibliographic data for each book or journal entry, including prices/subscription rates, and other essential acquisitions data.

For Sections I & II we have indicated current prices as far as available, and for which we have largely relied on information provided in publishers' catalogues. However, all prices are of course subject to change and some may no longer be current. Older titles which do not give an indication of price are likely to be out-of-print, but most will be found in major academic libraries.

Details of currencies/prices are given in their conventionally abbreviated forms. $ indicates US Dollars throughout, unless otherwise stated.

Telephone and fax numbers

All telephone and fax numbers are now given with their full international dialling codes. With the exception of UK listings, we have omitted the '0' figure following the country code and preceding the area code, and which should only be used when dialling from within the country. In many countries international network access is by dialling '00' ('011' in the US), followed by the country code, the area code and the number (though some countries, including several in Africa, require no area codes).

Data gathering

As already indicated in the preface, information for six sections in this book was collected through mailings of computer printouts from our database, and questionnaires for new entries or those requiring extensive revisions. Whereas overall the response was satisfactory, a number of organizations, institutions, publishers, etc. failed to reply and/or verify information, despite at least one chaser mailing. All these entries are marked either with the symbol † which indicates a repeat entry from the previous edition (updated, as far as possible, from secondary sources), or with the symbol Φ which indicates a *new* entry (for which, in the absence of a completed questionnaire, we have drawn unverified information from secondary sources). It goes without saying that information contained in entries with either of these two symbols must be used with caution.

Index

The index covers authors/editors (personal and corporate) and titles of books, titles of journals and continuing sources, names of journal editors, libraries and institutions, company names of publishers and of distributors and dealers, organizations, associations, foundations and donor agencies, and the names of awards/prizes. Names of personnel, other than journal editors, are not indexed. To provide additional means of access to the various listings, we have introduced a number of other, more general index entries which guide users to a *range* of entries and for which entry numbers appear in bold. It would be impossible, however, to provide a detailed subject index for a resource guide of this nature. For this edition we have also indexed the names of African publishers who are distributed by dealers in the UK or elsewhere although they may not have a main entry of their own, and the index entry may refer to the distributor.

Abbreviations and symbols

In order to save space this book contains a large number of abbreviations. Keys to abbreviations used for individual sections are provided at the beginning of each section. The following general abbreviations and symbols are also used throughout:

†   - indicates a repeat entry from the 1st edition (1989); information has not been verified; entry has been updated, as far as possible, from secondary sources

Φ   - indicates a provisional new entry, but questionnaire has not been completed; unverified information drawn from secondary sources

⌨   - indicates an electronic/online source

BP   - Boite Postal (PO Box)
Co   - Company
CP   - Caixa Postal/Case Postale (PO Box)
Email - Email address
Fax   - Facsimile address
Inc   - Incorporated
Ltd   - Limited Company
n/a   - not available/not disclosed
NGO   - non-government organization
plc   - Private Limited Company
PMB   - Private Mail Bag
POB   - Post Office Box
Tel   - Telephone (however, the abbreviation 'Tel' is generally omitted, and numbers only with country and area/STD codes are given immediately following the address. With the exception of UK telephone numbers, the initial '0' required for calls within the country has been omitted)

I. MAJOR GENERAL REFERENCE RESOURCES

This section provides a select listing of some of the key reference resources in the African studies field, primarily those written in English. It is confined to listings of *general* reference works and bibliographies only. For subject bibliographies, specialist resources, directories, etc. - for example on African art, African literature, African history etc. - consult Yvette Scheven's *Bibliographies for African Studies, 1970-1986*, and *1987-1993 (see* **34** *and* **35***)* or, for francophone Africa, Laurence Porges' *Sources d'Information sur l'Afrique Noire Francophone et Madagascar (see* **32***)*. For directories, dictionaries, handbooks, and other reference works consult John McIlwaine's *Africa: A Guide to Reference Material (see* **27***)*. The latter is also an excellent source for atlases, gazeteers and topographic reference works, which are *not* included in this section.

Africanist documentation and bibliography

1 Binns, Margaret. **"The Documentation of African Research."**
African Research and Documentation, no. 56 (1991): 1-34.
> A valuable survey of the current (as at 1991) state of documentation of Africanist research. Provides (1) an assessment of the major bibliographic tools covering African material, and their inclusion of material published in Africa; and (2) a study of African institutions to assess the work produced by them in the form of theses or research reports, and the extent to which this is documented in order to be accessible to others.

2 Guyer, Jane I. **African Studies in the United States. A Perspective.**
Atlanta, GA: African Studies Association Press, 1996. 106pp.
> An overview of the current status of African studies in the USA. Examines orientations in the scholarship on Africa in the US, linkages with Africa, patterns of advanced training in African studies, institutions involved in African studies and their future, and current debates and challenges. Also includes a variety of statistical analysis (e.g. on annual dissertation output), and a bibliography.

3 Larby, Patricia M. **New Directions in African Bibliography.**
London: SCOLMA, 1987. 159pp. £6.50
> The proceedings of SCOLMA's Silver Jubilee Conference, this collection of papers looks at future trends in African studies and their implications for libraries. Includes contributions and overviews on African studies research and documentation in Europe, North America, and Africa.

4 La Documentation africaniste en Europe. Africanist Documentation in Europe. Actes du colloque, Paris, 22-23 mars, 1986.
Strasbourg: Conseil européen des études africaines [3 rue de l'Argonne, F-67083 Strasbourg Cedex], 1987. 174pp.

> The proceedings of a conference held in Paris in 1986 and coinciding with the first General Assembly of the European Council on African Studies *(see **858***). Contains 17 papers on the state of Africanist documentation in Europe, including surveys of Africana library collections in several European countries. Two papers in English, the rest in French.

5 Otchere, Freda E. African Studies Thesaurus: Headings for Library Users. New York: Greenwood Press, 1992. 435pp. (Bibliographies and Indexes in Afro-American and African Studies, 29)

> Provides details of about 4,000 subject headings, including names of over 600 African peoples and some 600 African language headings. Includes Library of Congress classification numbers.

6 Sternberg, Ilse, and Patricia M. Larby. African Studies. Papers Presented at a Colloquium at the British Library, 7-9 January 1985.
London: The British Library in association with SCOLMA, 1986. 351pp. £17.95 (British Library Occasional papers, 6)

> Although not strictly a reference work, this volume is useful as a current (as at 1985) overview of the state of African studies in the UK and (to some extent) in Africa. The papers describe the resources available to researchers, the currency of guides and indexes to those resources, publishing and distribution problems for African studies in the UK, and international library and archival collaboration in the African studies field.

Annuals and yearbooks

7 Africa Contemporary Record. Annual Survey and Documents.
New York: Holmes & Meier, London: Rex Collings [1970-76] vol.I, 1968-69, published annually (later bi-annual), latest volume vol. XXII (1989-90), publ. 1996. 1,200pp. £295.00; forthcoming: vol. XXIII (1990-1992), due Winter 1996. ca. 1,500pp. Ed. by Colin Legum & John Drysdale [to 1988]; ed. by Marion Duro [from 1989]

> An annual work of analysis of political, economic, social, and constitutional developments covering all the countries on the African continent. Detailed articles and reviews on each African country. Also records the year's key documents from organizations such as the OAU, the UN, and the US House Committee on Foreign Affairs, and provides summaries and statistics regarding population growth, per capita GNP, oil and gas production, foreign aid, etc.

8 **Africa Review. The Economic and Business Report.** [1996 edition]
Saffron Walden: World of Information, 1996. 19th ed. 240pp. £40.00/$65.00
(in the US order from World of Information, POB 830430, Birmingham
AL 35283-0430)

> Annual economic and business survey of 53 African countries. Includes
> individual articles on economic and political developments and a general
> overview, together with chapters on each African country, each with analysis
> of the year's events, a country profile, key indicators, important facts, a
> business directory and business guide with listings of useful addresses, etc.
> Outline map for each country.

9 **Afrique noire politique et économique.** Paris: Ediafric-
La Documentation africaine, 1996. [1996 ed.] 304pp. FF220.00

> Annual survey charting political events and economic developments in the
> francophone countries of Africa. Issued as a special number each year of
> *Bulletin de l'Afrique Noire* (*see* **192**).

10 **New African Yearbook.** 10th ed. [1995-96 edition]
London: IC Publications Ltd, 1995. [in the US order from Hunter Publishing
Inc.] 496pp. £40.00/$65.00

> Annual publication covering all 53 African countries and offshore islands in
> alphabetical order, emphasizing basic factual material. Each country has
> sections on political history, the economy, politics, plus basic facts and the
> most up-to-date statistical data available. Also lists basic information and
> short profiles of the main African regional organizations. Outline map for
> each country.

11 **Africa South of the Sahara.** 25th ed. [1996 edition]
London: Europa Publications, 1989. 1,099pp. £180.00

> Annual survey and directory, covering political, social and economic
> developments during the preceding year in 52 African countries. Each country
> section includes background essays, economic, demographic and statistical
> survey/data, plus a wide-ranging directory of essential names and addresses
> most with telephone and fax numbers. Part one of the book, "Background to
> the Continent" provides a history of the continent and includes a series of
> essays by acknowledged experts on African affairs, covering topics such as
> recent political events, economic trends, evaluations of industrial and
> agricultural development prospects for sub-Saharan Africa, and of production,
> marketing and price movements in the principal African commodities. Part
> two, preceding the individual country surveys, provides details about the
> activities of African regional organizations. Each annual edition is
> substantially revised and updated to encompass the latest available facts,
> statistics and directory information.

Bibliographies and guides to sources

12 **African and African American Studies.**
Middletown, CT: CHOICE [100 Riverview Center, Middletown, CT 06457], 1992. 146pp. $22.00 (Choice Ethnic Studies Reviews)
> A cumulative volume of 754 book reviews which appeared in volumes 27-29 (September 1989-July 1992) of *Choice*, the publication of the Association of College and Research Libraries, a division of the American Library Association. Arranged by subject, with indexes by author and title.

13 **African Books in Print. An Index by Author, Title and Subject/Livres africains disponibles.** Ed. by Hans M. Zell. 4th ed.
London: Hans Zell Publishers, 1993. 2 vols. 1,520pp. £250.00/$400.00 set
> Lists 23,186 titles in print as at the end of 1991, from 745 publishers and research institutions with publishing programmes, in 45 African countries. Arranged under some 1,500 subject headings. Covers material in English and in French, plus a substantial number of titles in over 100 African languages. Cumulates the bibliographic listings in the quarterly *African Book Publishing Record (see 234)*. (New 5th edition of *ABIP* is to be published early in 1998.)

14 **APEX 96. African Periodical Exhibit 1996. Catalogue.**
Harare: Zimbabwe International Book Fair Trust [POX CY 1179], and London: Southern African Book Development Trust/SABDET [25 Endymion Road, London N4 1EE], 1996. 50pp. gratis
> Catalogue of 142 African periodicals, from 26 countries, displayed at a collective exhibit during the 1996 Zimbabwe International Book Fair, and which has now become an annual feature at ZIBF. Provides full address details for each journal and telephone/fax numbers, name of editor(s), year first published and latest issue, frequency, ISSN, subscription rates, together with a brief outline of contents.

15 Besterman, Theodore. **A World Bibliography of African Bibliographies.** Revised and updated by J.D. Pearson.
Oxford: Blackwell (Totowa, NJ: Rowman and Littlefield), 1975. 241 columns
> An extract of 1,136 titles from Besterman's *A World Bibliography of Bibliographies* (4th ed. 1963), together with a further 498 items added by J.D. Pearson, and published between 1963 and 1973. Entries are arranged under geographical divisions and thereafter in regional or subject division; plus an author and title index.

16 Blackhurst, Hector. **East and Northeast Africa Bibliography.**
Lanham MD, and London: Scarecrow Press, 1996. 301pp. $62.50 (Scarecrow Area Bibliographies, 7)
> A companion volume to the Southern Africa bibliography (*see 29*) listing some 3,800 entries covering Djibouti, Eritrea, Ethiopia, Kenya, Somalia,

Sudan, Tanzania and Uganda, published between 1960 and 1994, and arranged by subject headings. Author index.

17 Duignan, Peter, and Helen F. Conover. **Guide to Research and Reference Works on Sub-Saharan Africa.** Stanford: Hoover Institution Press, 1971. 1,102pp. (Hoover Institution on War, Revolution and Peace, Bibliographical Series, 46)

> A major and pioneering reference source for material published to 1969/70. 3,127 fully annotated entries arranged in topical and geographical sections, each with extensive details about bibliographies and other reference works, as well as serials. Indexes by author name, title, subject, and geographical location.

18 Fage, J.D. **A Guide to Original Sources for Precolonial Western Africa Published in European Languages: For the Most Part in Book Form.** Rev. ed. Madison, WI: African Studies Program, University of Wisconsin, 1994. 200pp. $30.00

> A core resource list. (Not examined)

19 Fenton, Thomas, and Mary Heffron. **Africa: Africa World Press Guide to Educational Resources from and about Africa.** Trenton , NJ: Africa World Press, forthcoming 1997. ca. 200pp. ca. $16.95

> An introductory guide to resources from and about Africa. 28 chapters - with printed material arranged by subject and sub-divided into books/pamphlets and serial publications, and audio-visual materials grouped by visual and audio resources - provide full bibliographic details and acquisitions data on a wide range of recommended materials. This covers a good proportion of African-published materials "to magnify the voices of those whose perspectives on Africa are not now adequately represented in the mainstream media and in materials used in libraries and schools in countries like the United States." The guide also includes extensive listings of organizations. (Not examined)

20 Gorman, G.E., and J. J. Mills. **Guide to Current National Bibliographies in the Third World.** 2nd rev. ed. London: Hans Zell Publishers, 1987. 392pp.

> Arranged alphabetically by country, this is a detailed survey of all Third World national bibliographies. Each entry includes full bibliographic citation, publisher address and current cost; a historical outline of the compilation; an objective statement of scope and contents; and an analysis of coverage together with critical commentary on usefulness and value. (A new 3rd edition of this book is scheduled for publication in 1999.)

21 Gorman, G.E., and J.J. Mills. **Guide to Current Indexing and Abstracting Services in the Third World.** London: Hans Zell Publishers, 1992. 278pp. £50.00/$85.00

> A companion volume to entry **20** above, which analyzes the contents of more than 120 current indexing and abstracting services published in the Third

World. Each entry gives full bibliographic citation and publication details, a statement of the scope and arrangement and a full description of contents, together with a critical assessment of the organization of each indexing and abstracting service and the accuracy of the information provided.

22 Gosebrink, Jean E. Meeh. **African Studies Information Resources Directory.** Oxford: Hans Zell Publishers (New York: K.G. Saur), 1986. 585pp.
Provides a comprehensive reference and research tool for identifying sources of information and documentation on sub-Saharan Africa located in the United States. Conceived as a partial revision of Peter Duignan's *Handbook of American Resources for African Studies,* it includes 437 entries (many with extensive sub-divisions) and is arranged alphabetically in four major sections: (1) Information Resources for African Studies; (2) Resources in Church and Mission Organizations; (3) Bookstores, Book Dealers and Distributors of Africa-related Materials; (4) Publishers. Includes an index to subjects, persons, places and institutions, and organizations mentioned in the text. Now somewhat dated, but still a valuable resource.

23 Howell, J.B., with Steven James Browne and Barbara M. Howell. **Index to the African Studies Review/Bulletin and the ASA Review of Books, 1958-1990.** Atlanta, GA: African Studies Association, 1991. 227pp. $7.00
An index to articles in the *ASA Bulletin* (later *ASA Review, see* **290**) to 1990; also provides indexes to book reviews in the latter and the *ASA Review of Books*, and the names of reviewers in these two sources.

24 **International African Bibliography 1973-1978; Books, Articles and Papers in African Studies.** Ed. by J.D. Pearson. London: Mansell, 1982. 374pp. £65.00/$130.00
Cumulates 24 consecutive issues (vols. 3-8) of *International African Bibliography (see* **171***)*, and adds some 3,000 further entries. Arrangement is by subject and regions, and thereafter sub-divided by country/subject.

25 International African Institute. **Cumulative Bibliography of African Studies.** Boston: G.K. Hall, 1973. Microfilm. Author catalog, 4 reels $200.00 Classified Catalog, 6 reels $300.00
Contains all the titles of books and articles listed in the quarterly bibliography published in the journal *Africa (see* **225***)*, from 1929 to 1970, and in the *International African Bibliography (see* **171***)* during 1971 and 1972.

26 Kagan, Alfred. **"Sources for African Language Materials from the Countries of Africa."** *IFLA Journal* [The Hague], 22, no. 1 (1996): 42-45.
A useful article which surveys the standard current reference sources for African language material, blanket and approval plan dealers who supply books in African languages, bookshops and publishers, printed and on-line library catalogues, and two microform collections.

27 McIlwaine, John. **Africa: A Guide to Reference Material.** London: Hans Zell Publishers, 1993. 592pp. £75.00/$145.00 (Regional Reference Guides, 1)
A highly acclaimed reference resource which evaluates the leading sources of information on Africa South of the Sahara, *other than* bibliographies (for the latter see the reference works by Yvette Scheven, *see* **34** and **35**). The volume includes 1,766 annotated entries, covering encyclopedias, dictionaries, directories, handbooks, gazeteers, almanacs, yearbooks, as well as topographical and statistical sources, and some other categories. Each title is described and analyzed for content, comprehension and ease of use. With a combined author, title and subject index.

28 McIlwaine, John. **Maps and Mapping of Africa. A Resource Guide.** London: Hans Zell Publishers, forthcoming 1997. ca. 350pp. ca. £60.00/$100.00
Contains some 1,500 bibliographical, partially annotated references to writings about maps, mapping and toponymy of Africa - both historical and contemporary - including bibliographies and catalogues, mapping and survey material, atlases and gazetteers, guides to map collections, together with a directory of overseas libraries and archives with African map collections. (Draft ms. copy only examined)

29 Musiker, Reuben, and Naomi Musiker. **Southern Africa Bibliography.** Lanham, MD, and London: Scarecrow Press, 1996. 287pp. $52.00 (Scarecrow Area Bibliographies, 11)
Aims to bring together all books published during the past half century (i.e. since 1945) dealing with Southern Africa: Angola, Botswana, Lesotho, Malawi, Mozambique, Namibia, South Africa Swaziland, Zambia, and Zimbabwe. Arrangement is alphabetical by country, subarranged by fairly broad subject fields, some of which have further sub-divisions. Author index. (*Note:* periodical or newspaper articles are not included. For these the reader is referred to a database available on CD-ROM: SARDIUS, the Southern African Research and Documentation and Information User Service, compiled at the Jan Smith House Library, Johannesburg, in association with the South African Institute of International Affairs, and Witwatersrand University Library: Grahamstown, 1994-)

30 Northwestern University. Melville Herskovits Library of African Studies. **Africana File Listing as of April 1988.** Evanston, IL: Melville J. Herskovits Library of African Studies, Northwestern University Library, 1988. 61 microfiche
An index of all major publications in Northwestern University Library's *(see* **468***)* extensive Africana vertical files, containing African government publications, political party and trade union materials, and company reports. 16,000 records are accessible by 37,000 index entries. Volume holdings of serials are included. There is a combined index by author, title, and added entry, in a single alphabetical sequence.

31 Pluge, John jr. **African Newspapers in the Library of Congress.**
Washington, DC: Library of Congress, Serial and Government Publications
Division, 1984. 144pp.
Lists over 900 newspapers, arranged by country, city, title, plus a title index.

32 Porges, Laurence. **Sources d'information sur l'Afrique noire
francophone et Madagascar. Institutions, répertoires, bibliographies.**
Paris: La Documentation française/Ministère de la coopération, 1988. 389pp.
FF150.00
A comprehensive guide to sources of information on francophone Black
Africa and Madagascar, containing 1,498 mostly annotated entries, and
several indexes. Part one lists sources for research institutions, associations
and societies, libraries and documentation centres, official publications,
magazines and periodicals, theses, and general and specialist bibliographies.
Part two provides an inventory of bibliographies, directories and other sources
of information on a country-by-country basis, with each country section also
including information about institutes, research centres and universities, as
well as museums, archival collections, and more.

33 **Répertoire de périodiques paraissant en Afrique au Sud du Sahara
(sciences sociales et humaines).** Comp. by M. Aghassian. Paris: Centre national
de la recherche scientifique, Centre de documentation sciences humaines, 1982.
83pp.
Lists 344 periodicals on Africa South of the Sahara in the social sciences and
the humanities, giving library locations and including a directory of libraries
in Paris and their addresses.

34 Scheven, Yvette. **Bibliographies for African Studies, 1970-1986.**
Oxford: Hans Zell Publishers, 1988. 637pp. £67.00/$110.00

35 - - - - **Bibliographies for African Studies, 1987-1993.** London: Hans Zell
Publishers, 1994. 198pp. £42.00/$70.00
The definitive resource for bibliographies published in the African studies
field. The volume covering the period 1970-1986 provides 3,245 annotated
references, with each entry giving information about the scope and number of
items in each bibliography, whether it is annotated, how it is arranged, and the
type of index(es) included. The continuation volume for 1987-1993 (and
which is a cumulation of the annual listings of new 'Africana Reference
Works' which have appeared in *The African Book Publishing Record, see*
234), gives details of a further 834 titles. Arrangement in the 1970-1986
volume is by some 100 subject and geographical sections; the supplementary
volume lists titles under Library of Congress subject headings. Author and
subject indexes facilitate access.

36 Schmidt, Nancy J. **"Africana Resources for Undergraduates: A Bibliographic Essay."** In *Africa* ed. by Phyllis M. Martin and Patrick O'Meara, 3rd ed. Bloomington, IN: Indiana University Press; London: James Currey, 1995. pp. 411-434.

A bibliographic essay - helpful both for undergraduates, and librarians who select materials for undergraduate collections - which forms a chapter in a popular introductory text for African studies courses. It describes general, easily accessible, resources for students starting off in African studies, with a focus on resources in English, published or reissued since 1980. It includes details of a number of audiovisual and computer resources, as well as journals and reference materials. Arranged under broad subject sections.

37 Shayne, Mette. **African Newspapers Currently Received by American Libraries.** rev. ed. Summer 1995. Evanston: Melville J. Herskovits Library of African Studies, Northwestern University, 1995. 32pp. gratis

A union list that aims to help researchers to locate African newspapers in US libraries. The list surveys the holdings of 17 libraries, and about 220 titles. Arrangement is by country of publication, with library location symbols indicated with each newspaper.

38 Travis, Carole, and Miriam Alman. **Periodicals from Africa: A Bibliography and Union List of Periodicals Published in Africa.** Boston: G.K. Hall, 1977. 619pp.

Lists 17,000 titles with locations in 60 British libraries, covering all countries except Egypt. *First Supplement* by D.S. Blake and C. Travis (Boston: G.K. Hall, 1984, 217pp.) gives a further 7,000 titles published through August 1979. A *Second Supplement*, by D.S. Blake is in preparation. Published for SCOLMA.

39 U.S. Library of Congress. African Section. **Africa South of the Sahara: Index to Periodical Literature, 1900-1970.** Boston: G.K. Hall, 1971. Microfilm 8 reels $365.00 First Supplement. 1973. 1 reel $135.00 Second Supplement. 1981. 3 reels $265.00 Third Supplement. 1985. 3 reels $265.00

Records serial articles relating to Africa South of the Sahara from 1900 onwards. The main work cites 80,000 references from 1,530 journals; arranged geographically with broad subject divisions. *First Supplement*: 14,100 entries; *Second Supplement*: 41,000 entries (1972-1976); *Third Supplement*: a further 4,199 citations of articles published in 1977.

40 Westfall, Gloria. **French Colonial Africa: A Guide to Official Sources.** London: Hans Zell Publishers, 1992. 224pp. £49.00/$85.00

Provides access to information on political, economic, social and cultural conditions in the former French colonial territories in Africa. Covers the basic reference tools, research guides and bibliographies, archival sources in France and in Africa, official and semi-official publications, and publications of colonial governments. With an index of authors, subjects, and distinctive titles.

41 Witherell, Julian. **The United States and Sub-Saharan Africa: Guide to US Official Documents and Government-Sponsored Publications, 1785-1975.** Washington, DC: Library of Congress, 1978. 949pp.

Over 8,800 annotated entries, in five chronological sections which are subdivided by region or country (and 1952-75 further sub-divided by subjects). Covers largely holdings at the Library of Congress, plus some at 45 other libraries; very extensively indexed. Continued by Witherell's *The United States and Sub-Saharan Africa: Guide to Official Documents and Government-Sponsored Publications, 1976-1980,* listing a further 5,074 entries. (1984. 721pp.)

42 The World Bank. **Bibliography of Publications, Technical Department, Africa Region, July 1987 to April 1996.** Ed. by P.C. Mohan. Washington, DC: The World Bank, 1996. 52pp. $16.95/£7.15 (World Bank Technical Paper, 329)

A complete annotated listing of all formal and informal publications produced by the staff and consultants of the Africa Technical Department of the World Bank, from July 1987 through April 1996, covering the Technical Department's work in Africa in all sectors. Arranged by departmental and divisional publications, and chronologically within each section; and information is given how to acquire these publications.

Biographical sources

43 **Africa Who's Who.** Publisher and editor-in-chief: Raph Uwechue. Senior Research Editor: Pramila Bennett. 3rd ed. London: Africa Books Ltd, 1996. 1,507pp. £195.00/$295.00

Biographical profiles of about 14,000 eminent Africans. Each entry includes full name and address (and telephone/fax numbers for many), date and place of birth and nationality, marital status, occupation, education, degrees awarded, education, career details and appointments held, current position/affiliation, major publications, and hobbies. The introduction does not provide details of the data gathering and data verification process (or whether all entrants in fact verified or updated their entries), however, for the most part information seems to be current as at the end of 1995, although some entries are dated. This impressive who's who includes not only politicians, diplomats, and statesmen/women, but also broadcasters, writers, journalists, artists, academics, librarians, civil servants, military personnel, trade unionists, lawyers and jurists, scientists, physicians, engineers, clergymen, sportsmen and women, as well as prominent figures from business and industry. This is probably the best biographical source currently available.

44 African Biographical Archive (AfBA)/Archives biographiques africaines/Afrikanisches Biographisches Archive. Microfiche edition. Editor: Victor Herrero Mediavilla. Munich: K.G. Saur Verlag. 1994-1997. Est. 450 fiches, to be delivered in 12 instalments [parts 1-6 issued to date]. DM19,800/$14,575 (diazo), DM21,840/$16,075 (silver) (in the US order from University Publications of America)

> This reference source on microfiche will, when completed in 1997, contain approximately 113,000 biographical entries for some 75,000 individuals, and drawing on 231 sources published between 1840-1993, in several Western languages. The sources used comprise a variety of biographical reference works and works of collective biography, e.g. encyclopedias, who's whos, historical dictionaries, and other sources. It covers eminent African personalities from all walks of life, including political and religious leaders, scholars, artists and writers. Post-1950 publications constitute about 80% of all sources from which material is reproduced; titles published prior to 1950 cover largely non-African persons such as explorers, colonial rulers and administrators, and missionaries. A complete list of sources is available free from the publishers. An index will be published upon completion of the collection. (Not examined)

'African Historical Dictionaries' series, *see* **55**

45 Brockman, Norbert C. An African Biographical Dictionary. Santa Barbara, CA & Oxford, England: ABC-Clio Ltd, 1996. 440pp. £59.95/$60.00

> 550 biographical sketches (some accompanied by photographs) of prominent Africans, as well as foreigners, who have affected the continent's history, with an emphasis on the 20th century. A number of appendices list individuals by country and by field of accomplishment, and there is also a listing of heads of state since independence.

46 Dictionary of African Biography/Encyclopaedia Africana. Accra: Encyclopaedia Africana Project; Algonac, MI: Reference Publications Inc, 1977- 20 vols.

Volume 1: **Ethiopia-Ghana.** 1977. 370pp. $75.00
Volume 2: **Sierra Leone-Zaire.** 1979. 374pp. $75.00
Volume 3: **South Africa-Botswana-Lesotho-Swaziland.** 1995. 304pp. $75.00

> An ambitious project that had its roots in an idea for a comprehensive 'Encyclopaedia Africana' first proposed as far back as 1909 by W.E.B. du Bois, and revived by Kwame Nkrumah in the early 1960s. Unfortunately, the project has been plagued by numerous problems, political upheavals, and funding difficulties. To date only three volumes have appeared. Written by Africanist scholars, each volume contains a series of full biographies (preceded by an historical introduction). Volume 1 contains 152 biographies on Ethiopia and 138 on Ghana; volume 2, 137 biographies on Sierra Leone, and 103 on Zaire. And the latest volume on Southern Africa published in 1995 contains 228 biographies, together with photographs, maps, a concise guide to names and terms, bibliographies, many cross-references, and an

extensive subject index. Further volumes are planned, but no precise publication schedule is available at this time.

47 Glickman, Harvey. **Political Leaders of Contemporary Africa South of the Sahara: A Biographical Dictionary**. Westport, CT: Greenwood Press, 1992. 364pp. £55.50/$65.00

Profiles of 54 major, politically influential personalities in Sub-Saharan Africa since 1945. Includes a chronology and an index.

48 Kirk-Greene, A.H.M. **A Biographical Dictionary of the British Colonial Service, 1939-1966**. London: Hans Zell Publishers, 1991. 420pp. £98.00/$165.00

A who's who of the British Colonial Service during the final quarter-century of Britain's imperial history. The dictionary consists of nearly 15,000 entries, listing every member of the British Colonial Service whose name appeared in the official Colonial Office Lists. It covers the professional as well as the administrative services.

49 Lipschutz, Mark R., and R. Kent Rasmussen. **Dictionary of African Historical Biography** 2nd ed., Berkeley: University of California Press, 1986. 328pp.

Arranged in dictionary form and contains some 850 biographical sketches of African historical figures. The second edition has a supplement that also covers 57 post-1960 political leaders.

50 **Makers of Modern Africa. Profiles in History**. Publisher and editor-in-chief: Raph Uwechue. Senior Research Editor: Appiah Sackey. 3rd ed. London: Africa Books Ltd, 1996. 733pp. £95.00/$145.00

Illustrated throughout with halftones and drawings, this volume sets out the life histories of some 600 distinguished Africans, both past and present (and both those living and dead) who have played a significant part - in a social, political, economic, or cultural sense - in shaping the continent that is Africa today. Each entry provides a fairly full biographical sketch. For those still alive, information is up-to-date to the end of 1995. Companion volume to *Africa Who's Who, see* **43**, and *Africa Today, see* **141**. (The three volumes are available as a set at a special price of £445.00/$670.00.)

51 **Profiles of African Scientists**. Nairobi: African Academy of Sciences [distr. by African Books Collective Ltd, Oxford], 1991. 2nd. ed. 661pp. £25.00/$45.00

Some 350 biographical profiles of African scientists and their work. Arranged by country, information for each entry includes biographical data and full contact address, professional/academic career, professional qualifications, achievements, major publications, and current research interests. With an index by name and scientific disciplines. Most entries include a small photograph. (*See also* entry **84**)

52 Rake, Alan. **Who's Who in Africa: Leaders for the 1990s.** Metuchen,
NJ: Scarecrow Press, 1992. 448pp. $59.50
'Penportraits' and chronological life histories of contemporary African
political figures. Arranged by country, with basic political data on each
country preceding the biographies.

53 Reich, Bernard. **Political Leaders of the Contemporary Middle East
and North Africa: A Biographical Dictionary.** Westport, CT: Greenwood
Press, 1990. 557pp. $79.95
Biographical essays on 70 prominent Middle Eastern and North African
political leaders who have made an impact on world events since World War
II. Includes bibliographies of works by, and about, the persons profiled.

54 Wiseman, John A. **Political Leaders in Black Africa: A Biographical
Dictionary of the Major Politicians since Independence.**
Aldershot, UK: Edward Elgar, [distr. in the US by Ashgate, Brookfield, VT]
1991. 248pp. £50.00/$74.95
Brief biographies for 485 Africans, primarily, though not exclusively, political
figures; with a chronology of major events since 1960 for each country, and a
geographical index.

Dictionaries and glossaries

55 'African Historical Dictionaries' series. Series Editor: Jon Woronoff.
Metuchen, NJ: Scarecrow Press, 1975- var. pp. £24.50/$48.50 to £58.00/$92.50
per volume [Full details available from publisher]
This excellent series currently comprises 47 volumes on individual African
countries (several titles have been updated since first published, and have
been published in revised editions). They provide, in dictionary form, basic
information about each country's geography, history, economic and social
aspects, events, institutions, and major persons and leaders. The biographical
entries cover past and present political leaders, statesmen, diplomats, military
leaders, educators, labour leaders, religious leaders, prominent traders and
business leaders, and entrepreneurs.

56 Grace, John, and John Laffin. **Fontana Dictionary of Africa since 1960:
Events, Movements, Personalities.** London: Fontana Books, 1991. 395pp.
£7.99
Covers political and some literary figures, and political groups, together with
some basic factual information about each country.

57 Kurian, George. **The Glossary of the Third World**. New York and
Oxford, UK: Facts on File, 1989. 320pp. £20.00/$35.00
> Defines over 10,000 words dealing with politics, culture, arts, customs, legal
> systems, military, agricultural, transportation, commerce, etc. covering some
> 120 countries.

58 Nuñez, Benjamin, **Dictionary of Portuguese-African Civilization**.
2 vols. Volume 1: **From Discovery to Independence**. Volume 2: **From
Ancient Kings to Presidents**. London: Hans Zell Publishers, vol. 1, 1995.
560pp. £65.00/$110.00; vol. 2, 1996. 502pp. £65.00/$110.00
> Volume 1 includes some 3,000 terms and phrases as they relate to the
> Portuguese presence in Africa, covering historical and political events, social
> life and customs, religion, geographical names, flora, fauna, artefacts,
> organizations, literature, culture, and more. Volume 2 provides over 2,000
> biographical sketches of Europeans, Africans, Arabs and others who played
> an important role in the making of the five Portuguese-speaking countries of
> Africa.

59 Olson, James S. **The Peoples of Africa: an Ethnohistorical Dictionary**.
Westport, CT: Greenwood Press, 1996. 681pp. $96.00/£79.50
> Provides brief descriptions (and population estimates for many) of some 1,800
> African ethnic groups, some of which are discussed in terms of their
> geographical settings, religion, population, and economy. Most entries - some
> rather eclectic - cite sources of information, and the volume is extensively
> cross-referenced. With a chronology of African history and a select
> bibliography.

60 Passevant, Christiane, and Lany Portis. **Dictionnaire black**.
Paris: Jacques Grancher, 1995. 528pp. FF185.00
> Chronicles the life histories of some 100 persons of African descent in Africa
> and the diaspora, covering writers, movie-makers, musicians, dancers, artists,
> and some sportsmen/women. (Not examined)

61 Shavit, David. **The United States in Africa: A Historical Dictionary**.
New York: Greenwood Press, 1989. 320pp $59.95
> Information about the persons, institutions (e.g. missionary societies and other
> groups), and events that have affected relations between the US and Africa
> over the last 200 years or so. Includes a short bibliographical essay for each
> country, as well as an index of individuals by profession and occupation.

62 Welsh, Brian W.W., and Pavel Butorin. **Dictionary of Development:
Third World Economy, Environment, Society**. New York: Garland, 1990
2 vols. 1,194pp. $150.00 (Garland Reference Library of Social Science, 487)
> Defines and describes major factors, concepts, and issues as they relate to the
> development process. Provides developing country indicator charts for
> African countries, with evaluations of issues and policies, together with a
> compendium of economic and social statistics, a listing of NGOs involved in

the development field, and a listing of journals and newsletters devoted to development topics. Lacks indexes.

Directories (General)

63 The African Book World & Press: A Directory/Répertoire du livre et de la presse en Afrique. Ed. by Hans M. Zell 4th rev. ed. Oxford: Hans Zell Publishers, 1989. 336pp. £87.00/$135.00

A reference tool on the African book world and print media providing comprehensive information on libraries, publishers and the retail book trade, research institutions with publishing programmes, magazines and periodicals, major newspapers, as well as the printing industries. Most entries are extensively annotated. Arranged in 52 country-by-country sections, the fourth edition includes 4,435 entries. Now somewhat dated.

64 African Publishers Networking Directory, 1997/98. 2nd ed. Oxford: African Books Collective Ltd, 1997. 60pp. £18.00/$30.00 [gratis to the book communities in Africa]

Lists almost 400 of the major and/or most active publishers in Africa today. In addition to full address details, and telephone, fax numbers, and Email addresses, provides a variety of extra specifics on each company, including names of chief executives, number of titles in print, nature of each publisher's list and areas of specialization, and overseas distributors in Europe and North America. Also includes a directory of African book trade journals, book trade organizations and details of major reference resources and bibliographic tools on African publishing.

65 Africana Librarians Council Directory. Comp. by Greg Finnegan. Cambridge, MA: Africana Librarians Council. [c/o Greg Finnegan, Tozzer Library, Harvard University, 21 Divinity Avenue, Cambridge, MA 02138-2089]. 1996. 18pp. gratis

Compiled for the use of members of the Africana Librarians Council of the (US) African Studies Association *(see* **854**), this directory lists the names of Africana librarians at the major institutions in the USA, as well as listing a small number of Africana book dealers. Gives 86 names and addresses, with telephone, fax numbers and Email addresses.

66 Current African Directories. 2nd ed. Beckenham, UK: CBD Research Ltd [Chancery House, 15 Wickham Road, Beckenham, Kent, BR3 2SJ], forthcoming 1997. ca. 300pp. ca. £87.00/$160.00

Supersedes *Current African Directories, Incorporating African Companies - A Guide to Sources of Information*, published in 1972. Arranged country-by-country, contains full bibliographic and acquisitions data and contents descriptions of (i) commercial directories and membership lists of trade associations and professional bodies, and (ii) guides to sources of information for company data. With index of titles, subject index and directory of publishers. (Not examined)

67 Fenton, Thomas P., and Mary J. Heffron. **Third World Resource Directory, 1994-1995. An Annotated Guide to Print and Audiovisual Resources from and about Africa, Asia & Pacific, Latin America & Caribbean, and the Middle East.** Maryknoll, NY: Orbis Books, 1994. 785pp. $75.00

> A rich source of reference for up-to-date - and sometimes hard-to-find - information and materials on Third World countries containing over 2,500 annotated entries, plus a directory of 2,300 international NGOs. The annotated listings provide full acquisitions data and prices of books, magazines and periodicals, pamphlets, videos, and other resources. Gives special attention to information and perspectives often overlooked in other reference publications: grassroots movements, economic and political alternatives, and issues of social justice. Fully indexed.
>
> *Note:* new 1998-1999 edition to be published by Pluto Press, London, and M.E. Sharpe, Armonk, NY, in Spring 1998. The contents of the 1994-1995 edition, along with the contents of recent issues of *Worldviews, see* **311**, are available on-line in a WAIS full-text database:
> 🖳 http://www.igc.org/worldviews/wvwais.html

68 Maja-Pearce, Adewale. **Directory of African Media**. Brussels: International Federation of Journalists/Fédération internationale des journalistes [rue Royale 266, 1210 Brussels, Belgium], 1996. 384pp. (price not reported) [also available in a French edition as *Annuaire de la presse africaine*]

> This is probably the most up-to-date directory on the press in Africa. However its title is somewhat misleading as the directory omits government-owned newspapers, and provides only listings of independent newspapers (and a number of magazines). Information for each entry is very full and includes name and address, telephone and fax numbers, name of publisher, managing editor and/or name of executive editor, date founded, frequency, format, circulation, and more. Listings are preceded by informative short essays presenting an overview of the state of the media in each African country.

69 Peters, Suzanne, and Jean-Pierre Poulet, *et al.* **Directory of Museums in Africa/Répertoire des musées en Afrique**. London: Kegan Paul International and UNESCO-ICOM, 1990. 211pp.

> Co-published with UNESCO/International Council of Museums Documentation Centre, this directory lists 503 museums in 48 African countries (excluding South Africa), though about half of the entries provide no more than a listing of the museum's name and address.

70 Stubbs, Lucy. **The Third World Directory 1997/98**. 3rd ed. London: The Directory of Social Change [24 Stephenson Way, London NW1 2DP], 1996. 216pp. £12.95

A guide to development organizations, volunteering opportunities and sources of funding, primarily addressed to those who might want to undertake volunteer work in Third World countries, or seek funding for projects. Part 1 lists over 200 UK-based organizations working in the development field, and Part 2 provides details of over 100 sources of funding for overseas development work. Also contains articles on working in a developing country, campaigning, and volunteering. With an index to organizations by the region and/or countries of their interest, and the main areas in which they are involved.

Directories of organizations

71 Belaouane-Gherari, Sylvie, and Habib Gherari. **Les Organisations régionales africaines. Receuil de textes et documents. Regroupements économiques, banques, organisations de mise en valeur, associations de producteurs.** Paris: Ministère de la coopération et du développement, La Documentation française, 1988. 472pp. FF250.00
  Directory of African regional organizations, with details of their aims and objectives, activities, charters, publications, etc.

72 **Contact Africa. A Directory of Organizations in Washington DC Involved in African Affairs.** Washington, DC: The African-American Institute, Washington Office, 1992. 69pp. $22.00
  Lists international organizations, NGOs, US government organizations and private consultant firms with offices in Washington DC.

73 **Directory of Development Institutions in Africa, 1991.** Addis Ababa: Pan African Development Information Systems/PADIS, UN Economic Commission for Africa, 1991. 112pp. (ST/ECA/PADIS/DAI/91)
  Profiles of 115 development institutions in Africa, giving full contact information, personnel, details of activities, publications issued, and other details.

74 DeLancey, Mark W., and Terry M. Mays. **Historical Dictionary of International Organizations in Sub-Saharan Africa.** Metuchen, NJ: Scarecrow Press, 1994. 515pp. $67.50 (International Organizations series, 3)
  An extensive research guide, in dictionary format, to international and inter-governmental organizations and NGOs active in Sub-Saharan Africa: regional, pan-African, sub-regional, African-European and African-Arab. Entries cover not only organizations - with descriptions of their roles and activities - but also include short entries and profiles of individuals who have played a significant part in the history of African international organizations. Additionally, the volume contains a very substantial bibliography of some 2,400 items by theme, a detailed chronology of organizations for 1885-1992, a list of acronyms and abbreviations, and three appendixes: African

organizations classified by field of activity; the charter of the Organisation of African Unity; and a listing of the past Secretaries General of the OAU and the Executive Secretaries of the UN Economic Commission for Africa.

75 Fredland, Richard. **A Guide to African International Organizations**. Oxford: Hans Zell Publishers, 1990. 324pp. £52.00/$85.00

Records and analyzes the activities of almost 500 international organizations which have appeared on the African continent in this century, and provides critical analysis and commentary on these organizations, together with historical background, etc. For organizations active today it also includes such details as addresses and names of executive personnel, though some of this information is now dated.

76 Söderbaum, Fredrik. **Handbook of Regional Organizations in Africa**. Uppsala, Sweden: Nordiska Afrikainstitutet, 1996. 161pp. £13.95 [distributed by Almqvist & Wiksell International, POB 4627, SE-11691 Stockholm, Sweden; distributed in the UK by Africa Book Centre Ltd, London]

Aims to provide an up-to-date, user-friendly, annotated reference guide to regional organizations currently in existence in Africa, with a focus on intergovernmental regional organizations. Includes some 200 entries. Part I covers the main regional and continental organizations in Africa, and for each organization gives an outline of its aims, history, structure, activities, member countries, publications issued, and secretariat/headquarters information with complete address and telephone and fax numbers. Part II covers other regional organizations in Africa, with the same type of information, but much briefer details. This is probably the best and most up-to-date guide to African organizations currently available; its only minor flaw is that it lacks an index of all the organizations listed in the book. An appendix provides an 'Alphabetical list of organizations in part II' (but without page references), and there is no index to the organizations in part I, although they are easily accessible through the contents page.

77 **Organizations with Exchange Programs or Interest in Sub-Saharan Africa**. Washington, DC: USIS, Bureau of Educational and Cultural Affairs, The African Working Group, 1995. 80pp.

Directory of over 150 organizations (NGOs, private, public, international and governmental), with interests in Sub-Saharan Africa. Provides contact information and details about their objectives. (Not examined)

Directories of research and teaching, and of African studies scholars

78 **African Studies Association. Membership Directory**. Atlanta, GA: African Studies Association, 1992 [latest edition; new edition to be published in 1997]. 84pp.

Periodically updated and re-issued, lists all the individual members of the ASA. Gives full address details, title, institutional affiliation, discipline(s), country or regional interests, office telephone, and Email address where available.

79 Deutsches Übersee-Institut. Übersee-Dokumentation. Referat Afrika. **Institutionen der Afrika-Forschung und Afrika-Information in der Bundesrepublik Deutschland und Berlin (West). Forschungsinstitute, Bibliotheken, Dokumentationsstellen, Archive.** 3rd ed. Comp. by Marion Gebhardt. Hamburg: Deutsches Übersee-Institut, 1990. 291pp. DM35.00 (Dokumentationsdienst Afrika, Reihe B, 5)

Directory of 210 research institutions, libraries, documentation centres, and archives in the German Federal Republic and Berlin. Arranged by cities, each entry provides full name and address, telephone/fax numbers, personnel, activities, area or subject focus, budgets, publications, and library holdings (with details of access and library hours, etc.) Alphabetical, geographical and subject indexes.

80 **Directory of African and Afro-American Studies in the United States.** Comp. by Annemarie Christy. 8th ed. Atlanta, GA: African Studies Association Press, 1993. 175pp. $20.00

Published by the African Studies Association *(see* **851***)*, this is a guide to 326 programmes of African and Afro-American studies in the United States, with entries listed state by state. Information given includes full name and address, telephone number, contact person, faculty and course listings, degree offerings, regional emphasis, special features, library holdings of Africana, and financial aid available at each institution. Contains an alphabetical index of institutions. Information was gathered by questionnaire mailings and institutions who failed to complete and return questionnaires are not included. This has resulted in some notable gaps.

81 **A Directory of Africanists in Britain.** Comp. by Anne Merriman and Richard Hodder-Williams. 3rd ed. Bristol: University of Bristol on behalf of the Royal African Society [order from Professor Hodder-Williams, Department of Politics, University of Bristol, Bristol BS8 1TH, UK], 1996. 165pp. £12.50

A who's who of Africanists in Britain, giving full names and address and institutional affiliations of 488 UK or UK-based African studies scholars, including telephone/fax numbers and Email addresses. Other information given includes subject/regional interests, primary research areas, research in progress, and major publications. Indexes by discipline and by country of research.

82 **Etudes africaines en Europe. Bilan et inventaire.** Comp. by the Agence de coopération culturelle et technique. Paris: ACCT & Editions Karthala, 1981. 2 vols. 655pp., 714pp.

Massive two-volume inventory (current as at 1980) of African studies research and African studies documentation in Europe. In addition to articles on various areas of African studies research, there are extensive 'Répertoire' sections, giving details about academic institutions throughout Europe which offer courses and undertake research in African studies, with information on staff, areas of specialization, etc. Indexes to names of institutions, individual scholars, disciplines, geographic area studied. Now inevitably out of date.

83 **International Directory of African Studies Research/Répertoire international des études africaines.** Ed. by the International African Institute and comp. by Philip Baker. 3rd ed. London: Hans Zell Publishers, 1994. 344pp. £95.00/$150.00

The most comprehensive and currently most up-to-date reference resource to African studies research and teaching worldwide. Provides information on over 1,800 academic institutions, research bodies, associations, and international organizations involved in African studies research in all parts of the world. Entries are set out in alphabetical order by name of institution, and include the following information: full name and address, telephone and fax numbers, and Email address where available; name of head/director and details of staff, including their fields of specialization; principal areas of current African studies research; courses offered and degrees awarded; library holdings; publications issued; and various other information such as sources of funding, and links with other institutions and organizations. Five indexes: thematic index by area/country; index of international organizations; index of ethnonyms and language names; index of serial publications; and index of personnel.

84 **Profiles of African Scientific Institutions, 1992.** Comp. by African Academy of Sciences and Network of African Scientific Organizations. Nairobi: Academy Science Publishers [distr. by African Books Collective Ltd, Oxford], 1992. 290pp. £24.00/$30.00

This is a companion volume to *Profiles of African Scientists (see* **51***)* which lists 186 institutions from 36 African countries. Covers institutions of higher education, research institutes, departments or agencies of government engaged in policy formation, a number of private sector agencies. Information provided for each entry includes full name and address and telephone numbers, names of executive officers and other personnel, budgets, a brief history of the institution, its mission and purpose, organizational structure, major current activities, publications, infrastructural facilities, and details of cooperative programmes with other organizations.

85 **Répertoire des enseignants et chercheurs des institutions membres de l'AUPELF-UREF. Afrique, Caraïbes, Océan Indien, monde arabe et Asie du sud-est, 1996-1997.** Montréal: Association des universités partiellement ou entièrement de langue française (AUPELF), 1996. 1,027pp. Can.$54.95

A directory of academics and researchers at AUPELF member institutions, with full address, telephone number, nationality, degrees, and areas of research. Index by name under countries. Companion volume to entry **86**.

Note: also available on the Internet :
⌨http://www.refer.qc/ca/ESF/FFI/SBD/REC/bwrec.htm

86 **Répertoire des établissements d'enseignement supérieur et de recherches membres de l'AUPELF-UREF, 1996/97**. Montréal: Association des universités partiellement ou entièrement de langue française (AUPELF), 1997. 1,339pp. Can $54.95
Companion volume to entry **85** which provides extensive details of teaching institutions in 34 (mostly francophone) countries, with information on teaching/departmental staff, courses offered, student services, library facilities, etc.
Note: also available on the Internet:
⌨ http://www.refer.qc.ca.ESF/FFI/SBD/RG/bwrg.htm

87 Trip, Aili Mari. **A Directory of Fellowships, Scholarships and Grants Available in the U.S. to African Women Students and Scholars**. 2nd ed. Madison, WI: Women's Studies Research Center, University of Wisconsin [1155 Observatory Drive, no. 107, Madison, WI 53706-1319], 1993. 21pp. $3.25 (Working Papers Series, 15)
(Not examined)

General interest reference sources

88 Asante, Molefi Kete. **The Book of African Names**. Trenton, NJ: Africa World Press, 1991. 64pp. $8.95 pap. $24.95 cased
Lists some 1,200 male and female names in two separate sections, under five African regions, and gives interpretations of their English meaning.

89 Madubuike, Ihechukwu. **A Handbook of African Names**. 2nd ed. Colorado Springs, CO: Three Continents Press, 1994. 158pp. $20.00
A guide to African male and female names, together with short essays on a number of African languages.

90 Room, Adrian. **African Placenames: Origins and Meanings of the Names for over 2000 Natural Features, Towns, Cities, Provinces, and Countries**. Jefferson, NC: McFarland, 1994. 234pp. $49.95
Etymologies of over 2,000 placenames (i.e. countries, capitals, rivers, lakes, mountains, deserts, islands, etc.), with an emphasis on Southern and Northern Africa. Includes a bibliography, plus an appendix providing a chronology of explorations of Africa, and a section giving basic demographic, linguistic and religious information.

91 **The Rough Guides**. London: The Rough Guides, [in the US order from Penguin USA, PO Box 999, Bergenfield, NJ 07621], var. pp. prices range from £6.99-£14.00/$12.95-$19.95
Although the 'Rough Guides' are essentially travel companions, they are really a great deal more than that, and provide excellent basic handbooks - some of near encyclopedic proportions - on African countries and regions. In addition

to practical information and advice on travel, sights and attractions, facilities, etc. each guide contains a well-researched "Contexts" section containing historical background, features on cultural life, languages, traditional society, religion, and more, together with annotated bibliographies. 'Rough Guides' are currently available for these countries and regions: Egypt, Kenya, Morocco, South Africa (due 1997)Tunisia, West Africa, and Zimbabwe & Botswana.

Guides to electronic sources and the Internet

92 Fung, Karen. **Africa South of the Sahara: Selected Internet Resources.** 💻 http://www-sul.stanford.edu/depts/ssrg/africa/guide.html
   A guide (in electronic form only) to Africana on the Internet, prepared by Karen Fung - who is Deputy Curator of Africana at the Hoover Institution *(see* **453***)* - for the Electronic Technology Group of the (US) African Studies Assocation. The site is constantly updated and expanded. Provides quick access to a wealth of Internet resources, including African studies programmes and organizations, current events, Email discussion groups/mailing lists concerned with Africa and African studies, grants, journals and newspapers, libraries and archives, student organizations, and many regional or subject specific sites.

93 Hubert, Muriel. **Inventaire: la recherche française sur le développement: panorama des banques de données/Directory: French Development Research Databases: An Overview.** Paris: OCDE, 1994. 126pp.
   An inventory of French development databases (both bibliographic databases, and those covering specific disciplines), providing an outline of contents, size of the database, and currency.

94 Kuntz, Patricia S. **"African Studies Computer Resources"** in *Internet Resources: A Subject Guide,* comp. by Hugh A. Thompson. Chicago: American Library Association, 1995, pp. 42-45 (originally published in *College & Research Library News* 55, no. 2, February 1994: 68-73).
   Guide to select African studies computer resources available in the USA with linkages to Africa, covering four computer network systems: Internet/Bitnet, Fidonet, UseNet, and BBS (dial-up bulletin board services).

95 Limb, Peter. **"An A-Z of African Studies on the Internet."** *African Research and Documentation,* no. 70 (1996): 58-68.
   A handy annotated guide to over 100 Africa-related listserv discussion groups and websites (current as at February 1996). Updates are promised for the future.
   💻 Accessible on-line, and regularly updated at:
   http://www.library.uwa.edu.au/sublibs/sch/sc_ml_afr.html
   also available at the H-Africa website at:
   http://www.h-net.msu.edu/~africa/internet/index.html#gen

96 Pfister, Roger. **Internet for Africanists and Others Interested in Africa**. Basel/Bern, Switzerland: Swiss Society of African Studies/Basler Afrika Bibliographien, 1996. 140pp. SFr. 10.00 [Order from Basler Afrika Bibliographien, Klosterberg 21, 4051 Basel]

> Both an introduction to the Internet and an inventory of over 500 Internet sites/services relating to sub-Saharan Africa, which are listed under four sections: (1) WWW, Gopher, FTP and Telnet, (2) ListServ mailing lists, (3) news groups, and (4) search engines. For the first section addresses are provided under 24 broad subject groups, and access is further facilitated by two indexes, one an alphabetical listing of keywords, and the other listing countries/regions alphabetically. For each entry it gives the name, URL (Uniform Resource Locator)/Email address, contact, and keywords. A helpful introductory section adds to the value of this publication.

Guides to film and video resources

A note about film and video resources:

During the course of 1997, the African Media Program (AMP) at Michigan State University, the publishers of item **101** below will create a new, definitive reference database by identifying, indexing, and critically reviewing all extant films and videos on Africa produced between 1981 and 1996. These reviews, with filmographies, will be disseminated electronically over the WWW and also published both in CD-ROM and print formats. In addition, the AMP expects to provide a database of other audio-visual materials (including transparencies, filmstrips, music, maps and globes) for teaching about Africa. For more information: Laura Arntson, Coordinator, African Media Program, African Studies Center, Michigan State University, 100 Center for International Programs, East Lansing, MI 48824-1035; tel. +1-517-432 0057, fax +1-517-432 1209, Email: AfrMedia@pilot.msu.edu

97 Ballantyne, James and Andrew Roberts. **Africa: A Handbook of Film and Video Resources**. London: British Universities Film & Video Council [55 Greek Street, London W1V 51R], 1986. 120 pp. (with Supplementary List, May 1987, 23pp.)

> Describes major archival collections of non-fiction films on Africa in Great Britain, together with a separate section with details of films on Africa which can be hired or borrowed, covering mostly history, politics and ethnography, the latter part arranged by subject with country subdivisions, and country, title and distributor indexes. The subject sections give details of distributor, year released, production company, length and other technical details, together with a brief annotation. Also includes a list of distributors' addresses and a bibliography.

98 California Newsreel. Library of African Cinema. **A Guide to Video Resources for Colleges and Public Libraries**. San Francisco, CA: Resolution Inc/ California Newsreel [149 Ninth Street, Suite 420, San Francisco, CA 94103]. n.d. [1991]. 35pp.

> Contains a brief introduction - 'Africa through African eyes' - to the African cinema and gives some pointers for viewing African films; thereafter provides reviews (with background material, maps, and photographs) of eight African films, plus a select filmography of other African films, and a listing of videos available from California Newsreel's Southern Africa Media Center.

99 Cyr, Helen W. **A Filmography of the Third World, 1976-1983. An Annotated List of 16mm Films**. Metuchen, NJ: Scarecrow Press, 1985. 285pp. £24.00

> Continues *Filmography of the Third World* (Scarecrow, 1976) and lists 1,300 new titles. Chiefly documentary but also short and feature-length fictional films, experimental cinema and cinema as art. Also lists distributors.

100 Lems-Dworkin, Carol. **Videos of African and African-related Performance: An Annotated Bibliography**. Evanston, IL: Carol Lems-Dworkin Publishers [POB 1646, Evanston, IL 60204-1646], 1996. 353pp. $57.00

> Somewhat oddly sub-titled "an annotated bibliography" this is in fact a videography, whose primary purpose is to help people locate videos showing aspects of African or African-related performance. This covers African music, dance, drama, rituals, oral tradition, storytelling, carnivals, folklore, ethnographic studies, women's studies, children's videos, and more. Also includes select videos from the African diaspora showing significant links to Africa (e.g. jazz, blues, gospel, steel pan, calypso, reggae). There are 1,390 entries, most quite extensively annotated. Each entry gives details of video formats and standards, duration, year released, names of directors/producers, etc., country of origin, and information about purchase/rental and distributor. A Distributors Index gives full names, addresses, and telephone and fax numbers (Email address and websites for some). An extensive 37 page subject index, and a names index, add to the value of this remarkable compilation.

101 Wiley, David S. **Africa on Film and Videotape: A Compendium of Reviews**. East Lansing, MI: African Media Program, African Studies Center [100 Center for International Programs, East Lansing, MI 488224-1035], 1982.

> Lists over 750 reviews of films and videotapes on Africa released between 1960 and 1981 which are available in the US. Includes critical annotations, and full details of length, date released, director/producer, distributor, etc. Indexed by topic, country, and by language. (See also note about film and video resources on p. 23).

Guides to library collections and archival sources

102 **African Language and Literature Collection, Indiana University Libraries**. Bloomington, IN: African Studies Program [221 Woodburn Hall], Indiana University, 1994. 515pp. $20.00

Indiana University (*see* **456**) has one of the largest collections of materials on African linguistics and texts in African languages. This guide to the collection (both catalogued and uncatalogued material, as well as field recordings housed in the Indiana Archives of Traditional Music), cites over 8,000 items in 700 languages, from 36 countries. Material is arranged by language and indexed by author.

103 Brown, Clare **Manuscript Collections in the Rhodes House Library, Oxford.** Oxford: The Bodleian Library, 1996. 171pp. £5.00

One in a series of guides to the Rhodes House Library's very substantial collections of archives and private papers relating to the colonial empire (other than India and Sudan). The guide contains almost 900 entries (of which over 60 are on Africa), covering accessions from 1978 to 1994. Material is divided into British Empire, non-African colonial regions, and some 20 individual African Territories. Each entry provides a short description on the nature of the deposit, together with its shelf number. With index to people, organizations and institutions, and an index of countries.

104 Conseil international des archives. **Sources de l'histoire de l'Afrique du Sud du Sahara dans les archives et bibliothèques françaises.** Volume 1: **Archives** Volume 2: **Bibliothèques** Volume 3: **Index.** Zug, Switzerland: Inter Documentation Co., 1976. 3 vols. 959pp., 932pp., 178pp. (Guides des sources de l'histoire des nations, 3 & 4)

Descriptions of archival holdings relating to Africa in libraries (public, government, private) in France. Extensively indexed. (For other volumes in the series *see* entries **107-115**).

105 Cook, Chris. **The Making of Modern Africa. A Guide to Archives.** New York: Facts on File, 1995. 218pp. $35.00/£29.95

Brings together, from many geographically diverse locations, archival information available in over 1,000 collections of personal papers and private archives "of value to the historian of modern Africa" (excluding governmental and offical archives however, which are well documented in other sources). The period covered is 1878 to the early 1990s. The guide is arranged by personal name, with each entry giving brief career details, followed by concise notes on the location and contents of the archive. With archive and subject indexes.

106 Geber, Jill **"Southern African Sources in the Oriental and India Office Collections (OIOC) of the British Library."** *African Research and Documentation,* no. 70 (1996): 1-35.

An extensive bibliographic essay that focuses on the range of sources to be found in the British Library's Oriental and India Office collections for the study of Southern Africa. Draws attention to almost 200 sources, including archival sources, manuscripts, official publications, those in the map collections, as well as illustrated material, paintings, prints, and printed books and serials.

"Guides to the Sources for the History of the Nations/Guides des sources de l'histoire des nations/Quellenführer zur Geschichte der Nationen"
Ed. by the International Council on Archives/Conseil international des archives. The aim of this vast project is to provide easy access to the rich source materials preserved in European libraries and archives relating to the history of countries formerly under colonial rule. In addition to entry **104** the following titles also cover archival holdings on Africa. (The complete 3rd series is available at DM 2,500).

107 *2nd series*
vol. 9:
Sources of the History of Africa South of the Sahara in the Netherlands. Comp. by M.P. Roessingh & W. Visser. Munich: K.G. Saur Verlag [for International Council on Archives], 1978. 241pp. DM88.00

108
vol. 10:
Indian Sources for African History: Guides to the Sources of the History of Africa and of the Indian Diaspora in the Basin of the Indian Ocean in the National Archives of India. Comp. by S.A.I. Tirmizi. Delhi: International Writers' Emporium, in association with UNESCO. 1988/89. 2 vols. 382pp.

109 *3rd series*
vol. 3, pt. 1:
Sources of the History of North Africa, Asia and Oceania in Denmark. Comp. by C. Rise Hansen. Munich: K.G. Saur Verlag, 1980. 842pp. DM298.00

110 vol. 3, pt. 2:
Sources of the History of North Africa, Asia and Oceania in Finland, Norway, Sweden. Comp. by Berndt Federley *et al.* Munich: K.G. Saur Verlag, 1981. 233pp. DM168.00

111 vol. 5:
Sources de l'histoire du Proche Orient et de l'Afrique du Nord dans les archives et bibliothèques françaises. Ed. by the Commission française du

guide des sources des nations. Part 1: **Archives** Part 2: **Bibliothèque Nationale** Munich: K.G. Saur Verlag, pt 1, 3 vols., 1996. 1,365pp. DM840.00 (set 3 vols.); pt. 2, 1984. 480pp. DM228.00

112 vol. 6:
Quellen zur Geschichte Nordafrikas, Asiens und Ozeaniens in der Bundesrepublik Deutschland bis 1945. Ed. by Ernst Ritter. Munich: K.G. Saur Verlag, 1984. 386pp. DM168.00

113 vol. 8:
Quellen zur Geschichte Nordafrikas, Asiens und Ozeaniens im Oestereichischen Staatsarchiv bis 1918. Ed. by the Generaldirektion des Oestereichischen Staatsarchiv. Munich: K.G. Saur Verlag, 1986. 272pp. DM198.00

114 vol. 9:
Sources of the History of Africa, Asia, Australia and Oceania in Hungary. With a Supplement: Latin America. Munich: K.G. Saur Verlag, 1991. 451pp. DM298.00

115 vol. 10:
Sources of the History of Africa, Asia, and Oceania in Yugoslavia. Ed. by the Union of Societies of Archivists in Yugoslavia. Munich: K.G. Saur Verlag, 1991. 164pp. DM168.00

116 Henige, David. **A Union List of African Archival Materials in Microform.** 2nd ed. Madison: University of Wisconsin, Madison Memorial Library, 1984. 45pp.
    Provides an inventory of the holdings in 18 libraries, and lists 299 titles; with country index and P.R.O. numerical list.

117 Hijma, B. **Gids van Afrika-Collecties in Nederlandse Bibliotheken en Documentatiecentra.** Leiden, Netherlands: Afrika-Studiecentrum [PO Box 9555, 2300 RB Leiden], 1986. 253pp.
    A guide to the Africana holdings of 123 libraries and documentation centres in the Netherlands. Gives full name and address, telephone numbers, contact personnel, services provided, collection size of books, serials and microfiche, a description of the collection and its special features, type of library catalogue maintained, and publications issued.

Institutionen der Afrika-Forschung und Afrika-Information in der Bundesrepublik Deutschland und Berlin (West), *see* **79**

118 Howell, John Bruce, and Yvette Scheven. **"Guides, Collections and Ancillary Materials to African Archival Resources in the United States."** *Electronic Journal of Africana Bibliography*, no. 1 (1996): (On-line version: Iowa City: University of Iowa Libraries; 🖳 http://www.lib.uiowa.edu/proj/ejab/ Also available as a hardcopy paper version from African Studies Program, University of Wisconsin [1454 Van Hise Hall, 1220 Linden Drive], 1996. 108pp. $18.00

> Primarily based on the holdings of the University of Iowa and the University of Illinois at Urbana-Champaign - but also including the collections at some other US research libraries - this is a list of published guides to the archives of Africa, especially those in microform, and includes inventories, records, catalogues, finding tools, indexes, annual reports, etc. arranged by regions and countries (excluding Egypt). Material covered includes titles in English, French, and Portuguese.

119 Mann, Michael, and Valerie Sanders. **A Bibliography of African Language Texts in the Collection of the School of Oriental and African Studies, University of London, to 1963.** London: Hans Zell Publishers, 1994. 448pp. £68.00/$105.00 (Documentary Research in African Literatures, 3)

> A massive inventory of over 7,000 African language titles in over 300 different languages. It covers the combined collections and archival holdings of African language texts at SOAS, the International Institute of African Languages and Culture (later International African Institute), and the Christian Literature Bureau for Africa (later International Committee on Christian Literature for Africa).

120 McIlwaine, John. **Writings on African Archives.** London: Hans Zell Publishers (for Standing Conference on Library Materials on Africa/SCOLMA), 1996. 297pp. £55.00/$95.00

> Provides an inventory of materials - monographs, articles, reports, conference papers and academic exercises - written about archives and manuscript collections within Africa, as well as about African-related archives located outside Africa. Contains 2,355 entries, many with brief annotations, and the volume is indexed by authors, editors, series titles, and names of individuals and institutions.

121 The New York Public Library. Schomburg Center for Research in Black Culture. **Schomburg Clipping File-Africa.** Cambridge: Chadwyck-Healey (Alexandria, VA: Chadwyck-Healey), 1986. 1,362 microfiche [with Index to the Schomburg Clipping File]

> A collection of newspapers and magazine clippings, pamphlets and ephemera on all aspects of the Black experience held by the Schomburg Center. This is a selection from the complete file, covering material devoted to the various countries of Africa. (*see also* **122**)

122 The New York Public Library. Schomburg Center for Research in Black Culture. **Index to the Schomburg Clipping File**. Cambridge: Chadwyck-Healey, 1986. 176pp. £35.00
> An index to the microfiche edition of the Schomburg collection of periodical and newspaper clippings. lists almost 7,000 subjects, of which 650 are on Africa and which are listed separately. *(see also* **121***)*

123 Northwestern University. **Catalog of the Melville J. Herskovits Library of African Studies, Northwestern University Library, and Africana in Selected Libraries**. Boston: G.K. Hall, 1972. 5,671pp. 8 vols. First Supplement. 1978. 4,380pp. 6 vols.
> Facsimile reproductions of the catalogue cards of this major library on African studies *(see* **468***)*. Altogether reproduces over 200,000 cards.

124 Pearson, J.D. **A Guide to Manuscripts and Documents in the British Isles Relating to Africa**. 2 vols. London: Mansell Publishing, Volume 1, 1993. 320pp. £100.00/$180.00; Volume 2, 1994. 576pp. £150.00/$265.00 (set 2 vols. £225.00/$400.00)
> This monumental and indispensable two volume guide is a much expanded and revised edition of Noel Matthews and Doreen Wainright's *Guides to Manuscripts and Documents in the British Isles Relating to Africa* (1991). It lists and describes manuscripts - both in African and Western languages - relating to Africa South of the Sahara held in public and private collections in Britain. Volume 1 covers institutions in London - including the extensive collections of the British Library - and volume 2 lists collections in the British Isles outside London, geographically grouped under England, Wales, Scotland, and Northern Ireland: under each of these, repositories are arranged alphabetically by cities of their location (including, for example, the large collections at Rhodes House Library in Oxford). A single combined index covers names, titles, and subjects.

125 Rhodes House Library. **Rhodes House Library Subject Catalogue**. Cambridge: Chadwyck-Healey, 1990. 477 microfiche.
> A reproduction, in microfiche format, of the original subject index cards at Rhodes House Library in Oxford *(see* **434***)* which houses extensive collections on Africa. Includes a *Guide and Listing to the Microfiche Edition*, compiled by Peter Wilkinson. (Not examined)

126 **The SCOLMA Directory of Libraries and Special Collections on Africa in the United Kingdom and in Europe**. Ed. by Tom French. 5th ed. London: Hans Zell Publishers (for Standing Conference on Library Materials on Africa/SCOLMA), 1993. 366pp. £55.00/$85.00
> Published on behalf of SCOLMA *(see* **865***)*, this is a valuable guide for all those who need to locate research material on Africa available in the libraries of the UK and in Europe. Contains 392 entries; each entry includes full name and address, name of chief librarian and/or person in charge of Africana collections, telephone/fax numbers, Email addresses, and (if information was

duly supplied) details of opening hours, conditions of access for external readers, size of library/collection, loan and reference facilities, the scope and depth of each collection, CD-ROM and on-line databases, audio-visual materials available, and publications issued. With an index covering institutions, organizations, subjects, and countries.

127 South, Aloha. **Guide to Federal Archives Relating to Africa.** Waltham, MA: Crossroads Press, 1977. 556pp.

Guide to federal archive holdings in the USA; lists over 800 record groups. Information for each entry includes details of footage of Africa-related material, geographic areas covered, etc. Extensively indexed.

128 South, Aloha. **Guide to Non-Federal Archives and Manuscripts in the United States Relating to Africa.** Oxford: Hans Zell Publishers (New York: K.G. Saur, Inc), 1989. 2 vols. 1,266pp.

This massive two-volume guide, published for the National Archives, Washington DC, describes textual and non-textual materials, relating to the African continent and offshore islands and which are located in public and private manuscript and archival depositories in the United States. Entries in the *Guide* indicate the scope and content of each collection, as well as the subject of documents contained in a collection or series. The types of documents include correspondence, letterbooks, journals, logbooks, photographs and slides, sound recordings and films. Includes an extensive 127pp. index.

129 Stenderup, Vibeke. **Nordisk Biblioteksguide för U-Lands-dokumentation. Nordic Library Guide to Documentation on Developing Countries.** Aarhus: Nordiska Vetenskapliga Bibliotekarieförbundet [distr. by Bibliothekcentralen, Telegrafvej 5, DK-2750 Ballerup, Denmark], 1981. 100pp.

A guide to Nordic research libraries with holdings of books, periodicals, reports and other material on developing countries. Covers 156 libraries. In addition to full name and address and address and telephone/telex numbers, each entry gives a brief description about the nature of each collection, information and documentation services provided by each library, publications issued, etc. Descriptions are all in Swedish, but there is an English subject/geographical index. Now somewhat dated.

130 Thurston, Anne. **Guide to Archives and Manuscripts Relating to Kenya and East Africa in the United Kingdom.** 2 vols. Volume 1: **Official Records.** Volume 2: **Non-Official Archives and Manuscripts.** London: Hans Zell Publishers, 1991. Vol. 1, 634pp., vol. 2, 576pp.

This two volume guide surveys official and non-official records in over 150 repositories in the United Kingdom. The earliest located sources are from the 17th century, although the bulk of the records described date from the end of the Second World War. Collections covered include the extensive holdings of the Public Record Office, the large number of manuscript holdings at the

Rhodes House Library in Oxford, as well as holdings of local record offices, university libraries, museums, Royal societies, and other special repositories.

131 Thurston, Anne. **Sources for Colonial Studies in the Public Record Office.** Volume 1. London: HMSO, 1995. 479pp. £60.00
Part of the British Documents on the End of the Empire (BDEEP) scheme, of which 'Series C' covers sources. This first volume in 'Series C' provides a companion to the records of the Colonial Office, with a successor volume (by the same author) to follow, and which will cover Cabinet, Foreign Office and Treasury records. Includes several historical overview chapters on the organization of the records, as well as information on how to use the records, and deals with questions of access, finding aids, registry codes, etc. There is a who-was-who of office holders in Colonial and Dominions Offices over two centuries, an extensive listing of PRO records, followed by an account of the records of the CO's Subject Departments. A highly detailed index completes this exemplary archival guide and working tool.

Guides to statistical sources, and economic and financial data

132 **African Economic and Financial Data.** Washington, DC: The World Bank, 1989. 204pp. $14.95 (UNDP/WB, StatSeries)
Provides African economic and financial statistics covering 1980-1987, including national accounts, external sector, debt and related flows, government finance, agriculture, and public enterprises; also monitors development programmes and aid flows.

133 **African Development Indicators 1996.** Washington, DC: The World Bank, 1996. 424pp. $45.00/£27.85 (UNDP/WB, StatSeries); also available on disk, $65.00/£40.50 [in the UK order from Microinfo Ltd., POB 3, Omega Park, Alton, GU34 2PG]
Economic and financial data on Africa with a broader range than the preceding entry (*see* **132**), employing new social and environmental indicators to monitor African development programmes and aid flows since 1980 and up to 1994. This latest revised and expanded edition provides the most detailed collection of social and development data available in one volume. Arranged in 254 separate tables or matrices for more than 300 indicators of development.

134 **African Official Statistical Serials, 1867-1982.** Cambridge: Chadwyck-Healey (Alexandria, VA: Chadwyck-Healey), 2,330 microfiche £5,500 for complete collection. For orders for single volumes or selections of volumes unit prices are: 1-49 microfiche £6.00, 50-99 microfiche £5.00, 100+ microfiche £4.00
Consists of general statistical compendia - economic, financial, social, demographic statistics - issued by the governments of nearly every African nation. Available as a complete collection or by individual countries.

135 Evalds, Victoria K. **Union List of African Censuses, Development Plans and Statistical Abstracts.** London: Hans Zell Publishers, 1985. 232pp.

Brings together the combined holdings of the collections in 13 major North American research libraries, of government documents concerned with African censuses, development plans and statistical abstracts. Entries cover the period 1945-1983 and are arranged in chronological order under each country (or former colonial territory). Holdings are noted for each library and locations are indicated using National Union Catalog symbols.

136 Johns, Michael. **US and Africa Statistical Handbook.** Washington, DC: American Heritage Foundation, 1991. 100pp. $8.00

Provides basic factual and statistical information for each African nation, plus import/export statistics for US and African countries. (Not examined)

137 Pinfold, John R. **African Population Census Reports. A Bibliography and Checklist.** London: Hans Zell Publishers (for Standing Conference on Library Materials on Africa/SCOLMA), 1985. 100pp.

Arranged in country and chronological order and containing some 600 entries, this inventory lists the published reports of every national population census carried out in Africa up to and including 1980. It also serves as a Union List surveying the holdings in 34 libraries in Britain and elsewhere in Europe. Location symbols are given for each entry.

138 **Statistics and Indicators on Women in Africa. 1986/Statistiques et indicateurs sur les femmes en Afrique. 1986.** New York: United Nations, Department of International Economic and Social Affairs, Statistical Office, 1989. 225pp. $23.50 (Social Statistics and Indicators, Series K, 7)

Drawing on a UN database, this volumes provides statistical information on the economic, social and legal status of women in Africa, including population distribution, education, health, etc.

Handbooks and encyclopedias

139 **Africa on File.** Comp. by Mapping Specialists Ltd. 2 vols. Volume 1: **East, Southern, and North Africa**; Volume 2: **West and Central Africa**: Regional issues. New York: Facts on File, 1995. 384pp. [looseleaf] $185.00/£140.00

A visual survey of the physical and human geography of 52 Sub-Saharan African countries. Includes over 1,000 maps, charts, factsheets and 'timelines' covering ethnic groups, language groups, population distribution, economic growth, migration, famine, civil wars, deforestation, daily calorie intake, interstate conflicts, and other topics. With a geographical and subject index.

140 **African History on File.** Comp. by The Diagram Group. New York: Facts on File, 1994. 288pp. [looseleaf] $165.00/£125.00

With more than 500 maps, charts, and diagrams, this historical atlas provides a visual presentation of African history from prehistory and the kingdoms of the Nile through to the establishment of modern nation states and 20th century Africa. (Not examined)

141 **Africa Today**. Publisher and editor-in-chief: Raph Uwechue. Senior Research Editor: Jonathan Derrick. 3rd ed. London: Africa Books Ltd, 1996. 1,684pp. £195.00/$295.00
[also available as a 3 volume set with *Africa Who's Who* and *Makers of Modern Africa, see* **43** and **50**)

A comprehensive source on the history, geography, economics, politics and current affairs, culture, language, and religions of Africa, with black and white maps for each African country, and 14 pages of 'Peters Projection' maps in full colour. The country surveys provide basic factual information for every African nation, each with extensive introductory material on geography, history and politics, the economy, and with details of government (as at April 1996), addresses of African and non-African diplomatic missions in each country and diplomatic missions abroad; plus many statistical tables, covering balance of payments, agricultural production and livestock, trade and industry, employment, education, health, environment and natural resources, and more. Additionally, the volume includes 25 essays contributed by prominent African/Africanist scholars such as Adebayo Adedeji, Samir Amin, Adu Boahen, Basil Davidson, Colin Legum, Ali Mazrui, Amadou-Mahtar M'Bow, Kole Omotoso, and Simon Gikandi, of which six are entirely new, and the others reprinted from the previous (1991) edition.

142 Arnold, Guy. **Political and Economic Encyclopaedia of Africa**. Harlow, UK: Longman (Detroit: Gale) 1993. 342pp. £80.00

Essential facts about African countries, organizations, institutions and some "personalities" (mostly political leaders). Primarily for the non-specialist.

143 **The Arts and Civilization of Black and African Peoples**. Ed. by Joseph Okpaku, Alfred Opubor, and Benjamin Oloruntimehin. New Rochelle, NY: The Victoria Corporation, 1987. 10 vols. $425.00 per set (institutions) $395.00 per set (individuals)

A ten volume encyclopedia - the outcome of a Colloquium on Black Civilization held during the 2nd World Black and African Festival of Arts and Culture in Lagos, Nigeria, in 1977 - covering practically every aspect of the evolution and cultures of Black people in all parts of the world. Contents of individual volumes range from the arts and literature, to philosophy, religion, education, and science and technology.

144 **The Cambridge Encyclopedia of Africa**. General Editors: Roland Oliver and Michael Crowder. Cambridge University Press, 1981. 492pp.

A one-volume encyclopedic guide to the past and present Africa, covering its physical environment, archaeology and history, natural resources, political economy, society, religion, art, tourism, and more. With contributions by almost a hundred African studies scholars, and a substantial amount of illustrative material in both black and white, and in full colour.

145 **The Encylopedia of Precolonial Africa**. General Editor: Joseph O. Vogel Walnut Creek, CA: Altamira Press. A Division of Sage Publications Inc, forthcoming 1997. ca. 600pp. $124.95

Encyclopedia of precolonial Africa with over a hundred articles by Africanist scholars, with maps, photographs, and figures. Each article includes a bibliography. Also included in the volume are a topical directory and an index. Subjects covered include: African environments, technology, people and culture, prehistory of Africa, histories of research, rock art, social complexity, trade and commerce, historical archaeology, etc. (Not examined)

146 **The Encylopedia of Sub-Saharan Africa**. General Editor: John Middleton. New York: Charles Scribner's Sons Reference Books, forthcoming 1997.

Compiled with the assistance of an impressive board of editorial advisers and consultants, this major new encyclopedia project has been in the making since 1992, and publication is now scheduled for sometime in 1997. Its goal is to provide a state-of-the-art account of Africa and "to produce a scholarly resource that will provide the social, cultural, and historical contexts and implications of facts, events, people, and practices pertinent to African studies." (Publisher's statement; not examined)

147 **Encyclopedia of the Third World**. 4th ed. Ed. by George T. Kurian. New York: Facts on File, 1992. 3 vols. 2,432pp. $225.00 (set 3 vols.)

A survey of 124 Third World countries, providing an overview of each nation's political, economic and social systems, including culture, religion, media, and more. Each national chapter follows the same format of 36 subject headings, with some 400 subtopics. Includes maps for each country and an extensive index.

148 Hall, David E. **African Acronyms and Abbreviations. A Handbook**. London: Cassell Academic/Mansell, 1996. 364pp. £60.00/$105.00

This remarkable compilation lists an astonishing 12,000 or so acronyms and abbreviations relating to Africa and African studies. Most relate to entities in Africa, i.e. official and unofficial bodies, political parties, educational establishments, institutions, business and trade organizations, etc., and also includes entries for other acronyms, which do not specifically relate to Africa but constantly recur in Africanist publications, for example those of international donor organizations, missions, and other bodies. The primary sources for the dictionary were the authority files which the compiler has maintained over 15 years of work on the *International African Bibliography (see* **171***)*. For each entry the country of origin is cited, as the same abbreviation frequently relates to different organizations (as many as 16 on the evidence of this dictionary). Both current and lapsed organizations are listed, and there are cross-references to changes of name or acronyms and alternative terms.

149 **Middle East and North Africa on File**. Comp. by Mapping Specialists Ltd. New York: Facts on File, 1995. 288pp. [looseleaf] $165.00/£125.00
A companion volume to entry **139**. Same format. Includes over 500 maps, charts, graphs and 'timelines' relating to the human and physical geography of the countries in the region. (Not examined)

150 Moroney, Sean. **Handbooks to the Modern World: Africa**. New York: Facts on File, 1989. 2 vols. 1,248 pp. $110.00/£85.00 set
Volume 1 contains basic factual information on each African country, covering topography, recent political and constitutional developments, the economy, social issues, education, the media, as well as some comparative statistical data and biographical profiles. Volume 2 comprises thematic and analytic essays contributed by 32 specialists in their disciplines. Includes maps, tables and charts and a comprehensive index.

151 Morrison, Donald G., Robert C. Mitchell, and John N. Paden. **Black Africa: A Comparative Handbook**. 2nd ed. New York: Paragon House and Irvington Publishers, 1989. 716pp. $169.50
A mammoth compilation of narrative, statistical and comparative data on 41 sub-Saharan African countries. Part 1 gives comparative profiles - most in tabular form as 154 tables and more than 300 indicators - under various topics such as demography, economic development and social mobilization, political developments, international relations, ecology and pluralism, etc. Part 2 contains country surveys, with maps, charts, tables, and chronologies. Data for the latter goes up to 1982. However, for more up-to-date data, and to stay current, the publishers offer a Black Africa Data Base on disk (PC or Macintosh versions), which costs $80.00 for the basic database; a four-disk subscription for updating costs $240.00. (Disks not examined)

152 Morrison, Donald G. **Understanding Black Africa: Data and Analysis of Social Change and Nation Building**. New York: Paragon House and Irvington Publishers, 1989. 237 pp. $39.50
A condensed, and relatively inexpensive, version of entry **151** above, containing over 80 tables.

153 **Peoples of Africa Series**. Comp. by Diagram Group. New York: Facts on File, forthcoming 1996/97. 6 vols. 672pp. $125.00/£85.00
Aimed primarily at middle and high school students, these six volumes profile the culture, and traditions of 20 major African ethnic groups. Volumes 1-5 are regional volumes covering Northern, East, West, Central and Southern Africa, and Volume 6 covers the nations of Africa from Algeria to Zimbabwe. Some 300 maps and illustrations are included in each volume. (Not examined)

Theses and dissertations

154 Boston University Libraries. **List of French Doctoral Dissertations on Africa, 1884-1961.** Boston: G.K. Hall, 1966. 334pp.
2,981 titles arranged by country and/or area.

155 Curto, Jose C., and Raymond R. Gervais. **Bibliography of Master's Theses and Doctoral Dissertations on Africa, 1905-1993.** Montréal: Canadian Association of African Studies, 1994. 311pp. Can.$18.00
Lists over 3,000 references, arranged by country, with indexes by author, subject and institutions. Also includes some information on African studies research in Canada. and funding for African studies.

156 Lauer, Joseph J., Gregory V. Larkin, and Alfred Kagan. **American and Canadian Doctoral Dissertations and Master's Theses on Africa, 1974-1987.** Atlanta, GA: African Studies Association/Crossroads Press, 1989. 377pp. $75.00
A continuation of entry **159**, providing details for more than 8,500 dissertations and theses. Arranged by country and region, with author, institution, and subject indexes. Kept up-to-date by the quarterly listings "Recent Doctoral Dissertations" _(see_ **174***)* which appear regularly in _ASA News (see_ **292**).

157 McIlwaine, J.H. St. J. **Theses on Africa, 1963-1975. Accepted by Universities in the United Kingdom and Ireland.** London: Mansell Publishing, 1978. 140pp.
Originally published as an annual publication 1966-1970 (published by Frank Cass, London on behalf of SCOLMA; six volumes published to the volume covering 1967-68), this volume covers theses presented at British academic institutions between 1963 and 1975. Contains 2,335 entries, arranged geographically and by broad subject headings, with an author index.

158 Price, Helen C., Colin Hewson, and David Blake. **Theses on Africa 1976-1988. Accepted by the Universities in the United Kingdom and Ireland**. London: Hans Zell Publishers (for Standing Conference on Library Materials on Africa/SCOLMA), 1993. 350pp. £60.00/$95.00
Continues entry **157** and earlier (annual) listings published by SCOLMA and provides details of 3,654 theses covering all regions of Africa and all subjects. Arranged by region, subdivided by country and subject, and with extensive subject and author indexes.

159 Sims, Michael and Alfred Kagan. **American and Canadian Doctoral Dissertations and Master's Theses on Africa, 1886-1974.** Waltham, MA: African Studies Association, Brandeis University, 1976. 365pp.
Lists 6,070 theses classified by geographical area and thereafter by discipline; indexed by subject and author. Continued by entry **156**.

II. CURRENT BIBLIOGRAPHIES AND CONTINUING SOURCES

Only the major *general* current bibliographies, continuing sources, and abstracting and indexing services are listed here; for more specialist continuing sources readers are again referred to the Scheven, McIlwaine, and Porges bibliographies *(see* **34** *&* **35**, **27, 32***)*.

160 **Accessions List Eastern and Southern Africa**
Nairobi: Library of Congress Field Office [POB 30598], 1968- Six times yearly
ISSN 1070-2717 gratis [also available on microfiche]
Edited by Winston Tabb

> A record of the publications acquired by the Library of Congress office, Eastern Africa, covering monographs and serials, and arranged by country. An Annual Publishers Directory, which appears at the end of each year, lists publishers whose monographs and serials have been included in the bimonthly *Accessions Lists* and in *Annual Serials Supplement.*

161 **Africa Bibliography**
Edinburgh: Edinburgh University Press (in association with the International African Institute), 1985- [in North America order from St. Martin's Press]
Annual ISSN 0266-6731 £40.00
Edited by Christopher Allen

> Records books, articles, pamphlets, and essays in edited volumes, principally in the social sciences, environmental sciences, humanities and the arts. Covers the whole of Africa (not confined to works in English); classified into a general section, subject, and geographically, and subdivided by broad groups. With author and subject indexes. The latest annual volume - covering works published on Africa during 1994 - included over 5,800 entries.

162 **"Africana Reference Works: An Annotated List of [1984/85-] Titles"**
The African Book Publishing Record, 12, no. 2 (1986)- *(see* **163***)*
Edited by Joe Lauer *et al.* [to 1988]; edited by Yvette Scheven *et al.* [1989-1992]; edited by Phyllis B. Bischof *et al.* [1993-1996]; edited by Mette Shayne *et al.* [1997-]

> A valuable annual listing which records, classifies and annotates new reference works on Africa published during the preceding year. It is generally limited to titles in European languages which have been examined by the compilers. Titles are arranged under LC subject headings.

163 **The African Book Publishing Record**
Oxford: Hans Zell Publishers, 1975- Quarterly ISSN 0306-0322
£120.00/$200.00 annually
Edited by Hans M. Zell and Cécile Lomer

> Provides systematic and comprehensive coverage of new and forthcoming African publications, giving full bibliographic and ordering information on new African-published material in English and French, as well as including significant titles in the African languages. Access is by subject, by author, and by country of publication. Cumulated every 4-5 years in *African Books in Print (see* **13***)*. In addition to its bibliographic coverage, *ABPR* also includes an extensive book review section, reviews of new African serials, articles on publishing and book development in Africa, and "Africana Reference Works", an annual annotated listing of reference works published during the preceding year *(see also* **162***)*.

164 **African Studies Abstracts** [succeeds *Documentatieblad. The Abstracts Journal of the African Studies Centre*, Leiden, 1967-1993]
London: Hans Zell Publishers (for the African Studies Centre, Leiden, Netherlands) [volume 25], 1994- Quarterly ISSN 1352-2175 £90.00/$153.00 annually institutional rate; £42.50/$76.50 annually individual rate
Edited by Elvire Eijkman, Tiny Kraan, Katrien Polman, Tineke Sommeling, and Marlene C.A. van Doorn

> Provides access to over 250 periodicals and edited works on Africa in the social sciences and the humanities. This includes all the leading journals in the field of African studies, as well as a number of other journals dealing with Third World countries and development studies in general. Each issue contains up to 450 abstracts, arranged geographically, with author, subject and geographical indexes, and a listing of the journals and edited works abstracted in each issue. A complete listing of all the journals that are scanned on a regular basis is included in the first issue of each volume.

165 **Ausgewählte neuere Literatur.../A Selected Bibliography of Recent Literature on Economic and Social Topics Concerning Africa/Bibliographie sélectionnée de littérature récente...**
Hamburg: Institut für Afrika Forschung, Dokumentations-Leitstelle Afrika, 1977- Quarterly

> Arranged geographically with subject sub-divisions; with (through 1982 only) subject, author, and geographical indexes.

166 **Bibliographie de l'Afrique sud-saharienne, sciences humaines et sociales: périodiques**
Tervuren, Belgium: Musée royal de l'Afrique centrale. 1925-1930, 1932- Annually
Compiled by Marcel d'Hertefelt and Anne-Marie Mouttiaux.

> Arranged by author, with detailed subject index and list of periodicals indexed. Beginning with 1986 (covering 1981-1983 publications) it indexes

only journal articles. First known as *Bibliographie ethnographique du Congo Belge et régions avoisinantes*; from 1962-1981 (covering 1960-1977) it was entitled *Bibliographie ethnographique de l'Afrique sud-saharienne*, and from 1978-1980 the title was *Bibliographie de l'Afrique sud-saharienne, sciences humaines et sociales*. No volume published since that covering the literature of 1989.

167 Bibliographie des travaux en langue française sur l'Afrique au sud du Sahara (sciences humaines et sociales)
Paris: Centre d'études africaines. 1977- Annually
Compiled by Zofia Yaranga.
   Lists monographs, articles, contributions to collected works, arranged by subject and geographically, with author and subject indexes.

168 A Current Bibliography on African Affairs
Farmingdale, NY: Baywood Publishing Co 1963- [New series 1968-] Quarterly
ISSN 0011-3255 $125.00 annually
   Each issue features articles and commentary, review articles and bibliographic essays, plus a topical and geographical list of books, documents, and periodical articles. An author index is included in each issue.

169 Index Islamicus. Current Books and Articles on Islam and the Muslim World
Cambridge: Cambridge University Library, 1958-1985. London: Mansell Publishing [as *Quarterly Index Islamicus*], 1986-1991. London: Bowker-Saur, 1992- Quarterly ISSN 0309-7395 £225.00/$340.00 annually
Edited by G.J. Roper and C.H. Bleaney
   Originally published in book form, this is a comprehensive continuing source on the literature of Islam and Middle Eastern Studies, which also includes a substantial number of citations for African countries, with sections for North and West Africa, Sudan and East Africa. Arranged by subjects and geographically. List some 6,000 new records annually. The fourth issue of each year is a hard-bound cumulation containing cumulated indexes for the year.

170 Index of African Social Science Periodical Articles/Index des articles de périodiques africains de sciences sociales
Dakar: CODESRIA [distributed by African Books Collective Ltd, Oxford], 1989- Annually ISSN 0850-9379 Volume 1: 1989, 112pp. £18.50/$38.00, Volume 2: 1993, 248pp. £19.95/$35.00
Compiled and edited by the CODESRIA Documentation and Information Center (CODICE)
   This is an important indexing and abstracting service of African social science journals, although thus far only two volumes have appeared: volume 1, 1989, which covered material published between 1985-1987, with 216 records from 24 African-published journals; and volume 2/3, 1990-1991 (published in 1993) which covered material for 1988-1989 and included 548 records from

49 journals. Abstracts are provided in the original language of publication, together with subject descriptors in English and French. Five indexes are included: authors, English subject descriptors, French subject descriptors, names of periodicals, and titles.

171 International African Bibliography. Current Books, Articles and Papers in African Studies

London: Mansell Publishing, 1971-1992; London: Hans Zell Publishers, 1993-Quarterly ISSN 0020-5877 £125.00/$215.00 annually
Edited by David Hall, in association with the Centre of African Studies at the Library, School of Oriental and African Studies, University of London

> Lists books, articles and papers in all fields of African studies, primarily in the social sciences and the humanities, but also includes scientific articles, especially relating to geography, natural resources and the environment. Includes some 4,000 entries annually, drawn from around 1,150 periodicals, about 250 of which are African serials. Entries are grouped under (1) Articles, and (2) Monographs, arranged geographically (for articles a full subject classification is indicated), with a subject index of articles. It covers articles in English, French, Italian, Dutch, Portuguese, and occasionally other European languages. An extensive cumulative index to each volume appears in the last issue of each volume, and consists of indexes by subject, authors and personalities, ethnic groups, languages, and other names and special terms.

172 Joint Acquisitions List of Africana

Evanston, IL: Melville J. Herskovits Library of African Studies, Northwestern University Library, 1962-1996 Six times yearly [ceased with volume 35, no. 6, November 1996] ISSN 0021-731X
Edited by Daniel Britz

> A joint list of monographs and serials acquired (in the current year and preceding five years) by 21 US libraries, and arranged by main entry. Annual cumulations for 1979, 1980, and 1981, but not thereafter, were published by G.K. Hall. Due to the changing on-line environment in many libraries, as well as increased access to on-line catalogues, the hardcopy version of *JALA* ceased publication at the end of 1996. However, the on-line version of *JALA* is available through the University of Michigan's on-line catalogue and will likely continue to be available at least through 1997. The database represents entries that originally appeared in *JALA* since July 1977. Its estimated file size is about 100,000 records.
>
> 💻 Access information: Telnet: HERMES.MERIT.EDU, at prompt "Which host?" enter MIRLYN, at first menu enter INDEXES, and first menu enter AFRI.

173 Quarterly Index to Periodical Literature, Eastern and Southern Africa

Nairobi: Library of Congress Office [POB 30598] 1991- Quarterly
ISSN 1018-1555 gratis

> An index to some 200 African-published serials, from 22 African countries, which are acquired regularly by the LC Nairobi office. Consists of a register

of citations by broad subject groups, followed by five indexes: author, geographical, subject term, title of article, and title of journal. For the most part coverage is restricted to scholarly serials, but some other types of journals (for example those in the areas of business and trade) are also included. A cumulated index to each year appears in the fourth issue of each volume.

💻 *Note:* the LC Nairobi Office offers a free bibliographic search service, whereby anyone with an Internet/Email address may search the periodicals database by field or by subject. Send an Email to serial@loc.sasa.unep.no with any subject of your choice, and with a body containing: find word word word, up to nine words.

174 **"Recent Doctoral Dissertations"** [in African studies]
Comp. by Joseph J. Lauer and Daniel Britz, *ASA News*, 1990- *(see* **292***)* Atlanta, GA: African Studies Association
     A supplementary and updating service to *American and Canadian Doctoral Dissertations and Master's Theses on Africa, 1974-1987 (see* **156***)*, which lists theses as reported in *Dissertation Abstracts International* and *Index to Theses with Abstracts Accepted for Higher Degrees by the Universities of Great Britain and Ireland*. Arranged by broad subject groups; includes the order number for each citation, and guidance on how to order copies.

175 **US Imprints on Sub-Saharan Africa: A Guide to Publications Catalogued at the Library of Congress**
Washington, DC: Library of Congress, African section, 1985- Annually
     Annual listing of titles catalogued during the previous year, arranged alphabetically by main entry and with title and subject indexes.

WorldViews: A Quarterly Review of Resources for Education and Action
see Section III: Journals and Magazines, entry **311**

Dealers' and distributors' catalogues (issued regularly)
(*see also* Section VI, pp. 170-185)

176 The Africa Book Centre Book Review
London: The Africa Book Centre Ltd [38 King Street, London WC2E 8JT]
1995- Quarterly £12.00 annually in the UK, £18.00 annually elsewhere
> Each issue (20-24pp. each) contains a small number of book reviews or a review essay of books on certain topics/countries, occasional interviews, plus two separate listings 'New Books from Africa' and 'New Books on Africa' arranged under broad subject groups, and providing a brief annotation on each title, prices and bibliographic data (but *not* names of publishers). All books listed can be ordered from the Africa Book Centre Ltd. *(see also* **663***)*.

177 African Books Collective Ltd Catalogue[s] no. 1- 1990- [latest catalogue, no. 13, 1996]
Oxford: African Books Collective Ltd [The Jam Factory, 27 Park End Street, Oxford OX1 1HU] Twice yearly gratis
> Extensively annotated biannual catalogues (64-96pp. each), providing full details of new and backlist titles from ABC member publishers (50 African publishers in 14 countries in 1996). Arranged by broad subject groups, with author/title index. All books are available from ABC's UK warehouse inventory of some 1,700 titles *(see* **664***)*. ABC also publishes a series of subject catalogues, currently in ten subject areas, which are issued regularly and periodically updated; other catalogues cover multicultural materials. All are available free on request.
> The complete ABC stocklist can be accessed from three websites:
> 🖥
> http://www.sas.upenn.edu/African_Studies/Publications/ABC_Menu.html *and*
> http://www.sas.upenn.edu/Africa_Studies/Books/bookmenu.html *and*
> http://wsi.cso.uiuc.edu/CAS

III. JOURNALS AND MAGAZINES

This is a *selective* listing of the major (for the most part *multidisciplinary*) African studies periodicals, as well as some more general interest magazines on Africa. It includes a number of journals not specifically on Africa - e.g. Black Studies, Third World studies, development, etc. - but which have strong Africa interests.

A substantial number of new journals have been added since publication of the first edition; those which have ceased publication have been deleted. Data was gathered through mailings of printouts and questionnaires. Journals were asked to verify and update information from the first edition; those with new entries were asked to complete questionnaires. Journals which did not respond, despite at least one chaser mailing, are marked with the symbols as set out below. A number of African-published journals who failed to respond have been dropped, as we have been unable to ascertain whether they are still being published.

Where forms were duly completed and verified, the following details are provided: full name and address (editorial address if different from main address); telephone and fax numbers (and Email addresses/Websites where available); year first published, ISSN, frequency, circulation, and subscription rates (surface postage unless otherwise indicated); name of editor/s and name/s of book review editor/s (and address if different from main address); a brief outline of contents and scope given in *italics*, and as provided by journal editors or publishers themselves; details of whether the publisher welcomes contributions and articles, and in what particular areas; average length suggested for contributions; payment offered (if any) and/or number of free copies of issue, or offprints, provided to contributors; type of illustrations used; and special editorial requirements.

Abbreviations and symbols used:

†   - repeat entry from 1st ed. (1989); information not verified; entry updated, as far as possible, from secondary sources

Φ   - provisional new entry, but questionnaire had not been completed; unverified information drawn from secondary sources

⌨   - indicates an electronic journal

Ann	- annually
Biwk	- bi-weekly
b/w	- black and white illustrations or photographs
Book rev	- journal carries book reviews
Book rev ed	- book review editor
char	- characters [number of, for contributions]
Circ	- circulation
col	- colour illustrations or photographs
Cont.	- content
Contrib	- contributions [welcomed in ...]
CRC	- camera ready copy
Dept	- department
d-s	- double-spaced
Ed/s	- editor/s
Edit req	- editorial requirements/style requirements
EU	- European Union
ext	- extension [for telephone numbers]
fn	- footnotes
h-t	- half-tones
Ill	- illustrations [type used]
indiv	- individual subscription rate
inst	- institutional subscription rate
ISSN	- International Standard Serial Number
L	- length [average length suggested for contributions]
line	- line illustrations
Mon	- monthly
2Mon	- twice monthly/fortnightly
NA	- North America
n/a	- no details provided
No contrib	- no contributions [does not publish unsolicited material]
NP	- no payment offered
occ	- occasional/occasionally
Offp	- offprints (or free copies to authors of articles)
P	- payment offered
photog	- photographs
pp	- pages [number of, for contributions]
Qtly	- quarterly
refs	- references
stud	- student subscription
Subs	- subscription rates [annually]

trans	- transparencies
w	- words [number of, for contribution]
Wk	- weekly
2Yr	- twice yearly
3Yr	- three times yearly
6Yr	- six times yearly/bi-monthly

EUROPE, ASIA, AUSTRALIA AND THE AMERICAS

Australia

178 **African Studies Association of Australasia and the Pacific Review and Newsletter**Φ
School of Social Sciences and Asian Languages
Curtin University of Technology
GPOB U1987
Perth WA 6001
+61-9-351 7648/351 7094
Fax: +61-9-351 3166
Email: gertzel@spectrum.edu.au
1978- 2Yr Circ: n/a Subs: A$25
Ed: Cherry Gertzel
Book rev
Cont: the journal and newsletter of the African Studies Association of Australia and the Pacific
Contrib: long and short contributions, correspondence and items for the News and Notes section are invited
Contributions on Africa-related research and teaching are particularly welcome

Austria

179 **Zeitschrift für Afrikastudien**†
Haydngasse 14/8
A-1060 Vienna
1987- ISSN 2235-89902 2Yr Circ: 500
Subs: AS360 inst AS180 indiv EU AS400 inst AS200 indiv elsewhere
Ed: Michael Neugebauer
Book rev Book rev ed: Bernhard Kittel, Waaggasse 12/6, A-1040 Vienna
'Promotes four political objects: anti-racism, anti-imperialism, anti-colonialism and anti-neocolonialism. Interdisciplinary approach. Learned journal for African studies'
Contrib: philosophy, labour unions, history, politics, economy, culture, literature, documents, international relations
L: 25pp NP 2 free copies Ill: line
Edit req: single side pp, disk provision (5¼" disk, 360 kbyte), software must be indicated, author's full name, address & affiliation, abstract of less than 150w in French or German language, refs, bibliography at end

Belgium

180 **Africa News Bulletin/Bulletin d'Information Africaine**
184 ave Charles Woeste
B-1090 Brussels
+32-2-420 3436 Fax: +32-2-420 0549
Email: paco@innet.be

1982- 2Mon; except in August
Circ: 1,000 Subs: $50 Africa $64
elsewhere
Ed: Paolo Costantini
Book rev
*'Information gathered from the press on
the main events in Africa during the
previous 2 weeks. Three sections: (1) press
reviews (2) short news items (3)
supplement of articles by African
journalists'*
Contrib: Africa. Analysis of current
events, background information and
opinions. Future developments
L: 900-1,000 P: $0.50 pw Offp

Brazil

181 **Africa: Revista do Centro de
Estudos Africanos**
CP 8105, C. Universitária
00508 São Paulo
+55-11-210 9416
Fax: +55-11-210 9416
Email: faam@usp.br
1978- ISSN 0100-8153 Ann
Circ: 1,500 Subs: $71 air
Ed: Fernando August Albuquerque
Mourão Book rev
*'Concentrates on human sciences in
general; dissemination of research on
Africa from Brazil and elsewhere;
establishment of interchange with
academic institutions; a cultural link
between Brazil and Africa. Articles are
published in Portuguese, French, English,
Spanish and Creole of Cabo Verde'*
Contrib: human sciences in general
L: 30pp NP 4 copies
Ill: photog, b/w
Edit req: 2 copies, d-s, 14, résumé of up to
10 lines, refs at end of articles; style sheet
available from ed

Canada

182 **African Literature Association
Bulletin**
Dept of Modern Languages &
Comparative Studies
University of Alberta
Edmonton
Alberta T6G 2E6
+1-403-4338510
Email: alab@planet.eon.net
1975- ISSN 0146-4965 Qtly
Circ: 1,000
Subs: $50 inst $40 indiv $10 stud
Ed: Stephen H. Arnold
Book rev
*'News, reviews, articles pertaining to
African literature and scholarship (plus
cinema and adjacent arts) in all
languages'*
Contrib: conference reports, memorial
tributes and historical occasions
L: 5pp NP 5 offp Ill: h-t, photog
Edit req: hard copy plus raw text in ASCII
on floppy disk, if possible

183 **Canadian Journal of African
Studies/Revue Canadienne des
Etudes Africaines†**
Centre for Urban and
Community Studies
University of Toronto
455 Spadina Avenue
Suite 426
Toronto Ontario M5S 2G8
+1-416-978 7067
1967- ISSN 0008-3968 3Yr
Circ: 1,000 Subs: Can$55
Can$20 Stud
Ed: Roger Riendeau
Book rev Book rev ed: Richard Maclure,
Faculty of Education, University of
Ottawa, 145 Jean Jacques Lussier, Ottawa,
Ontario K1N 6NE
*'The journal of the Canadian Association
of African Studies'*
Contrib: in English & French

184 Journal of Asian and African Studies

Dept of Sociology
York University
4700 Keele St, Downsview
Ontario M3J 1P3
+1-416-736 5507
Fax: +1-416-441 3035
1966- 2Yr Circ: n/a
Ed: K. Ishwaran
Book rev Book rev ed: Stephen Ndegwa, Government Dept, William and Mary College, POB 8795, Williamsburg, VA 23187-8795, USA
'Publishes scholarly studies on Asia and Africa; the focus of the journal is interdisciplinary'
Contrib: social sciences
L: 20pp NP 10 offp Ill: line, h-t, photog, b/w
Edit req: d-s; style sheet available from ed

France

185 Africa International

BP 172
F-75523 Paris Cedex 11
+33-1-44 93 85 95
Fax: +33-1-44 93 74 68 Email: 101445,2367@compuserve.com
1958- Mon Circ: 60,000 Subs: FF600
Ed: Marie Roger Biloa
Book rev
Contrib: n/a

186 Afrique Contemporaine

La Documentation française
29 quai Voltaire
F-75344 Paris Cedex 07
+33-1-402 15 70 00
Fax: +33-1-40 15 72 30
1962- ISSN: 0002-0478 Qtly Circ: 1,800
Subs: FF265 France
FF325 Europe FF410 elsewhere
Ed: Michel Gaud
Book rev Book rev ed: Jean-Yves Coutat

'Political, economic and social studies; extensive bibliography section of new publications, including material in English'
Contrib: as above
L: 40,000 char

187 Afrique Education

3 rue Carvès
F-92120 Montrouge
+33-1-42 53 72 09
Fax: +33-1-46 56 88 08
1993- ISSN 1247-5289 Mon
Circ: 20-30,000 Subs: FF200 France
FF480 Africa
Ed: Paul Tedga
Book rev
'Publishes a list of African universities each year as well as a special issue on the Baccalaureat in Africa'
Contrib: development issues
L: n/a NP Ill: photog

188 Afrique en Scènes

51 rue Sainte Anne
F-75002 Paris
+33-1-42 60 61 03
Fax: +33-1-42 60 60 82
Email: aec@pratique.fr
Website: http://www.ina.fr/AfricArt
1994- Qtly Circ: 4,000 Subs: FF280
Ed: Christian Genevier
'Notes on African artistes on tour outside Africa. Reports on African cultural events; a calendar of events'
Contrib: as above
L:500-1,500w NP Offp

189 Afrique Express

162 place du Dix-Neuf mars 1962
F-93100 Montreuil
+33-1-48 59 80 12
Fax: +33-1-48 59 80 12
1993- 46 yr Circ: 5,000 Subs: FF1,840
Ed: René Jacques Lique
Cont: n/a Contrib: all areas of Africa
L: n/a NP

190 Afrique MagazineΦ
57 bis rue d'Auteuil
F-756016 Paris
+33-1-44 30 19 60
Fax: +33-1-45 30 09 67
1983- Mon Circ:n/a Subs: FF1,300
Ed: Danielle Ben Yahmed
'Societies and people'
Contrib: n/a

191 Alternatives Africaines
DATFRO, 180 Avenue Henri
Ravera, BP 8
F-92220 Bagneux
+33-01-45 85 71 96
Fax: +33-01-45 85 71 96
1992- ISSN 1250-8411 Qtly Circ: n/a
Subs: FF100
Eds: n/a
Book rev Book rev ed: CEPED, 15 rue de
l'Ecole de médecine, F-75270 Paris Cedex
069
*'Social sciences, health, education,
economic issues, environment, women,
children, law, family, science and
technology'*
Contrib: as above; no political issues
L: 1,000w NP Offp Ill: photog

192 Bulletin de l'Afrique Noire
10 rue Vineuse
F-75784 Paris Cedex 16
+33-1-44 30 81 00
Fax: +33-1-44 30 81 11
Email: rosenwal@pratique.fr
1937- ISSN 0045-3501 45Yr Circ: n/a
Subs: FF5,600
Ed: Stephane Vigouroux
*'Economics, finance and politics, focus on
francophone Africa'*
No contrib

193 Cahiers d'Etudes Africaines
Ecoles hautes études sciences
sociales
54 boulevard Raspail
F-75006 Paris

+33-1-49 54 24 69
Fax: +33-1-49 54 26 92
Email: cahiers-Afr@ehess.fr
1960- ISSN 0008-0055 Qtly Circ: 600
Subs: FF420-480 inst FF270 indiv
Ed: Jean-Loup Amselle
Book rev
*'Anthropology, ethnology, history and
sociology'*
Contrib: as above
L: 25-30pp NP 30offp 1 free copy Ill: line,
b/w photog
Edit req: bibliographic references at the
end of article. Hard copy and disk (Word
5.1 for Macintosh)

**194 Etudes Littéraires Africaines:
Revue de l'Association pour
l'Etude des Littératures
Africaines APELA** (formerly
APELA Bulletin)
Université de Cergy-Pontoise
33 boulevard du Port
F-950011 Cergy-Pontoise
Cedex
+33-1-45 80 67 16
Fax: +33-1-45 80 67 16
1996- ISSN 0769-4563 2Yr Circ: 300
Subs: FF200/$40 inst FF150/$30 members
Ed: Daniel Delas
Book rev
*'Book reviews, bibliographic section,
association news, colloquium and
conference dates, covers anglophone,
francophone and lusophone Africa, and
West Indies'*
No contrib

195 Jeune Afrique†
57 bis rue d'Auteuil
F-75016 Paris
+33-1-47 66 52 42
Fax: +33-1-46 22 66 38
1960- ISSN 0021-6089 Wk Circ: n/a
Subs: FF620 France FF1,800 Africa
Ed: Hugo Sada
Book rev Book rev ed: Marcel Peju

'*Popular weekly news, current affairs and cultural magazine*'
Contrib: all areas
L: 1pp P: variable Ill: photog, drawings

196 **Jeune Afrique Economie**
58 rue de Lisbonne
F-75008 Paris
+33-1-53 75 29 02
Fax: +33-1-53 75 29 04
1981- ISSN 0962-1856 23Yr
Circ: 65,000 Subs: FF30 each
Ed: Blaise Pascal Talla
'*Fortnightly news magazine in French with summary pages in English*'
Contrib: n/a

197 **Journal des Africanistes**
Société des Africanistes,
Musée de l'Homme
17 place du Trocadéro
F-75116 Paris
+33-01-47 27 72 55
Fax: +33-1-47 04 63 40
Email: Ferry@mnhn.fr
1930- ISSN 0399-0346 2Yr
Circ: 1,000 Subs: FF300
Ed: M.P. Ferry
Book rev Book rev ed: Marc Piault
'*Original articles on human sciences in Africa: ecology, geography, prehistory, history, linguistics, physical, social and cultural anthropology, sociological studies of relations between Africa and the rest of the world*'
Contrib: as above
L: 30pp NP 25 offp
Edit req: summary and key word list

198 **La Lettre d'Afrique en Créations**
51 rue Sainte Anne
F-75002 Paris
+33-1-42 60 61 03
Fax: +33-1-42 60 60 82
Email: aec@pratique.fr
Website: http://www.ina.fr/AfricArt
1991- Qtly Circ: 4,000 Subs: gratis

Ed: Patrice Peteuil
'*News of contemporary African artistic endeavour; activities of Afrique en Créations*'
Contrib: as above
L: 250/500w NP Offp

199 **Marchés Tropicaux et Méditerranéens**Φ
René Moreux et Cie
190 blvd Haussmann
F-75008 Paris
+33-1-45 63 11 55
Fax: +33-1-42 89 08 72
1945- ISSN 0025-2859 Wk Circ: n/a
Subs: n/a
Ed: François Gaulme
Book rev
Cont: Current affairs, economics, development
Contrib: n/a

200 **Notre Librarie. Revue du livre: Afrique, Caraïbes, Océan Indien**
Club des lecteurs
d'expression française
(CLEF)
5 rue Rousselet
F-75007 Paris
+33-1-53 69 34 38
Fax: +33-1-43 06 14 9
1969- ISSN 0755-3854 Qtly
Circ:15,000 Subs: FF300
Ed: Marie Clotilde Jacquey
'*A critical literary publication, with articles in French, on French language literature from sub-Saharan Africa, Indian Ocean countries, and the Caribbean; interviews with authors and book reviews*'
Contrib: as above
L: 8pp article; 1p bk rev P: FF260 per printed p Offp Ill: b/w photog

201 **Nouvel Afrique Asie**
3 rue de Metz
F-75010 Paris

+33-1-40 22 06 72
Fax: +33-1-45 23 28 02
1969- ISSN 1141-9946 Mon
Circ: 100,000 Subs: FF340 Europe FF360
Africa $85 elsewhere (air)
Ed: Simon Malley
Book rev
Book rev ed: Odile Gundon
*'Information, analysis, opinions on
political, economic and social events in
Africa, Asia and Latin America'*
Contrib: as above
L: 4,-16,000w P Offp Ill: n/a
Contrib: concise, objective and well
documented.

202 Peuples Noirs, Peuples Africains†
82 ave de la Porte des
Champs
F-76000 Rouen
+33-2-35 89 31 97
1978- ISSN: 0181-4087 6Yr Circ: n/a
Subs: FF240; FF40 stud
Ed: Mongo Beti
*'All cultural and political subjects
concerning Black peoples'*
Contrib: as above
L: 1-5,000w NP 5 free copies Ill: none
[Ed. note: ceased?]

203 Politique Africaine
Karthala
22-24 boulevard Arago
F-75013 Paris
Editorial address:
Centre d'études d'Afrique noire, BP 101,
F-33405 Talence Cedex
+33-1-43 31 12 59
Fax: +33-1-56 37 45 37
1981- ISSN 0244-7837 Qtly
Circ: 2,000 Subs: FF320 France
FF395 Europe (air) FF490 NA (air)
Ed: Dominique Darbon
Book rev Book rev ed: Jean-Pascal Daloz
*'Current affairs, political life of (mostly)
Black Africa. Social and cultural topics'*

Contrib: field studies of political life in
contemporary Africa
L: 3-6,000w NP 3 offp Ill: photog

204 Présence Africaine. Revue Culturelle du Monde Noire†
Société Nouvelle Présence
Africaine
25 bis rue des Ecoles
F-75005 Paris
+33-1-43 54 13 74/43 25 96 67
1947- ISSN 0032-7638 Qtly Circ: n/a
Subs: FF300/$75
Ed: Yande Christiane Diop

Germany

205 Africana Marburgensia†
Universität Marburg
c/o Seminar für
Religiongeschichte
Am Plan 3
D-3550 Marburg/Lahn
+49-6421-283930
Fax: +49-6421-288968
1968- 2Yr Circ: 350 Subs: mainly
exchange
Ed: Christoph Elsas & Hans-Herman
Munkner
*'African studies - African religions;
African traditions and change (social,
economic and legal aspects)'*
Contrib: as above, preferably from
Africa/African authors
L: 10-20pp NP 10 offp Ill: none

206 Afrika Spectrum
Institut für Afrika-Kunde
Neuer Jungfernstieg 21
D-20354 Hamburg
+49-40-356 2523/524
Fax: +49-40-356 2511
Email: iak@hwwa.uni-hamburg.de
Website: http://bicc.uni-
bonn.de/coop/fiv/duei/iaa/info.html
1966- ISSN 0002-0397 3Yr Circ: 500
Subs: DM90

Ed: Dirk Kohnert
Book rev
'Africanist journal covering the social sciences in general (Africa South of the Sahara). Articles published in German, English, French. Each issue contains books reviews and reports on conferences and research activities'
Contrib: social, economic and political conditions and developments in Africa South of the Sahara
L: 20-25pp articles; 6-10pp reports NP 30 offp + 2 copies
Ill: line, h-t, b/w
Edit req: articles should contain 15-20 line summary

207 **Afrika Süd**
Königswinterer Strasse 116
D-53227 Bonn
+49-228-464369
Fax: +49-228-488177
1971- 6Yr Circ: 200 Subs: DM60
Ed: Hein Mollers
Book rev
'Political and economic development in southern Africa (South Africa, Namibia, Zimbabwe, Angola, Mozambique, Zambia, Botswana, Lesotho, Swaziland, Malawi, Tanzania, Zaire)'
Contrib: as above
L:1,200-2,400w P: DM0.50 p 7w 2 offp

208 **Afrika und Übersee-Sprachen, Kulturen**
Dietrich Reimer Verlag
Unter den Eichen 57
D-12203 Berlin 45
Editorial address:
Institut für Afrikanistik und Äthiopistik der Universität Hamburg,
Rothenbaumchausee 67-69, D-20148 Hamburg
+49-30-831 4081
Fax: +49-30-831 6323
1910- ISSN 0002-0427 2Yr Circ: n/a
DM148 each
Eds: E. Dammann, L. Gerhardt,

E. Köhler-Meyer
Book rev ed: Hilke Meyer-Bahlburg
'Articles mainly on African languages, on history in connection with languages, on traditional literature in connection with languages'
Contrib: African languages and linguistics
L: 30pp NP 25 offp

209 **Aktueller Informationsdienst Afrika/Africa Current Affairs Information Service**
Institut für Afrika-Kunde
Neuer Jungfernsteig 21
D-20354 Hamburg
+49-40-356 3523
Fax: +49-40-356 2511
Email: iak@hwna.uni.hamburg.de
1974- ISSN 0342-0396 Biwk
Circ: 200 Subs: DM195
Ed: Klaus Hemstedt
'Reproduction of articles from ca.20 African newspapers published in English, French and Portuguese and dealing with social, economic and political conditions and developments in Africa except northern Africa (covered by the Current Affairs Information Service published by the Deutsches Orient-Institut, Hamburg)'
No contrib

210 **Internationales Afrikaforum**
Weltforum Verlag
Marienburger Strasse 22
D-50968 Cologne
+49-221-937630
Fax: +49-221-937 6399
1964- ISSN 0020-9430 Qtly Circ: n/a
Subs: DM128
Eds: Hans-Gert Braun & Count Alois von Waldburg-Zeil
Book rev
'Chronik: (45 pp) political, social, economic, cultural development; essay section: forum for specialists and experts from various schools of thought; literary review'

Contrib: politics, social affairs, economics,
occasionally history
L: 10-15 pp NP 5 offp Ill: graphs,
diagrams, author must supply camera-
ready artwork

211 **Lusorama. Zeitschrift für
     Lusitanistik/Revista de estudos
     sobre os Países de Língua
     Portuguesa**
     Editora TFM
     Postfach 100839
     D-60008 Frankfurt am Main
Editorial address:
Amsterdamer Strasse 19B, D-13347 Berlin
+49-30-4560 6221
Fax: +49-30-4560 6222
1985- ISSN 0931-9484 3Yr Circ: n/a
Subs: n/a
Ed: Axel Schönberger
Book rev
*'Portugal, Brazil, Angola, Mozambique,
Cape Verde, São Tomé e Principe, Guinea
Bissau'*
Contrib: Literary criticism and linguistics

212 **Matatu. Journal for African
     Culture and Society**
     Damaschkeanger 139
     D-60489 Frankfurt am Main
     +49-69-761585 Fax: +49-69-761585
     Email: 100676,3042@compuserve.com
     1987- ISSN 0932-9714 2Yr
     Circ: 1,000 Subs: DM52
Ed: Holger Ehling
Book rev Book rev ed: Monika Trebert
*'Features all aspects of Black and African
cultural studies, with emphasis on
literature. Recent and forthcoming issues:
Littératures de Congo-Zaïre, Afrikaans
literature, children's literature, cinema,
Ghana; English and French'*
Contrib: as above, all aspects of Black and
African studies
L: 15-20pp P: variable 25 offp Ill: photog,
b/w drawing, lithographs
Edit req: MLA-Handbook style, summary
of 10-15 lines, self-addressed envelope

Greece

213 **Journal of Oriental and
     African Studies**
     Papadiamandi 228
     Aghia Barbara
     GR-12351 Athens
     +30-1-5613 643 Fax: +30-1-343161
     1989- Ann Circ: 500 Subs: $60
Ed: Athanasius T. Photopoulos
Book rev
*'Academic international,
multidisciplinary, and independent.
Covers Africa and Asia and their diverse
relations with the West. Promotes
academic research. Multilingual'*
Contrib: as above
L: 7,000w NP 25-30 offp
Edit req: hard & disk copy

India

214 **Indian Journal of African
     Studies**
     Dept of African Studies
     University of Delhi
     Delhi 110007
     +91-11-725 7828
     Fax: +91-11-725 7336
     1992- 2Yr Circ: 500
     Subs: $40 inst $20 indiv
Ed: Kay Matthews
Book rev Book rev ed: S.C. Saxena
*'Articles, book reviews, documents, special
features on African politics, economics,
history, sociology, geography, and
international relations'*
Contrib: as above
L: 8,000w NP 10 offp +1 free copy
Ill: n/a
Edit req: 2 copies d-s one side of paper, fn
and ref numbered at end

Italy

215 Africa. Rivista Trimestriale di Studi e Documentazione†
Istituto Italiano per l'Africa
16 via Ulisse Aldrovandi
I-00197 Rome
+39-6-321 6712 Fax: +39-6-322 5348
1946- ISSN 0001-9747 Qtly Circ: n/a
Subs: L40,000
Ed: Gianluigi Rossi

216 Nigrizia. Fatti e Problemi del Mondo Nero†
Vicolo Pozzo 1
I-37129 Verona
+39-45-596238 Fax: +39-45-800 1737
1883- ISSN 0029-0173 Mon
Circ: 30,000 Subs: L30,000 Italy L50,000
EU L70,000 Africa
Ed: Aurelio Boscaini
'Multidisciplinary, covering all aspects of African life, culture and religions etc.'

Netherlands

217 Journal of African Languages and Linguistics
Vakgroep Afrikaanse
Taalkunde
Rijkuniversiteit te Leiden
POB 9515
NL-2300 RA Leiden
+31-71-527 2245
Fax: +31-71-527 2615
Email: ameka@rulcri.Leidenuniv.nl
1979- ISSN 0167-6164 2Yr Circ: n/a
Subs: DM152 inst DM82 indiv
Ed: Felix K. Ameka
Book rev Book rev ed: Maarten Mous
'Each issue contains 2 to 4 articles on different aspects of African languages, extensive book reviews section, and list of recently published books on African languages'

Contrib: all aspects African languages, synchronic and diachronic, theoretical and data-oriented
L: n/a NP 24 offp
Edit req: copy in English or French

218 Journal of Religion in Africa
E.J. Brill Publishers
POB 9000
NL-2300 PA Leiden
Editorial address:
Dept of Theology and Religious Studies, University of Leeds, Leeds LS2 9JT, UK
+44(0)113-233 3640
Fax: +44(0)113-233 3654
Email: i.lawrie@leeds.ac.uk
1967- ISSN 0022-4200 4Yr
Circ: 2,000 Subs: NLG200 inst NLG148 indiv
Ed: Adrian Hastings
Book rev Book rev ed: David Maxwell, Dept of History, University of Keele, Keele, Staffs ST5 5BG, UK
'Concerned impartially with all aspects, present and past, of religion in Africa - traditional, Christian, Islamic - approached historically, anthropologically or theoretically. Most issues are focused upon one theme, e.g. on modern Islam'
Contrib: as above
L: 4-8,000w NP 25 offp Ill: occ. photog, maps
Edit req: 2 copies d-s, disk

Poland

219 Africana Bulletin
Karowa 20
Warsaw 00324
+48-22-268547 Fax: +48-22-261965
1962- 2Yr Circ: 800
Subs: $20 single copy
Ed: Bogador Winid Book rev
'All subjects dealing with African affairs'
Contrib: as above
L: 20pp NP 5 offp
Edit req: copy in English or French

Russia

**220 St. Petersburg Journal of
African Studies, The**
Evropeisky Dom
3 Furmanova Str
St. Petersburg 191187
+7-812-279 0833
Fax: +7-812-279 0833
Email: azic@evrdom.spb.su
1993- 2Yr Circ:1,000
Subs: $48 inst $28 indiv
Ed: Valentin Vydrine
Book rev
*'African linguistics, history, philology,
social anthropology (including economic
anthropology, ethnomusicology, etc.), art
studies, cultural studies, other humanities;
in English and French'*
Contrib: as above
L: max: 7,000w NP 2 offp + 1 free copy
Ill: b/w
Edit req: on disk if poss. in ASCII format;
all diacritics must be encoded using first
128 ASCII codes

Spain

221 Estudios Africanos
c/o Ramiro de Maeztu
Asociación Española de
Africanistas, a/c Colegio
Mayor Univ. NS Africa
Ciudad Universitaria
E-28040 Madrid
+34-1-5541 104 Fax: +34-1-5541 401
1985- ISSN 0214-2309 2Yr
Circ: 1,000 Subs: Pts2,000 Spain
Pts2,500 elsewhere
Ed: José W. Martinez Carreras
*'Studies and notes on history and current
affairs in Africa (society, culture,
literature, etc.)'*
Contrib: social sciences in general but all
areas considered
L: 20-25pp NP 5 offp
Edit req: d-s, a summary in English/French

Sweden

**222 Development Dialogue. A
Journal of International
Development Cooperation**
The Dag Hammarskjöld
Centre
Ovre Slottsgatan 2
SE-75310 Uppsala
+46-18-127272 Fax: +46-18-122072
1972- ISSN 0345-2328 2Yr Circ: n/a
Subs: gratis
Eds: Olle Nordberg & Sven Hamrell
Book rev
*'Contains mainly material arising from the
seminars and workshops organised by the
Foundation. The editors also, in certain
cases, commission articles. The issues
often feature a specific theme'*
No contrib

**223 Nordic Journal of African
Studies**
c/o Dept of Asian and African
Languages
Uppsala University POB 513
SE-75102 Uppsala
Editorial address:
Editor/NJAS, University of Helsinki, Box
13, Meritullinkatu 1B, FIN-00014
Helsinki, Finland
+358-9-1912 2677
Fax: +358-9-1912 2094
Email: ahurskai@waltari.helsinki.fi
or: arvi.hursakinen@ling.helsinki.fi
1992- ISSN 1235-4481 2Yr
Circ: ca. 500 Subs: SEK170 inst SEK140
indiv in Scandinavia SEK 215 elsewhere
Ed: Arvi Hurskainen
Book rev Book rev ed: Bernhard Helander,
Hässjevägen 13, SE-75647 Uppsala
*'Journal of the Nordic Association of
African Studies. Articles on social/cultural
anthropology, economic/cultural
geography, history, language, linguistics
and literature'*
Contrib: as above

L: max 30pp NP 2 free copies
Ill: simple diagrams, maps
Edit req: articles must be submitted on
disk, with no formatting

224 **Scandinavian Journal of**
   Development Alternatives and
   Area Studies
   POB 7444
   SE-10391 Stockholm
1980- ISSN 0280-2791 Qtly
Circ: 2,000 Subs: $50
Ed: Franklin Vivekananda
Book rev
'Main focus in Third World countries,
especially in Africa: economic
development, North-South relations,
environment, basic human need
satisfaction, migration, sociology, conflict
and peace, trade, finance'
Contrib: any issues on Africa; as above
L: 25pp Offp

United Kingdom

225 **Africa**
   International African Institute
   SOAS, Thornhaugh Street
   Russell Square
   London WC1H 0XG
Editorial address:
Dept of Anthropology, University College
London, Gower Street, London WC1E
6BT
+44(0)171-831 3068
Email: m.last@ucl.ac.uk
1928- ISSN 0001-9720 Qtly
Circ: 1,200 Subs: journal & annual
bibliography £132 inst £66 indiv journal
only £39.50 indiv
Ed: Murray Last
Book rev Book rev ed: Tom Young, Dept
of Economics and Political Studies,
SOAS, Malet Street, London WC1E 7HP
'The study of African societies and
cultures: encourages an inter-disciplinary
approach, involving the social sciences,

languages and culture and actively seeks
out international scholarly contributions'
Contrib: social sciences, history,
environmental and life sciences, languages
and culture
L: 8,000w NP 20 offp + 1 free copy
Ill: line, h-t, photog
Edit req: 2 copies, d-s, A4, abstract of not
more than 400w

226 **Africa Analysis**
   Ludgate House, Suite 71
   107-111 Fleet Street
   London EC4A 2AB
+44(0)171-353 1117
Fax: +44(0)171-353 1516
Email: africa-analysis@mcri.poptel.org.uk
1986- ISSN 0950-902X 2Mon
Circ: n/a Subs: £345/$595 inst
£245/$445 indiv
Ed: Ahmed Rajab
Book rev
'Fortnightly bulletin on financial and
political trends; business, stock market
and corporate update'
Contrib: Africa's finance, economy, and
inside politics
L: n/a P: £100 per 1,000w

227 **Africa Confidential**
   73 Farringdon Road
   London EC1M 3JB
+44(0)-171-831 3511
Fax: +44(0)-171-831 6778
1960- ISSN 0044-6483 2Wk
Circ: 2,500 Subs: £180/$468 NA (air)
£185 Africa £60 stud
Ed: Patrick Smith
'Exclusive features on African politics and
economics, and relations between Africa
and the rest of the world; short 'pointers'
on similar subjects'
Contrib: in depth political and economic
analysis
L: 500-1,000 P: £200 per 1,000w
Ill: maps

228 **Africa Economic Digest†**
26-32 Whistler Street
London N5 1NH
+44(0)171-359 5335
Fax: +44(0)171-359 9173
1980- ISSN 0144-8234 Wk
Circ: 6,000 Subs: £225
Ed: Jon Ofei-Ansah
*'Business and economic news on OAU
Africa'*
Contrib: commissioned only

229 **Africa Health**
Vine House
Fair Green Reach
Cambridge CB5 0JD
+44(0)1638-743633
Fax: +44(0)1638-743998
Email: paul@fsg.co.uk
1978- ISSN 0141-9536 6Yr
Circ: 6,000 Subs: £42 UK; £63 elsewhere
£8 health care indiv in Africa
Ed: Paul Chinnock
Book rev
*'Journal for doctors in Africa. Mainly
clinical but also readers' letters, news,
new products etc.'*
Contrib: clinical medicine
L: 1,700w max P: £100 per 1,700w article
Offp Ill: n/a

230 **Africa Now**
7 Rudolf Place
Miles Street
London SW8 1RP
+44(0)171-735 8071
Fax: +44(0)171-735 570
1981- ISSN 0261-5908 Mon
Circ: 30,000 Subs: £24
Ed: Peter Enahoro
Book rev Book rev ed: Ken Amankwah
*'Political, economic and cultural monthly
with specialised sections: News Analysis
Review; African Markets featuring
economics and business topics;
Despatches: incisive behind the news
reports; Karibu: travel, tourism and
culture. Occasional in-depth interviews'*

Contrib: politics, economics, business,
culture, travel, tourism, human interest,
profiles and interviews
L: 1,500 P: £80 per p Offp
Ill: witty cartoons welcome
Edit req: copy must arrive 15th preceding
month of publication

231 **Africa Research Bulletin**
Blackwells Publishers
108 Cowley Road
Oxford OX4 1JF
Editorial address:
Pines, Wykes Lane, Newton St Cyres,
Devon EX5 5AX
+44(0)1865-791100
Fax: +44(0)1865-791347
1964- ISSN A-political: 0001-9844
B-economic: 0001-9852 Mon
Circ: 600 Subs: Combined rate: £381 EU
$730 Africa NA £428 elsewhere
£285/$487 single subs
Ed: Pita Adams
*'Published in two separate parts.
Political: coverage, in form of digest, of
security, government relations in Africa.
Economic: digest: economic indicators,
budgets, commodities, industry, aid, trade'*
No contrib

232 **African Affairs**
SOAS, Thornhaugh Street
Russell Square
London WC1H 0XB
Editorial address:
Dept of Politics, University of Reading,
Whiteknights POB 218 Reading RG6 2AA
+44(0)1734-318503
Fax: +44(0)1734-753833
Email: p.r.woodward@reading.ac.uk
1901- ISSN 0001-9909 Qtly
Circ: 2,800 Subs: £38/$65
Ed: Peter Woodward
Book rev Book rev ed: Willie Henderson
*'Original articles on current or recent
social, economic and political
developments in Africa'*

Contrib: all areas concerned with Africa, written in style immediately accessible to non-specialists and specialists alike
L: 6,000w NP 25 offp Ill: maps, photog
Edit req: style sheet available from eds

233 **African Archaeological Review**
Institute of Archaeology,
University College
Gordon Square
London WC1H 0PY
+44(0)171-387 7050 ext.4429
Fax: +44(0)171-813 5241
Email: f.hassan@ucl.ac.uk
1983- ISSN 0263-0338 Qtly Circ: 400
Subs: $100 inst $35 indiv
Ed: Fekri Hassan
Book rev
'Authoritative articles on African archaeology. Emphasis on cultural continuities and discontinuities; interregional interaction; biocultural evolution; cultural dynamics; cultural ecology; role of cultural materials in politics and ideology'
No unsolicited contrib
L: 21,500w NP Offp Ill: photog, b/w line

234 **African Book Publishing Record, The**
Hans Zell Publishers
An imprint of Bowker-Saur
POB 56
Oxford OX1 2SJ
US Office: POB 130, Flagstaff
AZ 86002-0130
+44(0)1865-511428
Fax: +44(0)1865-311534
US tel & fax: +1-520-774 8862
Email: hzell@dial.pipex.com
US: 100255,1141@compuserve.com
1975- ISSN 0306-0322 Qtly
Circ: 500 Subs: £120/$220
Eds: Hans M. Zell & Cécile Lomer
Book rev
Book rev eds: Gary Gorman, School of Information Studies, Charles Sturt University, POB 588 Wagga Wagga, NSW

2650, Australia; Mark Delancey, Dept of Government and International Studies, University of South Carolina, Columbia SC 29208, USA
'Provides extensive bibliographic coverage of new and forthcoming African publications; also includes an extensive book review section and reviews of new African serials; plus news, reports, interviews, articles, etc. about African booktrade activities and developments'
Contrib: book reviews solicited only; articles welcomed on all aspects of African publishing and the booktrade, and African librarianship
L: 1,800-5,000w NP 3 free copies
Ill: b/w photog
Edit req: d-s, A4, refs with fn at end of articles (on disk if possible); all book reviews to be submitted through joint book review editors above; style sheet from eds

235 **African Business**
IC Publications Ltd
Coldbath Square
London EC1R 4LQ
+44(0)171-713 7711
Fax: +44(0)171-713 7970
Email: icpubs@dial.pipex.com
1966- ISSN 0141-3923 Mon
Circ: 16,539 Subs: £50/$90 £32/$50 stud
Ed: Anver Versi
Book rev
'Specialist magazine which charts the development business in Africa in the nineties. Concentrates Pan-African coverage on economics, business, industry, markets, commodities, finance and investment'
Contrib: anything on African economics and business
L: 900-1,000w £70 per 1,000w Offp
Ill: line, h-t, photog
Edit req: include 300-400w synopsis

236 **African Concord†**
Aare Abiola House
26-32 Whistler Street
London N5 1NH
+44(0)171-359 5335
Fax: +44(0)171-359 9173
1984- 2Mon Circ: 4,000
Subs: £225 Africa $245 EU £240
Ed: Jon Ofei-Ansah
'African issues and events - politics,
economics, culture and arts, ideas; events
and issues as they affect African people in
the diaspora, UK, Canada and the
Caribbean'
Contrib: opinions on African issues,
special news features on African affairs
and the diaspora
L: 1,000w P: £50-100 Ill: photog, cartoons
b/w, col

237 **African Farming & Food**
     Processing
27 Wilfred Street
London SW1E 6PR
+44(0)171-834 7676
Fax: +44(0)171-973 0076
Email: afed@alain.demon.uk
1979- 6Yr Circ: 9,000
Subs: £43.50/$75
Ed: Jonquil Phelan
Book rev
'All aspects of African agriculture and
food processing, including finance,
appropriate technology, crops, livestock,
irrigation, packaging, processing'
Contrib: commissioned only, as above
L: 1,500w P Offp Ill: photo, diagrams, b/w
& col
Edit req: welcomes relevant photographs
of Africa

238 **African Journal of Ecology**
Dept of Zoology
University of Cambridge
Downing Street
Cambridge CB2 3EJ
+44(0)1223-334455
Fax: +44(0)1223-336676

Email: ske1000@cus.cam.ac.uk
Website: http://www/blacksci.co.uk
1963- Qtly Circ: 600
Subs: £215 £53.50 members East African
Wildlife Society
Ed: F.I.B. Kayanja
Book rev Book rev ed: S.K. Eltringham
'Original scientific articles and book
reviews'
Contrib: African ecology
L: 3,500w NP 50 offp Ill: line, photog

239 **African Journal of**
     International and Comparative
     Law
Aberdeen House
22 Highbury Grove
London N5 2DQ
+44(0)171-704 0610
Fax: +44(0)171-704 0973
Email: 100632,3305@compuserve.com
1986- ISSN 0954-8890 Qtly Circ: n/a
Subs: £70/$120 inst £40 Africa £50 indiv
elsewhere £35 stud £30 African stud
Eds: E.K. Yakpo & Tahar Boumedra
Book rev
Book rev ed: Tahar Boumedra
'International and comparative law of
relevance to Africa'
Contrib: international law; domestic law in
comparative perspective, constitutional
law and human rights, humanitarian law,
environmental law
L:5000-10,000w NP 20 offp + 1 free copy
Ill: diagrams, maps
Edit req: original previously unpublished
work only; d-s A4; IBM/Macintosh disk
pref, numbered fn at end

240 **African Labour History**
POB 525
Oxford OX1 2TF
Fax: +44(0)1865-512409
1997- ISSN 0958-3149 Ann Circ: 750
Subs: £30/$60 inst £15/$30 indiv
Ed: Dwight Middleton
Book rev

'History of African labour worldwide: mainly in Africa; the Americas, Europe and the Middle East. Each volume includes a special feature, articles, review essays, sources and documents. Abstracts on English, French, and Spanish'
Contrib: scholarly articles on wide range of subjects, especially in economic and social history
L: max. 12,000w NP 1 free copy
Ill: camera ready artwork required
Edit req: d-s; if on disk indicate software used and supply hard copy; abstract 100w

241 African Languages and Cultures

SOAS, Thornhaugh Street
Russell Square
London WC1H 0XG
+44(0)171-637 2388
Fax: +44(0)171-436 3844
Email: mo1@soas.ac.uk or
mm3@soas.ac.uk
Website:http://www.oup.co.uk/jnls/list/aflang/subinfo
1988- ISSN 0954-416X 2Yr Circ: n/a
Subs: £27/$46 inst £16/$30 indiv $32 developing countries
Eds: Martin Orwin & Michael Mann
'Africa-oriented papers in descriptive linguistics, comparative linguistics and classification; oral literature, African writing in African and metropolitan languages; African art and music'
Contrib: as above
L: 25 pp NP 10 offp Ill: line, h-t
Edit req: d-s, A4, style sheet available from eds

242 African Literature Today

James Currey Publishers
73 Botley Road
Oxford OX2 0BS
Editorial address:
Fourah Bay College, University of Sierra Leone, Freetown, Sierra Leone
+44(0)1865-244111
Fax: +44(0)1865-246454

1968- ISSN 0852-5555 Ann
Circ: 4,000 Subs: £8.95 per vol
Eds: Eldred Durosimi Jones & Marjorie Jones
Book rev Book rev ed: James Gibbs, 8 Victoria Square, Bristol BS1 4ET, UK
'Each volume focuses on a special aspect of African literature, such as Women and African Literature, Poetry, Oral and Written, Drama, Prose, which is announced in advance'
Contrib: provided they fit into the announced topic
L: 3,500w NP 1 free copy
Edit req: d-s, A4, refs with fn at end of article

243 African Peoples Review

34-36 Crown Street
Reading RG1 2SE
+44(0)118-939 1010
Fax: +44(0)118-935 4442
Email: 01343,301@compuserve.com
1992- ISSN 0966-5781 3Yr
Circ: 10,000 Subs: £18 inst £12 indiv
Ed: Herbert Ekwe-Ekwe
Book rev Book rev ed: Nnamdi Nzegwu
'Inter- and multi-disciplinary journal of essays and reviews of publications by people of African descent worldwide'
Contrib: feature articles on African humanity, book reviews, arts/ films/ exhibitions reviews and criticism
L: variable NP 5 free copies Ill: welcome
Edit req: hard copy plus disk; Word/WP preferred; comprehensive notes and bibliography where applicable

244 African Research and Documentation

School of Library, Archive and Information Studies
University College London
Gower Street
London WC1E 6BT
+44(0)171-380 7206
Fax: +44(0)171-383 0557
Email: j.mcilwaine@ucl.ac.uk

1962- ISSN 0305-826X 3Yr
Circ: 400 Subs: £22/$50
Ed: John McIlwaine
Book rev Book rev ed: Terry Barringer,
Cambridge University Library, West Road,
Cambridge CB3 9DR
'Articles and news items on all aspects of
African studies, library and archive
collections relating to Africa, and African
bibliography'
Contrib: all aspects of African studies and
documentation
L: 6-8,000w NP 1 free copy
Ill: line, h-t, b/w

245 African Review of Business and
Technology
27 Wilfred Street
London SW1E 6PR
+44(0)171-834 7676
Fax: +44(0)171-973 0076
Email: afed@alain.demon.uk
1964- Mon Circ: 19,000
Subs: £55/$93.50
Ed: Jonquil Phelan
Book rev
'Finance, construction, computers and IT,
development issues, oil and mining,
power, business travel, commercial news,
transport and country profiles in sub-
Saharan Africa'
Contrib: commissioned only as above
L: 1,500w P Offp Ill: diagrams, b/w & col
photog
Edit req: relevant photographs of Africa

246 African Studies Association of
the UK Newsletter
33 Botley Road
Oxford OX2 0BS
Fax: +44(0)1865-246454
1995- Qtly Circ: 950
Subs: free with membership of ASAUK
and/or RAS (see **853, & 862**)
Ed: Douglas H. Johnson
'News and advance notices about
Africanist activities throughout the UK'

Contrib: announcements of forthcoming
meetings, workshops and conferences;
brief reports of past conferences and
events; announcements of appointments,
links and exchanges; new and forthcoming
books by ASAUK/RAS members;
obituaries; prizes and awards; any news of
general interest to Africanists
L: 300w NP Offp by arrangement
Ill: occ photog

247 African Textiles
Alain Charles House
27 Wilfred Street
London SW1E 6PR
+44(0)171-834 7676
Fax: +44(0)171-973 0076
Email: post@alain.demon.co.uk
1980- ISSN 0144-7521 6Yr
Circ: 9,367 Subs: £43.50/$75
Ed: Zsa Tebbit
Book rev
'Latest developments worldwide plus
reports on market trends, general
management skills and needs, projects,
company profiles and exhibition previews
and reviews'
Contrib: as above
L: 1,000w P: £90 per 1,000w Offp
Ill: line, h-t, photo, b/w & col

248 African Woman
London Women's Centre
Wesley House, 4 Wild Court
London WC2B 5AU
+44(0)171-405 0678
Fax: +44(0)171-831 3947
Email: amwa@gn.apc.org
1988- ISSN 0953-9816 2Yr
Circ: 5,000 Subs: £20 inst £8 indiv Africa
& UK £25 inst £10 indiv elsewhere
Ed: Bisi Adeleye-Fayemi
Book rev Book rev ed: Gloria Ogunbadejo
'Produced and edited by African women,
to articulate their needs, achievements and
aspirations. Economics, politics, culture
and development issues are all discussed
from an African woman's perspective.

Includes features, interviews, news, and reviews from across the continent and the diaspora'

Contrib: women and development
L: 2,000w NP Offp Ill: photog, maps

249 **Bulletin of Francophone Africa**
School of Languages
University of Westminster
9-18 Euston Centre
London NW1 3ET
+44(0)171-911 5000
Fax: +44(0)171-911 5870
1992- ISSN 0966-1018 2Yr
Circ: 2,000 Subs: £25 inst £15 indiv
Eds: Hélène Gill, Ethel Tolansky & Margaret Majumdar
Book rev Book rev ed: Aline Cook
'Articles and reviews of books concerned with issues regarding the francophone Maghreb area of North Africa and francophone regions of sub-Saharan Africa, of a social, political, economic or literary nature'
Contrib: as above in English or French
L: 5,000w NP Offp

250 **Bulletin of the School of Oriental and African Studies**
Oxford University Press
Journals Dept, Walton Street
Oxford OX2 6DP
Editorial address:
SOAS, Thornhaugh Street, Russell Square
London WC1H 0XG
+44(0)171-637 2388
Fax: +44(0)171-436 3844
Email: dm3@soas.ac.uk
Website: http://www.oup.co.uk//journals
1917- ISSN 0041-977X 3Yr
Circ: 1,000 Subs: £76/$134 inst £49/$79 indiv £60/$110 developing countries
Ed: C. Shackle
Book rev
Book rev ed: Diana Matias
'Original scholarly articles on the languages, culture, history and

archaeology, etc., *of Africa, the Near and Middle East and Asia'*
Contrib: as above
L: 10-12,000w NP 25 offp
Ill: line, h-t, photog, b/w
Edit req: d-s, single sided, fn d-s at end

251 **Communications Africa**
Alain Charles House
27 Wilfred Street
London SW1E 6PR
+44(0)171-834 7676
Fax: +44(0)171-973 0076
Email: afed@alain.demon.co.uk
1991- 6Yr Circ: 8,849 Subs: $75
Ed: Vaughan O'Grady
Book rev
'Telecommunications, broadcasting and IT news and features about, relating to, or of interest to, the African continent'
Contrib: mostly commissioned news

252 **Computers in Africa**
Aitec House, Church Walk
St. Neots PE 19 1JH
+44(0)1480-407477
Fax: +44(0)1480-407677
Email: aitec@geo2.poptel.org.uk
Website: http://www.web.co.za.aitec
1986- ISSN 0953-3257 11Yr Circ: 12,000
Subs: £20/$30
Ed: Alan Dickinson
Book rev
'Computer industry news from Anglophone Africa; guidelines and important international computing trends; regular software and hardware reviews; detailed surveys of national computer markets; new products; computer applications of particular relevance to Africa; expert advice; development of the Internet in Africa'
Contrib: as above
L: 200-1,000w P: £100 per 1,000w 1 free copy Ill: line, photog b/w & col

253 **Development Education Journal**
Development Education
Association, 3rd Floor
29-31 Cowper Street
London EC2A 4AP
+44(0)171-490 8108
Fax: +44(0)171-490 8123
Email: devedassoc@gn.apc.org
1994- ISSN 1354-0742 2Yr Circ: 350
Subs: £30 inst £10 indiv
Ed: Jill Brand
Book rev
'Reports and discusses current development education practice and theory in Britain and overseas; creates a forum for discussion of development education. Covers campaigns, public education and the media'
Contrib: from development agencies, DECs, academic institutions, schools and youth work worldwide.
L: 2,000w NP 1 free copy Ill: b/w photog with captions on back
Edit req: all articles assessed by editorial team

254 **Development in Practice**
Carfax Publishing Co
POB 25
Abingdon OX14 3UE
Editorial address:
c/o Oxfam, 274 Banbury Road, Oxford
OX2 7DZ
+44(0)1865-312148/9
Fax: +44(0)1865-312600
Email: oxfamedit@gn.apc.org
Website: http://www.oneworld.org/oxfam/
1991- ISSN 0961-4524 4Yr Circ: n/a
Subs: £125/$208 inst £50/$85 indiv
£25/$42 developing countries
Ed: Deborah Eade
Book rev Book rev ed: Caroline Knowles
'Forum for NGOs, official aid agencies, practitioners, policy makers, and academics to exchange information and analysis concerning the social dimensions of development and emergency relief work'

Contrib: as above
L: viewpoint 2,000w; notes 1,500w
NP 20 offp + 2 copies Ill: tables; figs
Edit req: send abstract to ed

255 **Development Policy Review**
Overseas Development
Institute, Portland House
Stag Place
London SW1E 5DP
+44(0)171-393 1600
Fax: +44(0)171-393 1699
Email: dpr@odi.org.uk
Website: http://www.oneworld.org/odi/
ISSN 0950-6764 Qtly Circ: n/a
Subs: £116/$183 inst £44/$70 indiv
Ed: Sheila Page
Book rev Book rev ed: Margaret Cornell
'Immediate questions and broader themes in development policy. New research and new thinking is complemented by an extensive book review section covering important works in the field'
Contrib: any articles in the field of development with an emphasis on, or direct relevance to, economic problems
L: 7-8,000w NP 25 offp + 1 free copy
Edit req: 2 copies d-s; style sheet available from eds

256 **Focus on AfricaΦ**
BBC World Service
Bush House, Strand
London WC2B 4PH
+44(0)171-257 2906
Fax: +44(0)171-379 0519
1990- Qtly
Ed: Robin White

257 **Gender and Development**
Oxfam
274 Banbury Road
Oxford OX2 7DZ
+44(0)1865-312106
Fax: +44(0)1865-312600
Email: csweetman@oxfam.org.uk
Website: http://www.oneworld.org/oxfam/

1993- ISSN 5598-3485 3Yr
Circ: n/a
Subs: £60 inst £25 indiv developing
countries £12
Ed: Caroline Sweetman
Book rev
*'Focuses on gender and development
issues internationally, making links
between theoretical and practical work.
Each issue is thematic, providing a
resource for researchers and
practitioners, combining factual rigour
with accessible language'*
Contrib: for 1997/8: gender and
organisations; masculinity; poverty in the
North; migration; education
L: 2,500-3,500w NP offp + 1 free copy
Ill: b/w
Edit req: to reach the widest audience
possible; clarity of language and all
technical words must be explained

258 Index on Censorship
Writers & Scholars
International Ltd
Lancaster House
33 Islington High Street
London N1 9LH
+44(0)171-278 2313
Fax: +44(0)171-278 1878
Email: indexoncenso@gn.apc.org
Website:
http://www.oneworld.org.org/index_oc/
1972- ISSN 0306-4220 10Yr
Circ: 5,500 Subs: £36 UK £42/$50
elsewhere £25/$35 stud
Ed: Ursula Owen
Africa ed: Adewale Maja-Pearce
*'As much as possible we like to publish the
banned material of particular artists.
Features on special artists/ journalists etc.
welcome. Recent trends in a country where
censorship has been tightened or
loosened'*
Contrib: news stories which are unreported
elsewhere; media freedom/diversity,
dissident voices, banned fiction

L: 2,500w P: £60 per 1,000w 2+ free
copies Ill: photog
Edit req: may require consultation with
country researcher

259 Internet Journal of African Studies⊟
Dept of Social and Economic
Studies
University of Bradford
Richmond Road
Bradford BD7 1DP
+44(0)1274-384771
Fax: +44(0)1274-385295
Email: g.littlejohn@Bradford.ac.uk
Website:
http://www.brad.ac.uk/research/ijas/
contents.htm.
1996- 3Yr Circ: n/a Subs: gratis
Ed: Gary Littlejohn
'African studies, mainly social sciences'
Contrib: as above
L: variable NP Ill: col
Edit req: on disk or by email

260 Journal of African Economies
Centre for the Study of
African Economies
University of Oxford
St. Cross Building
Manor Road
Oxford OX1 3UL
Editorial address:
Publications Office, 21 Winchester Road,
Oxford OX2 6NA
+44(0)1865-274556
Fax: +44(0)1865-274558
Email:
csae.publishing@economics.ox.ac.uk
Website: http://info.ox.ac.uk/csaeinfo or
http://www.oup.co.uk/jnls/list/jafeco
1992- ISSN 0963-8024 3Yr Circ: 400
Subs: £66/$118 $58 inst $40 indiv Africa
Ed: Paul Collier
Book rev Contrib: n/a
L: no details NP 25 offp Ill: b/w, charts,
graphs

261 **Journal of African History**
Cambridge University Press,
The Edinburgh Building
Shaftesbury Road
Cambridge CB2 2RU
Editorial address:
Dept of History, SOAS, Thornhaugh
Street, Russell Square, London WC1H
0XG
+44(0)1223-312393
Fax: +44(0)1223-315052
Email: da@soas.ac.uk
Website: http://www.cup.cam.ac.uk
1960- ISSN 0021-8537 3Yr
Circ: 1,850 Subs: £71/$123 inst £38/$61
indiv £30/$49 students
Eds: David Anderson, Louis Brenner,
Phyllis Martin, Tom Spear
Book rev Book rev ed: David Anderson
*'Covers the history of the whole African
continent, from prehistory to modern times
and includes articles on archaeology,
ethnology and linguistics'*
Contrib: as above; emphasis has recently
been given to themes in gender history,
ethnicity and environmental history
L: 6-8,000w NP 25 offp Ill:line, h-t
Edit req: style sheet available from eds

262 **Journal of Commonwealth
Literature**
Bowker-Saur , Maypole
House, Maypole Road
East Grinstead RH19 1HU
Editorial address:
Dept of English, University of Hull, Hull
HU6 7RX
+44(0)1428-465666
Fax: +44(0)1428-46564
Email: j.a.thieme@english.hull.ac.uk
1965- ISSN 0021-9894 2Yr
Circ: 1,000 Subs: £68/$120 inst £34/$60
indiv
Eds: John Thieme, Shirley Chew & Alan
Bower
*'Provides a focal point for discussion of
literature in English outside Britain and
the USA. The first two numbers of each*

*volume consist of an issue of critical
studies and essays; the third is the
bibliography issue, containing an annual
checklist of publications in each region of
the Commonwealth. Articles on all aspects
of subject and post-colonial theory,
African literature, bibliographic
contributions and checklists on prominent
authors*
Contrib: as above
L: 2,500-5,000w NP articles; P
bibliography [no details] 1 free copy Ill:
photog only occasionally
Edit req: style sheet available from eds

263 **Journal of Contemporary
African Studies†**
Carfax Publishing Company
POB 25
Abingdon OX14 3UE
+44(0)1235-521154
Fax: +44(0)1235-401550
Email: sales@carfax.co.uk
1983- ISSN 0258-9001 2Yr
Subs: £94 inst $154 NA £24 indiv $44 NA
Ed: Patrick McAllister *et al.*
Cont: an interdisciplinary journal of
research and writing in the human sciences
which seeks to promote a scholarly
understanding of developments and
change in Africa

264 **Journal of Modern African
Studies**
Huish, Mill Street
Chagford TQ13 8AR
+44(0)1647-433569
Fax: +44(0)1647-433355
1963- ISSN 0022-278X Qtly
Circ: 2,000 Subs: £78/$147 inst £37/$65
indiv £27/$47 contrib
Ed: David Kimble
Book rev
*'Offers a quarterly survey of politics,
economics, and related topics that is
designed to promote a deeper
understanding by both academics and*

practitioners of what is happening in Africa today'
Contrib: from all over the world as long as they are scholarly and 'readable'
L: 7-8,000w+ NP 25 offp + 1 free copy
Ill: tables, diagrams
Edit req: one copy (not original), d-s

265 Journal of Southern African Studies

Centre for Southern African Studies, University of York Heslington, York YO1 5DD
+44(0)1482-811227
Fax: +44(0)1482-815857
Email: csfl@york.ac.uk
1974- ISSN 0305-7070 Qtly Circ: 800
Subs: £114 inst £36 indiv £24 researchers in Africa
Eds: Saul Dubow, Liz Gunner & Debby Potts
Book rev Book rev ed: Jocelyn Alexander, JSAS, St Anthony's College, Oxford OX2 6JF
'Interdisciplinary scope...draws important connections within the humanities and social sciences...charts the progress of southern African studies in all fields...committed to developing further links between theory and the reality...special issues on topics in depth'
Contrib: as above
L: 8,000w NP 25 offp + 1 free copy
Ill: h-t, photog
Edit req: 3 copies

266 Leeds African Studies Bulletin

African Studies Unit University of Leeds Leeds LS2 9JT
+44(0)113-233 5069
Fax: +44(0)113-233 4400
Email: african-studies@leeds.ac.uk
1964- ISSN 0024-0249 Ann Circ: 500
Subs: n/a
Ed: Kate Banham
Book rev Book rev ed: Martin Banham

'Annual report on African studies activities at University of Leeds. Text of annual 'Leeds African Studies Lecture'. Articles on Leeds-based research projects. Abstracts of completed research theses; book reviews'
No contrib

267 Modern Africa†

57-59 Whitechapel Road London E1 1DU
+44(0)171-377 8413
Fax: +44(0)171-247 5407
1977- 6Yr Circ: 14,000
Subs: £36/$50
Ed: Patrick Smith
'Regional magazine for business people and government officials in sub-Saharan Africa. Articles on manufacturing and processing, raw materials, energy, transportation, communications, construction, banking, new government projects, etc. Also features on new technology, equipment and business developments in the industrialised countries; city reports and commodities monitor'
Contrib: as above
L: 6-800w P: £75 per 1,000w 1 free copy
Ill: h-t, line, maps, charts, colour trans

268 New African

IC Publications Ltd. 7 Coldbath Square London EC1R 4LQ
+44(0)171-713 7711
Fax: +44(0)171-713 7970
Email: icpubs@dial.pipex.com
1966- ISSN 0142-9345 Mon Circ: 26,763
Subs: £50/$90 £32/$50 stud
Ed: Alan Rake
Book rev Book rev ed: Baffour Ankomah
'Offers a balanced mix of political reporting, comment, economic and financial discussion, and features on social affairs including art, culture, music, and sport. Full colour supplement "New African Life" each quarter'

Contrib: commissioned only
L: variable P Offp as requested
Ill: col, b/w photog, slides
Edit req: consult with ed first

269 **New Internationalist**
55 Rectory Road
Oxford OX4 1BW
+44(0)1865-728181
Fax: +44(0)1865-793152
Email: newint@gn.apc.org
Website: http://www.oneworld.org/ni/
1972- 0305-9529 Mon Circ: n/a
Subs: £50 inst £24.85 indiv £14.70 stud
Eds: Vanessa Baird, Chris Brazier, Nikki
van der Gaag & David Ransom
Book rev Book rev ed: Vanessa Baird
*'Reports on the issues of world poverty
and inequality; to focus attention on the
unjust relationship between the powerful
and powerless in both rich and poor
nations; to debate and campaign for the
radical changes necessary within and
between those nations if the basic material
and spiritual needs of all are to be met;
and to bring to life the people, ideas and
the action in the fight for world
development'*
Contrib: short update features only - most
copy is commissioned
L: 1,000w max P Ill: col

270 **Newslink Africa**
7-11 Kensington High Street
London W8 5NP
+44(0)171-411 3111
Fax: +44(0)171-938 4168
Email: 101353,1745@compuserve.com
1982- Wk Circ: n/a
Ed: Shamlal Puri
Book rev
*'African development, economics, business
features'*
Also offers picture library on African
subjects colour and black and white
Contrib: African development, business,
economic features

271 **Oxford Development Studies**
University of Oxford
International Development
Centre
Queen Elizabeth House
21 St Giles
Oxford OX1 3LA
+44(0)1865-273600
Fax: +44(0)1865-273607
Email: ocls@sable.ox.ac.uk
Website: http://www.carfax.co.uk
1996- ISSN 1360-0818 3Yr Circ: 300
Subs: £198 EU £216 elsewhere
Eds: George Peters & Sanjaya Lall
*'Worldwide development issues of interest
to an international audience.
Multidisciplinary content not confined to
Africa'*
Contrib: development: economics, history,
anthropology, sociology
L: 6,000w NP 50 offp Ill: line
Edit req: abstract of 150 words. 3 copies
d-s. Disk if possible

272 **Reports on the Sessions of the
African Commission on
Human & Peoples' Rights**
African Journal of
International and
Comparative Law, Aberdeen
House, 22 Highbury Grove
London N5 2DQ
+44(0)171-704 0610
Fax: +44(0)171-704 0973 Email:
100632,3305@compuserve.com
1986- ISSN 0954-8890 Qtly Circ: n/a
Subs: £40 Africa £70/$120 inst £50 indiv
elsewhere stud £35 African stud £30
Eds: E.K. Yakpo & Tahar Boumedra
Book rev Book rev ed: Tahar Boumedra
*'The Report is a transcript of the
proceedings of the session of the African
Commission on Human and People's
Rights and related legal materials and
states reports as required by article 62 of
the AFRICAN Charter on Human Rights'*
No contrib

273 Review of African Political Economy
POB 678
Sheffield S1 1BF
+44(0)1226-741660
Fax: +44(0)1226-741661
Email: roape@mcr1.poptel.org.uk
1974- ISSN 0305-6244 4Yr
Circ: 2,500 Subs: £118 inst £28 indiv
Eds: Chris Allen & Jan Burgess
Book rev Book rev eds: Morris Szeftel, Ray Bush & Roy Love
'Bridges the gap between academia and political commitment, promoting scholarly work but relating it to Africa's on-going struggles for development and liberation. Includes briefings, debates, books lists and documents from movements in Africa'
Contrib: the super-powers, migrant population movements, grassroots activities, education, the military, culture, religion and activities specifically relating to women; political economy of development. Debates on democracy, labour movements
L: articles 8,000w briefings 3-4,000w NP 2 free copies Ill: line, h-t, photog

274 Review of the African Commission on Human & Peoples' Rights
African Society of International and Comparative Law
Aberdeen House
22 Highbury Grove
London N5 2DQ
+44(0)171-704 0610
Fax: +44(0)171-704 0973 Email: 100632,3305@compuserve.com
1991- ISSN 1353-6834 2Yr Circ: n/a
Subs: £20
Eds: Tahar Boumedra & Emile K. Yakpo
Book rev
'All works related to human and peoples' rights in Africa'

Contrib: Human rights, civil liberties, humanitarian law
L: 5-10,000w NP Offp + 1 free copy Ill: diagrams; maps

275 Safara Φ
Goldcity Communications Ltd, Suite F11
Shakespeare Business Centre
245a Coldharbour Lane
London SW9 8RR
+44(0)171-737 5933
Fax: +44(0)171-738 3613
1993- Qtly
Subs: £24/$50
Ed: Richard Paris
Cont: review of leisure and business in Africa

276 Social Identities. Journal for the Study of Race, Nation and Culture
Carfax Publishing Company
POB 25
Abingdon OX14 3UE
Editorial address:
Centre for the Study of African Economies, University of Oxford, 21 Winchester Road, Oxford OX2 6NA
+44(0)1235-521154
Fax: +44(0)1235-401550
1996- ISSN 1350-4630 3Yr Circ: n/a
Subs: £94 inst £40 indiv
Eds: Abebe Zegeye & David T. Goldberg
Book rev Book rev ed: Julia Maxted, University of Oxford, School of Geography, Mansfield Road, Oxford, OX1 3TB
'Furnishes an interdisciplinary and international focal point for theorizing issues at the interface of social identities. Especially concerned to address these issues in the context of the transforming political economies and cultures of postmodern and postcolonial conditions'
Contrib: as above
Edit req: 3 copies

277 **Southern Africa Monthly**
     Regional Bulletin - MRB
     POB 724
     London N16 5RZ
     +44(0)171-923 1467
     Fax: +44(0)171-923 2545
     Email: southscan@gn.apc.ord
     Website: http://www.gn.apc.org/southscan
     1992- ISSN 0966-8802 Mon Circ: n/a
     Subs: £130/$195 EU $245 elsewhere
     Ed: David Coetzee
     Book rev
     'News and analysis on the current business
     and econmic situation in Southern Africa'
     Contrib: business, economy
     L: 5-700w P: variable Offp

278 **Southscan**
     POB 724
     London N16 5RZ
     +44(0)171-923 1467
     Fax: +44(0)171-923 2545
     Email: southscan@gn.apc.org
     Website: http://www.gn.apc.org/southscan
     1986- ISSN 0952-7542 Wk Circ: n/a
     Subs: £210/$315 inst £95/$142 indiv
     Ed: David Coetzee
     Book rev
     'Weekly review of political and economic
     events concentrating on South Africa but
     taking in all of Southern Africa and based
     on correspondents in the field'
     Contrib: politics, economics
     L: 500w P: variable Offp

279 **Telecommunications in Africa**
     Aitec House, Church Walk
     St. Neots PE19 1JH
     +44(0)1480-407477
     Fax: +44(0)1480-407677
     Email: aitec@geo2.poptel.org.uk
     Website: http://www.web.co.za.aitec
     1995- ISSN 1359-978X 6Yr
     Circ: 6,000 Subs: £15/$20
     Ed: Richard Synge
     Book rev
     'Provides an overview of the
     telecommunications sector in Africa,

focusing on policy, strategy and
development issues; development of the
Internet in Africa'
Contrib: in above areas

280 **Third World Impact** †
     Hansib Publishing Ltd.
     Tower House
     139-149 Fonthill Road
     London N4 3HF
     +44(0)171-281 1191
     Fax: +44(0)171-263 9656
     1971- 2Yr Circ: 12,500
     Ed: Arif Ali
     'Comprehensive work of reference
     regarding the presence of the visible
     minorities in all spheres of British life with
     a who's who and reference section'
     Contrib: most of areas above
     L: 1,000w P: variable Ill: line, photog

281 **Third World Quarterly**
     Dept of Geography
     Royal Holloway College
     Egham TW20 0EX
     +44(0)1784-443579
     Fax: +44(0)1784-472836
     Website: http://www.catchword.co.uk
     1978- ISSN 0143-6597 5Yr Circ: 2,000
     Subs: paper/on-line: £162 inst EU £176
     elsewhere £53 indiv EU £42 elsewhere
     paper & on-line: £203 EU inst £53 EU
     indiv
     Ed: Shahid Qadir Book rev
     'Detailed analysis of global affairs.
     Regular source of information on
     contemporary social, economic, and
     political issues. Coverage of the
     Asia/Pacific region, Latin America and
     the Caribbean, Africa and the Middle
     East, devoting an entire section to
     literature and including reviews of recent
     research'
     Contrib: contemporary issues and events
     of importance to the Third World
     L: 5-7,000w NP 50 offp + 1 free copy
     Ill: camera-ready artwork
     Edit req: style sheet available from eds

282 **Third World Reports**
'Wild Acre', Plaw Hatch
Sharpthorne RH19 4JL
Editorial address:
Kob Cottage, 12 Harris Road, Kalk Bay,
Cape Peninsula 7975, South Africa
.+44(0)1342-810875
Fax: +44(0)1342-810875
1983- Mon Circ: n/a Subs: £50/$100
Ed: Colin Legum
*'Privately published newsletter, averaging
two reports a month; its main interest
focuses on Africa, but it regularly analyzes
developments affecting all Third World
countries'*
No contrib

283 **Wasafiri**
Dept of English, Queen Mary
and Westfield College
Mile End Road
London E1 4NS
+44(0)171-775 3120
Fax: +44(0)181-980 6200
Email: wasafiri@qmw.ac.uk
Website: http://www.qmw.ac.uk/~english/
wasafiri.html
1984- ISSN 0269-0055 2Yr Circ: 600
Subs: £16 inst £12 indiv £8 stud
Ed: Susheila Nasta
Book rev Book rev ed: Nigel Rigby
*'New creative writing, critical coverage of
new writing; a forum for current debate
concerning the teaching of multicultural
literature both at school and university
level. Focus issues have been on the
Caribbean, education and women, post-
colonial writing, African, Asian diaspora,
Black Britain'*
Contrib: literature and education in Africa,
the Caribbean, South-East Asia, Black
British writing, interviews with writers,
new creative writing
L: 5,000w NP 2 free copies Ill: line photog
Edit req: 2 copies, MLA style sheet,
d-s, typed, stamped addressed envelope,
pref docs in *WP* on disk

284 **West Africa**
43-45 Coldharbour Lane
Camberwell
London SE5 9NR
+44(0)171-737 2946
Fax: +44(0)171-978 8334
1917- Wk Circ: 24,000
Subs: £75 UK $190 NA £100 Africa 25%
discount stud
Ed: Maxwell Nwagboso
Book rev
*'Business and economy, political, social,
cultural, literary'*
Contrib: as above
L: 1,000w P: £50 No offp Ill: line, h-t,
photo b/w

United States

285 **Africa News**🖳
POB 3851
Durham NC 27702
+1-919-286 0747
Fax: +1-919-286 2614
Email: ans@afnews.org
Website: http://www.africanews.org
1973- ISSN 0191-6521 2Mon
Ed: Reed Kramer
Book rev Book rev eds: Sally Banker &
Tami Hultman
*'Online journal covering African politics,
economy, culture and US policy and
international issues affecting the
continent. Special features include new
publications section, bulletin board,
exclusive interviews and articles on
women, environment, wildlife and
development'*

286 **Africa Today**
Lynne Rienner Publishers
1800 30th Street, Suite 314
Boulder CO 80301-1026
Editorial address:
c/o Graduate School of International,
Studies, University of Denver, 2201
Gaylord Street Denver CO 80208

+1-303-871 3678
Fax: +1-303-871 2456
Email: afrtoday@du.edu
1954- ISSN 0001-9887 Qtly
Circ: 1,500 Subs: $64 inst $28 indiv $20
stud
Ed: Angelique Haugerud
Book rev Book rev ed: Naomi Reich
*Thematically arranged scholarly articles
on political, social or economic
developments in or related to Africa.
'Africa Rights Monitor', a survey of human
rights conditions on the continent, in each
issue'*
Contrib: all subject areas relating to
contemporary Africa
L: 3-5,000w NP 5 free copies to authors,
3 to book revs Ill: photo b/w line
Edit req: style sheet available from ed

287   **African Arts**
      The James S. Coleman
      African Studies Center
      10244 Bunche Hall
      UCLA
      Los Angeles CA 90095-1310
+1-310-825 1218
Fax: +1-310-206 2250
1967- ISSN 0001-9933 Qtly Circ: 4,000
Subs: US $42 elsewhere $50
Ed: Donald Cosentino
Book rev Book rev ed: Raymond A.
Silverman
*'Covers all the art forms of Africa
especially contemporary and traditional
art but not excluding dance, film, theatre
and popular decorative forms. Book and
show reviews relating to the above and
features on new museum acquisitions and
items of general interest. The African
continent is the focus, occasionally pieces
on the diaspora if there is a strong African
connection'*
Contrib: any areas, generally relating to
specific field work or research;
predominantly academics and specialist
scholars

L: 15-20 pp NP 2 free copies Ill: line, h-t,
photo, b/w & col
Edit req: d-s, glossy b/w trans

288   **African Economic History**
      University of Wisconsin
      African Publications
      205 Ingraham Hall
      1155 Observatory Drive
      Madison WI 53706
+1-608-262 2493
Fax: +1-608-265 5851
Email: afrsst@macc.wisc.edu
Website: www.wisc.edu/afr/
1972- ISSN 0145-2258 Ann
Circ: 350 Subs: $33 inst $16.50 indiv
Ed: David Henige
Book rev
*'Focuses on recent economic change in
Africa as well as the colonial and
precolonial economic history of the
continent'*
Contrib: in any areas of African economic
history, in English and French
L: 30-40pp NP 10 offp
Edit req: 2 copies d-s

289   **African Studies Quarterly**🖳
      Editorial Committee
      African Studies Quarterly
      Center for African Studies
      427 Grinter Hall
      University of Florida
      Gainesville FL 32611
+1-352-392 2183
Fax: +1-352-392 2435
Email: asq@africa.ufl.asq
Website:
http://www.clas.ufl.edu/africa/asq/
1997- Qtly Circ: n/a Subs: gratis
Ed: editorial committee
Book rev
*'African Studies Quarterly is an
interdisciplinary, fully-refereed, electronic
journal of the University of Florida,
Center for African Studies aimed at
Africanist scholars around the world using
the Internet'*

Contrib: all disciplines as long as there is significant Africa content
Ill: wide use of tables and graphics is discouraged
Spec edit req: all submissions must be made electronically either by FTP or by sending a disk to the address above

290 **African Studies Review**
African Studies Association
Credit Union Building
Emory University
Atlanta GA 30322
Editorial address:
Dept of Government and International Studies, University of South Carolina
Columbia SC 29208
+1-404-329 6410
Fax: +1-404-329 6433
1957- 3Yr Circ: n/a Subs: gratis ASA members only & libraries
Ed: Mark DeLancey
Book rev
'Includes scholarly articles from an interdisciplinary perspective on African studies plus book reviews. Frequently features special thematic issues'
Contrib: interdisciplinary African studies
L: 30-40pp NP 25 offp Ill: camera-ready artwork required
Edit req: d-s, Chicago Manual style
Note: The African Studies Association will relocate to Rutgers University, New Brunswick, NJ late in 1997.

291 **Africana Libraries Newsletter**
Africana Library
Michigan State University
East Lansing MI 48824-1048
+1-517-432 2218
Fax: +1-517-432 1445
Email: lauer@pilot.msu.edu
1975- ISSN 0148-7868 Qtly
Circ: 600 Subs: gratis
Ed: Joe Lauer
Book rev
'Produced to support the work of the Africana Librarians Council (ALC;

formerly Archives Libraries Committee) of the African Studies Association. Includes reports on meetings of ALC, CAMP and other relevant groups; also reports other items of interest including notes on vendors'
Contrib: areas of interest to African studies librarians
L: 5pp NP 1 free copy

292 **ASA News**
African Studies Association
Credit Union Building
Emory University
Atlanta GA 30322
+1-404-329 6410
Fax: +1-404-329 6433
Email: africa@emory.edu
Website: http://www.sas.upenn.edu/ African_Studies/Home_Page/ASA_Menu. html
1967- ISSN 0278-2219 Qtly Circ: n/a
Subs: gratis to ASA members
Ed: Chris Koch
'Reports current and future events of interest to members and Africanists, archives of the Association, bibliographical and news notes, opinion, editorial, and significant correspondence'
Contrib: announcements, letters, notes on seminars and conferences, short articles of interest to the Africanist community
L: 12pp NP 1 free copy Ill: camera-ready artwork required
Edit req: d-s, email or on disk preferred

293 **Callaloo**
Dept of English
University of Virginia
Charlottesville VA 22903
+1-804-924 6637
Fax: +1-804-924 1478
Email: callalloo@virginia.edu
1976 Qtly Circ: 3,000
Ed: Charles H. Rowell
Book rev Book rev ed: Trudier Harris
'Literary journal specializing in African American literature, art and culture.

*Features, essays, fiction, poetry,
interviews, drama, art, photography'*
Contrib: as above
L: n/a 25 offp

294 **Electronic Journal of Africana
     Bibliography**⌨
     University of Iowa Libraries
     Iowa City IO 52242
     +1-319-335 5867
     Fax: +1-319-335 5900
     Email: john-howell@uiowa.edu
     Website:
     http://www.lib.uiowa.edu/proj/ejab/
     1996- Circ: n/a Subs: gratis
     Ed: John Bruce Howell
     *'A refereed on-line journal of
     bibliographies on any aspect of Africa, its
     peoples, their homes, cities, towns,
     districts, states, countries, regions,
     including social economic sustainable
     development, creative writing, the arts,
     and the Diaspora (Issue no. 1 was Guides,
     Collections and Ancillary Materials to
     African Archival Resources in the United
     States, see* **118***)*
     Contrib: as above
     Edit req: bibliographies min 75 entries,
     pref with annotations, with intro and/or
     preface. Chicago style. Essay
     bibliographies on specific topics,
     bibliographies with French and/or
     Portuguese must have diacritics

295 **History in Africa**
     Memorial Library
     University of Wisconsin
     728 State St
     Madison WI 53706
     +1-608-262 6397
     Fax: +1-608-265 2754
     Email: henige@macc.wisc.edu
     1974- ISSN 0361 5413 Ann Circ: 4-500
     Subs: $43 inst $25 indiv
     Ed: David Henige
     *'Interested in problems of method,
     including historiography, source analysis,
     textual criticism, bibliography, and*

*epistemology. Also in comparative studies
relevant to understanding the African past'*
Contrib: as above; book review essays
L: 30-40pp NP 20-25 offp
Ill: line drawings, photog, b/w camera-
ready artwork required

296 **International Journal of
     African Historical Studies, The**
     African Studies Center
     Boston University
     270 Bay State Road
     Boston MA 02215
     +1-617-353 7306
     Fax: +1-617-353 4975
     Email: ascpub@asc.bu.edu
     Website:http://web.bu.edu:80/afr/
     publications.html
     1968- ISSN 0361-7882 Qtly Circ: 700
     Subs: $98 inst $35 indiv
     Ed: Norman R. Bennett
     Book rev
     *'Covers all aspects of African past
     including interactions between Africa and
     the New World. Articles are accepted in
     English or French, and the publication of
     original source material is encouraged'*
     Contrib: n/a Offp

297 **Issue: A Journal of Opinion**
     African Studies Association
     Credit Union Building
     Emory University
     Atlanta GA 30322
     Editorial address:
     Dept of Political Science, 236 Ullman
     Building, 1212 University Boulevard
     Birmingham AL 35294-3350
     +1-404-329 6410
     Fax: +1-404-329 6433
     Email: africa@emory.edu
     Website: http://www.sas.upenn.edu/
     african_studies/home page/asa_menu.html
     1970- ISSN 0047-1607 2Yr Circ: 4,000
     Subs: gratis to members of ASA
     Ed: Beverly Hawk
     *'Edited by a member of the Association's
     Current Issues Committee, presents*

*provocative and timely comment on events
in Africa and on developments in African
studies'*
Contrib: political or policy-oriented
questions relating to Africa or to African
studies
L: 15-20pp NP 1 free copy
Edit req: MS Word 5.0 or WP 5.1

298 **Journal of African Policy
Studies†**
The James S. Coleman
African Studies Center
UCLA, 10244 Bunche Hall
Los Angeles CA 90095-1310
+1-310-825 3686
Fax: +1-310-206 2250
1995- Qtly
Subs: $74 overseas
Ed: Edmund J. Keller

299 **Journal of Black Studies**
Sage Publications Inc
2111 West Hillcrest Drive
Newbury Park CA 91320
Editorial address:
Dept of African American Studies, Temple
University, Philadelphia PA 19122
+1-805-499 0721
Fax: +1-215-204 5953
1970- ISSN 0021-9347 Qtly Circ: 3,500
Subs: $211 inst $67 indiv
Ed: Molefi Kete Asante
Book rev Book rev ed: Molefi Kete
Asante
*'Sustains a full analytical enquiry into
African phenomena'*
Contrib: history, African studies,
afroethnicity
L: 5,000w NP Offp Ill: limited

300 **Northeast African Studies**Φ
Dept of History
Valparaiso University
Valparaiso IN 46383
+1-219 464 5265
Email: cschaefe@orion.valpo.eu
Ed: Charles Schaefer
Book rev

301 **Passages. A Chronicle of the
Humanities**
Program of African Studies
Northwestern University
620 Library Place
Evanston IL 60208
+1-847-491 7323
Fax: +1-847-491 3739
Email: rmark@nwu.edu
Website: http://nuinfo.nwu.edu/african-
studies/
1991- Irregular Circ: 3,000
Subs: gratis
Ed: R.M. Mark
Book rev
*'New and diverse writings in cultural
studies; most specifically, writing on
Africa and the African humanities in all
the possible sites of the production of
culture'*
Contrib: as above
L: variable NP 10 offp Ill: limited
Edit req: *WP* for Windows preferred

302 **Research in African
Literatures**
Indiana University Press
601 N. Morton Street
Bloomington IN 47404
Editorial address:
Ohio State University, POB 3789,
Columbus, OH 43210-0789
+1-614-292 9735
Fax: +1-614-292 3927
Email: ral@magnus.acs.ohio-state.edu
Website: http://www.indiana.edu/~iupress
1970- ISSN 0034-5210 Qtly Circ: 800

Subs: $68 inst US $35 indiv $45 African inst
Ed: Abiola Irele
Book rev
'Publishes scholarly articles on all aspects of African oral and written literatures. Also includes bibliographies and institutional research reports'
Contrib: African oral and written literatures
L: 20-30pp NP 10 offp + 1 free copy
Ill: prints, photo, b/w artwork
Edit req: MLA style manual

303 **Sage. A Scholarly Journal on Black Women†**
SWEP/SAGE
POB 42741
Atlanta GA 30311
+1-404-681 3643 ext.360
1984- ISSN 0741-8639 2Yr
Circ: 2,000 Subs: US $25 inst $15 indiv $31 inst $21 indiv $10 stud elsewhere
Ed: Patricia Bell-Scott
Book rev Book rev ed: Miriam Willis
'Articles, critical essays, interviews, resource listings, documents, announcements, photographs relating to lives of Black Women (women of African descent) wherever they reside'
Contrib: as above
L: 25pp NP 2 offp Ill: photog
Edit req: d-s, typed

304 **Studies in African Linguistics†**
The James S. Coleman
African Studies Center
UCLA 10244 Bunche Hall
Los Angeles CA 90095-1310
+1-310-825 3686
Email: imn6gs@uclamvs.bitnet
1920- ISSN 0039-3533 3Yr Circ: 350
Subs: $20 inst $12 indiv
Ed: Robert Botne
'Descriptive, comparative or theoretical linguistic articles in which the primary data source is languages native to the African continent'

Contrib: as above
L: 10-30pp NP 25 offp Ill: line, h-t
Edit req: abstract of 100-200w; style sheet available from ed

305 **Transafrica ForumΦ**
Transaction Publishers
Rutgers-The State University
New Brunswick NJ 08903
+1-908-445 2280
Fax: +1-908-445 3138
Qtly Subs: $96 inst $40 indiv
Ed: Courtland Lee
Cont: interdisciplinary journal serving as a forum for social scientists engaged in the analysis of the problems of black males

306 **Transition. An International Review**
1430 Massachussetts Avenue
4th Floor
Cambridge MA 02138
+1-6127-496 2847
Fax: +1-617-496 2877
Email: transition@fas.harvard.edu
1961; 1991- ISSN 0041-1191 Qtly
Circ: 3,000 Subs: $54 inst $24 indiv
Ed: Henry Louis Gates jr & Michael Vazquez
Book rev
'Award-winning journal of culture, politics and identity, and committed to the exploration of Africa and its diaspora'
Contrib: essays, photography, artwork
L: 2,500-5,000w NP Offp + 3 free copies
Ill: n/a
Edit req: 3 copies; no fn

307 **Ufahamu**
The James S. Coleman
African Studies Center
UCLA 10244 Bunche Hall
Los Angeles CA 90095-1310
+1-310-825 6518
Fax: +1-310-206 2250
1970- ISSN 0041-5715 3Yr Circ: 250
Subs: $22 inst $16 indiv

Ed: Mary Dillard
Book rev Book rev ed: Meghan Moore
'Contributions from anyone interested in Africa and related subject areas. Contributions may include political-economic analysis, commentaries, review articles, film and book reviews, and poetry'
Contrib: as above
L: 20-33 pp NP 1 free copy
Edit req: style sheet available from ed

308 **Washington Report on Africa**Φ
1413 K Street NW
Suite 1400
Washington DC 20005
+1-202-371 0555
Fax: +1-202-408 9369
1980- 2Mon Subs: $399
Ed: Rick Sherman
Cont: political analysis, business, development

309 **West African Research Association Newsletter**
POB 724 Howard University
Washington DC 20059
+1-202-806 9325
Fax: +1-202-806 4471
1995- 2Yr Circ: 200
Ed: Jeanne M. Toungara
No contrib

310 **World Development**
The American University
4400 Massachussetts Avenue NW
Washington DC 20016-8151
+1-202-885 2822
Fax: +1-202-885 2824
Email: jcraswe@american.edu
1972- ISSN 0305-750X Mon Circ: n/a
Subs: £164 inst
Ed: Janet L. Craswell
'Multi-disciplinary, policy-oriented journal of international development studies. Interdisciplinary work, primary research, policy analyses'
Contrib: any topic on international development
L: 10,000w NP 25 offp Ill: no col. ill
Edit req: 3 copies d-s, no copy by email

311 **WorldViews: A Quarterly Review of Resources for Education and Action** [formerly Third World Resources]
464 19th Street
Oakland CA 94612-2297
+1-510-835 4692 ext. 113 or 114
Fax: +1-510-835 3017
Email: worldviews@igc.org
Website: http://www.igc.org./worldviews/
1985- ISSN 1085-7559 Qtly
Circ: 1,500 Subs: $50 inst $25 indiv NA
$65 inst $45 elsewhere
Eds: Thomas P. Fenton & Mary J. Heffron
Book rev Book rev ed: Mary J. Heffron
'Notices and descriptive listings of organizations and newly released print, audiovisual, CD-ROM, on-line, and other educational resources on Third World regions and issues. Each issue contains a four-page insert with a comprehensive listing of organizations and resources on one region of the world, and a single focus-page listing of resources on a topic of current interest'
No contrib
(*see also* **67**)

AFRICA

Journals in Africa tend to lead a precarious existence, and many lag behind in their publication schedules; others are currently dormant. This is a small selection of African-published journals with a record of fairly regular publication in the past. It includes scholarly African studies periodicals, as well as a number of general interest/current affairs and literary or cultural magazines.

For more comprehensive coverage of African serials, including numerous specialist journals, consult *The African Book World & Press: A Directory/ Répertoire du livre et de la presse en Afrique (see 63)*, or the *APEX 96 Catalogue (see 14)*

Gabon

312 **Muntu**
   BP 770 CICIBA
   Libreville
   +241-76 12 71 Fax: +241-73 40 68
   1984- ISSN 0768-9403 2Yr
   Circ: 2,000 Subs: CFA8,000 Africa
   CFA10,000 elsewhere
   Ed: Vatomene Kukanda
   'Articles and features on Bantu civilisations'
   Contrib: linguistics, history, anthropology
   L: n/a NP 20 offp Ill: line, h-t, photog, b/w & col

Kenya

313 **Weekly Review, The**Φ
   POB 42271
   Nairobi
   +254-2-552233/66
   1975- Wk Circ: 20,000 Subs: Kshs50
   Ed: Jaindi Kisero

Cont: General interest current affairs and news magazine

Lesotho

314 **Review of Southern African Studies**
   Institute of Southern African Studies
   National University of Lesotho
   PO Roma 180
   +266-340601 Fax: +266 340000
   Email: iasa@isas.nul.ls
   1995- ISSN 1024-4190 2Yr Circ: 500
   Subs: $40 inst $20 indiv Africa $50 inst $25 indiv elsewhere
   Ed: Director of Institute
   Book rev Book rev ed: Janet Nyeko
   'Articles, book reviews, news from research institutes in the region, forthcoming titles from ISAS, News from ISAS'
   Contrib: Southern African studies, researched and original in arts, social and behavioural sciences
   L: 8,000w NP 1 free copy, 10 offp
   Ill: line, b&w photog
   Edit req: on disk, WP and hard copy; complete bibliographical references

Malawi

315 **Journal of Humanities**
   Faculty of Humanities
   Chancellor College
   University of Malawi
   POB 280 Zomba
   +265-522222
   1987- Ann Circ: n/a
   Subs: K5 indiv Malawi $8 elsewhere
   Ed: Didier N. Kaphagawani
   Book rev Book rev ed: Brighton Wedi-Kamanga
   'Due to the diverse specialities in the Humanities in general, the contents and scope vary from issue to issue;

classic, fine and performing arts,
literature and orature, linguistics,
theology and philosophy'
L: 20pp NP Ill: line, figures, photog
Edit req: 2 copies, d-s, refs & fn at end of
articles

Nigeria

316 **African ConcordΦ**
Plot 1, Block J
Isolo Industrial Estate, Lagos
+234-1-520357
1984- Wk Circ: 50,000
Ed: Lewis Obi

317 **Glendora Review. African**
Quarterly on the Arts
Glendora International
(Nigeria) Ltd
168 Awolowo Road
POB 50914 Ikoyi
Lagos
+234-1-269 2762
Fax: +234-1-262 8083
Email: 105271,11@compuserve.com
1995- ISSN 1118-146X Qtly
Circ: 2,000
Subs: £36/$40 inst £20/$24 indiv
Ed: Dapo Adeniyi
Book rev (as 'Supplement')
'Covers all fields of the arts: film, music,
theatre, visual arts, architecture,
photography etc. Special interest in
topical issues and discourse to benefit
researchers and general cultural workers.
Mode of presentation is intellectual yet
accessible'
Contrib: as above
L: variable NP Offp Ill: photog, line, col &
b/w
Edit req: relevance and clarity, for general
audience

318 **Newswatch**
3 Billingsway, Oregun
Industrial Estate
PMB 21499 Ikeja
Lagos
+234-1-496 0158
Fax: +234-1-962887
1985- Wk Circ: 100,000 Subs: n/a
Ed: Dan Agbese
Book rev
'Politics, economy, science, societal
issues. All the news that is fit to be
reported'
No contrib

319 **Nigerian Heritage: Journal of**
the National Commission for
Museums and Monuments
National Museum Onikan
PMB 12556 Lagos
+234-1-636005/636075/631134
1992- ISSN 1116-607X Ann
Subs: $40 inst $25 indiv (air)
Ed: L.I. Izuakor Book rev
'Subjects addressed comprise a wide
range of aspects of Nigerian culture,
including archaeology, ethnology,
museum studies and cultural resource
management'
Contrib: welcomes articles on any aspect
of Nigerian material and non-material
culture including, though not limited to,
archaeology, ethnography, natural history,
linguistics, history, art, drama and
architecture
L: 20-25pp NP 1 free copy
Ill: photog b/w
Edit req: 2 copies of ms, d-s, with notes
and refs gathered at end of text; good
quality b/w prints of photog; author status
and designation to be provided on a
separate page

320 **Okike. An African Journal of New Writing**
POB 53
Nsukka
Anambra State
+234-42 770981
Fax: +234-42 770981
1971- ISSN 0331-3566 3Yr
Subs: $56 inst $36 indiv $40 inst Africa
Founding ed: Chinua Achebe
Ed: Onuora Ossie Enekwe
Book rev
'Primarily a creative writing journal, featuring poetry, short fiction and short drama. Critical essays that give insight into the theory and practice of creative writing are valued. Aims to provide robust resource materials for scholars and students of African literature, both at home and in the diaspora'
Contrib: poems, short stories, one-act plays, essays, interviews, reviews
L: 15pp NP 1 free copy
Ill: photog, sketches, b/w
Edit req: d-s 2 copies, brief autobiographical note should accompany submissions
Note: has been dormant for a period, but recommenced publication with issue no. 31 (1996)

Senegal

321 **Africa Development/Afrique Développement**
CODESRIA
BP 3304
Dakar
+221-259822/23 Fax: +221-241289
Email: codesria@sonatel.senet.net
Website: http://www.wsl.cso.uiuc.edu/cas/codesria/codesria.htm
1976- ISSN 0850-3907 Qtly
Circ: 1,000 Subs: $32 inst $30 indiv
Ed: Tade Akin Aina
Book rev

'Bilingual journal; devoted to in-depth comprehensive and accessible analyses of the complex social, economic and political issues of contemporary Africa'
Contrib: original contributions which should not be under consideration by another publication at the same time; any field in the social sciences focused on Africa, or a comparative analysis of Third World issues; Africa and development in general, social movements and social change, gender questions
L: 30 pp NP 20 offp + 2 free copies
Ill: line
Edit req: d-s, with notes, fn, tables etc. on separate pages; CRC for maps, charts; abstract of 150-200w; author's name, academic status, current affiliation to be provided on separate covering page

322 **Afrika Zamani**
CODESRIA
BP 3304
Dakar
+221-259822/33 Fax: +221-241289
1993- ISSN 0850-3079 Ann Circ: 1,600
Subs: $10 Africa $15 elsewhere
Ed: Emmanuel Ghomsi
Book rev
'African history'
Contrib: history, particularly African history or areas of history that connect relations with Africa
L: n/a NP Offp Ill: n/a
Edit req: MS-DOS compatible disk + hard copy

323 **Ethiopiques. Revue Trimestrielle de Culture Négro-Africaine**
Fondation Léopold Sédar Senghor
rue el Hadji Seydou Nourou Tall
Angle René Ndiaye
BP 2035 Dakar
+221-21 53 55

1975- ISSN 0850-2005 Qtly Circ: 3,000
Subs: CFA8,000/FF160
Ed: Moustapha Tambadou
Book rev
*'Covers black African culture, literature
and art and its relations with the Black
world; francophone studies'*
Contrib: as above
L: 2-3,000w NP 10 offp Ill: photog
Edit req: must have a 20 line abstract in
English and French. Only articles in
French are published

South Africa

324 **Africa Insight**
Africa Institute of South
Africa
POB 630 Pretoria 0001
+27-12-328 6970
Fax: +27-12-323 8153
Email: africain@iafrica.com
1970- ISSN 0256-2804 Qtly
Circ: 1,000 Subs: R70/$35
Ed: Madeline Lass
Book rev
*'An independent publication which
promotes insight into the process of
change in Africa. Publishes scholarly
articles in the human sciences aimed at
the interested layperson and serious
student'*
Contrib: economics, political sciences,
anthropology, sociology and any other
human science field focusing particularly
on Africa
L: 6-10,000w NP 3 free copies
Ill: photog, maps, graphs

325 **African Studies**
Witwatersrand University
Press
PB 3 Wits 2050
Johannesburg
+27-11-484 5907
Fax: +27-11-484 5971
Email: 14bevh@cosmos.wits.ac.za
1921- ISSN: 0002-0184 2Yr Circ: 550

Subs: £20/$37 inst £12/$22 indiv
Ed: Deborah James
Book rev Book rev ed: Tom Lodge
*'Scholarly articles on topics relevant to
African anthropology, linguistics,
sociology and related studies'*
Contrib: as above
L: 10,000w NP 1 free copy Ill: b/w

326 **Development Southern Africa**
Development Bank of
Southern Africa
POB 1234
Halfway House
Midrand 1685
+27-11-313 3911
Fax: +27-11-313 3086
Email: cherylj@dbsa.org
1983- 0376-835X 2Mon Circ: 2,500
Subs: R75
Ed: Nick Vink
*'Articles to promote research and
discussion in development issues relating
to southern Africa'*
Contrib: development related
L: 8,000w max NP Offp Ill: occ
Edit req: 3 copies, d-s

327 **Mail and Guardian, The**
139 Smit Street
POB 32362
Braamfontein 2017
+27-11-403 7111
Fax: +27-11-403 1025
Email: newsdesk@wmail.misanet.org
Website:http://www.mg.co.za.mg/services/
goods/index.htm
1985- Wk Circ: 28-30,000
Subs: R300
Ed: Anton Harber
Book rev Book rev ed: Shaun de Waal
*'National news, Africa, media, business,
sports, arts & book reviews. Monthly
supplements: open Africa, PC review,
review of books'*
Contrib: current affairs and newsworthy
stories
L: variable P: per col/cm

328 Southern African Review of
BooksΦ
c/o Dept of History
Room B231
Beattie Building
University of Cape Town
PB Rondebosch 7925
+27-21-650 2965
Fax: +27-21-650 4038
Email: driver@beattie.uct.ac.za
Website: http://www.ucct.ac.za/depts/sarb
1987- ISSN 0952-8040 6Yr Circ: 3,000
Subs: R150 inst R75 indiv
Ed: Dorothy Driver
Book rev
Cont: deals with the cultural politics of
Southern Africa, and provides in-depth
reviews of new books relevant to the
region. Also includes essays, columns and
diaries dealing with the major issues of the
region

Zimbabwe

329 Africa Information Afrique.
Southern Africa Chronicle
6th Floor, Fanum House
57 Samora Machel Avenue
POB 7069 Harare
+263-4-756250 Fax: +263-4-757667
Email: aiazim@harare.iafrica.com
1988- 2Wk Circ: 150 Subs: $100
Ed: M. Dhiliwayo
'Development issues in the southern
African region'
Contrib: from SADC citizens in SADC
countries
L: 7-800w P: $0.15 pw

330 African Journal of Political
Science
African Association of
Political Science
POB MP1100
Mount Pleasant, Harare
+263-4-730403/795418
Fax: +263-4-730403

Email: aapp@harare.iafrica.com
1986- ISSN 1027-0353 2Yr Circ: 500
Subs: $20
Ed: Kwame Ninsin
Book rev
'Politics, social and development;
research notes mainly on Africa'
Contrib: political, social and developments
in Africa yesterday, today and tomorrow
L: 8,000w max NP Offp
Edit req: style sheet is sent to all
prospective contributors

331 Financial GazetteΦ
Modus House
27 Charter Rd
POB 66070 Kopje
Harare
+263-4-738722/29
Fax: +263-4-752831
1969- Wk Circ: 25-30,000
Subs: Z$220
Ed: Trevor Ncube
Cont: general interest; catering for the
financial community in particular

332 Journal of Social Development
in Africa
PB 66022 Kopje
Harare
+263-4-751815 Fax: +263-4-751903
Email: ssw@esanet.zw
1986- ISSN 1012-1080 2Yr Circ: 350
Subs: $40 inst $30 developing countries
Ed: Nigel Hall
'Social development issues, particular
concern with Africa and the Third World,
cross-disciplinarian, concerned with
developing appropriate intervention
strategies, and with issues of the poor and
marginalised'
Contrib: as above
L: 8-9,000w NP 5 offp + 1 free copy
Ill: line, diagrams, graphs, etc.
Edit req: 2 copies, single sided A4, d-s,
author's details on separate sheet, abstract
of 150-200w

333 Moto Magazine
POB 890, Gweru
+263-54-4886 Fax: +263-54-51991
Email: moto@hnetzim.wn.apc.org
1959- Mon Circ: 20,000
Subs: Z$30 $10 Africa $15 elsewhere
Ed: Donatus Bonde
'Coverage of church. cultural, social,
literary issues, as well as sports and other
light entertainment'
Contrib: as above with a bias toward the
Catholic Church
L: variable P: local currency Offp Ill: yes

334 Safere. Southern African
Feminist ReviewΦ
SAPES Trust
POB MP111
Harare
+263-4-727875
Fax: +263-4-732735
Email: sapes@mango.zw
1995- ISSN 1024-9451 2Yr
Subs: Z$80 Zimbabwe $50 NA
Book rev
Cont: focuses on gender issues in relation
to development - political, economic or
social.

335 Southern African Political and
Economic MonthlyΦ
SAPES Trust
POB MP111
Harare
+263-4-727875 Fax: +263-4-732735
Email: sapes@mango.zw
1987- Mon Circ: 2,000
Subs: Z$70 inst Z$50 indiv
Ed: Ibbo Mandaza
Book rev
Cont: focuses on debate and anlysis of
political, economic and social
developments, mainly in Southern Africa

336 Zimbabwean Review, The
3 Donaldson Lane
POB A763 Avondale
Harare
+263-4-304643 Fax: +263-4-333585
Email: zimreview@mango.zw
1995- ISSN 1026-2105 Qtly Circ: 700
Subs: £20/$30 £15/$23 Africa
Ed: Carole Pearce
Book rev
'Interdisciplinary reviews of books, films,
exhibitions etc. and articles emphasizing
the humanities and social sciences but
including topics of general interest to
Zimbabweans, Africans and Africanists
throughout the world'
Contrib: All topics of relevance to the
readers. Write to ed with synopsis
L: 1-3,000w P: Z$250 per 1,000w
1 free copy Ill: photog, line b/w

IV. MAJOR LIBRARIES AND DOCUMENTATION CENTRES

This section aims to identify the major libraries worldwide (outside Africa) with substantial African studies collections, either maintained as separate Africa-related collections, or with significant holdings of Africana material, though not separately maintained. African libraries are not included as they are extensively covered in another, albeit now rather dated, Hans Zell publication, *The African Book World & Press: A Directory/Répertoire du Livre et de la Presse en Afrique*, (4th ed., 1989; *see* **63**).

A number of additional libraries have been added to the database for this new edition, and a few others have been dropped. Data was gathered through mailings of printouts and questionnaires. Libraries were asked to verify and update information from the first edition and to add extra information as appropriate; those with new entries were asked to complete questionnaires. Libraries which did not respond despite at least one chaser mailing - but are known to hold sizeable African studies collections - are marked with the symbols as set out below.

Libraries are listed by countries, and alphabetically by keyword of institution (or town) within each country. Most libraries now include Email addresses and many of them have Websites and on-line hosts accessible via the Internet, as well as providing access to other electronic information services.

For smaller, more specialist libraries with African studies collections, users should consult two sources, (i) for Europe: *The SCOLMA Directory of Libraries and Special Collections on Africa in the United Kingdom and in Europe* (5th ed., 1993; *see* **126**); and (ii) for the USA: *African Studies Information Resources Directory* (1986, out-of-print, *see* **22**; although now rather dated, this directory remains a valuable source, describing collections in libraries and in many other types of repositories in the United States).

Where forms were duly completed and verified, the following information is given: full name and address, telephone and fax numbers;

Email (and Websites for many); the name of the person in charge of the African studies collection (where applicable); hours of opening; conditions of access; loan and reference/referral services or facilities; size of the African studies collection (number of books and current serials taken); on-line database and electronic information services provided; details of publications and finding aids issued; and a brief description of the collection, including any special features, or descriptions of major holdings of Africa-related manuscript and archival materials, or special audio-visual collections and collections of non-print media.

Abbreviations used:

†	- repeat entry from 1st ed. (1989); information not verified; entry updated, as far as possible, from secondary sources
Φ	- provisional new entry, but questionnaire has not been completed; unverified information drawn from secondary sources
Acc	- access [to the library collections]
AL/contact	- Africana or Collection development librarian (and/or other contact) in charge of African studies collections, or of collection in general
b	- books [number of books in collection]
Coll	- collection [size of]
cs	- current serials [number of current serials taken]
ext.	- extension [telephone numbers]
fac	- facilities
H	- hours of opening
ILL	- Inter-library loan
Loan/ref fac	- loan and reference/referral services and facilities are provided
On-line cat	- on-line catalogue [indicates that on-line catalogue is accessible to outside users, and access is through Internet, Telnet, etc.]
On-line dbs	- on-line database and electronic information services [details of systems]
OPAC	- On-line public access catalogue

photocop fac   - photocopying facilities [most libraries provide this, but
                  it is not usually specifically stated]
Publs   - publications and finding aids issued/available
Spec feat   - special features of the collection/s [i.e. collection
                  strength; special archival and manuscript holdings or
                  collections; collections of non-print media, etc.]

Australia

337 University of Melbourne
Library
Parkville
Victoria 3052
+61-3-9344 5379
Fax: +61-3-9348 1142
Website: http://www.lib.unimelb.edu.au
AL/contact: Juliet Flesch
H: term: Mon-Thur 08.30-11.00 Fri 08.30-
18.15 Sat & Sun 11.00-17.00 vacation:
Mon, Tues, Thur, Fri 08.30-17.00, Wed
08.30-21.00 closed weekends
Acc: open to public, loan only through
membership of the library
Loan/ref fac: loans to members, reference
to public and members, space to study,
access for disabled
Coll: 4,000b, 150cs
On-line dbs: all major on-line services
On-line cat: access through website above
Publs: *South Africa, a Changing Society:
an exhibition* (catalogue)
Spec feat: amongst the most significant
collections: *South Africa: internal and
foreign affairs 1945-1954; The CIA
Research Reports: Africa 1946-1976*
(microfilm); *South Africa: the making of
US policy 1962-1989*; Special Studies
Series: *Africa 1962-1988.* Carter-Karis
Collection based on materials collected by
Gwendolen M. Carter and Thomas Karis;
Trial transcripts: *The Treason Trial* and
*Prep Exom 1956-1961; The Rivonia
Sabotage Trial. The Black Consciousness
Movement of South Africa* (microform),
material from the collection of Gail M.
Gerhart.

338 University of Western
Australia
Reid Library
Nedlands WA 6907
+61-9-380 2348
Fax: +61-9-380 1012
Email: plimb@library.uwa.edu.au
Website: http://www.library.uwa.edu.au
AL/contact: Peter Limb & Professor
Norman Etherington (History)
nether@uniwa.uwa.edu.au
H: term: 08.00-22.00; vacation: 08.30-
18.00
Acc: open
Loan/ref: all members of library; reference
desk. Member of CAMP (Cooperative
Africana Microform Project)
Coll: 8-10,000b, 50-100cs
On-line dbs: ABN, UNCOVER,
FIRSTSEARCH, ABI (networked)
CURRENT CONTENTS, ERL, OVID,
SCALE (networked)
On-line cat: INNOPAC catalogue
available to Internet users
Publs: *Dept of History Library Lists;
An A-Z of African Studies on the Internet*
(*see* **95**)
http://www.library.uwa.edu.au/sublibs/sch/
sc_ml_afr.html
On-line database compiled by Peter Limb
updated periodically
Spec feat: one of the largest Africana
collections in Australia, mainly on
Southern African history. Includes
microfilm copies of: Carter-Karis
Collection; A.B. Xuma personal papers; A.
Luthuli papers; ICU Yase Natal records;
SA Dept Justice files selected by R. Edgar;
Wallerstein collection; newspapers such as
Umsebenzi, Guardian, Windhoek

Advertiser, Drum, Umvikele Thebe, Liberation, Fighting Talk; SA Parliamentary papers and debates; also *Ethiopian New Times* & *Ethiopian Observer* (full set); SA Inst Race Relations Archives (45 reels); SA Native Representative Council, Verbatim Report of Proceedings 1937-1946 (4 reels); SA Miscellaneous manuscripts 1911-1933 (1 reel); Papers of C. Kadalie from Univ of Wits; *Kunda ya Bantu*, the Negro Worker, *Imvo Zabantsundu* (selected years); John F. Kennedy National Security Files: Africa; Colin Legum's Press Cuttings 1936-86 and Writings; government publications relating to Tanganyika 1919-1961; *South Africa: a Collection of Political Materials 1902-1963*; World Missionary Archives; US State Dept. Files on Africa; *South Africa: the Making of US Policy, 1962-1989* (439 fiche). Some papers on Zaire, Zambia. Also holds audio-visual material, including recordings of the life of Sir Walter Coutts, Governor-General of Uganda; and substantial reference collection. Extensive monograph collection, strong on African (esp. Southern, Eastern) history, literatures (English and French) and anthropology. Pamphlet/govt. doc. collection: The Robert Dowse Collection: Ghana Politics and Economy, 1950s-1980 (includes writings of Kwame Nkrumah).

Austria

339 Universität Wien
Fachbibliothek für Afrikanistik
Doblhoffgasse 5/9
A-1010 Vienna
+43-1-407 4757
Fax: +43-1-405 227319
Email: Afrikanistik@univie.ac.at
AL/contact: Erich René Sommerauer
H: Mon-Thur 10.00-12.00, 13.00-16.00
Acc: students, faculty, and general public
Loan/ref: on request

Coll: 12,000b, 330cs
Spec feat: strong on African languages and linguistics, history, politics, literature; maps; 170 microfiches, 330 cassettes; some old rare books 16-19th century.

Belgium

340 Bibliothèque Africaine
65 rue Belliard
B-1040 Brussels
+32-2-501 3514/3544
Fax: +32-2-510 3669
AL/contact: Christine Bils-Lambert, Chief Librarian
H: Mon-Fri 9.00-16.00
Acc: n/a Loan/ref fac: interlibrary loans
Coll: 500,000b, 320cs
On-line dbs: BELINDIS (Belgian Information and Dissemination Service), available to outside users, user manual available on request
Publs: qtly list of acquisitions
Spec feat: in addition to very complete and exceptional collections of official and unofficial documents on the Congo and the former Belgian Congo, the library's collection contains rare books on Africa bought mainly by King Leopold II for his personal library.

341 University of Ghent
Dept of African Studies
Rozier 44
B-9000 Gent
+32-9-264 3818
Fax: +32-9-264 4180
Email: Henik.Pinxven@rug.ac.ge
AL/contact: Greta Van Daele
H: term: Mon-Fri 09.30-17.00
Acc: open Loan/ref fac:n/a
Coll: 20,000b, 50cs
Publs: card catalogue; database available shortly
Spec feat: African languages and literature, African history, traditional and modern African societies, anthropology.

342 **Koninklijk Museum voor**
     Midden-Afrika/Musée Royal
     de l'Afrique Centrale
     Steenweg op Leuven 13
     B-3080 Tervuren
     +32-2-695211
     Fax: +32-2-767 0242
     AL/contact: Danielle de Lame, Acting
     Librarian
     H: Tues-Fri 09.00-16.00
     Acc: one week ticket BF100; annual fee
     BF300
     Loan/ref fac: no loan fac; reading on the
     premises, photocop fac
     Coll: 105,000b, 3,000cs
     On-line dbs: access to database of the
     documentation service (social and cultural
     sciences)
     On-line cat: n/a
     Publs: catalogue available on request
     Spec feat: African varia in geology
     (samples, old maps, crystals); zoology
     (large collection of insects, fishes,
     amphibians, reptiles, birds, mammals,
     library on African zoology); cultural
     anthropology (large collection of artefacts,
     ethnic music records, etc.); history
     (archival material on Belgian presence
     overseas before 1960, Stanley Archives);
     social anthropology; significant library on
     all aspects of culture and society in Black
     Africa, including the most contemporary
     topics.

Canada

343 **Carleton University**
     Maxwell MacOdrum Library
     1125 Colonel By Drive
     Ottawa, Ontario K1S 5B6
     +1-613-520 2600 ext.2725
     Fax: +1-613-520 2750
     Email: poppie_rabalao@carleton.ca
     Website: http://www.library.carleton.ca
     AL/contact: Poppie Rabalao, Reference
     Services Department
     H: term: Mon-Fri 08.00-11.00, Sat-Sun
     10.00-11.00

Acc: open
Loan/ref fac: reference; maps, data, and
government information centre;
interlibrary loans
Coll: 13,198b, 245cs
On-line dbs: DIALOG, World News
Connection
On-line cat: see website above
Spec feat: the government documents
African collection comprises monographs
and serials from a wide variety of
countries for which a statistical count is
not available. Library holds a significant
collection of materials relating to Africa,
including books journals, government
documents and maps, focusing principally
on Anglophone Africa, in the post-1945
period. Has access to an ever-increasing
variety of electronic resources, including
CD-ROM databases and the Internet.

344 **McGill University†**
     McLennan Library
     Reference Dept
     3459 McTavish Street
     Montreal PQ H3A 1Y1
     +1-514-398 4755
     Fax: +1-514-398 7184
     AL/contact: The Librarian
     H: term: 08.30-23.00 vacation: 09.00-
     18.00
     Acc: open to serious scholars and
     university students
     Loan/ref fac: full service to institutional
     clientele, reduced service to external
     patrons
     On-line dbs: DIALOG, MINISIS/IRDC,
     Infoglobe, InfoMart, UTLAS
     On-line cat: via UTLAS, off-site access to
     institutional patrons only
     Spec feat: no special collections or
     holdings, concentration traditionally on
     anglophone West Africa and reference
     sources for the continent.

Denmark

345 Centre for Development Research Library
Gammel Kongevej 5
DK-1610 Copenhagen V
+45-33-251200
Fax: +45-33-258110
Email: cefuahwe@inet.uni-c.dk
Website: http://www.c.dk
AL/contact: Svend Erik Lindberg-Hansen, Chief Librarian
H: Mon-Fri 10.00-16.00 Acc: open
Loan/ref fac: full loan and ref fac
Coll: 40,000b, 450cs
Publs: series of 'C-papers', mainly library accessions list, catalogues, and occasional bibliographies
Spec feat: n/a

346 Mellemfolkeligt Samvirke/ Danish Association for International Development
Borgergade 10-14
DK-1300 Copenhagen
+45-33-326244
Fax: +45-33-144594
AL/contact: Helle Leth-Møller
H: Mon-Wed, Fri 13.00-16.00 Thur 13.00-18.00 Acc: open
Loan/ref fac: books 1 month, no lending of serials
Coll: 8,000b, 60cs
Publs: *Biblioteksnyt* (MS Library News); bibliographies, booklists
Spec feat: Africa, Asia, Latin America; development studies special collections; audio visual materials; minority MS library.

Finland

347 Department of Asian and African Studies
Helsinki University
Unioninkatu 38, POB 13

FIN-00014 Helsinki
+358-9-1911 2244
Fax: +358-9-1912 2094
Email: arvi.hurskainen@helsinki.fi
Website: http://www.helsinki.fi/hum/aakkl
AL/contact: Arvi Hurskainen
H: n/a Acc: apply for research purposes; also through Internet
Loan/ref fac: n/a
Coll: (total coll) ca. 10 millionb
On-line dbs: access through Internet to all the material. General purpose tools and also language-specific searching and retrieving tools available
On-line cat: see above
Spec feat: computer archives of Swahili language and folklore; contains 170 hours spoken language in Standard Swahili and dialects; wordlists in various dialects; a collection of newsaper texts; prose text from a number of books; Tanzanian Parliament discussions 1995-96; Bible translations, etc.

348 Helsinki University Library
Unioninkatu 36
POB 312
FIN-00171 Helsinki
+358-9-1912 2224
Fax: +358-9-1912 2094
Email: harry.halen@helsinki.fi
Website: htp://www.helsinki.fi/hum/aakkl/
AL/contact: Harry Halén
H: Mon-Fri 09.00-21.00 (summer to 18.00) Sat 09.00-18.00 (closed in July) Sun 12.00-18.00
Acc: open for research
Loan/ref fac: African material available only in reading rooms, no interlibrary loans, copies of microfiches and of articles in serials are provided
Coll: 64cs
On-line: DIALOG, Telesystems Questel
Spec feat: collection of Ovambo literature (Northern Namibia), ca. 400 vols to 1972; 19th century publications in the Ondonga languages, printed in Finland by the Finnish Missionary Society; several

dialects in 20th century material; most printing since 1901 in Ovamboland, literature printed after 1972 is included in the National Library Collection of the Library. The collection consists of religious books, school books, and practical guides; part was microfiched in 1985 for the Namibian National Library, copies are in the Library. The Emil Liljeblad Collections is a ms. collection consisting of folklore of the Ovambo peoples of Northern Namibia.

France

349 **Académie des sciences d'outre-mer, Bibliothèque**
15 rue La Pérouse
F-75116 Paris
+33-1-47 20 87 93
Fax: +33-1-47 20 89 72
AL/contact: Dominique Prince
H: Mon-Fri 14.00-17.30 Acc: open
Loan/ref fac: no loans, photocop fac
Coll: Asian & African: 50,000b, 3,000cs
5,000 brochures
Publs: *Mondes et cultures*
Spec feat: collection on French colonies: Indochina, francophone Africa, Caribbean, French Antilles (literature, sciences, politics, economics, ethnology). Important collection on Madagascar; 930 mss on Quebec.

350 **Bibliothèque de documentation internationale contemporaine**
6 allée de l'Université
BP 106
F-92001 Nanterre Cedex
+33-1-40 97 79 00
Fax: +33-1-40 97 79 40
AL/contact: Le Bibliothécaire en chef
H: Mon: 12.30-18.00 Tue-Fri: 10.00-18.00 Sat:10.00-18.00 reduced hours in August
Acc: public admission with card authorization, restricted access to documents

Loan/ref fac: no loans
Coll: 50,000b, 100cs
Spec feat: covers francophone, anglophone (particularly South Africa), hispanophone and lusophone Africa; politics, economics and social sciences from an international viewpoint; colonies and decolonisation in the 20th century; the two world wars in Africa. Collection of the Bibliothèque africaine et malgache, important papers on the colonial period and the early years of independence; collections of German documents published before 1945 on the German colonies. Documents are primarily those emanating from Europe, the US and USSR; few from Africa, apart from official journals. Photograph collection on the Sudan. Material on the Algerian war.

351 **Bibliothèque nationale de France**
58 rue Richelieu
F-75084 Paris Cedex 02
from 17th December 1996 also at:
11 quai François Mauriac,
F-75706 Paris Cedex 13
+33-1-4703 8126
Fax: +33-1-53 79 41 80
Email: mds@bnf.fr
Website: www.bmf.fr/
AL/contact: Paulette Lordereau
H: Dept des imprimés Mon-Fri 09.00-20.00 (closed at Easter) other depts 09.00-17/18.00
H: quai François Mauriac: Tues-Sat 10.00-19.00, Sun 10.00-18.00
Acc: primarily to scholars and students; others can apply for access authorization; at quai François Mauriac must be over 18
Loan/ref fac: for ref on premises only; some photocop fac also photog, microfiches, microfilms
Coll: 100,000b
On-line dbs: GEAC-BNOPALE, CD-ROM in prep
On-line cat: in reference rooms and website as above

Publs: *Littératures africaines à la Bibliothèque nationale, 1973-1983*; *Périodiques malgaches de la Bibliothèque nationale*; *Les Auteurs afro-américains, 1965-1982*; *Les Publications en série éditées au Sénégal, 1856-1982*, and various catalogues
Spec feat: the legal depository of the colonial period to 1960 has a rich collection of works in Malagasy; works in other African languages e.g. Fulani, Hausa, Kiswahili; the library of SEGOU, the collection of the Société de Géographie, voyages, expeditions and explorations in Africa. Current acquisitions are expanding literature holdings in French, English, Portuguese and the African languages. At quai François Mauriac 1,600 volumes dealing with African literature will be on open access.

352 Centre des archives d'outre-mer
29 chemin du Moulin Detesta
F-13090 Aix-en-Provence
+33-1-42 93 38 50
Fax: +33-1-42 93 38 89
AL/contact: Françoise Durand-Evrard
H: Mon-Fri 09.00-17.00 Acc: n/a
Loan/ref fac: n/a
Coll: (total coll) 100,000b
Spec feat: collections derive from the Ministry of the Colonies and administration of francophone possessions overseas; includes history of French colonies, geography, architecture and ethnology.

353 Centre d'études africaines, Bibliothèque†
54 boulevard Raspail
F-75006 Paris
+33-1-45 44 39 59
AL/contact: Olenka Darkowska-Nidzgorska
H: Mon-Fri 10.00-12.30, 14.00-17.00
Acc: letter of introduction required

Loan/ref fac: no lending facilities for external users
Coll: 16,000b, 300cs
Publs: *Cahiers d'études africaines, see* 193; *Bibliographie des travaux en langue française sur l'Afrique au sud du Sahara: sciences sociales et humaines* (ann, see 167); *Répertoire des thèses africanistes françaises*
Spec feat: collections strong in anthropology, history, sociology, folklore, geography, economic and social development, and politics.

354 Centre de recherches africaines, Bibliothèque†
9 rue Malher
F-75004 Paris
+33-1-42 18 33 22
AL/contact: Liliane Daronian
H: Tue-Wed 14.00-18.00
Acc: researchers and students at masters and doctorate level
Loan/ref fac: n/a
Coll: 12,000b, 450cs
Spec feat: the library is linked with the Universities of Paris Panthéon-Sorbonne, Sorbonne-Nouvelle and René Descartes, and is multi-disciplinary; covers the whole of the African continent; two distinct types of holdings - the first multi-disciplinary on history, ethnology, sociology, linguistics, and geography, and the second primarily historical.

355 Centre de recherches et d'études sur les sociétés méditerranéennes, Bibliothèque†
Maison de la Méditerranée
3 avenue Pasteur
F-13100 Aix-en-Provence
+33-3-23 03 86
AL/contact: Marie-José Bianquis
H: Tues-Fri 09.00-12.30, 13.30-17.00
Loan/ref fac: n/a
Coll: 22,000b, 220cs

Spec feat: acquires material in the social sciences and humanities on Morocco, Algeria, Tunisia, Libya and the Sahara; especially extensive holdings in the fields of history, geography, economics, law, political science, arts, literature, sociology, anthropology and demography.

356 La Documentation française, Bibliothèque

Fonds spécial Afrique et outre-mer
29 quai Voltaire
F-75344 Paris Cedex 07
+33-1-40 15 72 05
Fax: +33-1-40 15 72 30
Email: postmaster@ladocfrancaise.gouv.fr
Website:http://www.ladocfrancaise.gouv.fr
AL/contact: Marie-Edith Guinanmary
H: Mon-Fri 10.00-18.00 except Thur 10.00-13.00
Acc: open
Loan/ref fac: information; photocop fac; interlibrary loan; telephone information; CD-ROM EDOP available
Coll: 65,000, 130cs
On-line dbs: *see* entry **357** below
Publs: *Liste de nouvelles acquisitions de la bibliothèque* (mon); *Liste des publications de la Banque mondiale* (2Yr); *Liste des périodiques conservés à La Documentation française.*
Spec feat: collection was based on that acquired by the Agence économique des colonies which collected material from French colonies; since 1961 has specialized in works and periodicals about sub-Saharan Africa and Madagascar. Complete coverage until 1990 with an emphasis on social and human sciences, from 1990; no science, technology or agronomy.

357 La Documentation française, CIDIC Section Afrique

29 quai Voltaire
F-75340 Paris Cedex 07
+33-1-40 15 71 61

Fax: +33-1-40 15 72 30
Email: postmaster@ladocfrancaise.gouv.fr
Website:http://www.ladocfrancaise.gouv.fr
AL/contact: F. Corre, Z. Vatan
H: Mon-Fri 10.00-18.00
except Thur 10.00-13.00
Acc: open
Loan/ref fac: photocop fac
Coll: 701 'dossiers' for 54 countries 750cs
On-line dbs: minitel address: 3615 la doc.40 15 72 00 (same catalogue as CIDIC main library)
On-line cat: on-line database number above
Publs: *Catalogue des derniers documentaires: étranger et international - 1996*; *L'actualité internationale: chronologie sélective du CIDIC* (qtly)
Spec feat: books, periodicals, newspapers and press cuttings on all aspects of African affairs - legal, political, economic, social, cultural and scientific. Material is collected on all regions of Africa; official gazettes are received from all African countries, and there is a complete collection of all the bulletins and gazettes issued by the former French colonies in Africa from their earliest days. Another feature is a card index to the legislation of francophone African countries.

358 Musée de l'homme, Bibliothèque

Place du Trocadéro
F-75116 Paris
+33-1-44 05 72 03
Fax: +33-1-44 05 72 12
Email: duboijac@mnhn.fr
AL/contact: Jacqueline Dubois
H: Mon-Fri 10.00-17.00, except Wed 10.00-20.00
Acc: open to the public for reference purposes
Loan/ref fac: n/a Coll: 20,000b, 500cs
Spec feat: collects anthropological material on a worldwide basis; African coverage particularly strong for francophone countries. The Library also

houses the collection of the Société des africanistes *see* **863**.

359 ORSTOM - Institut français de recherche scientifique pour le développement en coopération

32 avenue Varagnat
F-93143 Bondy Cedex
+33-1-48 02 55 51
Fax: +33-1-48 47 30 88
Email: aldebert@orstom.fr
Website: http://www.orstom.fr
AL/contact: E. Aldebert
H: Mon-Fri 13.30-17.30
Acc: open
Loan ref fac: interlibrary loan, photocop, list of refs via mail, fax, Email
Coll: 50,000b, 300cs
On-line dbs: HORIZON (brochure available on request)
On-line cat: Telnet: horizon.orstom.fr or use website above
Spec feat: scientific articles and books; tropical zone, development, third world, environment, earth sciences, health, social sciences, oceanography, agronomy, fisheries, hydrology, soil science, demography, economics, anthropology, sociology, culture.

360 Service Afrique-Moyen Orient

Bibliothèque inter-universitaire des langues orientales
4 rue de Lille
F-75007 Paris Cedex 07
+33-1-44 77 87 20
Fax: +33-1-44 77 87 30
AL/contact: Nathalie Rodriguez
H: Mon 13.00-19.00, Tues-Fri 09.00-19.00, Sat 10.00-18.00; closed on Sat and restricted hours 14 July-1 October; closed certain holidays
Acc: public admission with card
Loans/ref fac: restricted to students and teachers of universities Paris III, VII, VIII and INALCO; interlibrary loans, photocop fac, photog & microfilms

Coll: (total coll) ca. 8,000b, ca. 350cs
On-line dbs: catalogue on CD-ROM
Spec feat: works on languages, literature and civilization; more than 70 languages, African linguistic material is now widely collected, Africa fiction in African and non-African languages.

361 Université de Bordeaux IV, Centre d'étude d'Afrique noire

Institut d'études politiques, Bibliothèque
BP 101 domaine universitaire
F-33405 Talence Cedex
+33-5-56 84 42 86
Fax: +33-5-56 84 43 24
Email: doccean@rsiep.iep.u_bordeaux.fr
Website:http://rsiep.iep.u_bordeaux.fr: 8001/cean/page0.html
AL/contact: Françoise Meynard
H: Mon-Fri 09.00-19.00
Acc: restricted to students, researchers and scholars
Loan/ref fac: full loan fac, photocop fac
Coll: 18,000b, 700cs
On-line dbs: document searching on the information system of the Institute
Publs: *Afrique politique* (ann), *Lusotopie* (ann), *Lettre du CEAN* (2yr), *Travaux et documents de CEAN* (qtly), *Multigraphiés du CEAN* (ann), *Bibliographies du CEAN* (2yr), *Politique africaine* (qtly see **203**)
Spec feat: specializes in Africa south of the Sahara; politics, economics, international relations, society, contemporary African religions and history; the press; collections of African newspapers and official journals of francophone countries.

Germany

362 Anthropos-Institut, Bibliothek

Arnold-Janssen Strasse 20
D-53754 Sankt Augustin
+49-2441-237318
Fax: +49-2441-205823

AL/contact: Ulla Hahn, Librarian
H: n/a Acc: n/a
Loan/ref fac: reference library
Coll: 8,000b, 30 cs
Publs: *Anthropos, Studia Instituti Anthropos, Collectanea Instituti Anthropos* (41 volumes since 1967, of which 22 are concerned with Africa)

363 Arnold-Bergsträsser Institut für Kulturwissenschaftliche Forschung, Bibliothek
Windaustrasse 16
D-79110 Freiburg
+49-761-85091
Fax: +49-761-892967
Email: abifr@ruf.uni-freiburg.de
AL/contact: Stephanie Gerum
H: Mon-Fri 08.00-18.00
Acc: open
Loan/ref fac: reference library, restricted loan facilities, inter-library loans
Coll: 30,000b, 100 cs
On-line dbs: information retrieval, acquisition lists, bibliographies
Spec feat: particularly strong collections in the fields of education and administration; collections of 'grey literature'.

364 Bayerische Staatsbibliothek
Ludwigstrasse 16
D-80539 Munich
+49-89-286380
Fax: +49-89-28638 293
Email: dir@bib.bvb.d400.de
Website: available shortly
AL/contact: Richard Mai (Acquisition department)
H: Main reading room: Mon-Fri 09.00-19.30 Sat to 16.30 Periodicals reading room: Mon-Fri 09.00-19.30 Lending department: Mon-Fri 10.30-12.30 14.30-16.30 Thur to 18.00
Acc: stock library, closed to the public
Loan/ref fac: full loan and ref fac
Coll: 40,000b, 120cs
On-line dbs: Informationsvermittlungsstelle (On-line

Information Service, access to DIMDI, DIALOG, DBI)
On-line cat: On-line public access (OPAC) accessible to outside users via Datex-P (45050982124) or Internet (BSB-LINE)
Spec feat: African collections not separately maintained; strong on African history, African-European relations, travel and exploration; substantial holdings of early (16th-19th century) literature.

365 Universitätsbibliothek Bayreuth
D-95440 Bayreuth
+49-921-553420
Fax: +49-921-553442
Website: http://www.ub.uni-bayreuth.de/w3opac/index.html
AL/contact: Rainer-Maria Kiel
H: Mon-Fri 09.00-18.00
Acc: open
Coll: 45,000, 220cs
On-line dbs: OPAC
On-line cat: use website above

366 Universitätsbibliothek Bielefeld
Universitätsstrasse 25
Postfach 100291
D-33502 Bielefeld
+49-521-106 3809
Fax: +49-521-106 4052
Email: sekretariat@ub.uni.bielefeld.de
Website: http://www.ub.uni-bielefeld.de
AL/contact: Johannes Rogalla von Biberstein
H: 08.00-13.00 Acc: open
Loan/ ref fac: interlibrary loan, JASON with more than 200,000 journal articles of which 75,000 are available on-line, SUBITO (from 1997) access to international special collections, JADE more than 24,000 journals with issues since 1987
Coll: 4,000b, 15cs
On-line cat: OPAC via Internet from 1997
Spec feat: collection strong in ethnology, sociology of development.

367 **Universität Bremen**Φ
Zentrum für Afrika-Studien,
Bibliothek
Postfach 33 04 40
D-2800 Bremen 33
+49-421-218 2387
Fax: +49-421-219 807
AL/contact: M. O. Hinz, Chief Librarian
H: Mon-Fri 09.00-16.30
Loan/ref fac: full loan and ref fac
Coll: 3-4,000b
On-line dbs: to external hosts worldwide
On-line cat: no; off-line cat on microfiches
Spec feat: 2,000 books entitled 'Black
Writings', from the collection of Janheinz
Jahn.

368 **Deutsches Institut für**
Tropische und Subtropische
Landwirtschaft GmbH,
Bibliothek
Steinstrasse 19 Postfach 1652
D-37213 Witzenhausen
+49-5542-60713
Fax: +49-5542-60739
AL/contact: Claudia Blaue
H: Mon-Fri 08.00-12.30
Acc: open to all bona fide academic
scholars
Loan/ref fac: most books can be loaned
Coll: 8,000b, 100cs
Publs: 'Topics in Applied Resource
Management in the Tropics'; *Der
Tropenlandwirt*
Spec feat: tropical and subtropical
agriculture, horticulture, botany, zoology;
history of German colonies; ethnology.
Total collection more than 55,000 books
and journals, mainly on tropical and
subtropical themes.

369 **Frankfurt Stadt-und-**
Universitätsbibliothek
Bockenheimer Landstrasse
134-138
D-60325 Frankfurt am Main
+49-69-212-397246/247

AL/contact: Irmtraud Wolcke-Renk &
Anne Kasper
H: Mon-Fri 11.00-16.30
Acc: open
Loan/ref fac: reading-room for ref books,
interlibrary loan
Coll: 100,000b
On-line dbs: library catalogue
On-line cat: Telnet: opac.server.uni-
frankfurt.de (login <opc); includes
holdings of other library collections in
Frankfurt
Publs: on-line *Neuerwerbungen Afrika;
Fachkatalog Afrika* (12 vols)
Spec feat: has the responsibility assigned
by the Deutsche Forschungsgemeinschaft
in 1964, for maintaining a special
collection for Africa South of the Sahara;
its aim is to provide a collection of all
relevant literature as completely as
possible, with materials being made
available for lending purposes. All
subjects except law, economics and natural
science.

370 **Frobenius Institut**
Völkerkundliche Bibliothek
Liebigstrasse 41
D-60323 Frankfurt am Main
+49-69-721012/2538
Fax: +49-69-1737258
AL/contact: Eleonore Schmitt
H: Mon-Thur 14.00-17.30 Fri 09.00-
12.00
Acc: open
Loan/ref fac: some restrictions on lending;
alphabetical catalogue, OPAC incl. subject
catalogue
Coll: 20,000b, 150cs
On-line dbs: OPAC
Spec feat: ethnology, cultural and social
anthropology, non-European prehistory
(rock paintings).

371 **Niedersächsische Staats-und**
Universitätsbibliothek
Göttingen†
Postfach 2932

Prinzenstrasse 1
D-3400 Göttingen
+49-551-395212
AL/contact: Fran Roth
H: Mon-Fri 09.00-18.00 Sat 09.30-13.00
Loan/ref fac: full loan and ref fac
Coll: 20,000b, 100cs
On-line dbs: several
On-line cat: yes, admission necessary
Publs: on-line databases
Spec feat: no specific Africa-related
collections but substantive African
holdings; comprehensive collections in all
subjects, rare book collections.

372 **Universität Hamburg**
Institut für Afrikanistik und
Äthiopistik,
Rothenbaumchaussee 67/69
D-20148 Hamburg
+49-40-4123 4874
Fax: +49-40-4123 5977
AL/contact: C. Geisenheyner, Chief
Librarian
H: Mon-Thur 10.00-16.00, Fri 10.00-
13.00
Acc: open
Loan/ref fac: alphabetical and keyword
catalogue; short loans only
Coll: 22,970b, 60cs
Spec feat: African languages especially
Swahili, Hausa, Amharic; African
literature; Pidgin/Creole languages;
Ethiopian studies; pre-colonial history;
African music and art; African Islamic
studies.

373 **Ifo-Institut für**
   Wirtschaftsforschung
Informationszentrum
Poschingerstrasse 5
D-81679 Munich
+49-89-9241 1350
Fax: +49-89-985369
AL/contact: The Librarian
H: Mon 13.00-17.00, Thur 09.00-13.00
Acc: for reference purposes only
Coll: 16,000b, 100cs

On-line dbs: IFOKAT at host GBI
On-line cat: collects material on the whole
of Africa in the field of economics,
development, and the social sciences.

374 **Institut für Afrika-Kunde,**
   Bibliothek
Neuer Jungfernstieg 21
D-20354 Hamburg
+49-40-356 2526/519
Fax: +49-40-356 2511
Email: iak@hwwa.uni-hamburg.de
AL/contact: Christine Hoffendahl &
Gertrud Wellman-Hofmeier, Chief
Librarians
H: Mon-Thur 09.00-12.30 13.30-17.00
Fri 09.00-12.30 13.30-16.00
Acc: open
Loan/ref fac: ref only, loans over weekend,
photocopy fac
Coll: 42,500b, 440cs
On-line cat: on request
Publs: *Neuerwerbungen der Bibliothek*
(Accessions Lists)
Spec feat: supported by the Deutsche
Forschungsgemeinschaft, the library
collects 'Report Literature' from sub-
Saharan Africa; collection of 40 daily or
weekly newspapers from Africa, cuttings
from which are published fortnightly in
Aktueller Informationsdienst Afrika (*see*
209). All acquisitions are indexed,
annotated and fed into the database of the
'Übersee Dokumentation' (ÜD), Hamburg.
The ÜD, through its Africa unit, publishes
the quarterly *Select Bibliography of Recent
Literature* and special bibliographies.

375 **Institut für**
   Auslandsbeziehungen,
   Bibliothek
Charlottenplatz 17
Postfach 102463
D-70020 Stuttgart
+49-711-222 5147
Fax: +49-711-226 4346
Email: 100631,115@compuserve.com
AL/contact: Udo Rossbach

H: Tue-Fri: 13.00-18.00 except Wed
10.00-19.00
Acc: n/a
Loan/ref fac: national and international
inter-library loan
Coll: 12,000b, 250cs
On-line dbs: Specialized Information
Network for International Relations and
Area Studies
Publs: *Biannual report: Zeitschrift für
Kulturaustausch; Materialien zum
Internationalen Kulturaustausch;
Literaturrecherchen*
Spec feat: foreign countries, cultural
relations with foreign countries, cultural
theory, ethnic stereotypes, research on
exchanges, developing areas and problems
of technical assistance and educational
training, history of emigration and
migration, ethnic minorities.

376 **Institut für Ethnologie und
Afrika-Studien, Bibliothek†**
Johannes Gutenberg-
Universität
D-6500 Mainz
+49(0)6131-395933/392798
Fax: +49(0)6131-393730
AL/contact: Anna-Maria Brandstetter,
Chief Librarian
H: by appointment
Acc: by appointment
Loan/ref fac: no loans
Coll: 25,000b, 218cs
Spec feat: in addition to the general
Africana collection, the institute houses
the 'Jahnheinz Jahn-Bibliothek', a
collection of African literature, including
literature in European and African
languages, children's literature, popular
literature and comics, literary journals -
10,000 titles and 173 journals.

377 **Institut für Weltwirtschaft,
Bibliothek**
Deutsche Zentralbibliothek
für Wirtschaftswissenschaften
Düsternbrooker Weg 120

D-24105 Kiel
+49-431-881 4383/498
Fax: +49-431-881 4520
Email: zbw.uni-kiel.de
Website: http://www.jp-a.129.143.3.25
AL/contact: A. Koch-Klose
H: Mon-Thur: 08.00-18.00
Fri 08.00-16.30
Acc: n/a
Loan/ref fac: lending library, inter-library
loan, catalogue and on-line searching
service based on written enquiries,
selective dissemination of information,
photocop fac
Coll: (total coll) 98,000, 2,100cs
On-line dbs: ECONIS (Economics
Information System) 22,700 records
referring to Africa
On-line cat: website as above - login
ozbw@x29t code 1313.opac
Spec feat: strong on economics statistics,
commercial and trade literature, official
publications, and publications from public
authorities, banks, trade unions, and
political parties.

378 **Universität zu Köln**
Institut für Afrikanistik
Bibliothek
Albertus-Magnus-Platz
D-5000 Cologne 41
+49-221-470 2708/3885
Fax: +49-221-470 5158
Email: ama01@aix370.rrz.uni-koeln.de
AL/contact: Helga Krüger
H: Mon-Fri 09.00-12.00 afternoon
opening hours by appointment
Acc: n/a
Loan/ref fac: on the premises only, reading
room, photocop fac
Coll: 15,600b, 100cs
Publs: *Afrikanistische Arbeitspapiere*;
'Afrikanistische Monographien'
Spec feat: oriented towards African
linguistics, particularly East Africa
(Nilotic, Cuslitic languages), Mande,
Bantu, Creole, Khoisan; gender studies;
anthropology (East Africa).

379 **Universität München**Φ
Institut für Völkerkunde und
Afrikanistik, Bibliothek
Ludwigstrasse 27/I
D-8000 Munich 22
+49-89-2180 2257
Fax: +49-89-284833
AL/contact: Falko Abeking, Librarian
H: Mon-Thur 09.00-12.00, 13.00-17.00
Fri 09.00-12.00, 13.00-15.00
Coll: 8,000b, 50cs
Spec feat: ethnography, linguistics,
archaeology.

380 **Universität des Saarlandes**
Zentrum Europa und Dritte
Welt, Bibliothek
Bau 30, D-66041
Saarbrücken
+49-681-302 2564
Fax: +49-681-302 2514
Email: ze70hsag@z.uni-sb.de
Website: http://www.uni-sb.de/z-einr/efb
AL/contact: Armin Goldschmidt
H: Mon-Thur 09.00-12.00
Acc: n/a
Loan/ref fac: ref library, author and sub
catalogue
Coll: 3,000b, 15cs
On-line dbs: see website above
Spec feat: social anthropology, culture,
psychology; development cooperation,
development aid and related topics;
migration and refugees.

381 **Staatsbibliothek zu Berlin,**
Preussischer Kulturbesitz
Haus 2 Potsdamer Strasse 33
Orientabteilung
D-10785 Berlin
+49-30-266 2489
Fax: +49-30- 264 5955
AL/contact: Meliné Pehlivanian
H: Mon-Fr 09.00-21.00 Sat 09.00-17.00
reading room of the Oriental dept:
Mon-Fri 09.00-17.00 Sat 09.00-13.00
Acc: open

Loan/ref fac: full loan and ref fac; interlibrary loan; photocop and microfilm fac
Coll: 56,000b, 400cs
Publs: catalogues of the African
manuscripts owned by German libraries,
also by the SBB, in the 'Katalogisierung
orientalischer Handschriften in
Deutschland' series; *Handbuch der*
historischen Buchbestände in
Deutschland, pt 1; *Kartographische*
Bestandsnachweise, 6 vols; *Pläne und*
Grundrisse afrikanerischer Städte (1550-
1945)
Spec feat: over 5,000 books on Africa
from 16th to mid-20th centuries covering
all fields, extensive coverage of German
colonies. Historical bibliographic
catalogues. Rich post-war Africana
holdings. Politics, history and African
languages. Excellent reference collection.
30,350 maps of Africa. 300 African
manuscripts mostly Ethiopic and Coptic.
39 African newspapers.

382 **Universitätsbibliothek**
Tübingen
Orientabteilung
Postfach 2620
Wilhelmstrasse 32
D-72016 Tübingen
+49-7071-297 3430
Fax: +49-7071-293123
Email: walter.werkmeister@uni-
tuebingen.de
Website: http://www.uni-tuebingen.de/
uni/qub
AL/contact: Walter Werkmeister
H: 08.00-20.00
Acc: open
Loan/ref fac: national and international
interlibrary loan; loan facilities only for
members of the University (students and
staff) and for residents of Tübingen
Coll: 65,000b, 350cs
On-line dbs: SSG-S document delivery
(books and articles)
On-line cat: TELNET: Telnet opac.ub.uni-
tuebingen.de (login: opac; password:

opac); http://www.ubka.uni-karlsruhe.de/hylib/suchmaske.html
Publs: *Neuerwerbungen Vorderer Orient* (Accessions List Near and Middle East)
Spec feat: African studies collection is part of the larger collection of books from and about the Near and Middle East; thus the relevant section contains literature pertaining to the countries of North and Northeast Africa - Morocco, Algeria, Tunisia, Libya, Egypt, Northern Sudan, Ethiopia, Horn of Africa.

383 Vereinigte Evangelische Mission, Bibliothek

Rudolfstrasse 17
Postfach 20 12 33
D-5600 Wuppertal 2
+49-202-890040
Fax: +49-202-890 0479
AL/contact: Reinhard Veller
H: Mon-Thur 09.00-15.00 Fri 09.00-13.00
Acc: n/a
Loan/ref fac: no loan fac
Coll: ca 5,000b , ca 10cs
Spec fac: archive files from ca 1800; Namibia, South Africa, Rwanda, Tanzania, Zaire, Cameroun, Botswana; religion, missions, ethnology, geography, history.

India

384 Centre of African Studies Library

University of Mumbai
Vidyanagari, Kalina Campus
Santacruz (East)
Mumbai 400098
+91-22-618 3201/5444 ext.265 & 297
Fax: +91-22-614 5722
Email: mvjnlib@giasbm01.vsnl.net.in
AL/contact: S. R. Ganpule, University Librarian
H: 09.00-19.00
Acc: open
Loan/ref fac: n/a
Coll: 12,000b, 15cs

Publs: *African Currents* (2yr); *Current Contents Africa* (mon, cumulated ann); special bibliographies; Current Awareness Service
Spec feat: primary and secondary source material on Africa; covers all Africa but especially Eastern and Western; primarily social sciences, holdings are substantial in history, political science, economics, sociology, geography and literature etc; reference works; 78 US doctoral dissertations in African studies; some primary source materials available on microfiche and microfilm.

385 International Crops Research Institute for the Semi-Arid TropicsΦ

ICRISAT Patancheru PO
502324 AP
+91-40-224016
Fax: +91-40-241239
Email: icrisat@cgnet.com
AL/contact: L.J. Haravu, Senior Manager Library and Documentation Services

Israel

386 Moshe Dayan Center for Middle Eastern and Africa Studies Library

Room 419 Gilman Building
Tel Aviv University
Ramat Aviv 69978
+972-3-640 9646
Fax: +972-3-641 5802
Email: marion@ccsg.tau.ac.il
AL/contact: Marion Gliksberg, Librarian
H: Sun-Thur 08.30-14.30
Acc: n/a
Loan/ref fac: no loans
Coll: 10,000b, 80cs
On-line dbs: fully indexed database featuring articles on the Middle East
Publs: *Current Contents of Periodicals on the Middle East; Middle East Contemporary Survey*

Spec feat: extensive economic holdings;
statistics; World Bank documents,
demography; yearbooks of the UN;
document colleciton of the BBC.

Italy

387 Biblioteca Nazionale
Piazza Cavalleggeri 1A
I-50122 Florence
+39-55-249191
Fax: +39-55-234 2482
Email: gloria@bncf.firenze.sbn.it
Website: 150.217.50.5 or
sbn.bncf.firenze.sbn.it
AL/contact: Antonia Ida Fontana, Director
H: Mon-Fri 09.00-19.00 Sat 09.00-13.00
Acc: identification required
Loan/ref fac: interlibrary loan except for
publications printed before 1886
Coll: n/a
On-line dbs: SBN: 1958-present; 851,000
titles, 341,000 authors
On-line cat: Telnet
Spec feat: no special African collections,
but library has sizeable collections of
travel books and historical maps and
atlases.

388 Curia Generalizia dei Missionari d'Africa (Padri Bianchi), Biblioteca
Via Aurelia 269
I-00165 Rome
+39-6-632314/318
Fax: +39-6-638 4623
AL/contact: Piet Horsten, Acting Librarian
H: 15.00-18.00
Acc: open
Loan/ref fac: ref only, no loans, photocop
fac
Coll: 8,000b, 34cs
Spec feat: African collection started in
1868; intended primarily as a resource for
those for whom the organization is
responsible, and its students; holdings
concentrate on subjects of interest to
missionaries e.g. history, ethnography,

archaeology, sociology, Islam, African
religions, African philosophy and
theology, development, and African
literature; most holdings in English and
French, but some in German, Italian and
Portuguese.

389 Food and Agriculture Organization of the United Nations (FAO) David Lubin Memorial Library
Library and Documentation
Systems Division
Via delle Terme di Caracalle
I-00100 Rome
+39-6-5225 3784
Fax: +39-6-5225 2002
Email: aglinet@fao.org or
FAO-Library-Loans@fao.org or
FAO-Library-Reference@fao.org
AL/contact: Jane M. Wu, Chief Librarian
H: n/a
Acc: not open to public; request admission
in writing or by telephone to the Reference
Section
Loan/ref fac: computerized literature
searches using CD-ROM and other
databases; loans and interlibrary loans,
selective dissemination of information;
microfiche reproduction of FAO docs;
acquisitions assistance; periodical and
table of contents circ; tours and briefings
Coll: (total coll) ca 1,000,000b, 7,000cs
On-line dbs: FAOBIB: FAO tech docs
since 1945 and library monograph
holdings since 1976; SERIAL: FAO
library serial holdings
Publs: electronic - *FAO Documentation
Current Bibliography*; *LOSA* (List of
Selected Articles) and New Books;
Catalogue of Serials Currently Received
Spec feat: collections grow by 2,500
monographs and 25,000 serial issues per
year. Consists of FAO documentation,
books and serials in FAO subject fields, a
comprehensive reference collection and
specialized Branch Library collections.
Covers agriculture, food and nutrition,

rural development, plant production, animal production, agricultural machinery, agro-industries, agro-forestry, forestry, fisheries, sustainable development, statistics, agricultural economics and other related subjects.

390 **Istituto Italiano per l'Africa e l'Oriente, Biblioteca**
Via Ulisse Alovandi 16
I-00197 Rome
+39-6-321 6712/322 1258
Fax: +39-6-322 5348
AL/contact: Carla Ghezzi, Chief Librarian
H: Mon-Fri 08.00-13.30 except Thur 15.00-17.00
Acc: identification required
Loan/ref fac: ref only, no loans, photocop fac
Coll: 65,000, 200cs
Publs: *La Letteratura Africana nella Biblioteca dell'Istituto Italo-Africano*
Spec feat: the library inherited the fund of the library of the Ministero per l'Africa Italiana, which ceased in 1953; unique material on Eritrea, Ethiopia, Libya and Somalia.

391 **Istituto per le Relazioni tra l'Italia e i Paesi dell'Africa, America Latina e Medio Oriente, Biblioteca**
Viale Tritone 62/9
I-00187 Rome
+39-6-679 2321/2311
Fax: +39-6-679 7849
AL/contact: Cristina Luciani
H: 09.00-12.30
Acc: open Loan/ref fac: n/a
Coll: 10,000b, 500cs
Publs: *Politica Internazionale*
Spec feat: n/a

392 **Istituto Universitario Orientale**
Biblioteca del Dipartimento di Studi e Ricerche su Africa e Paesi Arabi

Piazza San Domingo Maggiore 12
I-80134 Naples
+39-81-551 7840
Fax: +39-81-551 7901
AL/contact: Enrico Catemario, Chief Librarian
H: Mon-Fri 09.00-14.30
Acc: university students and bona fide scholars
Loan/ref fac: loan to university students, no special referral service
Coll: 25,000, 330cs
Spec feat: collections on African history, linguistics, Egyptology, Ethiopian studies; rare books on Berber studies; increasing collection on Arab studies, including the Maghreb and the Near East.

393 **Pontificia Universitas Urbaniana**
Pontificia Biblioteca Missionaria
Via Urbano VIII 16
I-00165 Rome
+39-6-6988 2351
Fax: +39-6-6988 1871
Email: puu@mvpuu.puu.urbe.it
AL/contact: Willi Henkel, Chief Librarian
H: Mon-Fri 08.30-13.00 14.00-18.30
Sat 08.30-13.00
Acc: academics free of charge; students L40,000 per 6 months
Loan/ref fac: n/a
Coll: ca. 13,000b, 45cs
On-line dbs: Telnet mvpuu.puu.urbe.it Aleph
On-line cat: data transfer requires permission
Publs: *Bibliographia Missionaria* (ann) 600 titles of books and periodicals on Africa; dictionary catalogue, linguistic catalogue with ca. 270 African languages
Spec feat: Borgia, Grottanelli (anthropology) collections; microfiches: IDC Wesley Missionary Society, London Missionary Society, Missionary Archives.

Japan

394 Center for African Area StudiesΦ
Kyoto University
46 Shimoadachi-cho
Yoshida Sakyo-ku
Kyoto 606-01
+81-75-753 7800
Fax: +81-75-753 7810
AL/contact: (Ms) Kyoko Tsuru, Librarian
Coll: 11,000b, 262cs

395 Institute for the Study of Languages and Cultures of Asia and Africa†
Tokyo University of Foreign
Studies, Library
4-51-21 Nishigahara, Kita-ku
Tokyo 114
+81-3-917 6111
Fax: +81-3-910-0613
AL/contact: The Librarian
H: Mon-Fri 09.30-17.00, Sat to 12.00
Acc: researchers of the Institute, teaching
staff of Tokyo University of Foreign
Studies; others apply in writing to the
Director
Loan/ref fac: loans limited, ref open to
public
Coll: 3-4,000b, 105cs
Spec feat: n/a

396 Institute of Development Economies Library†
42 Ichigaya-Hommura-cho
Shinjuku-ku
Tokyo 162
+81-3-3353 4231
Fax: +81-3-3226 8475
AL/contact: Koichi Nonaka, Librarian
H: 09.45-16.45
Acc: open
Loan/ref fac: loans service to members of
Institute
Coll: 25,000b, 90cs
On-line dbs: NIKKEI-Telecom & Atlas

Publs: *Ajia Keizai Shiryo Geppo* (Library
Bulletin, partly in English)
Spec feat: focus on social sciences of
modern Africa; economics, development,
sociology, politics, agriculture, industry.
The Institute maintains a separate
collection of statistics on Africa (1,762
titles, 12,300 vols, including monographs,
annuals, serials); large map collection.

Netherlands

397 Afrika Centrum Library
Rijksweg 15
NL-6267 AC Cadier en Keer
+31-43-4017 1226/407 1277
Fax: +31-43-407 3233
AL/contact: R. van Eijk, Chief Librarian
H: Mon-Fri 09.00-17.00
Acc: open
Loan/ref fac: identification required
Coll: 8,000b, 50cs
On-line dbs: n/a
Spec feat: religion, West Africa, culture
(anthropology, literature, art).

398 Afrika-Studiecentrum
The Library
Wassenaarseweg 52
PO Box 9555
NL-2300 RB Leiden
+31-71-527 3354
Fax: +31-71-527 3350
Email: derijk@rulfsw.leidenuniv.nl
AL/contact: E. de Rijk, Head Library and
Documentation
H: Mon-Fri 09.00-17.00
Acc: open
Loan/ref fac: loan fac restricted to books;
reading room, microfiche/film reader,
photocop fac; inter-library loan
Coll: 45,000b, 600cs
On-line dbs: PICA
On-line cat: OPAC available shortly
through Univ Leiden
Publs: *African Studies Abstracts* (*see* **164**);
acquisitions lists

Spec feat: collections emphasizing cultural anthropology, history, law, literature, politics, religion, and social and economic development; geographical coverage: North and sub-Saharan Africa.

399 University of Amsterdam Library†
PC Hoofthuis Section
Dutch/Afrikaans
Spuistraat 134
NL-1012 VB Amsterdam
+31-20-525 4532
AL/contact: E. van Hulsteijn
H: Mon-Fri 09.00-17.00 except Tue & Thur to 22.00
Acc: in principle for students and Faculty of Arts of the University, but others are admitted
Loan/ref fac: loans for students and faculty, others need special permission
Coll: n/a
On-line dbs: central system of the University Library
On-line cat: at local terminals (PC Hoofthuis and University Library); outside access on application
Spec feat: although officially restricted to Afrikaans, the collection is intended not to be racially biased; thus a limited number of books are held on South African history and current social and political affairs, together with holdings in current and past languages of South Africa.

400 Koninklijke Bibliotheek
Prins Willem Alexanderhof 5
PB 90407
NL-2509 LK The Hague
+31-70-314 0911
Fax: +31-70-314 0450
Website: http://www.honbib.nl
AL/contact: The Librarian
H: Mon-Fri 09.00-17.00 Sat 09.00-13.00
Acc: open to all with a borrower's card
Loan/ref fac: loans with a borrower's card: in person, by letter and by telephone; photocop fac

Coll: 13,000b, 133cs
On-line dbs: public access catalogue
On-line cat: see above website; direct dial +31-70-347 7778
Publs: union catalogue of periodicals, bibilographies, literature lists, *Koninklijke Bibliotheek: Gids voor Gebruikers* (user guide)
Spec feat: mainly humanities and the social sciences; depository library; covers all countries and regions, strongest representation being South Africa, Egypt, Zaire, Algeria, Morocco and Ghana; 40% of collection is history, 30% geography, and 30% other disciplines e.g. literature, linguistics and sociology; 275 titles published pre-1800, and 3,000 between 1800-1945.

401 Royal Tropical Institute Information, Library & Documentation
Mauritskade 63
NL-1092 AD Amsterdam
+31-20-568 8298
Fax: +31-20-665 4423
Email: ibd@support.nl
AL/contact: J. H. W. van Hartevelt
H: Mon-Fri 10.00-16.45
Acc: open
Loan/ref fac: loan and inter-library loan fac; photocop fac, information and bibliographical services by phone and by post
Coll: 40,000b, 1,600cs
On-line dbs: literature search services, on-line and on CD-ROM
On-line cat: request further details
Publs: *Agriculture and Environment for Development* (mon) abstract journal; 'Gender, Society and Development' book series; TROPAG and Rural CD-ROM; AIDS/STD *Health Promotion Exchange* newsletter
Spec feat: general collection covering international development, culture, history, health, rural development, social sciences and tropical agriculture.

Specialized collections cover: UN and international organizations; 24,000 thematic maps and atlases; a public library in the Tropenmuseum; and Resources Centre. Total collection approx. 215,000 books and 4,500 current serials.

402 Suid-Afrikaanse Instituut
Keizersgracht 141
NL-1015 CK Amsterdam
+31-20-624 9318
Fax: +31-20-638 2596
AL/contact: S. B. I. Veltkamp
H: Mon-Thurs 10.00-16.00 Fri to 15.00
Acc: open
Loan/ref fac: loans and interlibrary loans; photocop fac; information and bibliographical services by phone and mail.
Coll: 25,000b, 100cs
Spec feat: focuses on Afrikaans and South African English languages and literatures, including exile literature, literary criticism; history, socio-economic developments, politics, law, cultural anthropology, art and culture of South Africa. Special collections: archival material about the cultural relations between the Netherlands and South Africa from the 1880s onwards.

403 Universiteit Utrecht
Bibliotheek Centrum Uithof
Heidelberglaan 2
PB 80124
NL-3508 TC Utrecht
+31-30-253 2584/596
Fax: +31-30-253 1357
Email: w.karreman@ubu.ruu.nl
AL/contact: W. M. Karreman & P. F. Hermans
H: Mon-Thur 08.30-19.00 Fri 08.30-17.00
Acc: open
Loan/ref fac: on request
Coll: 25,000b, 80cs
On-line dbs: Library Catalogue University Utrecht
On-line cat: for a fee; uitleen@ubu.ruu.nl; fax: +31-30-253 8388; or contact: Univ

Library Utrecht, Witlevrouwenstraat 7-11, PO Box 16007, NL-3500 DA Utrecht
Spec feat: African publications in the field of geography, cultural anthropology and sociology, mostly sub-Saharan Africa.

New Zealand

404 National Library of New Zealand
PO Box 1467
Wellington
+64-4-743000 Fax: +64-4-743063
Email: atl@natlib.govt.nz
Website: http://www.natlib.govt.nz
AL/contact: G. Shaw, Manager, Reference and Research Service
H: Mon-Fri 09.00-17.00 Sat to 13.00
Acc: open (closed stacks)
Loan/ref fac: full ref & referral service; no loans to public except non ref publications on interlibrary loan; archives consulted only in the reading rooms of the Alexander Turnbull Library
Coll: 5,000b, 100cs
On-line: NZBN - multidisciplinary, records from NZ libraries and some overseas countries
On-line cat: both on-line and microfiche
Spec feat: African studies collection not separately maintained. The Manuscripts and Archives Section of the Alexander Turnbull Library, a division of the National Library, holds manuscript material relating to the South African War (1899-1902): diaries, letters and papers by members of the New Zealand Contingents in SA; records of the South African War Veteran Assoc 1937-1980 (also separate collections of the Waikato, Northland, Levin and Wellington branches); records of the Auckland Peace Association 1899-1906; and *O'er Veldt and Kopje, an Account of the Operations of the New Zealand Contingents in the Boer War* by James Arthur Shand, unpublished, ca. 1931. Some letters and diaries are held of New Zealand soldiers serving in North

Africa during World War II. Papers and records relating to New Zealand protests against apartheid and the debates about sporting contact with South Africa include the records of Halt All Racist Tours (HART) and the New Zealand Defence Aid Fund for South Africa. The Library's Photographic Archive includes Boer War. The Library's Oral History Centre holds relevant interviews, including interviews relating to sporting relationships with South Africa, in particular the protest movement against the 1981 Springbok Tour of New Zealand, and with New Zealand observers of the 1994 South African elections.

Norway

405 **Bergen University Library**
Social Science Library
H. Foss Gt. 6
N-5007 Bergen
+47-55-582631
Fax: +47-55-588380
Email: tom.johnsen@ub.uib.no
Website: http://www.rosin.ubb.uib.no
AL/contact: Tom Johnsen, Chief Librarian
H: Mon-Fri 08.00-15.45
Acc: open
Loan/ref fac: available
Coll: 9,000b, 75cs
On-line dbs: BIBSYS - Norwegian University Library on-line catalog OCLC, DIALOG and other international and national dbs
On-line cat: website http://www.bibsys.no/english.html
Spec feat: an important centre for Sudanese, Middle Eastern, Islamic and development studies; material held on other African countries also; national and UN depository library.

406 **Chr. Michelsen Institute Library**
Fantoftvegen 38
N-5036 Fantoft
+47-55-574000
Fax: +47-55-574166
Email: biblio@amadeus.cmi.no
AL/contact: Hilde E. Sperrevik, Librarian
H: Mon-Fri 08.00-15.00
Acc: open
Loan/ref fac: loan for books, not periodicals, photocop fac articles
Coll: 20,000b, 450cs
On-line dbs: catalogue is computerized; on-line access to international dbs service only
Publs: 'CMI Reports', 'CMI Working Papers'
Spec feat: the collection of Africa material is strongest on publications on the countries which cooperate with Norway: Eastern and Southern Africa; 95% of publications are in English; social sciences (economics, political science, anthropology).

Portugal

407 **Arquivo Historico Ultramarino**
Calcada da Boa-Hora 30
P-1300 Lisbon
+351-1-363 2414/8019
Fax: +351-1-362 1956
AL/contact: Maria Luisa Abrantes, Chief Librarian
H: Mon-Fri 13.30-19.00 Sat 09.30-12.00
Acc: n/a
Loan/ref fac: photocop fac
Coll: 4,000b, 8cs
Spec feat: extensive holdings of documentary material relating to the former Portuguese colonies. Colonial history, administrative and political history of Portuguese colonies, ethnology, anthropology of Portuguese colonies.

Spain

408 Biblioteca Nacional†
Sección de Africa y Mundo
Arabe
PO de Recoletos 20
E-28001 Madrid
+34-1-580 7800/7832/7817
Fax: +34-1-577 5634
AL/contact: Paloma Fernandez de Avilés
H: 09.00-21.00
Acc: bona fide researchers
Loan/ref fac: reading on the premises;
specialist bibliographic ref services
available; interlibrary loan
Coll: 41,500b, 2,000cs
Publs: *Nuevos Ingresos* (qtly); *Guída de
Bibliotecas y Centros de Documentación
Especializados, a Guide to the Sección*;
inventory of photographs
Spec feat: 634 volumes of miscellaneous
papers and transcriptions of archival
documents; personal archives of Garcia
Figueras, Guillermo Rotwagen and Juan
Fontan Lobé. Collections of the writings
and correspondance of El Raisuni.
Extensive collection of photographs on
Africa.

Sweden

**409 Nordiska Afrikainstitutet/The
Nordic Africa Institute Library**
POB 1703
SE-75147 Uppsala
+46-18-562270
Fax: +46-18-123775
Website: htpp://www.nai.uu.se
AL/contact: Louise Freden
H: Mon, Thur 10.00-19.00 Tues, Wed, Fri
10.00-16.00
Acc: open
Loan/ref fac: loans for books but not
newspapers, journals or government
documents; ref lists; photocop fac
Coll: 42,000b, 700cs

On-line dbs: free search on Internet;
guided searches on information resources
on Internet and CD-ROM. Own dbs
containing acquisitions since 1983
On-line cat: on Internet from summer 1997
Publs: *Africana i Nordiska
Afrikainstitutets Bibliotek* (ann, new
acquisitions), *Att Studera Afrika* (Studying
Africa)
Spec feat: collection of current
government documents and publications
from African countries, and documents
from the UN Economic Commission for
Africa. The only library in Nordic
countries specializing in contemporary
post-1945 Africa.

Switzerland

**410 Basel Mission Resource Centre,
Library**
Missionsstrasse 21
CH-4003 Basle
+41-61-268 8241
Fax: +41-61-268 8268
AL/contact: Marcus C. Buess, Librarian
H: Mon-Fri 08.00-12.00 14.00-17.00
Acc: open
Loan/ref fac: public library, national and
international loan
Coll: (total coll) 30,000b, 300cs
On-line dbs: catalogue of the university
libraries of Basel and Bern, through world
catalogue Switzerland
On-line cat: Telnet or Internet
Publs: *Cartes historiques/géographiques
correspondantes à disposition à la
bibliothèque de la Mission de Bâle*
Spec feat: n/a

411 Basler Afrika Bibliographien
Klosterberg 21
CH-4051 Basle
+41-61-271 3345
Fax: +41-61-271 3155
Email: bab@nethos.ch
Website: http://www.nethos.net/bab/

AL/contact: Carl Schlettwein & Dag Henrichsen
H: Tues-Fri 14.00-18.00
Acc: by prior arrangement access at other times as well
Loan/ref fac: photocop fac; no loans; computerized library
Coll: 10,000b, 100cs
Publs: regularly new titles on Africa topics, new archival registers, recent titles: *Personal Memories - Namibian Texts in Process, Internet for Africanists and Others Interested in Africa (see 96)*
Spec feat: Namibia Resource Centre: largest collection of books from Namibia in Europe, large collection of Namibian periodicals, photographs, posters and press cuttings on Namibia; Southern Africa Library: languages - English, Portuguese, German, Afrikaans, African languages.

412 L'Institut universitaire d'études du développement, Centre de documentation
24 rue Rothschild
CH-1211 Geneva 21
+41-22-906 5921
Fax: +41-22-906 5947
Email: hugo@uniza.unige.ch
Website: http://www.unige.ch/iued/
AL/contact: René Barbey
H: 09.00-18.00
Acc: open
Loan/ref fac: to residents in Switzerland
Coll: (total coll) 43,000b, 1,200cs
On-line dbs: computerized bibl index/cat; website as above
On-line cat: see above
Publs: *Bulletin Bibliographique*
Spec feat: specific documentation on developing countries; rich collection on French speaking Africa.

413 International Labour Office Central Library/ Documentation
CH-1211 Geneva 22
+41-22-799 8675/8682

Fax: +41-22-799 6516
Email: bibl@ilo.org
Website: http://www.ilo.org
AL/contact: Eleanor Frierson, Chief Librarian
H: 09.00-17.00
Acc: open
Loan/ref fac: documents, except those in ref collection, are available on loan to ILO officals, ILO Branch Offices and on interlibrary loan to other users; microfiches of texts of journal articles; photocop fac
Coll: 15,000b 440cs
On-line dbs: LABORDOC
On-line cat: via ESA-IRS, QUESTEL, ORBIT
Publs: *International Labour Documentation* (mon, current awareness and abstracting bulletin), *ILO Thesaurus: Labour, Employment and Training Terminology* (English, French, Spanish, German)
Spec feat: materials are in a multitude of languages, with English representing ca. 60%, French 20% and Spanish 10%; main subjects are industrial relations, labour law, employment and working conditions, social security, vocational training, labour related aspects of economics, social development, rural development, technological change, etc.

414 Stadtbibliothek Winterthur
Museumstrasse 52
Postfach
CH-8401 Winterthur
+41-52-267 5145
Fax: +41-52-267 5140
Email: bibliothek.stw@spectraweb.ch
AL/contact: Verena Amberg
H: Mon 10.00-18.00 Tues-Fri 08.00-18.00 Sat 08.00-16.00
Acc: open
Loan/ref fac: home loans - one month, reading & study room; photocop fac
Coll: 8,300b, 150cs
On-line cat: request instruction sheet and diskette from library

Publs: *Africana-Sammlung und Africana-Katalog in der Stadtbibliothek Winterthur* (3 vols, 1977, 1982, 1991)
Spec feat: African languages and literatures: linguistics, preference is given to dictionaries and grammar books; various forms of oral tradition - tales, myths, praise-songs, proverbs, either edited in books or recorded on discs; new African literature in African and European languages; literary history, criticism and sociology.

415 United Nations Library at Geneva

Palais des Nations
CH-1211 Geneva 10
+41-22-917 4181
Fax: +41-22-917 0028
Email: carol.davies@itu.ch
Website: www.unog.ch
AL/contact: Carol Davies, Acquisitions Librarian
H: 08.30-17.30
Acc: Masters, PhD level, with a referral letter from university professor, company or public library
Loan/ref fac: on production of referral letter
Coll: (total coll) 1,000,000b, 12,000cs
On-line dbs: UN Bibliographic Information Service
Publs: *UNDOC: Current Index, Monthly Bibliography; Part I books, government documents, serials; Part II periodical articles*
Spec feat: Africana not separately maintained; specialized material in the field of economics, finance, law and politics; collection includes a very complete collection of general reference works; definitive collection of works on international, constitutional and administrative law; international collection on economics, finance, social questions, atomic energy; archives of the League of Nations and complete collection of UN documents; maps and geographical works; 300,000 government publications.

416 Zentralbibliothek Zürich

Zähringerplatz 6
Postfach
CH-8025 Zurich
+41-1-268 3100
Fax: +41-1-268 3292
AL/contact: Hans-Peter Höhener & R. Mathys
H: 08.00-17.00
Acc: open
Loan/ref fac: n/a
Coll: ca. 23,000b
Spec feat: central library of the University of Zurich; Africana not separately maintained; on average some 500 new titles on Africa acquired every year.

United Kingdom

417 University of Birmingham

Information Services
Main Library
Birmingham B15 2TT
+44(0)121 414 5816
Fax: +44(0)121-471 4691
Email: library@bham.ac.uk
Website: http://www.bham.ac.uk
AL/contact: C.D. Field, Librarian & Director of Information Services
H: term: Mon-Thur 09.00-22.30
Fri 09.00-19.00 Sat 09.00-17.00
Sun 14.00-18.00 vacation: Mon-Fri 09.00-21.00 Aug open Mon-Fri 09.00-17.00
Acc: visitors welcome; prior written application preferred, essential if access to special collections is sought
Loan/ref fac: loan fac only to registered members of the University and to registered external borrowers, but are usually available on inter-library loan; ref fac available to all visitors
Coll: 30,000b, 200cs
On-line dbs: ESA-IRS, KNIGHTRIDER
On-line cat: access through JANET
Publs: *Information Sources in West African Studies*
Spec feat: systematic acquisition of Africana since 1963; extensive holdings of

material from anglophone West Africa; also from Francophone West African countries (which constitute the Library's specialization under the SCOLMA scheme). The collection includes some 500 17th, 18th and 19th century monographs; theses from the Centre of West African Studies; a collection of pamphlets, mainly from the papers of the the Church Missionary Society, the Cadbury Papers, and those of the British Cotton Growing Association.

418 British Library
Reader Services and
Collection Development
Great Russell Street
London WC1B 3DG
+44(0)171-412 7676
Fax: +44(0)171-412 7736
Website: http://www.portico.bl.uk/
or: http://www.portico.bl.uk/africa/
This website relates specifically to Africana collections including printed books and newspapers, audio, maps, pictures, photographs, stamps, bibliography, manuscripts and archives.
AL/contact: Carole Holden
H: Mon-Sat 09.00-17.00 Tues-Thur 09.00-21.00 in Main Reading Room
Acc: by readers ticket
Loan/ref fac: collections available for reading on the premises; some books and serials available for inter-library loan through the British Library Document Supply Centre in Boston Spa
On-line dbs: BLAISE
On-line cat: access to subscribers and through OPAC available through some university libraries in the UK
Publs: readers guides on the use of the catalogue etc., *African Studies. Papers presented at a colloquium at the British Library, 7-9 January 1985* (*see* **6**)
Spec feat: extensive African holdings including material of interest in the map, music, philatelic, manuscript and newspaper collections; a substantial

collection of books, serials and newspapers were received by colonial copyright deposit between the later 19th and mid-20th centuries from South Africa in particular, but also from Mauritius, Sierra Leone, East Africa, Gambia and Ghana; holdings of official publications from African countries are also strong, especially for those countries formerly under British control.
Note: The Library will be moving to its new building at St Pancras, 96 Euston Road NW1 2DB during 1997-98. The first reading room is scheduled to open at the end of November 1997.

419 British Library for Development Studies
Institute for Development Studies
University of Sussex, Falmer
Brighton BN1 9RE
+44(0)1273-678263
Fax: +44(0)1273-678420
Email: qdfd0@uk.ac.sussex.cluster
Website: http://www.ids.ac.uk or
http://devline.ids.ac.uk
AL/contact: Michael Bloom
H: Mon-Fri 09.30-22.00
Acc: n/a
Loan/ref fac: ref and inquiry services operate from 11.00-16.00; loans for inter-library users via inter-library loan
Coll: 250,000b, 8,000cs
On-line dbs: searching through major commercial hosts; ELDIS; Devline - see above website and through
Telnet://info.ids.ac.uk (login - lynx - password: <enter>)
On-line cat: ELDIS - Electronic Development Information System includes resources directory and gateway, Email discussion, links to databases, library catalogues, bibliographies etc. hosted with Devline. A range of enquiry, bibliographic, training and advisor services are available

Spec feat: concentrates on African publications of relevance to economic and social development, from both official and non-official sources within African countries. Material concerning African countries issued within the developed world is collected as far as is possible. Few items are in indigenous languages, the concentration being on European language publications. Specific areas of subject interest include amongst others, health, education, communication, industrial development, debt and adjustment, population studies, development theory, women and political development. IDS is a UN depository library. Most comprehensive collection of development studies literature in Europe.

420 British Library of Political and Economic Science
10 Portugal Street
London WC2A 2HD
+44(0)171-955 7229
Fax: +44(0)171-955 7454
Email: library@lse.ac.uk
Website: http://www.blpes.lse.c.uk
AL/contact: Lynne Brindley, Librarian & Director of Information Services
H: Mon-Fri 09.00-23.00 (July-Sept to 20.00) Sat & Sun 11.00-18.00 (closed July-Sept and Christmas vacation)
Acc: by arrangement for scholars and research workers
Loan/ref fac: individual loans to members of London School of Economics only; national back-up library in inter-library loans scheme; reference and referral; photocop fac
Coll: (total coll) 600,000b, 300cs
On-line dbs: library subscribes to a wide range of databases in the fields of the social sciences
On-line cat: access through JANET
Publs: *The International Bibliography of the Social Sciences*
Spec feat: extensive collections of government documents, especially from Anglophone Africa. Statistical

publications (except those on education) are collected as fully as possible and particular attention is paid to census reports, statistical year books and trade returns. Annual reports of relevant ministries are acquired whenever possible, and the library attempts to obtain all five-year plans and associated planning documents.

421 British Museum Ethnography Library
Museum of Mankind
6 Burlington Gardens
London W1X 2EX
+44(0)171-323 8031
Fax: +44(0)171-323 8013
AL/contact: Sheila Mackie
H: Mon-Fri 10.00-16.45
Acc: Fellows of the Royal Anthropological Institute; post-graduate researchers (reference); by appointment only where other sources are exhausted
Loan/ref fac: part of the stock is available for loan by fellows of the Royal Anthropological Institute only; otherwise for reference only
Coll: ca. 20,000b, ca. 250 cs
Publs: *Library Guide*
Spec feat: an anthropological collection, with its main emphasis on cultural anthropology and material culture. Its geographical scope is worldwide with a substantial section on Africa, the Library serves the Department of Ethnography in the British Musuem and, since 1976, has incorporated the library of the Royal Anthropological Institute.

422 University of Cambridge
African Studies Centre
Library
Free School Lane
Cambridge CB2 3RQ
+44(0)1223-334398
Fax: +44(0)1223-334396
Email: si106@cam.ac.uk
or african-studies@lists.cam.ac.uk

Website: http://www.african.cam.ac.uk/
asc_home_page/library.html
AL/contact: Sarah Irons, Librarian
H: Mon-Fri 09.00-17.30
Acc: by arrangement, for scholars and
research workers; visitors welcome
Loan/ref fac: individual loan to members
of the University of Cambridge; ref fac all
visitors
Coll: 27,000b, 100cs
On-line cat: see website above
Spec feat: supplements the holdings of
other Cambridge libraries, but is
particularly concerned with political,
social, economic, and developmental
literature. (*see also* **435**)

423 Commonwealth Secretariat Library
Marlborough House
Pall Mall
London SW1Y 5HX
+44(0)171-747 6164
Fax: +44(0)171-747 6168
AL/contact: Eileen Murtagh
H: Mon-Thur 09.15-17.00 Fri 09.15-17.00
Acc: by appointment, with permission
from the Librarian
Loan/ref fac: ref only
Coll: 3,000+cs
Publs: extensive, on various aspects of
Commonwealth (by Commonwealth
Secretariat); also periodicals -
*International Development Policies,
Commonwealth Law Bulletin,
Commonwealth Currents*, etc.
Spec feat: over 3,000 serials currently
received including official statistical
publications, development plans and
publications from international
organizations; emphasis is on current
Commonwealth development; subjects
include trade, agriculture, economics,
statistics, industry, politics, education,
women and development, and youth and
health. Archive of Commonwealth
Secretariat Publications.

424 University of Durham
University Library
Stockton Road
Durham DH1 3LY
+44(0)191-374 3018
Fax: +44(0)191-374 7481
Email: main.library@uk.ac.durham
Website: http://www.dur.ac.uk/library/
AL/contact: J. T. D. Hall, University
Librarian
H: Main Library-term: Mon-Fri 09.00-
17.00 restricted services Mon-Thur to
22.00 Fri to 19.00 Sat & Sun 14.00-22.00
vacation: Mon-Fri 09.00-17.00 closed
between Christmas and New Year and on
Public Holidays, except those in May
Acc: open to members of the University;
others apply in writing to the Librarian.
Prior contact in advance of a visit is
advised.
Loan/ref fac: stock is available for loan to
registered users, others ref only; Inter-
Library loans; photocop fac
Coll: n/a
On-line dbs: only to members of the
University
On-line cat: website as above; direct URL
for Web OPAC http://library.dur.ac.uk;
Telnet: library.dur.ac.uk
Publs: for electronic information on
archival collections see the Library's web
page URL: http://www.dur.ac.uk/library/
asc/index.html; *Summary Guide to the
Sudan Archive, Papers of Abbas Hilmi II*
(1874-1944) (summary list); *Catalogue of
the Papers of General Sir Reginald
Wingate (1861-1953) vol. 1 Sudan Papers*;
List of the Papers of Malcolm MacDonald.
Spec feat: substantial collections on
ancient, medieval and modern North
Africa, especially Sudan, with some
coverage of Africa South of the Sahara.
The Library's Middle East Documentation
Unit holds government publications and
primary documents (mainly 1960s
onwards) from and relating to the Middle
East and North Africa. The Library also
has two large archival collections relating
to North East Africa, the Abbas Hilmi II

papers and the Sudan Archive. Other
archival collections of interest to
Africanists include the Baring papers
(S. Rhodesia, Southern Africa, Kenya), the
Grey papers (primarily S. Africa), the
MacDonald papers (principally Kenya,
Rhodesia, Nigeria) and the Plomer
collection (South African literature).

425 Edinburgh University Library

George Square
Edinburgh EH8 9LJ
+44(0)131-650 3409/3384
Fax: +44(0)131-667 9780
Email: library@uk.ac.edinburgh
Website: http://www.lib.ed.ac.uk
AL/contact: Margaret Dowling, Social
Science Librarian
H: term: Mon-Thur 09.00-22.00 Fri 09.00-
17.00 Sat 09.00-17.00
vacation: Mon-Fri 09.00-17.00
Acc: non-members of the Unviersity must
write in advance to the University
Librarian
Loan/ref fac: ref fac normally free of
charge; other services including borrowing
available on subscriptions or fee
Coll: n/a
On-line cat: Telnet: //eulib.ed.ac.uk
Publs: *A Miscellany of Africana*
(exhibition catalogue)
Spec feat: African materials are integrated
with the general and special collections of
the 400-year old, large and decentralized
library system, and their size and extent
cannot be quantified. The Library acquired
material published in Malawi and Zambia
as part of the SCOLMA Area
Specialization Scheme. The Centre of
African Studies Library is held in the Main
Library. New College Library is rich in
material on Christian missions in Africa
and on non-Christian religion as is the
Centre for the Study of Christianity in the
non-Western world. The Centre of
Tropical Veterinary Medicine Library has
good collections on veterinary studies and
allied topics in Africa.

426 Foreign and Commonwealth Office Library

Room E213
King Charles Street
London SW1A 2AH
+44(0)171-270 3025
Fax: +44(0)171-270 3270
Website: http://www.fco.gov.uk
AL/contact: Louise Nation
H: Mon-Fri 09.30-17.30
Acc: by appointment only
Loan/ref fac: loans to other libraries only;
photocop fac
On-line cat: OPAC available on stand-
alone PC in reading room
Spec feat: extensive collection, mainly on
Anglophone Africa, especially on pre-
independence period; early works on
travel and exploration; treaty collections;
comprehensive and indexed collection of
legislation of Commonwealth countries in
Africa.

427 Institute of Commonwealth Studies Library

University of London
28 Russell Square
London WC1B 5DS
+44(0)171-580 5876
Fax: +44(0)171-255 2160
Email: d.blake@sas.ac.uk
Website: http://www.sas.ac.uk/ics/
AL/contact: David Blake, Librarian &
David Ward, Archivist
H: term: Mon-Wed 09.30-19.00
Thur & Fri 09.30-18.00
vacation: Mon-Fri 09.30-17.30
Acc: university staff, post-graduate
students; undergraduates may use the
library if their own library does not
contain the material they need. Others are
charged for using the library; details on
request
Loan/ref fac: ref only; interlibrary loans
within Britain
Coll: 40,000b, 1,000cs (including annual
reports)

On-line dbs: access to 34 other library catalogues from terminals in library; IBSS (MIDS); theses in progress in Commonwealth Studies
On-line cat: Telnet 193.62.18.239 or website as above
Publs: *Africa: New Titles Added to the Library* (qtly); *Theses in Progress in Commonwealth Studies* (ann), *The Southern African Material Project, 1973-1976; Current Periodicals: Africa*
Spec feat: covers the Commonwealth countries of Africa with particular emphasis on official material, research publications and bibliographies. Material from Sierra Leone and Gambia are collected under the SCOLMA Area Specialization Scheme. Archives include papers of anti-apartheid organizations and individuals collected during the Southern African Material Project (1973-76), the Ruth First Papers and papers of Sir Keith Hancock, head of the Buganda constitutional inquiry 1954. Special collections include political ephemera issued by political parties, trade unions and pressure groups in Commonwealth Africa and a collection of Foreign Office and Colonial Office Confidential Print. Microforms include the IDAF press cuttings (covering South Africa and Namibia), the papers of Albie Sachs and the Carter-Karis collection of Southern African Political Materials.

428 Institute of Education Library
University of London
20 Bedford Way
London WC1H 0AL
+44(0)171-612 6080
Fax: +44(0)171-612 6093
Email: lib.enquiries@ioe.ac.uk
Website: http://www.ioe.ac.uk/library
AL/contact: Diana Guthrie
H: Mon-Thur 09.30-21.00 Fri 09.30-19.00
Sat 09.30-17.00
Summer vacation: Mon-Fri 09.30-18.00

Acc: open to the general public, on payment of a fee
Loan/ref fac: loans only to members of the Library; ref and photocop fac
Coll: n/a, 20cs
On-line dbs: staff and institute students only
On-line cat: Telnet: library.ioe.ac.uk or 144.82.33.100 or website as above
Publs: *Catalogue of the Comparative Education Library*, 6 vols, (1971 + supplement, 1974)
Spec feat: extensive collection of official reports and statistics on education. Major CD-ROMs on education.

429 International Development Centre Library
University of Oxford
Queen Elizabeth House
21 St Giles
Oxford OX1 3LA
+44(0)1865-273629/590
Fax: +44(0)1865-273607
Email: sheila.allcock@qeh.ox.ac.uk
Website: http://www.qeh.ox.ac.uk/library/
AL/contact: Sheila Allcock, Librarian and Information Services Manager
H: term: Mon-Fri 09.00-18.00
vacation: Mon-Fri 09.00-17.00
Acc: open to the public, for reference use only
Loan/ref fac: to members of Oxford University
Coll: (total coll) 60,000b, 600cs
On-line dbs: Oxford University CD-ROM network, BIDS, FirstSearch
On-line cat: Oxford University Union Catalogue - OLIS
http://www.lib.ox.ac.uk/olis/
Publs: *Accessions List*; *Library Guide*; *Library Information*; *Book Marks*
Spec feat: books, pamphlets, newspapers, periodicals and official publications relating to current economic and political developments in the whole of Africa. Files of newspaper clippings on developing countries taken from the main English

dailies and some other newspapers 1945-
1995 (now discontinued). The library also
includes the collections (strong on
agricultural statistics, land economics and
population with particular reference to
food supply) of the former Institute of
Agricultural Economics, University of
Oxford. Formed in 1989 by the merger of
the libraries of the Institute of Agricultural
Economics and the Institute of
Commonwealth Studies.

430 **University of Leeds†**
      The Brotherton Library
      Leeds LS2 9JT
      +44(0)1133-243 1751
      Fax: +44(0)1133-233 5561
      AL/contact: R. H. Davis
      H: term: Mon-Fri 09.00-21.00 Sat to 13.00
      vacation: Mon-Fri 09.00-17.00 Sat to
      13.00 long vacation 12.30
      Acc: external user lending facilities
      Loan/ref fac: photocop fac
      On-line dbs: JANET
      Spec feat: general collections on Africa in
      the field of literature, history, geography,
      sociology, politics, economics, law and
      education, including official documents.
      The Library acquires publications from the
      Zaire Republic, Rwanda, Burundi and
      Zimbabwe under the SCOLMA Area
      Specialization Scheme.

431 **University of Manchester**
      John Rylands Library
      Oxford Road
      Manchester M13 9PP
      +44(0)161-275 3751
      Fax: +44(0)161-273 7488
      Website: http://www.rylibweb.man.ac.uk
      AL/contact: n/a
      H: term: Mon-Fri 09.00-21.30 Sat 09.00-
      13.00 vacation: Mon-Fri 09.00-17.30
      Sat 09.00-13.00
      Acc: student SCONUL agreement; public:
      3 annual visits fee for reference £25
      Loan/ref fac: no loans
      Coll: n/a

On-line dbs: for staff and students
On-line cat: available, [no access details
provided]
Spec feat: main strengths southern, central
Africa and Ethiopia, history and
anthropology, lusophone African
literature.

432 **Natural Resources Institute**
      University of Greenwich
      Central Avenue
      Chatham Maritime
      Chatham Kent ME4 4TB
      +44(0)1634-880088
      Fax +44(0)1634-880066/77
      Email: enquiries.library@nri.org
      Website: http://www.nri.org
      AL/contact: Tim Cullen
      H: Mon-Fri 10.00-14.45
      Acc: by appointment
      Loan/ref fac: reference, enquiry, inter-
      library loans, limited photocop fac
      Coll: (tropical agriculture) 250,000b,
      1,600cs
      On-line dbs: all major agricultural CD-
      ROMS, in-house computer system -
      CAIRS in a Microvax II; TRAIS (Tropical
      Agriculture Information Service), for
      ODA/ODNRI staff only, searching of
      specialised external dbs e.g. Agris,
      Agricola, CABI
      Publs: *Accessions Bulletin* (mon)
      Spec feat; specializes in the literature of
      tropical agriculture in the context of aid
      development and is recognized as a major
      world resource in this field. NRI is part of
      Greenwich University.

433 **Ordnance Survey**
      International Library
      Romsey Road
      Southampton SO16 4GU
      +44(0)1703-792659
      Fax: +44(0)1703-792230
      Email: rfox@ordsvy.gov.uk
      Website: http://www.ordsvy.gov.uk
      AL/contact: R. D. Fox
      H: Mon-Fri 09.00-16.30

Acc: bona fide researchers, developers, consultants
Loan/ref fac: ref only, but some published maps on sale; 40,000 maps; 500,000 air photographs; 5,000 files
Coll: 4,000b, 60cs
Publs: Data & Information Sheet, list of Ordnance Survey International mapping
Spec feat: maps, air photographs, survey data, and documents on international boundaries, on land legislation, and on survey legislation; mainly for the developing Commonwealth countries plus Liberia, Ethiopia, Sudan. Maps include all published DOS/OSD/Ordnance Survey International mapping plus many sheets produced by national survey organizations of the countries concerned; air photographs are vertical, black & white, scales usually 1:10,000-1:70,000, used for map-making, not for sale without country's permission. Survey data is mainly manuscript trigonometrical observations, descriptions, coordinates, not copyable without country's permission.

434 Rhodes House Library
University of Oxford
South Parks Road
Oxford OX1 3RG
+44(0)1865-270909
Fax: +44(0)1865-270912
Email: john.pinfold@chl.ox.ac.uk
AL/contact: John Pinfold
H: term: Mon-Fri 09.00-19.00
Sat to 13.00 vacation: Mon-Fri 09.00-17.00 Sat to 13.00
Acc: open to all members of the University of Oxford and to those holding a Bodleian Library reader's ticket
Loan/ref fac: ref only; books are lent to other libraries for use in those libraries
Coll: 125,000b, 220cs
On-line dbs: access to wide variety of on-line services via Telnet, gopher,www etc.
On-line cat: available [no access details provided]

Publs: *Manuscript Collections* (excluding Africana), *Manuscript Collections of Africana*, *Manuscript Collections of Africana: supplement*, *Manuscript Collections (Africana and non-Africana): accessions 1978-1994 (see also* **103***)*
Spec feat: specializes in the social, political and economic history of the Commonwealth, the United States and sub-Saharan Africa. As a department of the Bodleian Library, it receives British copyright publications; foreign books and periodicals are purchased. Commonwealth government publications are available in long runs. The Library is strong in manuscript material relating to British colonial administration. It holds the papers of Cecil Rhodes, of Arthur Creech Jones, of the Fabian Colonial Bureau, of the Africa Bureau and of the Anti-Apartheid Movement, and it has collected the papers of many former colonial officials.

435 Royal Commonwealth Society Collections
Cambridge University
Library
West Road
Cambridge CB3 9
+44(0)1223-333000/ 333198
Fax: +44(0)1223-333160
Email: tab@ula.cam.ac.uk
AL/contact: Terry A Barringer, Librarian
H: Mon-Fri 10.00-17.30
Acc: scholars and accredited students (as for main university library)
Loan/ref fac: individual loans to members of the University of Cambridge; photocop fac; copies of photographs by arrangement
Coll: 15,000b
On-line cat: card cat in reading room; RCS cat records are being added to Main Cambridge University Library Catalogue (on-line). African material will be added over next two years
Publs: *Subject Catalogue of the Royal Empire Society*, vol. 1 (1930, repr. 1967); *Subject Catalogue of the Library of the*

Royal Commonwealth Society, vols 3-4 (1971); *Biography Catalogue* (1961), *Manuscript Catalogue* (1975); *RCS Photograph Collection* (microfilm, 1988); *Library Notes with List of Accessions* (6yr) Spec feat: major collections on all African Commonwealth countries and on South Africa, and extensive material on the former colonial territories of other European countries. There are numerous original collections of works on African exploration, and there is a substantial pamphlet collection on the slave trade. Long runs of older periodicals have been extensively catalogued, and there is much official material. The Manuscript Collection, though not large, contains important historical material, and there are some 20,000 photographs of Africa, catalogued in detail. More details about the collections available on request; or from the *Cambridge University Library Readers' Handbook* series of leaflets, sections D2 & D3. (*see also* **422**)

436 Royal Institute of International Affairs

Chatham House
10 St James Square
London SW1Y 4LE
+44(0)171-957 5700
Fax: +44(0)171-957 5710
Email: riialibrary@gn.apc.org
Website: http://www.riia.org
AL/contact: John Peel
H: Mon-Fri 10.00-18.00
Acc: members and research staff of the Institute; bona fide post-graduate researchers on payment of fee (advance contact essential)
Loan/ref fac: members only, or through BLDSC
Coll: 5,000b, 64cs
On-line dbs: FT-profile, EUROBASES, BLAISE-LINE (members and staff only)
Publs: *Index to Periodical Articles 1950-1989 in the Library of the RIIA* (2 vols and 3 supplements, 1964-1990), *Classified*

Catalogue of the Library of the RIIA [to 1983] (Fiche, 1981-84). Monthly lists of articles newly indexed and of books added available on subscription.
Spec feat: African-related material is integrated in the Institute's general collection on international affairs world-wide. Current main strengths are in international politics, economics and security. Apart from primary sources, the main focus of acquisitions and holdings is the most recent 30-35 years. Special collections include subject files of press cuttings (1924-39 on microfilm at Chatham House; 1940-71 in hard-copy at the British Library Newspaper Library; 1972 to date in hard-copy at the RIIA), and the Institute's own archives, including records of meetings, and study groups.

437 School of Oriental and African Studies, Library

University of London
Thornhaugh Street
Russell Square
London WC1H 0XG
+44(0)171-637 2388
Fax: +44(0)171-636 2834
Email: rt4@soas.ac.uk
Website: http://www.soas.ac.uk/library
AL/contact: Barbara Turfan
H: term: Mon-Thur 09.00-20.45 Fri 09.00-19.00 Sat 09.30-13.00 (17.00 for ticket holders) vacation: as above except Summer: Mon-Fri 09.00-17.00 Sat 09.30-13.00 (17.00 for ticket holders)
Acc: staff and students of the School and to anyone else on application
Loan/ref fac: most monograph material available for loan; rare books; manuscripts, microforms, serials and materials designated 'Reference' restricted to the Library
Coll: 71,000b, ca. 500cs
On-line dbs: Internet access to other libraries; CAMP (Cooperative Africana Microform Project) membership (loan and

purchase); contributor to NISC CD-ROM 'African Studies' (1996-)
On-line cat: via Telnet: lib.soas.ac.uk and www as above
Publs: *Library Guide*. Subject guides for each region and for the archives and manuscripts collection, general services and CAMP; home pages on www
Spec feat: collects material on and from the whole of Africa in the humanities and social sciences, and is particularly strong in its coverage of African languages and their literatures. In addition to published monographs and periodicals, holdings include maps, photographs, slides, sound recordings and microforms as well as a number of important collections of archives and private papers, and manuscripts in European and African languages. Under the SCOLMA Area Specialization Scheme, SOAS undertakes responsibility for the acquisitions of the publications of Somalia, Djibouti, Ethiopia, Tunisia, Algeria, Morocco, Mauritania, Liberia, Botswana, Lesotho, Swaziland, Madagascar and Nigeria.
Special collections include: Hardyman Madagascar Collection, donated by Mr & Mrs James Hardyman (published material catalogued, archival material pending); Society for Libyan Studies library (held on permanent loan).

438 **University of York†**
J.B. Morrell Library
Heslington
York YO1 5DD
+44(0)1904-433867
Fax: +44(0)1904-433433
Email: librl@uk.ac.york
AL/contact: The Librarian
H: term: Mon-Fri 09.00-22.00 Sat to 17.15 vacation: Mon-Fri 09.00-21.00 July & August: Mon-Fri 09.00-17.15
Acc: all bona fide enquirers
Loan/ref fac: ref use only for non-member of the University; material may be borrowed through the Interlibrary Loans Services. Photocop and photog fac

Coll: n/a, 70cs
On-line dbs: available, charged at cost
On-line cat: access through JANET and PSS. JANET name:
UK.AC.YORK.LIBRARY Numeric address 00000610001240
Publs: *University of York Library*; *Southern African Studies: Guides to Literature Searching, York University. Centre for Southern African Archives in the University of York; Guide to the Tanganyikan Papers of Marian Lady Chesham.*
Spec feat: the collection covers all aspects of Southern Africa (Angola, Botswana, Lesotho, Malawi, Mozambique, Namibia, South Africa, Swaziland, Zambia and Zimbabwe). There is a good collection of bibliographical guides to the area and a wide selection of official publications. The substantial archive collection is held at the Borthwick Institute of Historical Research, University of York, St Anthony's Hall, Peasholme Green, York YO1 2PW; tel: +44(0)1904-437233.

United States

439 **Boston University**
African Studies Library
771 Commonwealth Avenue
Boston MA 02215
+1-617-353 3726
Fax: +1-617-353 2084
Email: gwalsh@bu.edu
Website: http://web.bu.edu/library/asl.html
AL/contact: Gretchen Walsh, Head
H: term: Mon-Thur 09.00-20.00 Fri-Sat to 17.00 vacation: Mon-Fri 09.00-17.00
Acc: open to all scholars (in-house privileges only); write or call to make arrangements
Loan/ref fac: interlibrary loan
Coll: 155,000b, 500cs
On-line dbs: commercial dbs in main library

On-line cat: using a 1200 baud modem
dial 617-353 9601 at a >connect library;
Telnet: library.bu.edu
Publs: *A Guide to African Language
Materials in the Boston University
Libraries*
Spec feat: particularly strong in
publications of African national
governments, regional and international
agencies. Collects for the entire continent,
with strength in sub-Saharan Africa. The
social sciences and economics are
emphasized, although the collection
includes all academic disciplines.

**440 University of California,
       Berkeley**
390 Main Library
Berkeley CA 94720
+1-510-643 6649/1586/3143
Fax: +1-510-643 6650
Email: pbischof@library.berkeley.edu
Website: http://www.lib.berkeley.edu/
collections/africana
AL/contact: Phyllis B. Bischof
H: variable; longer hours during term;
vacation minimum service from 09.00-
17.00 on weekdays. Closed on some
holidays
Acc: open; purchase of a card possible at
cost of $100 for one year, but card is
unnecessary in order to use the collections
Loan/ref fac: ref/referral, interlibrary loan
(for a fee non-UCB readers), photocop fac
Coll: 100,000b, 1,000cs
On-line dbs: access to dbs services
On-line cat: both Berkeley's GLADIS and
the UC Systemwide MELVYL catalogues
are available on a no-cost basis - for
assistance call 510-643 9999, or with a
UNIX account Telnet: gladis.berkeley.edu
or Telnet: melvyl.ucop.edu; for library
Internet services: Telnet
library.berkeley.edu and login as <guest>
Publs: *Africana Library Collections*
Spec feat: extensive runs of serials and of
foreign, domestic, and international
government publications. Main Library
collects social sciences and humanities,

including economics, geography,
linguistics, political science, sociology,
and African history well documented by
secondary sources. Excellent reference
collection. Literary works by African
writers collected in depth. Branch libraries
collecting Africana include anthropology,
business/economics, education-
psychology, environmental design, bio-
sciences, music, and public health
libraries. Africana maps and atlases
collected continent-wide, with extensive
collections of ethnographic and
geographic slides and videos. Fine
collection of Mauritian books; pre-eminent
Yoruba collection. Rare book collection
includes early voyages and travels.

**441 University of California, Los
       Angeles**
University Research Library
Los Angeles CA 90095-1575
+1-310-825 1518
Fax: +1-310-206 4974
Email: rbellgam@library.ucla.edu
AL/contact: Ruby Bell-Gam, African
Studies Bibliographer
H: Mon-Thur 08.00-23.00 Fri to 18.00
Sat 09.00-17.00 Sun 13.00-23.00
Acc: open
Loan/ref fac: reference referral, interlibrary
loan, etc.
Coll: 200,000b, 1,000cs
On-line dbs: listed on OCLC, MELVYL
(Univ California system), and ORION via
access to campus Office of Academic
Computing
Spec feat: special strengths are the
collection of maps, government
documents, publications in African
languages (including Arabic and
Amharic), newspapers and manuscripts
(including archival materials on
microfilm). Geographical areas of strength
are East Africa, West Africa, and Northern
Africa (which is covered by the Near
Eastern bibliographer).

442 University of California, San
DiegoΦ
Central Library/0175R
La Jolla CA 92093-0175
+1-619-534 5398
Email: rcoates@ucsd.edu
AL/contact: Ronnie Coates, African
Studies Bibliographer

443 University of California, Santa
BarbaraΦ
Reference Services Library
Santa Barbara CA 93106-9010
+1-805-893 8022
Fax: +1-805-893 4676
Email: curtis@library.ucsb.edu
AL/contact: Sylvia Y. Curtis, Black
Studies and Dance Librarian

444 Center for Research Libraries
6050 South Kenwood Avenue
Chicago IL 60637
+1-773-955 4545 ext. 323
Fax: +1-773-955 4339
Email: rudeen@crlmail.uchicago.edu
AL/contact: Marlys Rudeen, Microform
Projects & Preservation Coordinator
H: Mon-Fri 09.00-17.00
Acc: members via ILL, free; non-members
fee-based ILL
Loan/ref fac: n/a
Coll: 10,000b cs n/a
On-line cat: Telnet:
crlcatalog.uchicago.edu or 128.135.73.2
(login -password <guest>)

445 Columbia University
308 Lehman Library
International Affairs Building
420 West 118th Street
New York NY 10027
+1-212-854 8045
Fax: +1-212-854 3834
Email: jc93@col2umbia.edu
Website: http://www.columbia.edu/cu/
libraries/indiv/area/Africa

AL/contact: Joseph Caruso, African
Studies Librarian
H: variable
Acc: visiting readers must apply to Library
Information Office, Columbia University,
234 Butler Library, New York, NY 10027;
212-854 2271, 3533;
or Email: lio@columbia.edu
Loan/ref fac: interlibrary loan; specialized
references assistance on topics relating to
Africa south of the Sahara. Orientation
lectures and tours are also arranged.
Coll: 200,000b, 1,700cs
On-line dbs: Telnet
columbianet.columbia.edu select CLIO
On-line cat: contains records processed
since 1981 only
Publs: *Use of the Columbia University*
Libraries: Visiting Readers
Spec feat: collections on Africa south of
the Sahara emphasize the arts, economic
development, geography, history, law,
literature, political science, sociology and
anthropology. Some materials are acquired
in Arabic and African languages. Over
1,500 maps of Africa.

446 Cornell University
Africana Studies and
Research Center Library
310 Triphammer Road
Ithaca NY 14853
+1-607-255 3822/5299
Fax: +1-607-255 0784
Email: africana_library@cornell.edu
Website:
http://www.library.cornell.edu/africana
AL/contact: Thomas Weissinger, Head
H: Mon-Thur 10.00-23.00 Fri 10.00-17.00
Sat closed Sun 14.00-23.00
vacation: Mon-Fri 10.00-17.00
Acc: open
Loan/ref fac: loans restricted to holders of
Cornell University ID card or library card;
reference information and assistance
provided in person, by telephone, mail,
Email; interlibrary loan through Cornell
Univ Library

Coll: 15,000b, 125cs
On-line dbs: hundreds of dbs and
periodical indexes available. Also Black
Studies on disk, extensive CD-ROM
database and the library's Africana Studies
website
On-line cat: Cornell University Library cat
including Africana Library, use Telnet or
TN3270 - see website for instructions for
accessing the catalogue
Spec feat: the Africana Library provides a
specialized collection concentrating on the
social and political dimensions of the
history and culture of peoples of African
descent. It includes basic books, complete
collections of works by important writers
and highly selective research materials.

447 Dartmouth College
Baker Library
Hanover NH 03755
+1-603-646 2868
Fax: +1-603-646 2167
Website:
http://www.dartmouth.edu/~library/
AL/contact: The Librarian
H: n/a
Acc: open; library users who are not
members of the College community or fee-
paying guest borrowers must use material
in the library
Loan/ref fac: n/a
Coll: 7,800b, 350cs
On-line cat: website as above
Spec feat: disciplines emphasized in
collection development are art,
anthropology, government, history, music
and literature; the geographic emphasis
has been placed on West Africa, but the
scope of the collection has been expanded
to encompass increasing interest in
Southern and East Africa.

448 Duke University
International and Area
Studies
Perkins Library
POB 90195

Durham NC 27708
+1-919-660 5847
Fax: +1-919-684 2855
Email: hsb@mail.lib.duk.edu
Website: http://www.lib.duke.edu/iaj/
hsb.html or: www.lib.duke.edu
AL/contact: Helene Baumann, African
Studies Bibliographer
H: Mon-Thur 08.00-24.00 Fri & Sat
08.00-22.00 Sun 10.00-24.00
Acc: open access to the public; visiting
researchers must use the materials within
the library
Loan/ref fac: interlibrary loan, photocop
fac
Coll: 50,000b, 3,180cs
On-line dbs: numerous CD-ROM
(including Sociofile and PAIS); and
DIALOG, BRS, VUTEXT
On-line cat: see website above
Publs: reference dept issues a variety of
finding aids on many subjects
Spec feat: collection emphasis is on
Anglophone Africa. Subject strengths
include history, economics, political
science, women and development studies;
also numerous government documents.
Close cooperation with the University of
North Carolina at Chapel Hill (includes a
common on-line catalogue), whose
Africana collection focuses on Franco-and
Lusophone Africa, and the North Carolina
State University, which collects technical
and agricultural African material. Aside
from a collection of Swahili texts to
support languages teaching, material
collected are primarily in European
languages. Strong manuscript holdings in
British colonial history, the slave trade and
nineteenth century European travellers'
accounts. In November 1995, Duke
University Libraries established the John
Hope Franklin Research Center for
African and African American
Documentation that will collect
manuscript materials related to 20th
century Africa.

449 **Emory University**
Robert W. Woodruff Library
Atlanta GA 30322
+1-404-727 6953
Fax: +1-404-727 0053
Email: libemb@emory.edu
AL/contact: Elizabeth A. McBride,
Coordinator for the Social Sciences
H: 24hrs for selected services
Acc: open access; monographs may be
circulated but use of periodicals is limited
to the library
Loan/ref fac: Emory University libraries
hold Africa-related materials in the Special
Collections Department of the Robert W.
Woodruff Library, and in the Pitts
Theology Library of its Chandler School
of Theology
Coll: 15,000b, 300cs
On-line dbs: OUC, Nexis/Lexis, Eureka,
www, wide selection of dbs, Galileo,
Silver platter etc.; many dbs restricted to
Emory Univ
On-line cat: http://www.library.emory.edu
for web-based version
Spec feat: n/a

450 **Fisk University Library**
Special Collections
Fisk University
Nashville TN 37203
+1-615-329 8646/8580
Fax: +1-615-329 8761
AL/contact: Ann Allen Shockley
H: Mon-Fri 08.00-17.00
vacations: closed June & July: closed
Acc: special collections may be used by
bona fide scholars and researchers;
advance arrangement preferred
Loan/ref fac: no loans, photocop fac
Coll: n/a
Publs: *Dictionary Catalog of the Negro
Collection of the Fisk University Library*,
6 vols
Spec feat: Special Collections contains
some of the oldest and most definitive
collections of African-American history
and culture. Comprises three divisions:

reference - housing books, periodicals,
microfilm, ephemeral materials, journals,
newspapers, and non-print holdings of
photographs, records, and tapes; archives -
which hold the records of the University,
including papers of the Jubilee Singers,
past presidents, faculty/staff, and
administrators, as well as other records of
organizations; and the Black Oral History
Collections contain taped interviews with
persons who have been eyewitnesses,
participants, or contributors to the black
experience.

451 **University of Florida**
George A. Smathers Libraries
140 Library West
Gainesville FL 32611-2048
+1-352-392 4919
Fax: +1-352-392 8118/7251
Email: petmala@nervm.nerdc.ufl.edu
Website: http://www.ufl.edu/hss/africana/
AL/contact: Peter Malanchuk, Africana
and Political Science Bibliographer
H: Mon-Thur 08.00-13.00 Fri 08.00-22.00
Sat 10.00-18.00 Sun 10.00-13.00
Acc: open
Loan/ref fac: contact Africana
bibliographer or main ref staff at +1-352-
392 0361
Coll: 75,000b, 500cs
On-line cat: use
http://www.uflib.ufl.edu/luiscat.html or
Telnet: luis.nerdc.ufl.edu
Publs: *Africa-Related Dissertations and
Theses at the University of Florida, 1956-
1995*
Spec feat: broad Africa-related collection,
consisting mainly of resources dealing
with the social sciences and the
humanities. There are extensive holdings
on rural development, tropical agriculture,
agricultural development and food
production in Africa. Strong collections
on Eastern and Southern Africa.
Specialized holdings in Shona language
and linguistics (George Fortune
collection); Gwendolyn Carter collection
and papers, South Africa; René Le

Marchand collection, Rwanda, Burundi and Chad; Ronald Cohen Collection, field notes and materials on Northern Nigeria; George Shepperson collection on Rhodesia.

452 **Harvard College Library**
Sub-Saharan Africa
Collection Development
Department, Widener 85
Cambridge MA 02138
+1-617-495 3559
Fax: +1-617-495 0403
Email: jill_coelho@harvard.edu
AL/contact: Jill Young Coelho, Librarian
H: Mon-Fri 09.00-17.00
Acc: members of Harvard University students, staff & faculty
Loan/ref fac: interlibrary loan is available as a fee-based service
Coll: n/a
On-line dbs: the HOLLIS on-line catalogue via http://hplus.harvard.edu/alpha/hollis.html or Telnet: hollis.harvard.edu
On-line cat: as above
Spec feat: Harvard's resources for African studies are extensive, but not assembled in one collection or one library. The HOLLIS on-line catalogue provides access to the holdings of all research collections' books and serial collections. Widener Library, the principal graduate library, holds most of the humanities and social science research collections. In Widener, collecting is done by place and/or language of publication, with Africana collected at a research level in all European languages, as well as in Arabic for North Africa. The Tozzer Library of Anthropology has extensive collections of Africana. Other university libraries include Africana in their specialized collections, such as art, design, zoology, botany and geology.

453 **Hoover Institution**
Africa Collection
Stanford University
Stanford CA 94305
+1-415-725 3505
Fax: +1-415-725 4655
Email: fung@hoover.stanford.edu
AL/contact: Karen Fung, Deputy Curator
H: Mon-Fri 08.00-17.00
Acc: open access to the public for on-site use, library stacks are closed, loan privileges to Stanford students, faculty and staff only
Loan/ref fac: interlibrary loan, General Reference tel: +1-415-723 2058, photocop fac on pay machines
Coll: 70,000b, 560cs
On-line dbs: over 60 commercial research dbs including RLIN, OCLC (World Catalog), Lexis-Nexis, Uncover, MEDLINE, Agricola, Anthropological Lit, GeoRef, MAGS, NEWS, ABI/INFORM, Dissertation Abstracts, Index to Foreign Legal Periodicals, Public Affairs Information Service, Washington Alert, etc.
On-line cat: Telnet: forsythetn.stanford.edu (login <socrates>)
Publs: *History of the Library and Archives of the Hoover Institution, Guide to the Hoover Institution Archives*
Spec feat: strengths: colonial history, political ephemera (election material, broadsheets, posters, etc.), African newspapers, Southern Africa, Nigeria, Zaire (Belgian Congo). ca. 200 special/archival collections. Collections of Jay Lovestone, Herbert Weiss, William H. Friedland, L. Gray Cowan, S. Herbert Frankel, L.H. Gann, Harvey Glickman, Ernest W. Lefever, Rene Lemarchand, Paul Lubeck, Robert K. Middelmas, Frederick Quinn, Claude E. Welch, Brian Weinstein, L.P. Hartzler, Martin Lowenkopf, Brian Reid, I. William Zartman, Harvey Glickman, A.H.M. Kirk-Greene, Garland Farmer, Virginia Thompson and Richard Adloff, Victor LeVine, Bruce Fetter, David Brokensha,

Wilson C. Flake, Arthur J. Lewis, George Reppas, William D. Moreland, Jerry Eckert, Louise Fortmann and Emery Roe, William H. Hutt, Ferdinand Klein, Frederick Russell Burnham, Keith Middlemas, William Henry Vatcher, Frank A. Salamone, George D. Jenkins, David B. Abernethy, Thomas Henriksen, Charles Darlington.

454 Howard University
Moorland Springarn Research Center
500 Howard Place NW
Washington DC 20059
+1-202-806 7266/56
Fax: +1-202-806 6405
AL/contact: Marva Bett, Reference Librarian, African Bibliographer
H: Mon-Thur 09.00-16.45 Fri 09.00-16.30
Acc: closed stacks
Loan/ref fac: non-circulation of materials; no ILL of original materials; photocop fac
Coll: 65,000b, 70cs
Publs: *African Newspapers in the MSRC*, in-house acquisitions lists
Spec feat: a wealth of information on the history and culture of black people in Africa, the Caribbean and US. Includes ca. 1,600 books and pamphlets on slavery, unique collection of black authors in 20 languages, a teaching museum, archives, oral history, music department and prints and photographic unit. Undertakes a global acquisitions program.

455 University of Illinois Library
Africana Room 328
1408 W. Gregory Drive
Urbana IL 61801
+1-217-333 6519
Fax: +1-217-333 2214
Email: akagan@uiuc.edu
Website: http://wsi.cso.uiuc.edu/cas/
AL/contact: Al Kagan, Africana Bibliographer
H: Mon-Fri 08.30-17.00

Acc: open access to Illinois residents; visiting scholars welcome, may obtain building and stacks use permits
Loan/ref fac: full loan and ref fac; interlibrary loan service includes both lending and photocop fac; participates in international interlibrary loan
Coll: 143,000, 1,000cs
On-line dbs: searches from a wide variety of on-line dbs; numerous CD-ROMs also available throughout the library, and can be searched without cost
On-line.cat: Telnet or dial access, see website above
Publs: *Africana in the University of Illinois Library* (brochure describing the collection and services); *Selected Africana Acquisitions* (3yr). All are free on request from Africana Bibliographer
Finding aids: key indexes, general indexes, women, statistics, newspapers, etc.
Spec feat: strong subject holdings include agriculture, anthropology, art history, economic and social development, music education, geography, geology, history, library science, linguistics, literature, and political science. Over 200 African languages are represented, and about 45,000 African maps. A fine collection of nineteenth century geographical journals and general publications of the European colonial powers, as well as current development plans, journals, censuses, and statistical materials from African countries. Seven collections in the University Archives include the American Library Association archives, the Avery Brundage Collection (sports), University of Illinois programmes in Sierra Leone, Malawi, Kenya; 19th century Arabic manuscripts.

456 Indiana University Libraries
Bloomington IN 47405
+1-812-855 1481
Fax: +1-812-855 8068
Email: schmidtn@indiana.edu
Website: http://www.indiana.edu:80/~afrist/
AL/contact: Nancy J. Schmidt

H: term: Mon-Fri 08.00-24.00 Sat from
10.00 Sun from 11.00
Summer: shorter hours
Acc: open
Loan/ref fac: Indiana University students
and staff and residents of Indiana with
proper identification may borrow books
and serials, microforms and manuscripts
do not circulate. ref, interlibrary loan,
photocop fac
Coll: 100,000b, 1,400cs
On-line dbs: 200+ CD-ROM dbs free of
charge, Internet and www available
On-line cat:
http://www.indiana.edu/~libweb
Publs: *African Music and Oral Data: A
Catalog of Field Recordings 1902-1975,
African Studies Periodicals and Other
Serials Currently on Subscription,
Bibliography of Africana in the Institute
for Sex Research, Bibliography of
Africana in the Lilly Library, African
Language and Literature Collection (see
*102), Finding List of Materials on
Somalia and in the Somali Language*
Spec feat: in addition to books and current
serials, holds the largest collection of
audio recordings on Africa in the US in
the Archives of Traditional Music,
including music, linguistics, literature,
folklore and politics. 30,000 uncatalogued
government publications and 50,000
uncatalogued pamphlets. Main strength of
holdings is sub-Saharan Africa:
humanities, social sciences and African
languages materials. Boxer travel literature
collection, Noma Award Archives in Lilly
Library, slides in the Fine Arts Library,
maps in the Geography-Map library
inventoried on a web page; Human
Relations Area Files, and films in Audio-
Visual Services Department.

457 University of Iowa Libraries
Iowa City IA 52242-1420
+1-319-335 5885
Fax: +1-319-335 5900
Email: john-howell@uiowa.edu
Website: oasis.uiowa.edu <enter>

AL/contact: John Bruce Howell
H: office hrs 07.30-17.00 central library
07.30-24.00
Acc: open to UoI students, faculty, staff
and Iowa residents; open to all schools
members of CIC
Loan/ref fac: interlibrary loan (2-4 weeks)
Coll: 60,000b, 2,540cs
On-line dbs: AFRC: African Conference
Papers Index; AGRI, AGRICOLA, ANTH:
Anthropological Literature, CCTC,
CCAB: current contents (Feb 1995-),
ERIC, MLAB (1963-), PAIS (1980-),
PERI (1986-), PSYJ & PSYB (1967-),
WLS1 & WLS2 (1982-)
On-line cat: website as above
Publs: *Electronic Journal of Africana
Bibliography (see* **294**). *no.1: Guides,
Collections and Ancillary Materials to
Africana Archival Resources in the United
States*
Spec feat: Iowa's collections consist
primarily of monographs and serials from
Nigeria, Burkina Faso, Kenya, Tanzania,
South Africa and Zimbabwe, and other
states in southern Africa. The collections
are strong in African art and literature in
English, French, Swahili, and Yoruba. A
recent DOE grant was devoted to
collecting health/ medical journals from all
sub-Saharan Africa. Iowa continues to
fund many of the titles first acquired
through the grant. Iowa has the Paul F.
Cranefield Archive of East Coast Fever in
East and Southern Africa.

458 University of Kansas Library
Lawrence KS 66045
+1-913-864 3038
Fax: +1-913-864 5311
Email: klohrent@ukanvm.bitnet
AL/contact: Kenneth P. Lohrentz,
Africana Bibliographer
H: Mon-Thur 08.00-24.00 Fri 08.00-20.00
Sat 10.00-18.00 Sun 12.00-24.00
Acc: open; borrower's card available to all
current Kansas residents (required for
borrowing)

Loan/ref fac: interlibrary loan free; photocop fac; Uncover/Reveal available free to KU faculty and students; specialized reference assistance available on topics relating to sub-Saharan Africa; orientation and tours by arrangement
Coll: 30,000b, 200cs
On-line dbs: commercial CD-ROM databases at main library and branches
On-line cat: Telnet: ukanmvsvt.cc.ukans.edu or 913-864 3366 for handout with details for accessing catalogue; may be faxed on request
Spec feat: broad, study-level collection, consisting primarily of materials in the social sciences and humanities for anglophone Africa. Recent collection development efforts include francophone Africa and study collections for Swahili and Hausa language instruction, with procurement of a representation of scholarly materials emanating from African publishers. Africana holdings are integrated into the general collections as determined by Library of Congress classification. Special collections include holdings of Onitsha market literature at the Spencer Research Library and strong cartographic holdings in the T.R. Smith Map Collection. The Library also has the Human Relations Area Files. Kansas State University, located 90 miles away (Manhattan, KS) maintains collections in agriculture and development, and has a strong collections of Botswaneana.

459 Library of Congress
African and Middle Eastern Division
Washington DC 20540
+1-202-707 7937/2933
Fax: +1-202-252 3180/1724
Email: amed@loc.gov
Website: http://lcweb.loc.gov/
AL/contact: Beverly Gray, Chief
H: Mon-Fri 08.30-17.00 general reading rooms Mon, Wed, Thur 08.30-21.30
Tues, Fri, Sat to 17.00

Acc: open access to anyone over high school age; valid photo ID to obtain photographic reader registration card for access to reading rooms
Loan/ref fac: reference, photocop fac, microform duplication, interlibrary loan
Coll: n/a, holdings dispersed primarily by subject
On-line dbs: in-house use of on-line catalogue is accessible to users: MUMS, SCORPIO
On-line cat: indirectly through vendors (e.g. DIALOG) and machine-readable catalogue (MARC) tapes are available for purchase through the Library's Cataloguing Distribution Service; directly at http://lcweb.loc.gov/
Publs: information about recent publications is available in the brochures: *The African Section in the Library of Congress, La Section africaine de la Bibliothèque du Congrès*
Spec feat: pre-eminent collections on sub-Saharan Africa encompassing all geographic areas and every major field of study except technical agriculture and clinical medicine, which are under the jurisdiction of the National Agricultural Library and the National Library of Medicine, respectively. Holdings in economics, history, linguistics, and literature are especially strong. Most of the materials are housed in the Library's general book and periodical collections. Impressive holdings may also be found in special collections of legal publications, manuscripts, maps, microforms, music, newspapers, prints, photographs and films in the various custodial divisions of the Library. In addition, an uncatalogued pamphlet collection of some 20,000 items is housed in the African Section.

460 University of Maryland Baltimore County†
Albin O. Kuhn Library and Gallery
5401 Wilkens Avenue

Baltimore MD 21228
+1-301-455 2232
AL/contact: The Librarian
H: Mon-Thur 08.00-24.00 Fri to 18.00
Sat 12.00-18.00 Sun 12.00-24.00
Acc: open
Loan/ref fac: circulating material through interlibrary loan
Coll: n/a
On-line dbs: available to persons on University of Maryland campuses and by local dial-up access
Publs: in-house bibliographies
Spec feat: several special collections on microfilm. There are ca. 579 reels of microfilm of materials from the Schomburg collection. There are 181 reels of microfilm of materials for the books from the Black culture collection from Atlanta University. The collection emphasis is on microfilm including Black Workers (selected years) during the era of the Great Migration, Black abolitionist papers and some early papers of the NAACP.

461 Michigan State University Libraries
Africana Library
East Lansing MI 48824-1048
+1-517-355 2366
Fax: +1-517-342 1455
Email: 20676oez@msu.edu
Website:http://www.lib.msu.edu/coll/main/africana
AL/contact: Onuma Ezera
H: Mon-Fri 08.00-12.00 13.00-17.00
Acc: open
Loan ref/fac: interlibrary loan, ref dbs
Coll: 150,000b, 600cs
On-line dbs: BRS, DIALOG
On-line cat: OCLC, MAGIC via MSU net or MERIT - dial 517-353 8500
Publs: *Select Recent Acquisitions* (qtly), *Africana in Microfilm in the Michigan State University Library*
Spec feat: most of the Africana holdings are integrated into the general research

collections. The Africana Area Files, a large collection of pamphlets and fugitive material, is housed in the Africana library. Congo Collection: consists of de Ryck's (a former governor of Belgian Congo) private library. There are more than 10,000 volumes including periodical titles, maps and about nine linear feet of manuscript material pertaining to Zaire, Burundi and Rwanda from 1880-1962. The Audio, Maps and Microforms, Special Collections, Government Documents and Voice Library also have strong Africana content.

462 National Museum of African Art Branch Library
Smithsonian Institution
950 Independence Avenue SW
Washington DC 20560
+1-202-357 4600 ext.285
Fax: +1-202-357 4879
Email: libem010@sivm.si.edu
Website: http://www.sil.si.edu
AL/contact: Janet L. Stanley
H: Mon-Fri 09.00-17.15
Acc: open to the public by appointment
Loan/ref fac: full range of ref services, interlibrary loan, literature searching
Coll: 22,000b, 250cs
On-line cat: Telnet: siris.si.edu
Publs: *Library Acquisition List* (6Yr)
Spec feat: the collections emphasize the visual arts, performing arts, ethnography, religion, oral tradition, and history. They also include material on African retentions in the New World. The Library maintains extensive vertical files on aspects of African art, history and culture.

463 New York Public Library
Schomburg Center for Research in Black Culture
515 Malcolm X Blvd
New York NY 10037-1801
+1-212-491 2218
Fax: +1-212-491 6760
Email: showard@nypl.org

Website: http://www.nypl.org
AL/contact: Sharon M. Howard, Head of
Acquisitions
H: General Research & Reference
divisions: Mon-Wed 12.00-20.00 Thur-Sat
10.00-18.00 Special Collections divisions:
Mon-Wed 12.00-17.00 Fri-Sat 10.00-
17.00
Acc: materials do not circulate; Special
Collections divisions require identification
and completion of registration forms
Loan/ref fac: interlibrary loan with
members of RLG and METRO (NY
Metropolitan Reference and Research
Library Agency)
Coll: 151,139b, 500cs
On-line cat: website as above
Publs: *Kaiser Index to Black Resources,
Dictionary Catalog of the Schomburg
Collection of Negro Literature and
History*
Spec feat: The Schomburg Center for
Research in Black Culture of The New
York Public Library is one of the foremost
research facilities in the world devoted to
documenting the experiences of peoples of
African origin and descent. The collections
(which include extensive holdings of
serials, microforms, photog, mss
collections and organizational records,
film and videotapes, recorded music,
spoken arts recordings, art and artefacts)
are strongest in three areas: Afro-
Americana throughout the Western
hemisphere; sub-Saharan Africa; and Afro-
Caribbeana. Since 1972 the Schomburg
Center's emphasis has been placed in the
humanities and the social sciences.

464 New York University

Elmer Holmes Bobst Library
70 Washington Square South
New York NY 10003-1113
+1-212-998 2437
Fax: +1-212-995 4366
Email: sinnotte@elmer1.bobst.nyu.edu
AL/contact: Elisabeth Sinnot, Africana
Bibliographer

H: Mon-Thur 08.00-23.00, Fri 08.00-
19.00, Sat 08.00-23.00, Sun 08.00-23.00
Acc: RLG constitutents; METRO referral
cards; telephone reference (limited to
ready reference and catalogue reference)
Loan/ref fac: interlibrary loan, general
reference assistance available
Coll: n/a
On-line cat: bobcat.nyu.edu or
128.122.128.132
Spec feat: disciplines emphasized in
collection development are anthropology,
cinema studies, economics, history,
journalism, literature, museum studies,
performance studies, political science, and
sociology. A special strength of the
Africana collection lies in motion pictures
from sub-Saharan Africa and the diaspora.
Especially well represented are Ethiopia
and the Republic of South Africa.

465 State University College†

Sojourner Truth Library
New Paltz NY 12561
+1-914-257 3680
Fax: +1-914-257 3670
Email: nyquistc@snynewvm.bitnet
AL/contact: Corinne Nyquist
H: n/a
Acc: open
Coll: 22,000b, 100cs
Spec feat: the World Study collection of
SUNY collects materials on the entire
continent of Africa, in all subjects, but
social science materials dominate. The
collection is strongest on Eastern and
Southern Africa, and in the fields of
anthropology, education, geography,
history, music and politics.

466 State University of New York at Buffalo

Lockwood Memorial Library
Buffalo NY 14260
+1-716-645 2817
Fax: +1-716-645 3859
Email: woodson@acsu.buffalo.edu
Website: http://www.buffalo.edu/libraries

AL/contact: Dorothy C. Woodson
H: Mon-Thurs 08.00-22.45 Fri to 21.00
Sat 09.00-17.00 Sun 12.00-22.45
Acc: open
Coll: 23,000b, 12,500cs
On-line dbs: all DIALOG and BRS
databases, numerous CD-ROM
On-line cat: access via website above
Publs: *African Studies Resources in
Lockwood Memorial Library*; wide range
of reference and finding aids
Spec feat: extensive collection of
secondary source material, no appreciable
primary source materials.

467 Northern Illinois University
Founders Memorial Library
DeKalb IL 60115
+1-815-753 9845
Fax: +1-815-753 9845
Email: ljharicombe@niu.edu
AL/contact: Lorraine J. Haricombe, Head
Circulation Dept & Rob Ridinger
H: Mon-Thur 07.30-02.00 Fri 07.30-10.00
Sat 09.00-22.00 Sun 13.00-02.00;
telephone for holiday hours
Acc: open
Loan/ref fac: loans vary; interlibrary loan:
subject specialist reference facilities
Coll: 3,500b, 60cs
On-line dbs: Wilson indexes; ERIC;
MEDLINE; IBIS; Carl Uncover;
Firstsearch; a wide array of CD-ROM
products in various subject areas
On-line cat: 815-753 6600 Telnet
nil.lib.niu.edu <enter>; at "welcome"
screen <b> and <enter>
Publs: *African Studies Research Guide*;
*African Archaeology: A Selective
Bibliography*
Spec feat: sizeable collection of British
parliament papers on Africa.

468 Northwestern University
Library
Melville J. Herskovits
Library of African Studies
Evanston IL 60208-2300

+1-847-491 7684/3084
Fax: +1-847-491 8306
Email: africana@nwu.edu
Website: http://www.library.nwu.edu/
africana/
AL/contact: David L. Easterbrook, Curator
of Africana
H: Mon-Fri 08.30-17.00, other times by
special arrangement
Acc: open
Loan/ref fac: interlibrary loan, all aspects
of ref and referral service
Coll: 245,000b, 2,500cs
On-line dbs: most of the Herskovits
Library's collection can be found in
NUcat; a special catalog AFRC, provides
access to individual papers presented at
African studies conferences world-wide
which are held by the library
On-line cat: access to Nucat via NUNET
or Telnet using tn3270 version. Internet
address is library.ucc.nwu.edu (IP address
+ 129.105.54.2), from menu choose nucat
or access from home page www as above
Publs: *Africana File Listing as of April
1988* (a microfiche index to items in the
Herskovits Library's vertical file as of
April 1988, *see* 30), *Joint Acquisitions List
of Africana (JALA)* (6yr 1962-1996,
ceased with vol. 35, no.6, November 1996,
see 172); various bibliographies, guides,
and finding aids; *Africana Conference
Paper Index* (AFRC) is a special on-line
file available as part of the on-line
catalogue providing access to ca. 70,000
conference papers (see above)
Spec feat: largest separate Africana
collections in the world; scope is continent
wide, and subject matter ranges from art,
history, literature, music, and religion to
communications, management, and
cooking. The collection focuses primarily
on the social sciences and humanities, with
major geographic emphasis on sub-
Saharan Africa. Also included are some
materials from North Africa, mostly in
French. Holdings include a rare book
collection of more than 3,500 titles,
including early accounts of exploration by

Europeans; and a large collection - much of it unique - of uncatalogued material covering statistical publications, development plans, commission reports, censuses, laws, and debates, pamphlet materials from trade unions, political parties, and national liberation movements. Ca. 11,500 publications in some 300 African languages.

Materials from and about Africa also exist elsewhere in Northwestern's library system: African maps are in the Map Collection; publications from the United States government and from international agencies are located in Government Publications; videos are in the Marjorie Mitchell Multimedia Library; most newspaper and microform material is in the Newspaper/ Microtext Room; sound recordings and some books on African music are in the Music Library; the Seeley G. Mudd Science and Engineering Library, the Geology Library, and the Transportation Library all contain some African material; Africana archives related to Northwestern University are in the University Archives; language tapes are available in the Language Laboratory (Kresge Hall).

Note: for more information apply for a copy of the Herskovits Library brochure.

469 **Ohio State University Libraries**Φ

1858 Neil Ave Mall
Columbus OH 43210
+1-614-292 2393
Fax: +1-614-292 7859
Email: edaniel@magnus.ircc.ohio-state.edu
AL/contact: Eleanor Daniel, Black Studies Librarian

470 **Ohio University Libraries**

Park Place
Athens OH 45701-2978
+1-614-593 2703/2569
Fax: +1-614-593 0138

Email: fosterth@ohiou.edu
Website: http://www.library.ohiou.edu/
AL/contact: Theodore S. Foster
H: 08.00-22.00 during term
Acc: open
Loan/ref fac: interlibrary loan
Coll: 90,000b, 250cs
On-line cat: www as above;
Telnet: alice.library.ohiou.edu
Publs: browse website
Spec feat: beyond basic support for the whole of Africa, the collection focuses on West Africa (Nigeria & environs); East Africa (Kenya, Tanzania, Uganda) and Southern Africa (especially Botswana and Swaziland).

471 **Princeton University**Φ

Firestone Library
Princeton NJ 08544-2098
+1-609-258 5962
Fax: +1-609-258 4105
Email: pressman@phoenix.princeton.edu
AL/contact: Nancy Pressman Levy, African Studies Selector

472 **Syracuse University**

Ernest Stevenson Bird Library
222 Waverly Avenue
Syracuse NY 13210-2010
and
Martin Luther King, jr. Memorial Library
Dept. of African American Studies, 200 Sims Hall V
Syracuse NY 13244-1230
+1-315-443 2730/4243
2. +1-315-443 4302/9349
Fax: +1-315-443 9510/1725
Email: personalid@hawk.syr.edu
Website: http://web.syr.edu/libweb
AL/contact: vacant (Africa and African-American Bibliographer)
H: 08.00-12.00 extended hours during finals; 2. Mon-Wed 10.00-20.00 Thur-Fri 11.00.00-17.00

Acc: open access; borrowing privileges for those affiliated with Syracuse University and with special permission
Loan/ref fac: interlibrary loan, all aspects of reference services
Coll: 20,587b, 200cs
On-line dbs: SUMMIT, Syracuse University's on-line catalogue; access 443 4804 (a SUnix account is required for dial access)
On-line cat: Telnet: summit.syr.edu or Telnet 128.230.31
Publs: *Africana Microfilms at the E.S. Bird Library, Syracuse University: An Annotated Guide to the Kenya National Archives*
Spec feat: collection strength is in materials relating to Eastern Africa, but there are also considerable holdings on Southern and West Africa. Special collections: Kenya National Archives microfilmed materials; Sir Richard Francis Burton papers; Francis G. Hall papers; the Laubach collection. Since 1993, Syracuse University included Zimbabwe as a centre for the Division of International Programs Abroad (DIPA). In 1994, for the first time since its existence in the early 1970s, Martin Luther King jr. Memorial Library's collection was added to SUMMIT the on-line catalog of Syracuse University Library system.

473 **United Nations†**
     Dag Hammarskjöld Library
     United Nations Plaza
     New York NY 10017
+1-212-963 7412
AL/contact: Jakob van Heijst
Acc: open to delegations, permanent missions to the UN and authorized users. Qualified researchers must obtain permission to use the collection
Loan/ref fac: n/a
Coll: (total coll) 400,000b, 4,000cs
On-line dbs: reference searches
Publs: *UNDOC: Current Index* (10yr), *Index to Proceedings ... of the General*

Assembly; *Current Bibliographical Information* (10yr)
Spec feat: specialized international library which combines the functions of an international affairs bureau with those of a research library in the social sciences. Maintains complete collections of all the documents and publications of the United Nations, its affiliated bodies and specialized agencies, as well as those of the League of Nations. Government documents and official publications from African countries are held, also population censuses and statistics.

474 **University of Virginia†**
     Alderman Library
     Charlottesville
     VA 22903-2498
+1-804-924 4984
Fax: +1-804-924 1431
Email: gtc@virginia.edu
AL/contact: George T. Crafter, Africana Bibliographer
H: Mon-Thur 08.00-24.00 Fri to 22.00 Sat 09.00-18.00 Sun 12.00-24.00
Acc: materials in general collections circulate to card holders
Loan/ref fac: full range of interlibrary loan services 804-924 3987; full range of reference services
Coll: 30,000b, 384cs
On-line dbs: BRS, DIALOG, OLCL, PAIS on CD-ROM. Services available in-house
On-line cat: yes, contact library for instruction on accessing; library has NOTIS
Publs: *African Languages, A Guide to the Library Collection of the University of Virginia* (1986); *Africana Related Periodicals and Serials Currently Received at Alderman Library, University of Virginia* (1988)
Spec feat: pamphlets, predominantly government publications and departmental reports from East and South Africa during the period 1930-1960 (1,000). African language dictionaries, grammars and language learning aids, some with audio

cassettes (1,000). Human Relations Area Files on micro-fiche. The Special Collections Department houses 42 collections containing material on Africa: particularly the Vieira correspondence regarding the Angolan grain trade, 1942-43; the Dillar Family Papers, 1923-38, regarding various educational missions; the Stettinius Papers regarding records of the Liberia Company, 1946-1949; and the Terrell & Cocke Collections of letters, 1834-1865 to former masters from freed men settled in Liberia.

475 Wayne State University Φ
Purdy/Kresge Library
Room 231
Detroit MI 48202
+1-313-577 8006
Fax: +1-313-577 4172
Email: dward@cms.cc.wayne.edu
dward@wayneest1.bitnet
AL/contact: Dane Ward, Reference Librarian

476 University of Wisconsin
Memorial Library
728 State St
Madison WI 53706
+1-608-262 6397
Fax: +1-608-265 2754
Email: henige@vms.macc.wisc.edu
AL/contact: David Henige, Africana Bibliographer
H: Sun-Thur 08.00-24.00 Fri-Sat 10.00-22.00
Acc: all materials are in general stacks and freely accessible, though entry to general library requires pass available on presentation of reasonable ID
Loan/ref fac: semester loans available to all citizens of Wisconsin and staff of CIC universities; large ref dept open same hours as above
Coll: 60,000b, 5-600cs
On-line dbs: BRS, ERIC, DAI, etc. over 200 electronic dbs, most networked, are available

On-line cat: some available; specific arrangements to be made either with General reference dept in Memorial Library or relevant branch libraries (over 20)
Publs: specialized guides (e.g. Africana in microform) issued from time to time; the General System as well as Memorial Library have several guides to holdings, hours, conditions of use, etc.
Spec feat: particularly strong on Zaire, Central Africa (esp. Francophone CA), Nigeria, and Zimbabwe, and on materials published before ca.1960. Archival materials held by both Memorial Library and the library of the State Historical Society of Wisconsin.

477 Yale University Library
African Collection
PO Box 208240-130
130 Wall Street
New Haven CT 06520-8240
+1-203-432 1882/1883 (voicemail)
Fax: +1-203-432 7231
Email: crossey@yale.vm.ycc.yale.edu
Website:
http://www.library.yale.edu/africa/html
AL/contact: Moore Crossey, Curator
H: 08.30-17.30
Acc: RLG member institutions with ID (including undergraduates); graduate students, faculty (academic staff), other adult researchers with campus ID and/or driving licence or passport; non-RLG undergraduates require letter from their library stating need
Loan/ref fac: personal loans by arrangement with lending libraries; interlibrary loan office tel: 203-432 1788; privileges tel. 203-4324 1853
Coll: 100,000+b, 3,000cs
On-line dbs: ORBIS (on-line cat), DIALOG, MEDLINE etc.; CD-ROM, eds of PAIS, Dissertation Abstracts History Abstracts, Psych. Abstracts, etc.; RLIN (Eureka), OCLC (Firstsearch), etc.

On-line cat: ORBIS via
http://webpac.library.edu/orbis_Telnet.ycc.
yale.edu (port 06520) <enter>;
orbis_tn3270.ycc.yale.edu <enter>
Publs: *Guide to Library Resources for the
Study of Southern Africa*, general guides
from the Reference Department, Divinity
Library, etc.; *African Studies: a select
bibliography*
Spec feat: concentrated in the Sterling
Memorial (main) Library, the Seeley
Mudd (storage) Library, and in the
Divinity, Law, Medical, Kline Science,
Social Science, and other special libraries.
There are extensive collections in all
languages (including African languages
and Arabic) in all humanities and social
science, disciplines, and less extensive
collections in biological sciences, geology,
education, medicine, agriculture
(technical), criminology, etc. Coverage of
anglophone West and Southern Africa
nears comprehensiveness in some subject
fields. Special collections include:
Economic Growth Center Collection (in
the Social Science Library), statistics,
development plans, budgets, etc; the Day
Missions Collection in the Divinity
Library; South African law in the Law
Library; tropical forestry and ecology in
the Forestry Library; Historical Medical
Library in the Medical Library; the Garvan
Sporting Books Collection - big game
hunting - in the Seeley Mudd Library. Ms.
collections in the department of
Manuscripts and Archives has a strong
concentration of original and microform
mss. on Southern and Western Africa -
also postcards, photographs, political
ephemera; the Map and Atlas Collection
has good holdings of modern maps and old
maps of South Africa. ORBIS contains
2,000,000+ titles of materials including
books, journals, manuscript and archival
collections, maps, musical scores, sound
recordings, and other formats.

V. PUBLISHERS WITH AFRICAN STUDIES LISTS

This section provides details of the major publishers with significant African studies lists. It covers publishers who produce scholarly/ academic works on African and development studies (both monographs and reference works), and textbooks at tertiary level; also those publishing African literature and creative writing by African authors. Publishers of general and trade titles on Africa, e.g. coffee-table type of books, travel and guidebooks, etc., are not included.

Arrangement is alphabetical by country, with a separate section providing details of a number of scholarly publishers in Africa. Those requiring up-to-date contact details for other African publishers should consult ABC's *African Publishers Networking Directory (see* **64***)*

Data was gathered through mailings of computer printouts from our database, and questionnaires for new entries. Publishers who did not respond despite at least one chaser mailing - but are known to be active in the African studies area - are marked with the symbols as set out below. A number of publishers listed in the first edition have been deleted.

The full addresses of UK/European distributors of North American publishers are given, as are North American distributors of UK/European publishers, unless the distributor also appears as a main entry elsewhere in the directory, in which case a cross-reference is given. Space restrictions do not permit us to list stock-holding distributors in areas other than North America and UK/Europe.

Details and guidance provided by publishers with regard to submission of manuscript proposals varies considerably. However, most will want to see a synopsis, contents lists, and sample chapters in the first instance, along with details about the author or a CV. Sending complete, unsolicited manuscripts to publishers is definitely *not* recommended.

Where forms were duly completed and verified a full entry includes: name and address, telephone and fax numbers, Email address (and

Websites for some); ISBN prefix, year founded; names of chief executive and editor/contact person for African studies list; details of approximate number of titles published annually and those in-print in the African studies field; series published in African studies; areas of specialization in Africa (or development, or Third World) studies; information regarding areas/levels in which manuscript submissions are invited, preferred length of manuscripts, and details of any editorial or other requirements concerning manuscript submissions. Finally, details of North American distributors of European publishers, or vice-versa European/UK distributors of North American publishers, including their addresses, are given where the information was provided.

Abbreviations and symbols used:

†	- repeat entry from 1st ed. (1989); information not verified; entry updated, as far as possible, from secondary sources
Φ	- provisional new entry, but questionnaire has not been completed; unverified information drawn from secondary sources

ABC	- African Books Collective Ltd. [distributor, *see* **664**]
ann	- annually [number of titles]
AS contact	- African studies contact person/editor
AS titles	- African studies titles [published]
Chief exec	- chief executive
CRC	- camera-ready copy
d-s	- double spaced
Edit req	- editorial requirements [for manuscript submissions]
Found	- year founded
ip	- in print
ISBN	- International Standard Book Number prefix(es)
ms	- manuscript
MS L	- manuscript length [preferred length]
MS subm	- manuscript submissions [areas/levels in which invited]
NA distr	- North American distributor
pp	- pages [number of]
Ser	- series [published in African studies]
Spec	- area/s of specialization
UK distr	- United Kingdom and/or European distributors

w   - words [number of]
WP   - WordPerfect [software]

EUROPE AND NORTH AMERICA

Canada

478 **Galerie Amrad African Arts Publications**
42 Anwoth, Westmount
Montreal H3Y 2E7
+1-514-931 4747
Fax: +1-514-931 4747
Email:gaaap@odyssee.net
Website:
http://www.odyssee.net/~gaaap.htm
Found: 1985
ISBN 0-9693081; 1-896341
Chief exec and contact: Esther A. Dagan
UK distr: Art Books International,
London, UK; US distr: Baker & Taylor;
Canada distr: Diffusion Ubert
AS titles: 1 ann, 13 ip
Ser: *Cherisamba: the Hybridity of Art*,
first title in a series on contemporary
African artists
Spec: arts-related
MS subm: PhD scholarly level in various
fields but specifically in relation to African
arts

479 **University of Calgary Press**
2500 University Drive NW
Calgary, Alberta T2N 1N4
+1-403-220 7578
Fax: +1-403-282 0085
Email: sonn@aoss.ucalgary.ca
Website:
www.ucalgary.ca/uofc/departments/up
Found: 1980
ISBN 1-895176; 0-919813
Chief Exec: n/a
AS contact: Shirley A. Onn, Director

UK distr: Trevor Brown Associates, 114-
115 Tottenham Court Road, Midford Place
London W1P 0BY
AS titles: 1 ann, 8 ip
Ser: 'African Occasional Papers'
Spec: archaeology

France

480 **Editions Pélissier**
Montamets
F-78630 Orgeval
+33-1-1397 57 265
Found: 1978
Chief Exec: René Pélissier
AS titles: 11 ip
Ser: 'Ibero-Africana'
Spec: Lusophone Africa; Spanish-
speaking Africa; history, politics,
bibliography, travel literature, Timor

481 **L'Harmattan, Edition-Diffusion**
7 rue de l'Ecole
Polytechnique
F-75005 Paris
+33-1-40 46 46 79 20
Fax: +33-1-43 25 82 03
Found: 1975 ISBN: n/a
Chief exec: Denis Pryen
NA: L'Harmattan Inc *see* **645**
AS titles: 120 ip
Ser: 'Alternatives paysannes', 'Encres
noires', 'La Légende des mondes', 'Polars
noirs', 'Grandes figures d'Afrique'
Spec: social sciences and humanities,
literatures and arts, also development
studies (distributor for ORSTOM
publications)
MS subm: as above
MS L: no restrictions
Edit req: n/a

482 Karthala Edition-Diffusion†
22-24 boulevard Arago
F-75013 Paris
+33-1-43 31 15 59
Fax: +33-1-45 35 27 05
Found: 1980 ISBN 2-86537
Chief exec: Robert Agenau
AS titles: 30 ann, 250 ip
Ser: 'Les Afriques', 'Reliu', 'Contes et
légendes'
Spec: essays on current social and political
issues, economic and political studies,
technical works (agronomy, health etc.),
oral literature, history, languages
MS subm: commissioned; direct
submissions also considered

483 ORSTOM Editions⚘
31 avenue Henri Varagnat
F-94143 Bondy Cedex
(bookshop at Point Librarie,
ORSTOM, 213 rue La Fayette
F-75480 Paris Cedex 10)
+33-1-48 02 55 00
Fax: +33-1-48 47 30 88
Website: http://www.orstom.fr/
ISBN 2-7099
AS titles: 800 ann (development studies in
general)
Spec: ORSTOM (Institut français de
recherche scientifique pour le
développement en coopération) is a
national public, scientific and technical
establishment under the supervision of
both the Ministry of Research and the
Ministry of Co-operation. Its task is to
initiate targeted basic research that
contributes to the development of regions
in the tropics, especially through the study
of the physical, biological and human
environments in the countries concerned
and through experimental research aimed
at conferring mastery of development

484 Présence Africaine†
25 bis rue des Ecoles
F-75005 Paris
+33-1-43 54 13 74
Fax: +33-1-43 25 96 67
Chief exec: Yande Christiane Diop
NA distr: Editions Hurtubuise HMH 7360
Boulevard Newman, La Salle, Quebec
HBN 1X2, Canada
Spec: African literature (fiction, drama,
poetry), critical studies on African
literature, children's books, history,
politics, economics, philosophy, religion

485 SEPIA Editions⚘
6 ave du Gouverneur Général
Binger
F-94100 Saint Maur
+33-1-43 97 22 14
Fax: +33-1-43 97 32 62
Chief exec: Patrick Hérand
Spec: books on African art, architecture,
and anthropology, and social sciences

Germany

486 Institut für Afrika-Kunde
(Institute of African Affairs)
Neuer Jungfernstieg 21
D-20354 Hamburg
+49-40-356523
Fax: +49-40-356 2511
Email: iak@hwwa.uni-hamburg.de
Found: 1963 ISBN 3-928049
Chief exec: Rolf Hofmeier
AS contact: Dirk Kohnert
AS titles: 6-8 ann, 90 ip
Ser: 'Hamburger Beiträge zur Afrika-
Kunde', 'Arbeiten aus dem Institut für
Afrika-Kunde', 'Hamburg African Studies'
Spec: social sciences (contemporary
political, economic and social
development) in sub-Saharan Africa
MS L: minimum 100pp (in printed form)
Edit req: ms pref in German language; ms
in English and French accepted in
exceptional circumstances

487 **Lektorat Afrika**
LIT Verlag
Grindelberg 15a
D-20144 Hamburg
+49-40-446446
Fax: +49-40-441422
Email: lit@lit.hh.eunet.de
Found: 1981
ISBN 3-8258; 3-88660; 3-89473
AS contact: Veit Dietrich Hopf
NA distr: Transaction Publishers, c/o
Rutgers University, *see* 566
UK distr: WorldView Publications *see* 538
AS titles: 40 ann, 300 ip
'Classics in African Anthropology',
'Monographs from the International
African Institute', 'Nomadic Peoples',
'Social Research on Africa', 'Research on
African Languages and Cultures', 'Beiträge
zur Afrikaforschung', 'Studien zur
Afrikanischen Geschichte', 'Mainzer
Beiträge zur Afrikaforschung', Beiträge
zur Afrikanistik', 'Bremer Afrika Studien',
'Afrikanische Studien'
Spec: African studies, history,
anthropology, economics, international
politics, linguistics/language, literature,
development, gender studies
MS subm: textbooks, PhD theses,
collections, conference papers,
monographs, dictionaries, reference guides
(in German and English)
MS L: 200-350pp (in printed form)
Edit req: synopsis and author cv

488 **K.G. Saur Verlag GmbH &
Co**
Ortlerstrasse 8
Postfach 701620
D-81316 Munich
+49-89-769020
Fax: +49-89-769 02150
Email: 100730,1341@compuserve.com
Found: 1974 ISBN 3-598
Chief exec: Klaus G. Saur
AS titles: 1ann, 20 ip
Ser: 'Guides to the Sources for the History
of the Nations'

Spec: 'African Bibliographic Archive' on
microfiche; occasional reference works in
the African studies field

489 **Verlagsgruppe Deutscher
Wirtschaftsdienst**
Marienburger Strasse 22
D-50968 Cologne
+49-221-937630
Fax: +49-221-937 6399
ISBN 3-8039
AS contact: Axel Halbach
AS titles: ca. 200 ann
Ser: 'Afrika-Studien', 'Afrika-Studien-
Sonderreihe', 'Ifo-Forschungberichte'
Spec: publishes the results of leading
research institutes in the field of the
politics of international development and
works in related areas. Publications
include series produced by the following
institutions: Ifo-Institute for Economic
Research, Munich; German Overseas-
Institute, Hamburg; Arnold-Bergsträsser-
Institute, Freiburg Br.; Federal Ministry
for Economic Cooperation and
Development, Bonn; German
Development Institute, Berlin (*see* also
Weltforum Verlag, entry **490**)

490 **Weltforum Verlag GmbH**
Guntherstrasse 23
D-80639 Munich
+49-89-173672
Fax: +49-89-173672
Found: 1964 ISBN 3-8039
Chief exec: Peter Johan von Freyend
AS contact: Rena Sutor
AS titles: 5 ann
Ser: 'Afrika-Studien,' 'Afrika-Studien
Sonderreihe', 'Ifo-Forschungsberichte',
'Ifo-Studien zur Entwicklungsforschung',
'Ifo-Studien-Sondereihe'
Spec: all areas
MS subm: all areas and levels concerning
Africa
(*see* also Verlagsgruppe Deutscher
Wirtschaftsdienst, entry **489**)

Netherlands

491 African Studies Centre
Wassenaarseweg 52
NL-2338 AK Leiden
+31-71-527 3372
Fax: +31-71-527 3344
Email: veerman@rulfsw.leidenuniv.nl
Found: 1958
Chief exec: G. Hesseling
AS contact: Dick Focken
NA & UK distr: Ashgate/Avebury, *see* **501**
AS titles: 5 ann, 3 ip
Ser: 'African Studies Centre Leiden
Research Series'
Spec: political and economic
liberalization, ethnicity, labour, nutrition,
globalization, language and literature
(African), religion, land law and
constitutional law, environment and
management of natural resources
MS subm: as above
MS L: 200-250pp (in printed form)

492 A. A. Balkema Publishers
Vijverweg 8
POB 1675
NL-3000 BR Rotterdam
+31-10-414 5822
Fax: +31-10-413 5947
Email: balkema@balkema.nl
Website: http://www.jcn.nl/ima/balkema
Found: 1972
ISBN 90-5410; 90-6191
Chief exec and contact: A.T. Balkema
NA & UK distr: Ashgate/Avebury, *see* **501**
AS titles: 5 ann, 100 ip
Spec: earth sciences & archaeology, flora
and fauna of Africa, South African history
MS subm: earth sciences, civil
engineering, flora of Africa
MS L: 300pp (in printed form)
Edit req: in English on disk + hard copy

493 E.J. Brill Publishing Company
POB 9000
NL-2300 PA Leiden
+49-71-535 3500
Fax: +49-71-531 7532
Found: 1683 ISBN 90-04
AS contact: D. Orton
AS titles: 10 ann, 39 ip
Ser: 'Studies on Religion in Africa'
MS subm: post-doctoral level
MS L: 60,000w

494 Editions Rodopi B.V.
Keizersgracht 302-304
NL-1016 EX Amsterdam
+31-20-622 7507
Fax: +31-20-638 0948
Email: E.van.broekhuizen@rodopi.nl
Found: 1968 ISBN 90-4200
Chief exec: Eric van Broekhuizen
AS contact: Fred van der Zee
NA distr: Editions Rodopi, 2015 South
Park Place, Atlanta GA 30339, USA
AS titles: 3 ann, 20 ip
Ser: 'Cross/Cultures - Readings in the
Post-Colonial Literatures in English'
(includes other continents)
Spec: literature, culture
MS subm: as above
MS L: 200-500pp

495 KIT Press - Royal Tropical Institute
POB 95001
NL-1090 HA Amsterdam
+31-20-568 8272
Fax: +31-20-568 8286
Email: kitpress@kit.support.nl
Found: 1985 ISBN 90-6832
Chief exec: W. Campschreur
AS contact: (Ms) R. Gunn
AS titles: 5-10 ann, ca 50 ip
Ser: 'Development-oriented Research in
Agriculture'
Spec: health care - primarily at district &
village level, but also health management
information systems; natural resources

management - including agriculture,
livestock, farming systems; culture
MS subm: tropical agriculture, natural
resource management, health care, rural
development, research management
MS L: 200pp (in printed form)
Edit req: send proposal first, mss should
cover action-oriented applied research,
have an inter-disciplinary approach, and
include participation of the user group

496 TOOL
Sarphatistraat 650
NL-1018 AV Amsterdam
+31-20-626 4409
Fax: +31-20-627 7409
Email: tool@tool.nl
Website: http://www.tool.nl
Found: 1974
AS contact: M.P.C. Tiepec
AS titles: n/a
Spec: technology, food processing, gender
studies, renewable energy, environment,
information management (especially
relating to developing countries)

Sweden

497 Scandinavian Institute of
African Studies
POB 1703
SE-751 47 Uppsala
+46-18-562200
Fax: +46-18-695629
Email: nai@nai.uu.se
Found: 1962 ISBN 91-7106
Chief exec: Lennart Wohlgemuth
AS contact: Karl Eric Ericson
AS titles: 15-20 ann, 400 ip
Ser: 'Research Reports', 'Discussion
Papers', 'Seminar Proceedings', 'Current
African Issues'
Spec: social and political science
MS subm: as above
MS L: 100-150 pp (in printed form)

United Kingdom

498 ABC-CLIO Ltd.
Old Clarendon Ironworks
35A Great Clarendon Street,
Oxford OX2 6AT
+44(0)1865-311350
Fax: +44(0)1865-311358
Email: 100567,2650@compuserve.com
Found: 1971 ISBN 1-85109
Chief exec: Anthony J. Sloggett
AS contact: Robert G. Neville
NA distr: ABC-CLIO Inc, *see* 541
AS titles: 4 ann, 50 ip
Ser: 'World Biographical Series'
Spec: bibliographies of individual African
countries, multi-disciplinary
MS subm: bibliographies, school and
library reference works and trade reference
MS L: 150-200,000w
Edit req: on disk and hard copy

499 Addison Wesley Longman
Edinburgh Gate
Harlow CM20 2JE
+44(0)1279-623623
Fax: +44(0)1279-623949
ISBN 0-582
AS contact: Jenny Pares
NA distr: Longman Inc, Gessler Publising
Co Inc, 10 E Church Ave, Roanoke
VA 24001
AS titles: 6 ann, 200 ip
Ser: 'Longman African Writers'
Spec: African history, African literature,
undergraduate textbooks for African
universities
MS subm: fiction, undergraduate (first
year) level textbooks MS L: n/a
Edit req: typed copy of ms

500 Africa Books Limited
3 Galena Road
Hammersmith
London W60 0LT
+44(0)181-746 3646
Fax: +44(0)181-741 4890

Found: 1977 ISBN 0-903274
Chief exec: Chief Raph Uwechue
AS titles: 3 ann, 6 ip
Ser: 'Know Africa Reference Series'
Spec: reference works

501 **Ashgate Publishing Ltd/
     Avebury**
     Gower House, Croft Road
     Aldershot GU11 3HR
+44(0)1252-331551
Fax: +44(0)1252-317446
Email: ashgate@cityscape.co.uk
Website: http://www.ashgate.com/
publishing/
Found: 1967 ISBN 1-85972
Chief exec: Nigel Farrow
AS contact: Sarah Markham
NA distr: Ashgate Publishing Co, Old Post
Road, Brookfield VT 05036-9704, USA
AS titles: 15 ann, 60 ip
Ser: 'The Making of Modern Africa'
Spec: economics, rural/agricultural
studies, planning, urban development,
ethnic and gender studies, gerontology,
regional studies, environment
MS subm: research monographs, upper
level/post graduate studies, subject areas
include all of above plus general social
science and philosophy
MS L: 50-150,000w
Edit req: initial approach with synopsis,
list of contents, sample chapters and
author cv

502 **Berghahn Books**
     3 Newtec Place
     Magdalen Road
     Oxford OX4 1RE
+44(0)1865-250011
Fax: +44(0)1865-250056
Email: berghahnuk@cityscape.co.uk
Found: 1993 ISBN 1-57181
Chief exec: Marion Berghahn
AS contact: Sarah Miles
NA distr: Berghahn Books Inc, 165 Taber
Ave, Providence RI 02906, USA

AS titles: ca 3/4 ann, 3 ip
Ser: 'Cameroon Studies', 'Refugee and
Forced Migration Studies'
Spec: refugee studies history,
anthropology, social studies, politics
MS subm: tertiary, academic
MS L: 100,000w
Edit req: submit brief proposal initially

503 **Cambridge University Press**
     The Edinburgh Building
     Cambridge CB2 2RU
+44(0)1223-312393
Fax: +44(0)1223-315052
Email: jkuper@cup.cam.ac.uk
Found: 1584 ISBN 0-521
Chief exec: Anthony Wilson
AS contact: Jessica Kuper
NA distr: Cambridge University Press,
32 East 57th Street, NewYork
NY 10022-4211, USA
AS titles: 3-4 ann, 110 ip
Ser: 'African Studies Series'
Spec: none
MS subm: post PhD, not theses; history,
sociology, anthropology, politics,
economics
MS L: up to 100,000w
Edit req: typed clean copy

504 **Frank Cass & Co Ltd**
     Newbury House
     890-900 Eastern Avenue
     Newbury Park
     Ilford IG2 7HH
+44(0)181-599 8866
Fax: +44(0)181-599 0984
Email: info@frankcass.com
Found: 1957 ISBN 0-7146
Chief exec: Frank Cass
AS contact: Robert Easton
NA distr: ISBS, 5804 NE Hassalo St,
Portland OR 97213-3644, USA
AS titles: 8 ann, 800 ip
Spec: all areas
MS subm: academic
MS L: 80-100,000w

505 **Cassell Academic**
Wellington House
125 Strand
London WC2R 0BB
(see also separate entries for Pinter **526,**
Mansell **521,** *Leicester Unversity Press*
519)
+44(0)171-420 5555
Fax: +44(0)171-240 8531
Email: 100321,2277@compuserve.com
Website: http://www.bookshop.co.uk/
cassell/
Found: n/a
ISBN 0-86187; 0-304; 0-7185; 0-7201
Chief exec: Janet Joyce
AS contact: Janet Joyce (arts &
humanities) Petra Recter (politics &
economics)
NA distr: Cassell, PO Box 605, Herndon
VA 22070, USA
AS titles: 5-10 ann, 30 ip
Ser: African studies titles published under
all four academic imprints
Spec: economics, political economy,
international relations, agriculture,
anthropology, history, reference works,
religious studies media and cultural studies
MS subm: as above, all levels including
textbooks, reference and monographs
MS L: 80-130,000w max, longer if
reference
Edit req: outline and cv to be sent initially;
all proposals will be peer-reviewed; no
dissertations

506 **Catholic Institute for**
International Relations
Unit 3, Canonbury Yard
190A New North Road
London N1 7BJ
+44(0)171-354 08838
Fax: +44(0)171-359 0017
Found: 1940
ISBN 0-946848; 1-85287
Chief exec: Ian Linden
As contact: Loraine Sweeney
NA distr: Novalis, div. of Unimedia,

49 Front St. E, 2nd floor, Toronto, Ontario
M5E 1B3, Canada
AS titles: 6 ann, 28 ip
Spec: Southern Africa, politics, theology,
development, conflict resolution and peace
building
MS subm: commissioned only

507 **Centre for the Study of**
African Economies
Institute of Economics and
Statistics
University of Oxford
St Cross Building
Manor Road
Oxford OX1 3UL
+44(0)1865-271084
Fax: +44(0)1865 281447
Email: csaeinfo@sable.ox.ac.uk or
csae.publishing@economics.oxford.ac.uk
Website: http://info.ox.ac.uk/~csaeinfo/
Found: 1991
Chief exec: Professor Paul Collier
AS contact: Christine Ayorinde & Sana
Mallinson
AS titles: 30 ann, 55 ip
Ser: 'CSAE Working Paper Series',
'Monographs on African Economies' (with
Macmillan)
Spec: study of African economies through
applied social science

508 **James Currey Publishers Ltd**
73 Botley Road
Oxford OX2 0BS
+44(0)1865-244111
Fax: +44(0)1865-246454
Email: jamescurrey@dial.pipex.com
Found: 1985 ISBN 0-85255
Chief exec: James Currey
AS contact: Douglas Johnson
AS titles: 20 ann, 200 ip
Ser: 'Eastern African Studies', 'African
Literature Today' (ann), 'Studies in African
Literature', 'Social History of Africa',
'African Issues'
Spec: studies in history, politics,
economics, anthropology; study and

criticism of African literature; economic
development in the Third World, politics,
Caribbean history, sociology, economics
MS subm: scholarly works and
monographs in all above areas
MS L: 70-120,000 w
Edit req: submit abstract, contents and cv
first; do not send typescript unless asked to
do so; send disks only after agreement to
publish

509 Earthscan Publications Ltd
120 Pentonville Road
London N1 9JN
+44(0)-171-278 0433
Fax: +44(0)-171-278 1142
Email: earthinfo@earthscan.co.uk
Website: http://www.earthscan.co.uk
Found: 1987 ISBN 1-85383
Chief exec and contact: Jonathan Sinclair
Wilson
NA distr: Island Press, Center for
Resource Economics, 1718 Connecticut
Ave NW, Suite 300, Washington
DC 20009
AS titles: 6-12 ann, 12 ip
Ser: 6-12 [no details provided]
Spec: feminism, economics, urban studies,
agriculture (arid, semi-arid and wetland),
industry, social studies, geography, health
studies, development studies
MS subm: as above
MS L: not less than 35,000w
Edit req: typed scripts only, d-s; all floppy
disks to be IBM compatible and, where
possible, in WP or MS Word

510 Edinburgh University Press
22 George Square
Edinburgh EH8 9LF
+44(0)131-650 4218
Fax: +44(0)131-662 0053
Email: university.press@ed.ac.uk
Website: http://www.ed.ac.u/~eup/
Found: 1948 ISBN 0-7486
Chief exec: David Martin
AS contact: Jane Feore

NA distr: Blackwell US, 238 Main St.,
Cambridge MA 02142, USA & Columbia
University Press, 562 West 113th St., New
York NY 10025, USA
AS titles: 1-2 ann, 9 ip
Ser: 'International African Library',
'International African Library Seminar
Series', 'Africa Bibliography' (ann)
Spec: anthropology; publishes on behalf of
the International African Institute, London
see 825
MS subm: see below
MS L: less than 100,000w
Edit req: all ms must be submitted through
International African Institute, School of
Oriental and African Studies, Thornhaugh
Street, Russell Square, London WC1A
0XG

511 Heinemann Educational
Publishers
Halley Court, Jordan Hill
Oxford OX2 8EJ
+44(0)1865-311366
Fax: +44(0)1865-314169
Email: export.repp@bhein.rel.co.uk
Website: http://www.heinemann.co.uk
Found: 1890 ISBN 0-435
Chief exec: William Shepherd
AS contact: Natalie Warren-Green
NA distr: Heinemann, US *see* 552
AS titles: 5-8 ann, 170 ip
Ser: 'African Writers Series', 'UNESCO
History of Africa'
Spec: literature
MS subm: fiction
MS L: 200-250 pp A4
Edit req: typed scripts, d-s; author must
retain copy of ms as not responsible for
loss or damage

512 Hurst & Co Publishers
38 King Street
London WC2E 8JT
+44(0)171-240 2666
Fax: +44(0)-171-240 2667
Email: hurst@atlas.co.uk
Found: 1967

ISBN 1-85065; 0-905838; 0-903983
Chief exec: Christopher Hurst
AS contact: Christopher Hurst & Michael
Dwyer
AS titles: 5 ann, 75 ip
Spec: history, politics, social studies,
neocolonialism, autobiography; also Asia:
southwest, south, south east, east and
Soviet central
MS subm: research, tertiary
MS L: no preference
Edit req: no ms submissions before
synopsis has been submitted and approved

513   IC Publications
7 Coldbath Square
London EC1R 4LQ
+44(0)171-713 7711
Fax: +44(0)171-713 7898
Email: icpubs@dial.pipex.com
ISBN 0-905268
Chief exec: Afif Ben Yedder
AS contact: Jean Tomlinson
AS titles: 1 ann, 1 ip
Ser: 'New African Yearbook'
Spec: reference

514   Institute for African Alternatives
23 Bevenden Street
London N1 6BH
+44(0)181-251 1503
Fax: +44(0)181-253 0801
Email: ifaanet@gn.apc.org
Found: 1986 ISBN 1-870425-05
Chief exec: Mohamed Suliman
AS titles: 6 ann, 4 ip
Spec: economy, environment, conflict,
gender
MS subm: academic monographs
MS L: 200pp (in printed form)

515   Institute of Development Studies
University of Sussex
Brighton BN1 9RE
+44(0)1273-678269/ 606261
Fax: +44(0)1273-691647/ 621202

Email: ids.books@sussex.ac.uk or
ids.subs@sussex.ac.uk
Website: http://www.ids.ac.uk/ids/ids.html
Found: 1966 ISBN 1-85864
Chief exec: John Toye
AS contact: Acting Publications Manager
AS titles: 10 ann, 50 ip
Ser: 'IDS Discussion Papers', 'IDS
Working Papers', 'IDS Research Reports',
'IDS Development Bibliographies'
Spec: agriculture and rural development,
environment, political and economic
development, employment and technology,
gender education, trade
MS subm: commissioned by IDS from IDS
fellowship only
MS L: variable
Edit req: adherence to house style

516   Intermediate Technology Publications
103-105 Southampton Row
London WC1B 4HH
+44(0)171-436 9761
Fax: +44(0)171-436 2013
Email: itpubs@gn.apc.org
Website: http://www.oneworld.org/itdg
Found: 1967 ISBN 1-85339
Chief exec and contact: Neal Burton
AS titles and related: 180 ip
Spec: appropriate technology, and the
technical and economic aspects of
development studies
MS subm: in areas above: practical
manuals, case studies of technical
development, economic assessment of
technical assistance
MS L: max. 80,000w
Edit req: authors should provide
information about target audience for
whom they are writing, and what the
practical objectives of the book are; and
confirm that ms is not a unique copy

517 Karnak House
300 Westbourne Park Road
London W11 1EH
+44(0)171-221 6490
Fax: +44(0)171-221 6490
Found: 1975 ISBN 0-907015
Chief exec and contact: Amon Saba
Saakana
NA distr: Africa World Press/ Red Sea
Press *see* **542**
AS titles: 8 ann, 35 ip
Ser: 'Ancient Afrikan History/Civilization'
Spec: African-American, Afro-Caribbean,
Africa; religion, history, linguistics,
literature, anthropology, sociology, art,
folk tales, proverbs, African languages,
ancient Egypt, women's studies, politics,
development studies, education
MS subm: all areas above, academic and
general
MS L: 50-100,000w
Edit req: covering letter, biographical note,
prepaid international coupon with name
and address, synopsis, sample chapters,
contents page

**518 Kegan Paul International
Ltd**
POB 256
London WC1E 3SW
+44(0)171-580 5511
Fax: +44(0)171-436 0899
Email: books@keganpau.demon.co.uk
Website: http://www.demon.co.uk/
keganpaul/
Found: n/a ISBN 0-7103
Chief exec: Peter Hopkins
AS contact: Kaori O'Connor
NA distr: Columbia University Press, 562
West 113th Street, New York NY 10025,
USA
AS titles: 4-6 ann, 42 ip
Ser: 'African Studies Series' (for African
Studies Centre, Leiden *see* **398**);
publications in association with the
International Institute London

Spec: African studies, history, art,
sociology, anthropology, language and
linguistics, medicine, politics
MS subm: as above
MS L: 180pp min (in printed form)
Edit req: disk and hard copy

519 Leicester University Press
Wellington House
125 Strand
London WC2R 0BB
+44(0)171-420 5555
Fax: +44(0)171-240 8531
Email: 100321,2277@compuserve.com
Website: http://www.bookshop.co.uk/
cassell/
ISBN 0-7185
Chief exec: Philip Sturrock
AS contact: Janet Joyce
NA distr: Cassell, PO Box 605, Herndon
VA 22070, USA
AS titles: 4 ann, 6 ip
Spec: cultural studies, art, religion
MS subm: academic monographs
MS L: 80-120,000w
Edit req: synopsis and/or introduction,
contents list, cv

520 Macmillan Press Ltd
Houndmills
Basingstoke RG21 2XS
+44(0)1256-29242
Fax: +44(0)1256-479985
Found: 1843 ISBN 0-333
Chief exec: D.J. Knight
AS contact: T.M. Farmiloe
AS titles: 30 ann, 100 ip
Spec: economics, history, politics,
sociology
MS subm: tertiary
MS L: 80,000w
Edit req: typed, d-s ms and disk

521 Mansell Publishing Ltd
Wellington House
125 Strand
London WC2R 0BB
+44(0)171-420 5555

Fax: +44(0)171-240 8531
Email: 100321,2277@compuserve.com
Website: http://www.bookshop.co.uk/
cassell/
Found: 1966 ISBN 0-7201
Chief exec: Philip Sturrock
AS contact: Veronica Higgs
NA distr: Cassell, PO Box 605, Herndon
VA 22070, USA
AS titles 4 ann, 9 ip
MS subm: reference guides,
bibliographies, handbooks, directories,
library and information science
MS L: 80-120,000w
Edit req: synopsis and/or introduction,
contents list, cv

522 New Beacon Books
76 Stroud Green Road
London N4 3EN
+44(0)171-272 4889
Fax: +44(0)171-281 4662
Website: http://www.newbeacon.books.
com
Found: 1966 ISBN 0-901241
Chief exec and contact: John la Rose
AS titles: 2 ann, 12 ip
Spec: politics, cultural studies, history,
literary theory, poetry
MS subm: no unsolicited mss

523 Oxford University Press
Walton Street
Oxford OX2 6DP
+44(0)1865-56767
Fax: +44(0)1865-56646
Website: http://www.oup.co.uk
Found: 1478 ISBN 0-19
Chief exec: James Arnold-Baker
AS contact: Editorial Director,
Arts/Reference Division
NA distr: Oxford University Press Inc, 200
Madison Ave, New York NY 10016, USA
AS titles: 5 ann, 17 ip
Ser: 'Oxford Studies in African Affairs'
Spec: politics, history, development
studies, geography, economics
MS subm: all areas, tertiary level

524 Pathfinder Press
47 The Cut
London SE1 8LL
+44(0)171-261 1354
Fax: +44(0)171-928 7970
Email:101515,2702@compuserve.com
Found: 1970
ISBN 087348; 0913460; 0947083
Chief exec: Marcella Fitzgerald
AS titles: 1 ann, 7 ip
Spec: politics, development

525 Pentland Press, TheΦ
1 Hutton Close
South Church
Bishop Auckland DL14 6XB
+44(0)1388-776555
Fax: +44(0)1388-766766
ISBN 1-85821
Chief exec: N.S. Law
AS contact: J.A. Phillips
Spec: autobiography and memoirs of
former African colonial officers

526 Pinter
Wellington House
125 Strand
London WC2R 0BB
+44(0)171-420 5555
Fax: +44(0)171-240 8531
Email: 100321,2277@compuserve.com
Website: http://www.bookshop.co.uk/
cassell/
Found: 1973 ISBN 1-85567
Chief exec: Philip Sturrock
AS contact: Petra Recter
NA distr: Cassell, PO Box 605, Herndon
VA 22070, USA
AS titles: 4 ann, 8 ip
Spec: politics, economics, history,
geography, development studies,
environmental studies
MS subm: academic monographs
MS L: 80,120-000w
Edit req: synopsis and/or introduction,
contents list, cv

527 **Pluto Press**
345 Archway Road
London N6 5AA
+44(0)181-348 2724
Fax: +44(0)181-348 9133
Email: pluto@pluto6ks.demon.co.uk
Found: 1987 ISBN 0-7453
Chief exec and contact: Roger van
Zwanenberg
NA distr: InBook, 1436 West Randolph
St, Chicago IL 60607, USA
AS titles: 5-10 ann, 20 ip
Ser: 'Africa and the Caribbean'
Spec: all aspects of political economy
broadly defined, from African cultural
studies e.g. music and art, to African
women's studies, African history, society
and politics
MS subm: undergraduate, graduate,
popular political analysis
MS L: 60,000w min
Edit req: d-s, send return postage if ms is
sent or send table of contents and two or
three page outline

528 **Radcliffe Press**Φ
45 Bloomsbury Square
London WC1A 2HY
+44(0)171-916 1069
Fax: +44(0)171-916 1068
ISBN 1-85043
AS contact: Anthony Kirk-Greene
NA distr: St. Martin's Press *see* **567**
AS titles: ca 12 ip
Spec: specializes in memoirs, biographies,
and collections of letters and diaries,
which relate accounts of experiences in
Africa, the Caribbean, Asia and the
Pacific, the Near and Middle East and the
Mediterranean by authors who worked and
lived in those regions. Authors include
diplomats, military officers, colonial
administrators, professional and technical
staff, as well as other individuals with a
story to tell
MS subm: as above

529 **Routledge, Chapman and
Hall**†
11 New Fetter Lane
London EC4P 4EE
+44(0)171-583 9855
Fax: +44(0)171-842 2302
ISBN 0-416
Chief exec: David Croom
AS contact: Sarah Lloyd
NA distr: Routledge, Chapman and Hall,
Inc, 29 West 35th Street, New York NY
10001, USA
AS titles: 2-5 ann, 12 ip
Ser: 'Routledge Introduction to
Development', 'Development and
Underdevelopment'
Spec: rural, urban, economic,
environment, women, industrialization,
political development
MS subm: all areas to do with Third
World, mainly tertiary - undergraduate and
above, plus a few A-level and professional
level
MS L: 100,000w (80-120,000)
Edit req: proposal consisting of an
overview (2-4pp outline of book), list of
contents, list of tables, maps, diagrams etc.
(a rough indication of how many), a letter
explaining why the book is being written,
a description of the level and what market
book is aimed at; what, if any, access to
word processors, laser printers etc., with
description of type and make, length of
ms, date of expected delivery

530 **School of Oriental and
African Studies**†
University of London
Thornhaugh Street
Russell Square
London WC1H 0XG
+44(0)171-637 2388
Fax: +44(0)171-436 3844
Found: 1917 ISBN n/a
AS contact: M.J. Daly
AS titles: 2-3 ann, 55 ip
Spec: principally language, literature,
history

MS subm: normally only publishes for staff or close associates of the School

531 Serif Publishers
47 Strachan Road
London E3 5DA
+44(0)181-981 3990
Fax: +44(0)181-981 3990
Found: 1993
AS contact: Paul Westlake
AS titles: 1 ann, 4 ip
Spec: current affairs, politics, history, literature
MS L: 80,000 w
Edit req: ms not initially required, synopsis only

532 I.B. Tauris & Co Ltd
45 Bloomsbury Square
London WC1A 2HY
+44(0)171-916 1069
Fax: +44(0)171-916 1068
Email: mail@ibtauris.com
Website: www.ibtauris.com
Found: 1985
Chief exec: I. Bagherzade
AS contact: Lester Crook
NA distr: St. Martin's Press *see* **567**
AS titles: 10 ann, 50 ip
Ser: 'International Library of African Studies'
Spec: modern history, international relations, politics, economics
MS subm: serious journalistic to dissertation level
MS L: 150,000w max
Edit req: disk; occ for specialized topics require CRC or a grant/subvention as sales will not cover costs; ms submitted are evaluated on their conceptual merits (including independent academic referees) before consideration of financial issues

533 UCL Press Ltd
University College London,
Gower Street
London WC1E 6BT
+44(0)171-380 7707

Fax: +44(0)171-413 8392
Email: c.wintersgill@ucl.ac.uk
Website: http://www.bookshop.co.uk/ucl/
Found: 1991 ISBN 1-85728
Chief exec: Roger Jones
AS contact: Caroline Wintersgill
NA distr: Taylor & Francis Inc
AS titles: 0-5 ann, 6 ip
Spec: migration, gender and development, comparative politics
MS subm: as above
MS L: 70-100,000w
Edit req: detailed book proposal in first instance, including academic rationale, competition, market, length and submission date, and detailed description of each chapter

534 Virago Press
Brettenham House
Lancaster Place
London WC2E 7EN
+44(0)171-911 8000
Fax: +44(0)171-911 8101
Found: 1972 ISBN 1-86049
Chief exec: Philippa Harrison
AS contact: Lennie Goodings
Spec: fiction, poetry, non-fiction, women's writing
Edit req: synopsis and sample chapter, 2 months response time

535 VSO Books
Voluntary Service Overseas
317 Putney Bridge Road
London SW15 2PN
+44(0)181-780 2266
Fax: +44(0)181-780 1326
Email: sbernau@vso.org.uk
Website: http://www.oneworld.org/vsobooks/
Found: 1990 ISBN 0-9509050
AS contact: Penny Amerena & Jo Rogers
AS titles: 2-4 ann, 10 ip
Ser: 'Working Papers in Development' (new series published electronically on website)

Spec: practical manuals for development workers in all sectors: agriculture, water supplies, skills transfer etc., handbooks for teachers in low-resource contexts
MS subm: no unsolicited mss for the most part
Edit req: mss should draw upon or be able to include practical examples and information based on VSO volunteers' and their overseas colleagues' professional experience

536 **Women's Press, The**
    34 Great Sutton Street
    London EC1V 0DX
    +44(0)171-251 3007
    Fax: +44(0)171-608 1938
    Found: 1978 ISBN 0-7043
    Chief exec and contact: Kathy Gale & Mary Hemming
    NA distr: Trafalgar Square Publishing, Howe Hill Road, North Pomfret VT 05053, USA
    AS titles: 10 ann, 100 ip
    Spec: fiction, accessible non-fiction, women's writing
    MS L: 60,000w

537 **World of Information**
    2 Market Street
    Saffron Walden
    Essex CB10 1HZ
    +44(0)1799-521150
    Fax: +44(0)1799-524805
    Email: waldenpub@easynet.co.uk
    Found: 1977 ISBN 0-903339
    Chief exec and contact: Anthony Axon
    AS titles: 1 ann
    Ser: 'Africa Review'
    Spec: business and economics, reference
    MS subm: no unsolicited mss

538 **WorldView Publications**
    9 Park End Street
    PO Box 595
    Oxford OX1 6YH
    +44(0)1865-201562
    Fax: +44(0)1865-201906

Email: worldview@patrol.inway.co.uk
Found: 1994 ISBN 1-872142
Chief exec and contact: Toby Milner
AS titles: 5 ann, 5 ip
Ser: 'African Studies Series', 'Women and Development Series', 'Development Management Reprints Series'
Spec: development, NGOs, gender, anthropology, history, social studies, humanities
MS subm: tertiary and post-graduate, professional
MS L: n/a

539 **Zed Books**
    7 Cynthia Street
    London N1 9JF
    +44(0)171-837 4014
    Fax: +44(0)171-833 3960
    Email: zed@zedbooks.demon.co.uk
    Found: 1977 ISBN 0-86232/ 1-85649
    AS contact: Robert Molteno
    NA distr: Humanities Press International Inc, *see* **554**
    AS titles: 5 ann, 80 ip
    Ser: 'African Energy Policy Resarch Series'
    Spec: economics, political economy, development, politics, women, health, environment, culture
    MS subm: academic, activist, areas as above, particularly with reference to the Third World
    MS L: 70-90,000w
    Edit req: ms or proposal including chapter abstracts, rationale and sample text

540 **Hans Zell Publishers**
    An imprint of Bowker-Saur
    Div. of Reed Elsevier (UK) Ltd
    POB 56
    Oxford OX1 2SJ
    +44(0)1865-511428
    Fax: +44(0)1865-311534
    Email: hzell@dial.pipex.com
    ISBN 1-873836; 0-905450
    Chief exec: Charles Halpin

AS contact: Hans M. Zell (Consultant)
NA distr: Bowker-Saur/Reed Reference
Publishing *see* **545**
AS titles: 6 ann, 80 ip
Ser: 'New Perspectives in African
Literature', 'African Discourse'
(Monograph series now discontinued),
'Bibliographical Research in African
Literatures', 'Documentary Research in
African Literatures'
Spec: all areas of African/Third World
studies (reference works only since 1994)
MS subm: reference works annotated, or at
least partially annotated, in all areas of
African/Third World studies
MS L: 200pp min (in printed form)
Edit req: outline/synopsis of scope and
contents must be submitted with sample
chapters/specimen pages and indication of
its relationship to existing or competing
works, and proposed length; special author
proposal form available on request

United States

541 **ABC-CLIO**
   501 South Cherry Street
   Suite 350
   Denver CO 80222
+1-800-368 6868/ 303-333 3003
Fax: +1-303-333 4037
Found: 1955 ISBN 87436
Chief exec: Ronald J. Boehm
AS contact: Heather Cameron
UK distr: ABC-Clio Ltd, *see* **498**
AS titles: 2-5 ann, 20 ip
Ser: numerous titles covering African
countries in the 'ABC-CLIO World
Bibliographical Series'
Spec: historical bibliography, areas studies
bibliographies, biographical dictionaries,
single-volume, subject encyclopedias
MS subm: biographical dictionaries,
handbooks, subject encyclopedias
MS L: 150-200,000w
Edit req: request details from publisher

542 **Africa World Press Inc/**
   The Red Sea Press Inc
   11-D Princess Road
   Lawrenceville
   NJ 08648-2319
+1-609-844 9583
Fax: +1-609-844 0198
Email: africawpress@nyo.com
Found: 1983
ISBN 0-86543; 0-932415; 1-56902
Chief exec: Kassahun Checole
AS contact: Nanjiku Ngugi
UK distr: Turnaround Publishers Services
Ltd., Unit 3, Olympia Trading Estate,
Coburg Road, Wood Green, London N22
6TZ
AS titles: 80 ann, 200 ip
Ser: 'African Writers Library', 'African
Women Writers'
Spec: economics, politics, history, public
health, linguistics, cultural studies, literary
criticism, development studies, women's
studies, agriculture, anthropology, religion
MS subm: as above
MS L: 250-400pp (in printed form)
Edit req: on disk, WP 5.1+; index,
bibliography

543 **Africana Publishing**
   Company†
   Holmes & Meier Publishers
   Inc, 160 Broadway
   Suite 900 East Wing
   New York NY 10038
+1-212-254 4100
ISBN 0-8419
Chief exec: Miriam Holmes
UK distr: B.R.A.D., 244a London Road,
Hadleigh SS7 2DE

544 **ASA Press** [formerly
   Crossroads Press]
   African Studies Association
   Credit Union Building
   Emory University
   Atlanta GA 30322
+1-404-329 6410

Fax: +1-404-329 6433
Email: africa@emory.edu
Website: http://www.sasa.upenn.edu/
African_Studies/Home_Page/ASA_menu.
html
Found: n/a ISBN 0-918456
Chief exec and contact: Chris Koch
Note: this is the publishing arm of the
African Studies Association *see* **851**
AS titles: 4-5 ann, 35 ip
Ser: 'The Arts of Africa: An Annotated
Bibliography' (ann)
Spec: development, bibliographies,
medical studies, history, humanities
MS subm: as above
MS L: n/a
Edit req: ms must be submitted with
review from two scholars, preferably
members of the ASA, author must be
prepared to undertake any revisions,
editing, and to prepare the ms to CRC

545 **Bowker-Saur/Reed**
     Reference Publishing
     121 Chanlon Road
     New Providence NJ 07974
     +1-908-665 3576
     Fax: +1-908- 665 6688
     Email: info@bowkersaur.com
     Website: http://www.reedref.com
     Chief exec: Carol Cooper
     AS contact: Hans M. Zell, POB 56,
     Oxford OX1 2SJ, UK
     Note: distributor in North America of the
     Hans Zell Publishers list
     Spec: *see* Hans Zell Publishers, entry **540**

546 **Carolina Academic Press**
     700 Kent Street
     Durham NC 27701
     +1-919-489 7486
     Fax: +1-919-493 5668
     Email: cap.press@worldnet.att.net
     Found: 1972 ISBN 0-89089
     Chief exec: Keith R. Sipe
     AS contact: Russ Bahorsky
     UK distr: Basil Blackwell Ltd, 108
     Cowley Road, Oxford OX4 1JF

AS titles: 2-3 ann, 6 ip
Spec: African poetry, African literature,
African history, African studies textbooks,
all at academic or scholarly level
MS subm: especially interested in books
with an international or global perspective,
also interested in the areas listed above
MS L: 250pp min (in printed form)
Edit req: scholarly/academic

547 **Duke University Press**Φ
     905 West Main Street
     POB 90660
     Durham NC 27708-0660
     +1-919-687 3600
     Fax: +1-919-688 4574
     Website:http://www.duke.edu/web/
     dupress/
     AS contact: Jean Brady

548 **Feminist Press at CUNY,**
     The
     311 East 94th Street
     New York NY 10128
     +1-212-360 5794
     Fax: +1-212-348 1241
     Found: 1970 ISBN 1-55861
     Chief exec: Florence Howe
     UK distr: Gazelle Book Services Ltd,
     Falcon House, Queen Square, Lancaster
     LA1 1RN
     AS titles: 1 ann, 2 ip
     Ser: in prep 'Women Writing Africa', a
     seven volume series of written and oral
     narratives by women in Africa, both
     historically, and in the present
     Spec: texts by African women: fiction,
     autobiography, short stories, etc. Also
     "lost" writings by women in other parts of
     the "Third World"
     MS subm: as above
     MS L: n/a
     Edit req: n/a

549 **Garland Publishing Inc**†
     717 Fifth Avenue
     New York NY 10022
     +1-212-751 7441 Fax: +1-212-308 9399

Found: 1969 ISBN 0-8240
Chief exec: Gavin Borden
AS contact: Gary Kuris, Editor
Europe distr: Garland Publishing,
10 Storey's Gate, London SW1P 3AY, UK
Spec: literature, the arts, education,
women's studies, reference works
AS subm: as above MS L: 250-400pp
Edit req: prospectus, sample chapters

550 **Greenwood Publishing**
   Group Inc†
   88 Post Road West
   POB 5007
   Westport CT 06881
   +1-203-226 3571
   Fax: +1-203-222 1502
   Found: 1967
   ISBN 0-313; 0-275 (Praeger)
   Chief exec: Robert Hagelstein
   AS contact: Cynthia Harris
   Europe distr: Westport Publications Ltd,
   3 Henrietta Street, London WC2E 8LT,
   UK
   AS titles: 20-25 ann, 500 ip
   Ser: 'Contributions in Afro-American and
   African Studies', 'Bibliographies and
   Indexes in Afro-American Studies',
   'African Special Bibliographical Series'
   Spec: spectrum from literary criticism to
   behavioural sciences, with an emphasis on
   political and economic affairs and military
   studies
   MS subm: as above at university level
   MS L: 350 pp max, d-s (in ms form)
   Edit req: prefer to see a prospectus and cv
   prior to actual ms submissions; the
   prospectus should indicate scope,
   organization and length of the project and
   if or when a completed ms is available

551 **Haworth Press Inc, TheΦ**
   10 Alice Street
   Binghamton
   NY13904-1580
   +1-607-722 5857
   Fax: +1-607-722 6362
   ISBN 1-56024

552 **Heinemann**
   361 Hanover Street
   Portsmouth NH 03801
   +1-603-431 7894
   Fax: +1-603-431 7840
   Email: info@heinemann.com
   Website: http://www.heinemann.com
   ISBN 0-435
   Chief exec: Michael Gibbons
   AS contact: Jean Hay
   UK distr: Heinemann, *see* **511**; James
   Currey Publishers Ltd, *see* **508**
   AS titles: 20 ann, 100 ip
   Ser: 'Studies in African Literature', 'Social
   History of Africa', 'Classics in Context',
   'African Issues', 'African Writers Series'
   Spec: history, literature and literary
   criticism, religion, anthropology,
   development studies, women's studies,
   political science
   MS subm: college level texts, specialist
   monographs, books aimed at general
   readership
   MS L: 80,000w max
   Edit req: prefer synopses, contents lists,
   sample chapters in first instance, along
   with cv

553 **Howard University Press**
   1240 Randolph Street
   Room 106
   Washington DC 20017
   +1-202-686 6696
   Fax: +1-202-806 9029
   Found: 1972 ISBN 0-88258
   Chief exec and contact: Edwin J. Gordon
   UK distr: Baker & Taylor International
   AS titles: 2-3 ann, 16 ip
   Spec: African diaspora studies
   MS subm: women's studies, governmental
   policy, literature, literary criticism, and
   biography
   MS L: 3-600pp, d-s (in ms form)
   Edit req: letter of inquiry, table of
   contents, sample chapter, cv and self-
   adressed envelope

554 Humanities Press International Inc
165 First Avenue
Atlantic Highlands
NJ 07716-1289
+1-201-872 1441
Fax: +1-201-872 0717
Email: hpmail@humanitiespress.com
Website: http://www.humanitiespress.com
Found: 1952 ISBN various imprints
Chief exec and contact: Keith Ashfield
Note: firm is distributor for Zed Books
UK *see* **539** and Oxfam UK *see* **909** and
Ireland
AS titles: 25 ann, 100 ip

555 Indiana University Press
601 North Morton Street
Bloomington
IN 47404-3797
+1-812-335 4773
Fax: +1-812-855 8507
Email: iupress@indiana.edu
Website: http://www.indiana.edu/~iupress
Found: 1950 ISBN 0-253
Chief exec: John Gallman
AS contact: Janet Rabinowitch
UK distr: Open University Press, Celtic
Court #22, Ballmoor MK18 1XW
AS titles: 8-10 ann, 100 ip
Ser: 'African Systems of Thought',
'Traditional Arts of Africa'
Spec: history, politics, anthropology,
folklore, gender studies, cultural studies,
film, literature
MS subm: scholarly books, upper division
texts
MS L: 75,000w
Edit req: initial enquiry by letter; all ms to
be typed, d-s

556 Edwin Mellen Press
POB 450
415 Ridge Street
Lewiston NY 14902-0450
+1-716-754 2788/2266
Fax: +1-716-754 4056

Email: mellen@ag.net
Website: http://www.mellen.com
Found: 1974 ISBN 0-88946
Chief exec: Herbert Richardson
AS contact: John Rupnow
UK distr: The Edwin Mellen Press Ltd,
Lampeter, Dyfed, Wales SA48 8LT
AS titles: 5 ann, 64 ip
Ser: 'African Studies', 'Studies in African
Education', 'Studies in African Health and
Medicine', 'Studies in African Literature',
'Studies in African Economic and Social
Development'
Spec: as above
MS subm: as above
MS L: 150pp (in printed form)
Edit req: indicate general topic of
proposed work, and specific contribution
to field of scholarship, describe contents,
noting major parts/chapters, give personal
scholarly background - attach cv, give
present state of ms and projected date of
completion

557 Monthly Review Press
122 West 27th Street
New York NY 10001
+1-212-791 2555
Fax: +1 212-727 3676
Email: mreview@igc.apc.org
Website: http://www.monthlyreview.org/
monthlyreview
Found: 1951 ISBN 0-85345
Chief exec: Paul Sweezy & Harry Magdoff
AS contact: Renee Pendergrass
UK distr: Central Books, *see* **668**
AS titles: 2 ann, 25 ip
Spec: development and transition, socialist
theory
MS subm: as above

558 Ohio University Press
Scott Quadrangle 223
Athens OH 45701-2979
+1-614-593 1155 Fax: +1-614-593 4536
Email: gillian.berchowitz@ohiou.edu
Found: 1964 ISBN 0-8214
Chief exec: David Sanders

AS contact: Gillian Berchowitz
UK distr: Academic University Publishers
Group Ltd, 1 Gower Street, London
WC1E 6HA
AS titles: 10 ann, 50 ip
Ser: 'Eastern African Series', 'Ohio
University Center for International Studies
African Series'
Spec: Eastern and Southern Africa, some
West Africa
MS subm: scholarly manuscripts of
interest to university scholars and libraries
MS L: 250-400pp ms (in ms form)
Edit req: typed, d-s, one side only, disk

559 **Orbis Books**
POB 308 Maryknoll
NY 10545-0308
+1-914-941 7590
Fax: +1-914-945 0670
Email: orbisbooks@aol.com
Website: http://www.maryknoll.org/orbis/
mklorbhp.htm
Found: 1970 ISBN 0-88344/ 1-57075
Chief exec: R.J. Gormley
AS contact: Susan Perry & Willliam
Burrows
UK distr: Alban Books, 79 Park Street,
Bristol BS1 5PF
AS titles: 4 ann, 35 ip
Ser: 'Religious Studies/Theology'
Spec: as above
MS subm: as above
MS L: 400pp max (in ms form)

560 **Passeggiata Press, Inc**
[formerly Three Continents
Press]
POB 636
Pueblo CO 80301
+1-719-544 1038
Fax: +1-719-546 7889
Email: passeggia@aol.com
Website: http://www.members.aol.com/
passeggia/passeggiata.htm
Found: 1996 ISBN 1-57889
Chief exec: Donald E. Herdeck
AS titles: 3-5 ann, 11 ip

Spec: creative literature (prose, short
stories, poetry), literary criticism, some
cultural studies, music, architecture, other
humanities; books in these areas from the
non-Western world: Africa, the
Caribbean/Latin America, the Middle East
(Morocco to Iran), Asia and the Pacific
Islands
MS subm: as above, primarily university
level but original fiction and poetry also
for high school and below
MS L: 125-250 pp (in printed form)
Edit req: enquire first, do not send ms
unless requested, ms to be as polished as
possible; if a translation (from French,
Arabic, etc.) submitted by translator, an
introduction is requested by the translator
placing the author in literary/cultural
context, with some discussion of
biographical material and particular work
being presented; a brief bibliography and
glossary may also be requested; if a critical
work, a substantial bibliography, which
the author is often requested to compile
and index, is essential
Note: rights to the former Three
Continents Press backlist titles were sold
to Lynne Rienner Publishers in October
1996, *see* entry **564**

561 **Path Press**
53 West Jackson Boulevard,
Suite 724
Chicago IL 60640-3610
+1-312-663 0167
Fax: +1-312-663 5318
Email: bjjiii@aol.com
Found: 1969 ISBN 0-910671-00-0
Chief exec and contact: Bennett J. Johnson
AS titles: 1 ann, 1 ip
Spec: Afro-American and Third World
peoples
MS subm: as above

562 **Princeton University Press**
41 William Street
Princeton NJ 08540-5237
+1-609-258 4900
Fax: +1-609-258 6305
Website: http://www.pup.princeton.edu
Found: 1917 ISBN 0-691
Chief exec: Walter Lippincott
AS contact: Mary Murrell
UK distr: John Wiley & Sons Ltd,
1 Oldlands Way, Bognor Regis PO22 9SA
AS titles: 2 ann, 20 ip
Spec: n/a
MS L: under 400pp (in ms form)

563 **Reference Publications Inc**
218 St Clair River Drive
PO Box 344
Algonac MI 48001
+1-810-794 5722
Fax: +1-810-794 7463
Found: 1975 ISBN 0-917256
Chief exec and contact: Aline Irvine
AS titles: 11 ip
Ser: 'Encyclopedia Africana-Dictionary of
African Biography'
Spec: biography, botany, encyclopedias
and reference works
MS subm: commissioned only

564 **Lynne Rienner Publishers
Inc**
1800 30th Street, Suite 314
Boulder CO 80301
+1-303-444 6684
Fax: +1-303-444 0824
Found: 1984
ISBN 0-931477; 1-55587; 0-89410
Chief exec and contact: Lynne Rienner
Europe distr: Eurospan Ltd, 3 Henrietta
Street, London WC2E 8LU
AS titles: 8-10 ann, 80 ip
Ser: 'SAIS African Studies Library'
Spec: all areas
MS subm: tertiary through post-doctoral
work in history, politics, sociology,
anthropology, economics, agriculture,
literature, and literary criticism

Edit req: prefer letter of enquiry with cv,
including proposed outline or table of
contents, estimated length and completion
date, and intended market
Note: acquired rights to many Three
Continents Press titles in October 1996

565 **Norman Ross Publishing
Inc**
330 W 58th Street
New York NY 10019
+1-212- 873 2100
Fax: +1-212-765 2393
Email: info@nross.com
Website: http://www.nross.com
Found: 1972 (as Clearwater Publ)
ISBN 0-88354
Chief exec: Norman A. Ross
AS contact: Todd Bludeau
Spec: clearing house for microfilms and
microfiche worldwide, selling primarily to
libraries in the US and Canada; represents
major publishers of Africana material in
microform such as Inter Documentation
Company (IDC), Microform Academic
Publishers, World Microforms, etc.
MS subm: ideas for microform collections,
whether the original materials to be filmed
are in the US, Africa, Europe or elsewhere

566 **Rutgers University Press**
POB 5062
Livingston Campus
Building 4161
New Brunswick
NJ 08901-1242
+1-908-445 7762
Fax: +1-908-445 7039
Email: dtgross@rci.rutgers.edu
Website: http://sociology.rutgers.edu/
rupress
Found: 1936 ISBN 0-8135
Chief exec: Marlie Wasserman
AS contact: Leslie Mitchner
UK distr: John Ramsay Marketing, 16
Devon Square, Newton Abbot TQ12 1HR
AS titles: 3 ann, 10 ip

Spec: cultural studies, women, public health
MS subm: professional and scholarly, college supplemental reading
MS L: 100,000w
Edit req: complete proposal, assessing market and competing books

567 St. Martin's Press Inc†
257 Park Avenue South
New York NY 10010
+1-212-982 3900
Fax: +1-212-420 9314
Found: 1952 ISBN 0-312
Chief exec: Thomas McCormack
AS contact: James Fitzgerald
AS titles: 100 ip
Ser: 10-15 [no details provided]
Spec: politics, history, economics
MS subm: upper division undergraduate/graduate level
MS L: 80-100,000w

568 Scarecrow Press Inc
4720 Boston Way
Lanham MD 20706
+1-301-459 3366
Fax: +1-301-459 2118
Found: 1950 ISBN 0-8108
Chief exec: James E. Lyons
AS contact: Shirley Lambert
UK distr: Shelwing Ltd, 127 Sandgate Road, Folkestone CT20 2BL
AS contact: 8 ann, 60 ip
Ser: 'African Historical Dictionaries'
Spec: reference material; a few monographs on librarianship, language, literature
MS subm: historical dictionaries or other reference materials
MS L: 250pp min (in printed form)
Edit req: d-s, typed, one recognised style to be followed (Chicago, APA, MLA); if a bibliography, annotations preferred; appropriate indexes, chronologies, or bibliographies are invited

569 Smithsonian Institution PressΦ
470 L'Enfant Plaza SW
Suite 7100
Washington DC 20560
+1-202-287 3738
Fax: +1-202-287 3184/ 3637
AS contact: Ruth W. Spiegel

570 University of California Press
2120 Berkeley Way
Berkeley CA 94720
+1-415-642 4247
Fax: +1415-643 7127
Found: 1893 ISBN 0-520
Chief exec: James H. Clark
AS contact: Monica McCormick
UK distr: University Presses of California, Columbia & Princeton Ltd, 1 Oldlands Way, Bognor Regis PO22 9SA
AS titles: 4 ann, 100 ip
Ser: 'African Studies Center' series (monographs), 'Marcus Garvey and the Universal Negro Improvement Association Papers', 'Perspectives on Southern Africa', 'UNESCO General History of Africa'
Spec: history, anthropology
MS subm: all areas and levels
MS L: n/a

571 University of Chicago Press
5801 South Ellis Avenue
Chicago IL 60637-1496
+1-312-702 7700
Fax: +1-312-702 9756
Email: tdb@press.uchicago.edu
Website: http://www.press.uchicago.edu
Found: 1891 ISBN 0-226
Chief exec: Morris Philipson
AS contact: T. David Brent
UK distr: John Wiley & Sons Ltd, 1 Oldlands Way, Bognor Regis PO22 9SA
AS titles: 5 ann, 100 ip
Spec: West African anthropology, history, African music, South African and Tswana studies

MS subm: as above, graduate and
professional level
MS L: 90-120,000w
Edit req: d-s typed, author cv

572 University of Massachusetts Press
505 East Pleasant Street
Amherst MA 01002
+1-413-545 2217
Fax: +1-413-545 1226
Website: http://www.vyne.com/
umasspress/
Found: 1964
ISBN 0-87023; 1-55849
Chief exec: Bruce Wilcox
AS contact: Clark Dougan
UK distr: Eurospan Ltd, 3 Henrietta Street,
London WC2E 8LU
AS titles: 5 ann, 25 ip
Spec: African history and literature as well
as a much larger list in African American
studies
MS L: 300pp
Edit req: standard procedure is to invite
submission of a manuscript only after
receiving an abstract or prospectus, table
of contents, and perhaps one or two
sample chapters

573 University Press of America
4720A Boston Way
Lanham ML 20706
+1-301-459 3366
Fax: +1-301-459 2118
Email: nulrich@univpress.com
Found: 1974 ISBN 0-8191/ 0-7618
Chief exec: James E. Lyons
AS contact: Nancy J. Ulrich
UK distr: Eurospan Ltd, 3 Henrietta Street,
London WC2E 8LU
AS titles: 5 ann, 30 ip
Spec: comparative government. language
studies
MS subm: as above, upper-level university
MS L: 250-300pp

Edit req: send xerox non-returnable copy
for review; laser or CRC ms for
publication

574 University of Washington Press
1326 Fifth Avenue
Suite 555
Seattle WA 98101-2604
+1-206-543 4050
Fax: +1-206-685 3460
Email: uwpord@u.washington.edu
Found: 1902 ISBN 0-295
Chief exec: Pat Soden
AS contact: Naomi B. Pascal
Distr: Trevor Brown Associates, 114-115
Tottenham Court Road, London W1P 0BY
AS titles: 2 ann, 25-30 ip
Spec: art, anthropology, folklore,
environmental studies
MS subm: as above
MS L: 200-350pp d-s (in ms form)
Edit req: d-s, consecutive numbers

575 University of Wisconsin Press
114 North Murray Street
Madison WI 53715-1199
+1-608-262 4928
Fax: +1-608-265 6696
Email: uwiscpress@macc.wisc.edu
Found: 1936 ISBN 0-299
Chief exec: Allen N. Fitchen
AS contact: Rosalie M. Robertson
UK distr: Eurospan Ltd, 3 Henrietta Street,
London WC2E 8LU
AS titles: 2 ann, 80 ip
Spec: history, anthropology, development,
folklore
MS subm: scholarly and trade titles in
African history and anthropology
MS L: 200-450pp (in ms form)
Edit req: proposals or full ms, d-s, may be
submitted

576 Waveland Press Inc
PO Box 400
Prospect Heights IL 60070
+1-847-634 0081
Fax: +1-847-634 9501
Email: info@waveland.com
Found: 1975 ISBN 0-917974; 0-88133
Chief exec: Neil J. Rowe
AS contact: Thomas J. Curtin
AS titles: 4 ann, 20 ip
Spec: college/university level textbooks
and supplement
MS subm: as above
Edit req: submit contents and prospectus
initially

577 Westview Press
5500 Central Avenue
Boulder CO 80301-2877
+1-303-444 3541
Fax: +1-303-449 3356
Website: http://www.hcacademic.com
Found: 1975 ISBN 0-8133
Chief exec: Marcus Boggs
AS contact: Laura Parsons
UK distr: Oxford Publicity Partnership,
12 Hids Copse Road, Cumnor Hill,
Oxford OX2 9JJ
AS titles: 20 ann
Ser: 'African Modernization and
Development', 'Monographs in
Development Anthropology'
Spec: history, politics-society,
international relations, regional security,
development, anthropology, gender
studies, cultural studies
MS subm: as above
MS L: 95-100,000w
Edit req: full guidelines for authors
available on request

**578 Markus Wiener Publishing
Inc**
114 Jefferson Road
Princeton NJ 08540
+1-609-921 1141
Fax: +1-609-921 1140
Email: wiener95@aol.com

Found: 1981 ISBN 1-55876
Chief exec and contact: Markus Wiener
UK distr: B.R.A.D., 244A London Road,
Hadleigh SS7 2DE
AS titles: 4-5 ann, 15 ip
Ser: 'Topics in World History'
Spec: history, literature, African-American
history
MS subm: African history, Islam, Middle
East and Africa, colonialism
MS L: 90-100,000w
Edit req; send letter and sample chapter,
final requirement for ms: hard copy and
disk

579 Winston-Derek Publishers
1722 West End Avenue
Nashville TN 37203
+1-615-321 0535
Fax: +1-615-329 4824
Email: jillmerry@aol.com
Found: 1974 ISBN 1-55523
Chief exec: James W Peebles
AS contact: William Pain
UK distr: Pepukayi Book Distribution
Service, 34 Church Road,
London N17 8AO
AS titles: 5-10 ann, 22 ip
Spec: religion, ancient culture, artefacts,
the African World Order, contemporary
literature
MS subm: children (K-12), fiction, non-
fiction, history, social affairs, African life
(general/college level) religion,
philosophy, education (college level)
MS L: fiction 2-300pp, non-fiction no
limit
Edit req: d-s, typed, title and page number
on each page

580 WorldViews
[formerly Third World
Resources]
464 19th Street
Oakland CA 94612
+1-510-835 4692
Fax: +1-510-835 3017
Email: worldviews@igc.org

Website: http://www.igc.org/worldviews/
Found: 1984
Chief exec: Tom Fenton
AS contact: Mary J. Heffron or Tom
Fenton
Spec: resources in English language,
written, audiovisual, CD-ROM from and
about the African continent; quarterly
review of new resources on Africa and
other Third World regions (*see* **311**)

581 **Yale University Press**
     302 Temple Street
     New Haven CT 06520
+1-203-432 0900
Fax: +1-203-432 2394
Email: yupacq@yalevm.ycc.yale.edu
Website: http://www.yale.edu/yup/
Found: 1908 ISBN 0-300
Chief exec: John Ryden
AS contact: Charles Grench
UK distr: Yale University Press, 23 Pond
Street, London NW3 2PN
AS titles: 2-3 ann, 47 ip
Spec: languages
MS subm: scholarly
MS L: 400pp min (in ms form)
Edit req: covering letter, prospectus,
author's cv, table of contents, sample
chapter, the estimated length of ms,
examples or descriptions of artwork and
total number of illustrations, and the
estimated potential audience for the work

AFRICA

Cameroon

582 **Editions CLEΦ**
     BP 1501
     Yaoundé
+237-223554/232709
Fax: +237-231660
Found: 1963 ISBN 2-7235
Chief exec: Comlan Prosper
AS contact: Ngandu Tshimanga
Europe distr: L'Harmattan, Paris, *see* **481**
Spec: African literature and some
scholarly titles, Christian literature

Côte d'Ivoire

583 **EDILIS, Editions Livres du
     Sud SA**
     10 BP 477
     Abidjan 10
+225-24 46 50
Fax: +225 24 46 51/ 22 59 60
Website: http://www.c.i.refer.org/tur/edic
Found: 1992 ISBN 2-909238
Chief exec: (Mme.) Mical Drehi
Lorougnon,
AS titles: 4 ann, 30 ip
Ser: 'Littérature générale', 'Livres d'art',
'Parascolaire', 'Alphabétisation en français
en langues', 'Préscolaire', 'Livres scolaires'
Spec: all levels, children, adult, teenagers,
poetry, literature, criticism, teaching and
study works
MS subm: all levels from pre-school to
adult
MS L: no preference
Edit req: typed

584 **Editions CEDAΦ**
     Centre d'édition et de
     diffusion africaines
     Immeuble 60
     Logements Plateau
     04 BP 541 Abidjan 04

+225-246510/246511
Fax: +225-250567
Found: 1961 ISBN 2-86394
Chief exec: Venance Kacou
AS contact: Boare Dramane
NA distr: Schoenhof's Foreign Books,
Cambridge, Massachussetts, USA
AS titles: n/a
Spec: scholarly, general and children's

585 **Nouvelles Editions**
   Ivoiriennes, LesΦ
   1 boulevard de Marseille
   01 BP 1818, Abidjan 01
   +225-240766/240825
   Fax: +225-242456
   Found: 1992 ISBN 2-910190
   Chief exec and contact: Guy Lambin
   Spec: educational: primary, secondary,
   tertiary, academic; general trade, African
   literature, children's literature

586 **Presses Universitaires de**
   Côte d'Ivoire†
   Université de Côte d'Ivoire
   BP V334, Abidjan
   +225-448248
   Fax: +225-448248
   Email: poiria@refer.org
   Found: 1964 ISBN 2-7166
   Chief exec and contact: Alain Poiri
   Spec: academic and scholarly

Ethiopia

587 **Addis Ababa University**
   Press
   POB 1176
   Addis Ababa
   +251-1-119148
   Fax: +251-1-550655
   Found: 1968
   Chief exec: Taddesse Tamrat
   AS contact: (Ms) Messelech Habte
   AS titles: ca 3 ann, 8 ip
   Ser: 'Acta Aethiopica'
   Spec: botany, geography, history,

hydrology, languages, literature, and
ornithology
MS subm: as above at tertiary level
MS L: 150-300pp (in printed form)
Edit req: careful assessment by recognised
scholars in the field always required

Ghana

588 **Afram Publications**
   POB M18
   Accra
   +233-21-74248
   Fax: +233-21-778715
   Found: 1973 ISBN 9964-70
   Chief exec and contact: Eric Ofei
   Distr: ABC, *see* **664**
   AS titles: 2 ann, 2 ip
   Spec: music
   MS subm: contemporary African music
   MS L: 40-60,000w
   Edit req: d-s

589 **Anansesem Publications**
   POB 39, TUC Post Office
   Accra
   +233-21-225581
   Fax: +233-21-231390
   Found: 1994 ISBN 9988-552
   Chief exec and contact: Charles Wereko-
   Brobby
   US distr: Anansesem Publications
   4260 via Arbolada # 213
   Los Angeles CA 90042
   Spec: the study and recording of the
   history, culture, scholarship, traditions of
   Africa from within Africa itself.
   MS subm: as above including history,
   economics, media, literature, and
   children's literature
   MS L: consult publisher

590 **Ghana Publishing**
   CorporationΦ
   Publishing Division
   PB Tema
   Accra

+233-281 2921/2521
Found: 1965 ISBN 9964-1
Chief exec: Fuachie Sobreh
AS contact: Yaw Owusu-Kwarteng
Distr: ABC, *see* **664**
AS titles: n/a
Spec: academic and educational, African
literature

591 **Ghana Universities Press**
POB 4219
Accra
+233-21-761051
Fax: +233-21-501930
Email: scs@ug.gn.abc.org
Found: 1962 ISBN 9964-3
Chief exec: K.M. Ganu
AS contact: Linda Tseni
Distr: ABC, *see* **664**
AS titles: 6 ann, 140 ip
Spec: social sciences, history, religion,
African music
MS subm: tertiary, university
MS L: 200pp
Edit req: typed A4 d-s, tables and figures
numbered consecutively, style sheet
available from publisher

592 **Sankofa Educational**
    Publishers
POB C 1234
Cantonments
Accra
+233-21-774107/777866
Fax: +233-21-778839
Found: 1990
Chief exec: Adu Boahen
AS contact: Yaw Aye Odame
Distr: ABC, *see* **664**
AS titles: 2 ip
Spec: African history, textbooks for
schools
MS subm: scholarly, academic works on
Africa, literature and creative writing,
textbooks at tertiary level
MS L: no restriction
Edit req: d-s, typed, ms on disk WP 6.0

593 **Sedco Publishing Ltd**
Sedco House
POB 2051
Accra
+233-21-221332
Fax: +233-21-220107
Found: 1975 ISBN 9964-72
Chief exec: C.K. Segbawu
AS contact: E.K. Sallah
AS titles: 3 ip
Spec: school books, tertiary, and children's
MS subm: educational and tertiary level
texts

594 **Woeli Publishing Services**
POB K601
Accra New Town
+233-21-229294/227182
Fax: +223-21-229294/ 777098
Found: 1984 ISBN 9964-978
Chief exec and contact: Woeli Dekutsey
Distr: ABC, *see* **664**
AS titles: 3 ann, 12 ip
Spec: creative writing (novels, poems,
plays), women's studies, development
studies
MS subm: no restrictions
MS L: 150-300pp
Edit req: typed, disks MS Word or WP

Kenya

595 **Academy Science Publishers**
POB 14798
Nairobi
+254-2-884401-405
Fax: +254-2-884406
Email: aas@arcc.permanet.org
Found: 1989 ISBN 9966-831
Chief exec: Thomas R. Odhiambo
AS contact: Serah W. Mwanycky
Distr: ABC, *see* **664**
AS titles: 2-5 ann, 40+ ip
Spec: science (including social science)
and technology
MS subm: scholarly books at tertiary and
research levels

MS L: no restrictions
Edit req: typed, d-s, for journals apply to
ed for style sheet, for books clear English

596 East African Educational
Publishers Ltd
Mpaka Road
Woodvale Grove
POB 45314
Nairobi
+254-2-444700/445260
Fax: +254-2-448753
Email: hchakava@arso.gn.apc.org
Found: 1965 ISBN 9966-46
Chief exec: Henry Chakava
AS contact: Jimmy Makotsi
Distr: ABC, *see* **664**
AS titles: 5 ann, 80 ip
Spec: literature and literary criticism,
education, law, history (African), political
science and government, theology and
religious studies, sociological and
anthropological studies, population
studies, philosophy (African), economics
and economic development, and health
sciences
MS subm: academic, scholarly levels,
especially on Kenya and East Africa
MS L: 100-200,000w
Edit req: typed, d-s, disk acceptable

597 ICIPE Science Press
International Centre for Insect
Physiology and Ecology
POB 72913
Nairobi
+254-2-442233
Fax: +254-2-442649
Email: icipe-isp@5:7311/30.42
Found: 1988 ISBN 92-9064
Chief exec: Agnes Katama
AS contact: Hans R. Herren
Distr: TMB International, Kent, UK
AS titles: 10 ann 30 ip
Ser: 5 [no details provided]
Spec: tropical agricultural pests, disease
vectors, host-insect relationships,

integrated pest management, commercial
insects, economic entomology
MS subm: tertiary level tropical insect
science, environmental physiology,
regulation of development and
reproduction, chemical ecology, natural
products chemistry, plant resistance,
vector biology, farming of insects
MS L: depends on subject and title
Edit req: papers must have abstract of ca.
200w in English and French, copyright
transferred to ICIPE Science Press, papers
are peer-reviewed

598 Initiatives Ltd
POB 69313
Nairobi
+254-2-569986
Fax: 254-2-565173
Email: acts@arso.sasa.unon.org
Found: 1988 ISBN 9966-42
Chief exec and contact: Elizabeth Larson
Distr: Zed Books *see* **539** (selected titles
only)
AS titles: 3 ann, 45 ip
Ser: 'Ecopolicy', 'Biopolicy', 'Drylands',
'Technology Policy', 'Environmental
Policy'
Spec: environment, especially biodiversity
studies and genetic resources
MS subm: scholarly researched material
MS L: variable ca. 250pp (in printed form)
Edit req: mss reviewed by editorial board,
send synopsis, outline or first chapter
before sending ms

599 Macmillan Kenya
Publishers
POB 30797
Kijabe Street
Nairobi
+245-2-220012/ 224485
Fax: +254-2-212179
Found: 1970 ISBN 9966-885
Chief exec: David N. Muita
AS contact: David Ng'ang'a
Distr: Macmillan Companies and
Associates

AS titles: 5 ann, 35 ip
Ser: 'AIDS Awareness Readers', 'Hadithi
za Kukumbuka'
Spec: literature, creative writing
MS subm: fiction, prose, Kiswahili
language
MS L: 20-150pp
Edit req: typed, d-s

600 Nairobi University Press
University of Nairobi
Jomo Kenyatta Memorial
Library, POB 30197
Nairobi
+254-2-226451/331894
Fax: +254-2-336885
Found: 1984 ISBN 9966-846
Chief exec: F. Karani
AS contact: J. Kimaita Kirimania, Acting
Sec
Distr: ABC, *see* **664**
MS subm: academic
MS L: not restricted
Edit req: typed or computer print out d-s

**601 Oxford University Press
Eastern Africa†**
POB 72532, ABC Place
Waiyaki Way, Westlands
Nairobi
+254-2-226184/339169
Fax: +254-2-443972
Found: 1952 ISBN 9966-19
AS contact: A.M. Fondo
Spec: academic, educational and general

Lesotho

**602 Institute of Southern
African Studies**
The National University of
Lesotho
PO Roma 180
+266-340601/ 340347
Fax: +266-340000/ 340004
Email: isas@nul.ls
Found: 1979 ISBN 99911-31

Chief exec: G. Prasad
AS contact: Janet Nyeko
Distr: ABC, *see* **664**
AS titles: 5 ann, 54 ip
Ser: 'Research Reports', 'Southern African
Studies', 'Working Papers'
Spec: human rights, gender and
environmental studies, Southern African
studies
MS subm: Southern African studies,
gender and environment, tertiary level,
original research or reviews of studies
accomplished
MS L: variable
Edit req: A4, d-s and disk in WP 6.1 or
below, full bibl ref, statement to the effect
it has not been published elsewhere;
request more details from ed

Namibia

**603 Gamsberg Macmillan
Publishers (Pty) Ltd**
19 Faraday Street
POB 22530
Windhoek
+264-61-232165
Fax: +264-61-233538
Found: 1987 ISBN 086848
Chief exec: Herman van Wyk
AS contact: Clare Galloway & Joseph
Auala
Distr: Macmillan, Basingstoke & Colletts,
Solihull, UK
AS titles: 10 ann, 60 ip
Ser: 'Colonial Era Studies' and others
Spec: ecological and environmental
awareness, African fauna and flora,
sociology, history, African literature
MS subm: as above
MS L: 50-300pp (in ms form)
Edit req: disk WP5.1, Pagemaker

604 New Namibia BooksΦ
POB 21601
Windhoek
+264-61-235796/221134
Fax: +264-61-235279

Email: nnb@granny.mac.com.na
ISBN 99916-31
Chief exec and contact: Jane Katjavivi
Distr: ABC, *see* **664**
Spec: academic, educational and children's

605 Out of Africa (Pty) Ltd
POB 21841
Windhoek
+264-61-221494
Fax: +264-61-221270
Found: 1994 ISBN 99916
Chief exec: Wieda Lochner
AS contact: Peter Reiner & Martha
Namuandi
Distr: Macmillan, Basingstoke & Colletts,
Solihull, UK
AS titles: 10 ann, 20 ip
Spec: history of the Royal families,
Owambo ethnic peoples and Caprivi
MS subm: African studies in social
awareness, politics, history
MS L: 40-250pp (in ms form)
Edit req: printed ms & disk WP 5.1 and/or
Pagemaker

Nigeria

606 African Book Builders Ltd
2 Awosika Avenue
UI POB 20222
University of Ibadan
Ibadan, Oyo State
+234-2-810 1113
Found: 1989 ISBN 978-2015
Chief exec: Chris W. Bankole
AS contact: Sherifat Oladokun
AS titles: 10-12 ann, 30 ip
Ser: joint publications with IFRA on
various subjects
Spec: tropical agriculture, agricultural
economics, urban sociology, anthropology,
political science, archaeology, economics
MS subm: intermediate technology,
tropical medicine, African studies,
literature and history
MS L: 50pp min (in printed form)

Edit req: d-s, English or French, disks WP
5.1/6.0

607 Evans Brothers (Nigeria) Publishers Ltd
Jericho Road
POB 5164 Ibadan
Oyo State
+234-22-241 3708/ 241 4287/
241 4394
Fax: +234-22-241 0757
Found: 1966 ISBN 978-167
Chief exec: B.O. Bolodeoku
AS contact: Damola Ifaturoti
UK distr: Evans Brothers Ltd, 12A
Portman Mansions, Chiltern Street,
London W1M 1LE
AS titles: variable, 51 ip
Spec: scholarly/academic works on
African and development studies and
textbooks at tertiary level, also African
literature and creative writing by African
authors
MS subm: as above
MS L: no restrictions
Edit req: d-s, A4

608 Fourth Dimension Publishers Co Ltd
Plot 64A City Layout
PMB 01164 Enugu
Enugu State
+234-42-459969/453739
Fax: +234-42-453298/456904
Email: nwankwov@infoweb.abs.net
Found: 1976 ISBN 978-156
Chief exec: Chief Victor Nwankwo
AS contact: Frank Onwe
Distr: ABC, *see* **664**
AS titles: 30 ann, 100 ip
Ser: 'Nsukka Studies in African Literature'
Spec: African view points
MS subm: scholarly works in law,
literature, African history, social studies,
and children's literature
MS L: 200-300pp (in printed form)

Edit req: ms must be typed d-s, and bound,
or pref on disk MS Word for PC or
Macintosh

609 Heinemann Educational
Books (Nigeria) PlcΦ
1 Ighodaro Road, Jericho
PMB 5205
Ibadan
Oyo State
+234-22-241 2268/241 0943
Fax: +234-22-241 1089/241 3237
Found: 1962 ISBN 978-129
Chief exec: Ayo Ojeniyi
AS contact: Ezekiel M Ojo
Distr: ABC, *see* **664**
Spec: educational, academic, law, African
literature, children's

610 Ibadan University PressΦ
University of Ibadan
PMB 16 UI Post Office
Ibadan, Oyo State
+234-22-8102 0704
Found: 1952 ISBN 978-121
Chief exec and contact: Festus A.
Adesanoye
Distr: ABC, *see* **664**
Spec: academic

611 Malthouse Press LtdΦ
8 Amore Street
Off Toyin Street
Ikeja, Lagos State
+234-1-820358
Fax: +234-1-269 0985
Found: 1985
ISBN 978-023; 978-2601
Chief exec: Dafe Otobo
AS contact: (Mrs) C.O. Oyetunji
Distr: ABC, *see* **664**
Spec: academic, general, children's,
African fiction and poetry

612 Obafemi Awolowo
University Press Ltd†
PMB 004
Obafemi Awolowo University
Ile-Ife, Osun State
+234-36-230284
Found: 1968 ISBN 978-1360
Chief exec: Akin Fatokun
Distr: ABC, *see* **664**
AS titles: 6 ann, 25 ip
Ser: 'Ife History Series'
Spec: African and Third World history
MS subm: as above, tertiary level
MS L: 200-350pp (in ms form)
Edit req: clearly typed, d-s, on quarto
paper, submitted in duplicate

613 Spectrum Books Ltd
Sunshine House
1 Emmanuel Alayande Street
PMB 5612 Ibadan
Oyo State
+234-22-231 2705
Fax: +234-22-231 8502
Email: berkhout@infoweb.abs.net
Found: 1978 ISBN 978-246
Chief exec: Chief Joop Berkhout
AS contact: Tony Igboekwe
Distr: ABC, *see* **664**
AS titles: 2 ann, 30 ip
Spec: democratization, economic, gender
studies, local government matters,
minority group activities
MS subm: as above
MS L:120-300pp (in printed form)
Edit req: high density disk Wordstar 4.0,
WP 5.0, Corel Ventura 4.0 and hard copy

614 University of Lagos Press
POB132
University of Lagos Post
Office
Akoka, Lagos
+234-1-825048
Found: 1978
ISBN 978-2264; 978-017
Chief exec: S. Bodunde Bankole

AS contact: Bukola Olugasa
Distr: ABC, *see* **664**
AS titles: 5 ann, 45 ip
Spec: economics, education, law, business, medicine, language, engineering, social sciences, computer studies
MS subm: as above tertiary level
MS L: n/a
Edit req: typed on A4, d-s

615 University of Port Harcourt Press

East-West Road, Choba
PMB 5323 Port Harcourt
Rivers State
+234-84-300440 ext.376
Found: 1986 ISBN 978-2321
Chief exec: E. J. Alagoa
AS contact: Ozo-Mekuri Ndimele
Distr: ABC, *see* **664**
AS titles: 1 ann, 9 ip
Ser: 'Delta Monograph Series'
Spec: Niger Delta
MS subm: history, archaeology, anthropology, language, commerce, economics, politics, environment
MS L: 30-65pp [?]
Edit req: ms in duplicate d-s printed hard copy and disk

616 Vantage Publishers (Int) Ltd

POB 7669 Secretariat
Ibadan, Oyo State
+234-2-810 0341
Found: 1986 ISBN 978-2458
Chief exec and contact: 'Poju Amori
AS titles: 3 ann, 21 ip
Ser: various series in English and Yoruba
Spec: African languages (Yoruba, Igbo and Hausa), political science, education, philosophy, guidance and counselling
MS subm: educational, fiction, non-fiction, biography, autobiography
MS L: 25-250,000w
Edit req: typed, d-s

Senegal

617 CODESRIA

BP 3304
Dakar
+221-259822/23
Fax: +221-241289
Email: codesria@sonatel.senet.net
Found: 1973 ISBN 2-86978
Chief exec: Achille Mbembe
AS contact: Tade Akin Aina
Distr: ABC (English language titles), *see* **664**; Karthala (French language titles), *see* **482**
AS titles: 10 ann, 65 cs
Ser: 'CODESRIA Book Series', 'CODESRIA Monograph Series'
Spec: social sciences
MS subm: ms must be based on findings of original research which deserve to be accessible to the research community in Africa and elsewhere. The work may be case studies, theoretical debates or both
MS L: variable
Edit req: contact ed for copy of the CODESRIA 'Guidelines for Authors'

618 Nouvelles Editions Africaines du Sénégal, Les

10 rue Amadou Assane Ndoye
BP 260 Dakar
+221-211381
Fax: +221-223604
Found: 1989 ISBN 2-7236
Chief exec: Doudou Ndiaye
AS contact: Mamadou Kassé & Djibril Faye
AS titles: 15 ann, 40 cs
Spec: wish to give opportunities to black African writers in the following fields: academic, educational, general, African literature
MS subm: literature, history, children's literature, school books, economics, law, sport, art
MS L: 100-200pp (in ms form)

Edit req: no specific limitations as long as ms deals with "African realities"

South Africa

619 Jonathan Ball Publishers Φ
[incorporating AD Donker Publisher, Delta Books, Harper Collins SA and Who's Who of Southern Africa]
POB 33977
Jeppestown 2043
+27-11-622 2900
Fax: +27-11-622 7610
Found: 1978 ISBN 86850
Chief exec: Jonathan Ball
AS contact: Francine Blum
Spec: non-fiction, literature, academic and scholarly works, South African history, reference, religious, Africana, business, politics

620 Heinemann Publishers (Pty) Ltd
POB 781940
Sandton 2146
+27-11-784 8619
Fax:+27-11-784 8360
Email: sabeloz@heinemann.cna.co.za
ISBN 1-86853
Chief exec: Kevin Kroeger
AS contact: Sabelo Zulu
Distr: Heinemann International, *see* **552**
AS titles: 30 ann, 150 ip
Ser: 'Adult Readers Collection', 'GAP Books for Teenagers'
Spec: schoolbooks and undergraduate texts in the humanities and social sciences, essays, poetry
MS subm: junior primary to undergraduate tertiary level
MS L: n/a
Edit req: disk, MSWord 7 or equivalent, abstract and summary

621 International Thomson Publishing Southern Africa (Pty) Ltd
POB 2459
Halfway House 1685
+27-11-805 4819
Fax: +27-11-805 3648
Email: lmartini@thrasher.co.za or ewessels@thrasher.co.za
Website: http://www.thomson.co.za
Found: 1995 ISBN 1-86864
Chief exec: Fergus Hall
AS contact: Leanne Martini & Eloise Wessels
Distr: International Thomson Publishing
AS titles: 1/2 ann, 4 ip
Spec: development studies, undergraduate and graduate levels
MS subm: tertiary education from 1st year to 4th/honours
MS L: 2-500pp (in ms form)
Edit req: contact ed for guidelines

622 Juta & Co Ltd
POB 14373
Kenwyn 7790
+27-21-797 5101
Fax: +27-21-762 7424/797 0121
Email: RCooke@juta.co.za
Website: http://www.jutastat.com
Found: 1853 ISBN 0-7021
Chief exec: Richard Cooke
AS contact: Eve Horwitz & Simon Sephton
Distr: B.R.A.D., 244a London Road, Hadleigh SS7 2DE, UK
AS titles: 75 ann, 300 ip
Spec: South African law, business studies, Southern African college texts
MS subm: as above
MS L: 80,000w
Edit req: in first instance submit brief abstract and motivation, plus contents list

623 **Oxford University Press**
POB 1141
Cape Town 8000
+27-21-457266
Fax: +27-21-457265
Email: oxford@oup.co.za
Found: 1915 ISBN 0-1957
Chief exec: Kate McCallum
AS contact: Hanri Pieterse Distr: n/a
AS titles: variable, ca 23 ip
Spec: literature in English & African
languages, public administration,
economics in developing countries,
history, primary health care
MS L: n/a
Edit req: typed or on disk

624 **David Philip Publishers
(Pty) Ltd**
POB 23408
Claremont 7735
+27-21-644136
Fax: +27-21-643358
Email: dpp@iafrica.com
Found: 1971 ISBN 0-86486
Chief exec: David H. Philip
AS contact: Russell Martin
UK distr: Central Books (distributor), *see*
668/Africa Book Centre (agent), *see* **663**
AS titles: 30 ann, 275 ip
Ser: 'The People of Southern Africa',
'Africasouth Paperbacks', 'South African
Archaeological Society Series', 'Mantis
Poets', 'Africasouth Learners Series',
'Africasouth New Writing'
Spec: Southern African history, politics,
sociology, economics, anthropology,
archaeology, religious studies and natural
history; biography, fiction, drama and
poetry; educational texts for pre-school,
primary, secondary and adult learners;
books for the children of Africa
MS subm: all of the above
MS L: n/a
Edit req: ms typed or printed out from
computer disks and d-s, or neatly hand-
written and photocopied; preferably
initially one or two page synopses of

scripts with contents page and sample
chapter

625 **Ravan Press (Pty) Ltd**
POB 145
Randburg 2125
+27-11-789 7636
Fax: +27-11-789 7653
Found: 1972 ISBN 0-86975
Chief exec: G.E. de Villiers
AS contact: Ipuseng Kotsokoane
UK distr: Africa Book Centre, *see* **663**;
NA distr: Ohio University Press, *see* **558**
AS titles: 5 ann, 70 ip
Spec: Southern Africa: history, literature,
children's books, politics, sociology,
labour studies, business studies,
economics
MS L: 450pp max (in ms form)
Edit req: hard copy + disk - MS Word or
WP 5.1

626 **South African Institute of
International Affairs**
POB 31596
Braamfontein 2017
+27-11-339 2021
Fax: +27-11-339 2154
Email: 160mig@cosmos.wits.ac.za
Website: http://www.wits.ac.za/wits/if/
main2.html
Found: 1934 ISBN 1022-0461
Chief exec: Gregory Mills
AS contact: Alan Begg & Elizabeth
Stanley
AS titles: 6 ann, 50 ip
Ser: 'Bibliography Series', 'Yearbook'
(ann), 'Southern Africa Series' (ann)
Spec: emphasis on but not confined to,
Southern Africa region. All aspects:
political security, socio-economic and
environmental. Also research in parallel
areas developmentally: S.E. Asia and Latin
America, relations with EU countries
generally
MS subm: as above
MS L: 7,000w max

Edit req: original work not currently under consideration for publishing elsewhere. To be accompanied by 150w abstract & brief cv. Endnote style. In disk format WP 5.1 ASCII or compatible plus d-s hard copy; alternatively by Email + hard copy

627 University of Cape Town Press (UCT Press)
University of Cape Town
Hiddingh Campus
PB Rondebosch 7700
+27-21-244519 Fax: +27-21-232453
Email: uctpress@hiddingh.uct.ac.za
Website: http://www.uct.ac.za/org/uctpress
Found: 1993 ISBN: 1-919713
Chief exec: Rosemary Meny-Gibert
AS contact: Glenda Younge
AS titles: 1-15 ann, 5 ip
Distr: Africa Book Centre/Global Book Marketing, *see* **663**
Spec: cultural studies, economics and development studies and environmental studies, gender and women's studies, religion and comparative religion
MS subm: as above
MS L: 70-90,000w
Edit req: 3 hard copies of ms, plus indication of extras: index, illustrations, tables and diagrams

628 University of Natal Press
Private Bag X01
Scotsville 3209
+27-331-260 5225
Fax: +27-331-260 5599
Email: books@press.unp.ac.za
Found: 1948 ISBN 0-86980
Chief exec and contact: (Ms) M.P. Moberly
UK distr: Africa Book Centre/Global Book Marketing, *see* **663**
NA distr: I.S.B.S., 5804 NE Hassalo Street, Portland OR 97213-3644, USA
AS titles: 8-10 ann, 70 ip
Ser: 'Killie Campbell Africana Library Manuscript Series', 'Killie Campbell

Africana Library Publications Series', 'Colin Webb Natal and Zululand Series'
Spec: Natal and Zulu people, literature and history, Natal plants, ornithology, South African literature, women's issues
MS subm: as above
MS L: 100,000w

629 Witwatersrand University Press
PO Wits
Johannesburg 2050
+27-11-484 5906-5910
Fax: +27-11-484 5971
Email: wup@iafrica.com
Website: http://www.wits.ac.za/wup.htm/
Found: 1922 ISBN 1-86814
Chief exec: Francoise McHardy
AS titles: Pat Tucker
Distr: Africa Book Centre/Global Book Marketing, *see* **663**
AS titles: 6 ann, 30 ip
Ser: 'Bushman Research Series', 'Cambridge/WUP African Studies Series'
Spec: oral studies, Bushman studies, archaeology, social anthropology, development
AS subm: as above
MS L: 100-500,000w
Edit req: 2 copies, d-s + disks pref WP6 for Windows

Tanzania

630 Dar es Salaam University PressΦ
POB 35182
Dar es Salaam
+255-51-49192
Fax: +255-51-48274
Found: 1979 ISBN 9976-60
Chief exec and contact: N.G. Mwitta
Distr: ABC, *see* **664**
Spec: academic and scholarly

631 **Tanzania Publishing
HouseΦ**
47 Samora Machel Avenue
POB 2138 Dar es Salaam
+255-51-32164/5
Found: 1966 ISBN 9976-1
Chief exec and contact: Primus Isidor
Karugendo
Distr: ABC, *see* **664**
Spec: educational, occasional scholarly
titles

Uganda

632 **Fountain Publishers Ltd**
Fountain House
55 Nkrumah Road
POB 488
Kampala
+256-41-259163/251112
Fax: +256-41-251160
Email: jamest@imul.com
Found: 1988 ISBN 9970-02
Chief exec and contact: James Tumusiime
Distr: ABC, *see* **664**
AS titles: 10 ann, 50 ip
Ser: 'Ugandans in History', 'Our Heritage',
'East African Studies'
Spec: politics, development issues, history,
education, fiction
MS subm: children's books, general,
scholarly
MS L: 4-10,000w
Edit req: hard copy and disk

Zambia

633 **University of Zambia Press**
University of Zambia
POB 32379 Lusaka
+260-1-293580 ext.1379
Fax: +260-1-253952
Email: press@admin.unza.zm
Website: http://www.unza.zm
Found: 1938 ISBN 9982-03
Chief exec: (Ms) Monde Sifuniso
AS contact: Samuel Kasankha

AS titles: 2 ann, 43 ip
Ser: 'Zambian Papers'
Spec: social research in Africa, especially
in sociology and social anthropology,
psychology, economics, human geography
and demography, history and political
science
MS subm: as above
MS L: 10,000w max
Edit req: 3 copies + disk, d-s, contact ed
for house style

Zimbabwe

634 **Anvil PressΦ**
POB 4209
Harare
+263-4-751202/ 739681
Fax: +263-4-751202
Found: 1987 ISBN 0-7974
Chief exec: Paul Brickhill
AS contact: Felix Nyabadza
Spec: development-oriented books,
academic and children's

635 **Baobab Books**
An imprint of Academic
Books (Pvt) Ltd
4 Conald Road
Graniteside
POB 567 Harare
+263-4-755035/755036
Fax: +263-4-759052
Found: 1988 ISBN 0-908311
AS contact: Irene Staunton
Distr: ABC, *see* **664**
AS titles: 3 ann, 30 ip
Spec: tertiary, children's and new fiction
from Zimbabwe and region
MS subm: as above
MS L: 50-75,000w
Edit req: d-s, typed, preferably with back-
up disk

636 **College Press Publishers**
     (Pvt) Ltd
     POB 3041
     Harare
     +263-4-754145/754255
     Fax: +263-4-754146
     ISBN 0-86925; 1-77900
     Chief exec: Ben Mugabe
     AS contact: Mazvita Patricia Madondo
     AS titles: 4-5 ann, 50 ip
     Spec: teacher education, historical and
     popular reference, political/topical issues,
     African literature
     MS subm: all areas/levels although little
     tertiary/highly specialized materials i.e.
     theses
     MS L: 250pp min
     Edit req: typed, d-s, author must retain
     copy, min 3 months for full assessment,
     Macintosh disk Pagemaker 5/6 or
     Windows 5

637 **Longman Zimbabwe**
     Publishers (Pvt) Ltd
     POB ST125
     Southerton
     Harare
     +263-4-621611-617
     Fax: +263-4-621670
     Email: cs@longman.co.zw
     Found: 1964 ISBN 1-77903
     Chief exec: Nda Dlodlo
     AS contact: C. Sithole
     AS titles: 35 ann, 700 ip
     Ser: 'Zimbabwe Writers Series'
     Spec: primary and secondary level
     textbooks; novels, plays, poems, historical
     works; children's literature
     MS subm: primarily areas above by
     Zimbabwean authors
     MS L: 200pp max
     Edit req: typewritten ms preferred,
     accompanied by a synopsis and note on
     author

638 **Mambo Press†**
     Senga Road
     POB 779
     Gweru
     +263-54-4016/4017
     Fax: +263-54-51991
     Found: 1958 ISBN 0-86922
     Chief exec: L. Fischer
     AS contact: Vonai B. Paradza
     UK distr: Africa Book Centre, *see* **663**
     AS titles: 6 ann, 70 ip
     Spec: history, anthropology, development
     studies, cooperatives, missiology
     MS subm: as above
     MS L: 25-30,000w
     Edit req: typed, d-s, ms accepted, typed on
     one side only

639 **Southern Africa Printing**
     and Publishing
     House/SAPES TrustΦ
     POB 111
     Mount Pleasant
     Harare
     +263-4-727875/790815
     Fax: +263-4-732735
     Email: sapes@mango.apc.org
     Found: 1988 ISBN 0-7905
     Chief exec: Ibbo Mandaza
     AS contact: Jonathan Kadye
     Distr: ABC, *see* **664**
     Spec: academic, socio-economic, political
     economy

640 **Southern African Research**
     and Documentation Centre
     POB 5690
     Harare
     Zimbabwe
     +263-4-738695/6
     Fax: +263-4-738693
     Chief exec: Phyllis Johnson
     AS contact: Patience Zonge
     Distr: ABC, *see* **664**
     AS titles: 2 ann, 2 ip
     Spec: research, analysis and dissemination
     of information on social, political,

economic and cultural issues in the
Southern African region
MS subm: invites ms on social, political
and economic issues when we need
contributions to book chapters
MS L: 10-12,000w for book chapter

641 University of Zimbabwe
PublicationsΦ
POB MP 203
Mount Pleasant
Harare
+263-4-303211 ext.1236
Fax: +263-4-333407/3352249
Email: uzpub@esanet.zw
Found: 1972 ISBN 0-908307
Chief exec: vacant (Director of
Publications)
Distr: ABC, *see* **664**
Spec: academic and scholarly

642 Zimbabwe Publishing
House (Pvt) Ltd
POB 350
Harare
+263-4-497548-558
Fax: +263-4-497554
Found: 1981 ISBN 0-9449932
Chief exec: David Martin
AS contact: Sam Mtetwa,
Promise Mojo & Ellen Mtetwa
Distr: ABC, *see* **664**
AS titles: 20 ann, 200 ip
Ser: 'African Writers', 'African History'
Spec: political history of southern Africa,
literature
MS subm: as above, primary, secondary
and tertiary levels
MS L: 100,000w
Edit req: typed ms, d-s; full list of
copyright material used with title and
publisher of original work; if permission
already granted, letter from copyright
holders

VI. DEALERS AND DISTRIBUTORS OF AFRICAN STUDIES MATERIALS

This is a 'names & numbers' listing of the principal dealers, booksellers and distributors of African studies material in Europe, North America and a small number in Africa. Many of those listed also stock CDs and cassettes, posters, arts and crafts, prints, etc. The list includes a number of general booksellers and retailers holding sizeable stocks of Africana, either new or antiquarian.

Entries marked with a † dagger symbol are unverified, and we have been unable to verify whether these dealers are still trading and/or currently stocking African studies materials.

EUROPE AND NORTH AMERICA

Austria

643 **Shakespeare & Co Booksellers**
Sterngasse 2
A-1010 Vienna
+43-1-535 505311
Fax: +43-1-535 503316

Belgium

644 **Librairie des Etangs**
319 Chaussée d'Ixelles
B-1050 Brussels
+32-2-646 9786
Fax: +32-2-646 9473
International bookshop which carries stocks of books by African authors.

Canada

645 **L'Harmattan Inc**
55 Saint-Jacques
Montréal, Quebec H2Y 1K9
+1-514-286 9048

Fax: +1-514-286 8267
Canadian branch of the Paris bookseller and publisher (*see* **481, 650**).

646 **Liberation Books Inc†**
2015 Drummond Street
Montréal, Quebec H3G 1W7
+1-514-287 9739

647 **Three World Plus**
65 Rutherford Avenue
POB 2033 Deep River
Ontario K0J 1P0
+1-613-687 8322

Denmark

648 **ALOA. Centre for Literature from Africa, Asia, Latin America and Oceania**
Bakkegårds Allé 9 kld
D-1804 Frederiksberg C
+45-31-310900 Fax: +45-31-310900
Mainly stocks literary titles. Catalogues issued.

France

649 Elliot Klein SARL†
47 rue Saint-André-des Arts
F-75006 Paris
Antiquarian only; mainly ethnology.

650 L'Harmattan Edition-Diffusion
16 rue des Ecoles
F-75005 Paris
also at:
7 rue de l'Ecole
Polytechnique
F-75005 Paris
+33-1-43 26 04 52/43 54 79 10
Fax: +33-1-43 25 82 03
The leading bookshop in France with the most extensive stocks of African materials, both in French and in English. Regular catalogues issued. Branch in Montréal (*see* **645**)

651 Librairie Présence Africaine
25 bis rue des Ecoles
F-75005 Paris
+33-1-43 54 15 88
Fax: +33-1-43 25 96 67
Long established specialist bookshop in the heart of Paris' Quartier Latin district.

Germany

652 Books on African Studies†
Jerry Bedu-Addo
Postfach 1224
D-6905 Schriesheim
+49-6203-62976
Specialist dealer in Germany, with stocks of some 2,000 items in English and in German.

653 Buchhandlung Fremde Welten
Konstantin von Harder
Müllerstrasse 43
D-80469 Munich
+49-89-260 5916

654 Das Arabische Buch
Horstweg 2
D-14059 Berlin
+49-30-322 8523
Fax: +49-30-322 5183
Specializes in books in the social sciences on the Middle East, Asia and Africa. Publishes regular catalogues.

655 Galerie Marisuto. Afrika Buch- und Kunsthandlung
Brüsselerstrasse 5
D-50674 Cologne
+49-221-923 2884
Fax: +49-221-923 2886
New African bookshop and art gallery which opened in Cologne in 1996.

656 Versandbuchhandlung Volker Bauch
Wehrstrasse 28
D-04639 Gössnitz
+49-34493-30944
Fax: +49-34493-30944
Specialist in African and Latin American literatures. Catalogues issued.

Netherlands

657 Erasmus Antiquariaat en Boekhandel
POB 19140
NL-1000 GC Amsterdam
+31-20-627 6952
Fax: +31-20-620 6799
Carries stocks of both new and antiquarian titles.

658 Houtschild International Booksellers
POB 30716
NL-2500 The Hague
+31-70-360 7889
Fax: +31-70-361 5355

659 **W. J. van Hoogstraten, BV**
     Boekhandel
     98 Noordeinde
     NL-23145 The Hague
     +31-70-365 2845

Norway

660 **Narvesen Distribution**
     Bertrand Narvesens Vei 2
     Postboks 6219 Etterstad
     N-0602 Oslo
     +47-2257 3010
     Fax: +47-2268 2465

Portugal

661 **Livraria Académica**
     rua Martires da Liberdade 10
     P-4050 Porto
     +351-2-005988
     Fax: +351-2-315373
     Leading Africana dealer in Portugal;
     mostly antiquarian. Regular catalogues
     issued.

662 **Livraria Historica e**
     Ultramarina Lda†
     Travessa da Queimada 28-1°
     P-1200 Lisbon
     +351-1-36 85 89

United Kingdom

663 **The Africa Book Centre Ltd**
     38 King Street
     London WC2E 8JT
     (Also trading as Global Book Marketing)
     +44(0)171-240 6649/836 3020
     Fax: +44(0)171-497 0309
     Email: africabooks@dial.pipex.com
     The major retail outlet in the UK for
     African books, at a central London
     location just off Covent Garden. Carries a
     stock of some 6,000 books - including
     extensive stocks of African-published
     material - as well as CDs, cassettes,
     magazines and some newspapers.
     Information on new titles is published in
     the quarterly *Africa Book Centre Book
     Review* (£12 annually in the UK, £18
     elsewhere); also issues specialist lists, and
     provides a mail order service. The Africa
     Book Centre acts as distributor or agent
     for the following publishers (those
     *asterisked are distributed by Central
     Books Ltd. *see* **668**)
     Africa Refugee Publishing Collective, UK;
     African Research and Information Bureau,
     UK; African Rights, UK; Bayreuth African
     Studies, Germany; *Camerapix, Nairobi;
     *Environmental Policy & Society (EPOS),
     Sweden; *Haan Publishers, UK &
     Somalia; *Human Rights Watch, USA; IC
     Publications, UK; *Indicator Press, South
     Africa; *Interkont, Finland; Ithemba!
     Publishing, South Africa; *Kwela Books,
     South Africa; Mambo Press, Zimbabwe;
     Maskew Miller Longman, South Africa;
     Mayibuye Centre, South Africa; Mosuro
     Publishers, Nigeria; *David Philip, South
     Africa; Phuthadikobo Museum, Botswana;
     *Ian Randle Publishers, Jamaica; *Ravan
     Press, South Africa (selected titles only);
     Ring Road Publishers, UK; *Scandinavian
     Institute of African Studies, Sweden;
     Selwyn Publishers, Ghana; Third World
     Publishing, Zimbabwe; Three Continents
     Press, USA; *University of Cape Town
     Press; *University of Natal Press, South

Africa; University of the Western Cape, South Africa; Vita, UK; *Witwatersrand University Press, South Africa.

664 African Books Collective Ltd
The Jam Factory
27 Park End Street
Oxford OX1 1HU
+44(0)1865-726686
Fax: +44(0)1865 793298
Email: abc@dial.pipex.com
Website: http://www.sas.upenn.edu/
African_Studies/Publications/ABC_Menu.
html (*see also* **177**)
Founded in 1989, African Books Collective is a major self-help initiative by a group of African publishers to promote their books in Europe, North America, and in Commonwealth countries outside Africa. It is collectively owned by its founding member publishers. From an initial 17 founder member publishers in 1989, membership has grown rapidly and ABC now provides a single source of supply for the books from 50 African publishers, with a stock inventory of over 1,700 titles. A wide range of catalogues are issued, including a 64pp. catalogue of new titles which is published twice yearly, catalogues of multicultural materials, and a series of subject catalogues which are regularly updated and reissued. Standing Order plans for libraries. A full list of ABC member publishers follows:
Academy Science Publishers, Kenya; Afram Publications, Ghana; Africa Christian Press, Ghana; Africa Community Publishing & Development Trust, Zimbabwe; African Council for Communication Education, Kenya; Baobab Books, Zimbabwe; Bookcraft Ltd, Nigeria; Buchu Books, South Africa; Council for the Development of Social Science Research in Africa (CODESRIA), Senegal; Dar es Salaam University Press, Tanzania; East African Educational Publishers, Kenya; Editions de l'Océan Indien, Mauritius; Environmental Development Action in the Third World

(ENDA), Senegal; Foundation for Education with Production, Botswana; Fountain Publishers, Uganda; Fourth Dimension Publishing Co. Ltd, Nigeria; Freedom Publications, Ghana; Ghana Publishing Corporation, Ghana; Ghana Universities Press, Ghana; Heinemann Educational Books (Nigeria) plc, Nigeria; Ibadan University Press, Nigeria; Institute of Southern African Studies, National University of Lesotho, Lesotho; Malthouse Press Ltd, Nigeria; Mkuki na Nyota Publishers, Tanzania; Multimedia Zambia, Zambia; Nairobi University Press, Kenya; New Horn Press Ltd, Nigeria; New Namibia Books (Pty) Ltd, Namibia; Nigerian Institute of International Affairs, Nigeria; Obafemi Awolowo University Press, Nigeria; Sankofa Educational Publishers, Ghana; Sankore Publishers; Nigeria; Saros International Publishers; Nigeria; Skotaville Publishers, South Africa; Southern Africa Printing and Publishing House/SAPES Trust, Zimbabwe; Southern African Research and Documentation Centre (SARDC), Zimbabwe; Spectrum Books Ltd, Nigeria; Tanzania Commission for Science and Technology, Tanzania; Tanzania Publishing House, Tanzania; University of Lagos Press, Nigeria; University of Maiduguri Press, Nigeria; University of Nigeria Press, Nigeria; University of Port Harcourt Press, Nigeria; University of Zimbabwe Publications; University Press plc, Nigeria; Woeli Publishing Services, Ghana; Zimbabwe Book Publishers Association, Zimbabwe; Zimbabwe Publishing House, Zimbabwe; Zimbabwe Women Writers, Zimbabwe.

665 BAC Bookshop
Lavender Hill, Battersea
London SW11 5TF
+44(0)171-223 6557
Black writers/fiction, children's, and women's studies.

666 **B.H. Blackwell Ltd**
50 Broad Street
Oxford OX1 3EL
+44(0)1865-792792
Fax: +44(0)1865-794143
Oxford's famous bookshop. Has a good
(though declining) Africana section with
stocks of about 600 titles.

667 **Bookmarks**
265 Seven Sisters Road
Finsbury Park
London N4 2DE
+44(0)181-802 6145
Fax: +44(0)181-802 3835
Socialist bookshop in North London; also
mail order service.

668 **Central Books Ltd**
99 Wallis Road
London E9 5LN
+44(0)181-986 4854
Fax: +44(0)181-533 5821
This is not a retail operation, but this firm
distributes a number of African and
African studies publishers for which the
Africa Book Centre Ltd act as agents. (*see*
Africa Book Centre, entry **663** for names
of publishers).

669 **Centreprise Bookshop**
136 Kingsland High Street
London E8 2NS
+44(0)171-254 9632
Fax: +44(0)171-923 1951
Community bookshop with a large stock
of black fiction and non-fiction.

670 **Dillons Bookstore**
82 Gower Street
London WC1E 6EQ
+44(0)171-6363 3435
Fax: +44(0)171-580 7680
Approximately 500 Africana titles held in
stock; also some African news magazines.

671 **Francis Edwards**
The Old Cinema
Castle Street
Hay-on-Wye HR3 5DF
+44-(0)1497 820071
Fax: +44(0)1497-821004
Antiquarian and secondhand; mostly
travel, natural history and ethnography.

672 **W. & G. Foyle**
113-119 Charing Cross Road
London WC2H 0EB
+44(0)171-437 6807
Fax: +44(0)171-434 1580
This huge and famous bookshop in the
centre of London has a good selection of
African studies titles.

673 **Frontline Books**
1 Newton Street, Piccadilly
Manchester M1 1HW
+44(0)161-236 1101
Fax: +44(0)161-236 1103
Manchester's alternative bookshop;
specialists in feminist, socialist, black, and
Third World books.

Global Book Marketing, *see* Africa
Book Centre Ltd **663**

674 **Halewood & Sons**
68 Friargate
Preston PR1 2AT
+44(0)1772-252 2603
Antiquarian and secondhand; specialists in
maps, atlases and travel books.

675 **Heffers Booksellers**
20 Trinity Street
Cambridge CB2 3NG
+44(0)1223-358351
Fax: +44(0)1223-410464
Major bookshop, carrying about 800
Africana titles.

676 Heritage Books & Consultancy
52 Topsfield Parade
Tottenham Lane, Crouch End
London N8 8PT
+44(0)181-347 6463
Fax: +44(0)181-340 2120
Booksellers and library suppliers, and
specialists in multicultural books.

677 Hogarth Representation
1 Birchington Court
Birchington Road
London N8 8HS
+44(0)181-341 6570
Fax: +44(0)-341 0284
Email: 100265,51@compuserve.com
Largely a library supplier, and one of the
leading blanket order/approval plan
dealers for African imprints, including
government and official publications and
'grey' literature. Also offers a search
service. Extensive range of lists and
catalogues issued.

678 Independent Bookshop
69 Surrey Street
Sheffield S1 21H
+44(0)114-273 7722
Stock mostly on literature and politics.

679 Index Bookcentre
10/12 Atlantic Road
Brixton
London SW9 8HY
+44(0)171-274 8342
Areas of specialization include Third
World and Afro-Caribbean.

680 Multicultural Book Shop
Rashid House
Westgate
Bradford BD1 3AA
+44(0)1274 731908
Fax: +44(0)1274 390176
Carries stocks over over 3,000 titles on
Asia, Africa, and the Caribbean.
Catalogues issued.

681 New Beacon Books
76 Stroud Green Road
London N4 3EN
+44(0)171-272 4889
Fax: +44(0)171-281 4662
Website: http://www.newbeacon-
books.com/new.htm
Extensive stocks of ca. 20,000 titles
covering fiction and non-fiction
from/about Africa, the Caribbean, Afro-
America and Black Britain. New Beacon
Books are the joint organizers of the
International Book Fair of Radical Black
and Third World Books, held biennially in
London, usually in March.

682 Oriental and African Books
4 Kingsland Court
26 Kennedy Road
Shrewsbury SY3 7AB
+44(0)1743-352575
Fax: +44(0)1743-354699
Antiquarian only. Issues catalogues of out-
of-print books on Africa.

**683 Pepukayi Book Distribution
Services**
34 Church Road
London N17 8AQ
+44-(0)181-801 0205
Fax: +44(0)-181-801 0205
Distributors and wholesalers of books by,
for and about Black/African people
worldwide.

**684 Arthur Probsthain Oriental
Bookseller**
41 Great Russell Street
London WC1B 3PH
+44(0)171-636 1096
Fax: +44(0)171-636 1096
Long established firm specializing in
Oriental and African studies, both new and
antiquarian books. Catalogues issued.

685 **Raddle Bookshop**
70 Berners Street
Leicester LE2 0AF
+44(0)116-262 4875
Fax: +44(0)116-2624875
Large number of titles stocked, with on-approval service for libraries, multicultural centres and community organizations.

686 **Sceptre Books Ltd**
257 High Street
Walthamstow
London E17 7BH
+44(0)181-521 3669
Fax: +44(0)181-521 8313
Areas of specialization include children's and multicultural books, Black and ethnic writing, women's studies, atlases and travel.

687 **Silver Moon Women's Bookshop**
64-68 Charing Cross Road
London WC2H 0HB
+44(0)171-836 7906
Fax: +44(0)171-379 1018
Prominent women's bookstore in the centre of London, which has a large Black and Asian writers section.

688 **Soma Books Ltd**
Independent Publishing Company
38 Kennington Lane
London SE11 4LS
+44(0)171-735 2101
Stocks especially strong on creative writing and children's books.

689 **Harriet Tubman Bookshop**
27-29 Grove Lane
Handsworth
Birmingham B21 9ES
+44(0)121-554 8479
Many titles on black and African/Caribbean studies and Black Britain.

690 **Rowland Ward's**
at Holland & Holland Ltd
33 Bruton Street
London W1Y 8JS
+44(0)171 499 4411
Fax: +44(0)171 499 4544
Antiquarian only.

691 **Wycliffe Associates**
23 Armorial Road
Coventry CB3 6GH
+44(0)1203-414676
Antiquarian, mainly linguistics, anthropology and African missionary history.

Trinidad & Tobago

692 **Places, Peoples & Perspectives**
Bookshop
PO Box 511 Port of Spain
Trinidad
+1-809-663 9708
Fax: +1-809-663 9708
New, and the only, bookstore in Trinidad and Tobago which specializes in African books. Also sells CDs and audio cassettes.

United States

693 **African American Book Center†**
7524 South Cottage Grove Avenue, POB 730
Chicago IL 60619
+1-312-651 0070
Part of the Institute of Positive Education.

694 **African Imprint/Caribbean Imprint Library Services**
POB 350
55 Ridgeview Drive
Falmouth MA 02574
+1-508-540 5378
Fax: +1-508-548 6801
Email: ailscils@sprintmail.com
Website: http://www.africanbooks.com

Primarily library supplier and blanket order dealer for virtually all printed materials published anywhere in Africa, including government and official publications and more elusive material. Numerous lists issued.

695 **Bennett-Penvenne Livros,**
Books & Pamphlets on Africa & the Portuguese & Spanish Worlds
162 Oak Street
Duxbury MA 02332
Email: bennett@pcix.com
Extensive stocks on lusophone Africa. Catalogues issued.

696 **Larry W. Bowman Bookseller**
458 Middle Turnpike
Storrs CT 06268
+1-203-486 3355
Email: bowman@uconnvm.uconn.edu
Antiquarian, especially books, maps and prints on the Indian Ocean islands. Catalogues issued.

697 **Ethnographic Arts Publications**
1040 Erica Road
Mill Valley CA 94941
+1-415-383 2998
Mostly books on African art, artefacts, material culture.

698 **Firebird Distributing**
1945 P Street
Eureka CA 95501
+1-707-444 1434

699 **The Foreign Book Service**
POB 649
Falmouth MA 02541
+1-508-540 7147
Fax: +1-508-540 7755
Email: foreignbks@aol.com
Supplier of African-published materials; blanket order plans; lists issued.

700 **Shelley Higgins**
Promoting Trade with Africa
12021 Wilshire Boulevard
792
Los Angeles CA 90025
+1-310-828 3321
Fax: +1-310-829 6383

701 **Livres de l'Afrique Centrale**
1531 Walnut Street
Berkeley CA 94709
+1-510-841 6732
Email: wdrake@sirius.com
Supplies publications from Zaire and Congo-Brazzaville. Catalogues issued.

702 **McBlain Books**
POB 5062
Hamden CT 06518
+1-203-281 0400
Email: mcblain@pcnet.com
Scarce and rare books on sub-Saharan Africa. Catalogues issued.

703 **Malikah's Books, Plus**
POB 2063
Mount Vernon NY 10550
+1-212-234 7238

704 **New Leaf Distributing Company**
5425 Tulane Drive SW
Atlanta GA 30336-2323
+1-404-691 6996

705 **Océanie-Afrique-Noire**
15 West 39th Street 2nd floor
New York NY 10018-3806
+1-212-840 8844

706 **T'Olodumare Bookstore†**
2440 Durant Avenue
Berkeley CA 94704
Mailing address:
POB 32386
Oakland CA 94604

+1-415-843 3088
Specialists in African literature; also CDs, videos, prints, etc.

707 **Simon Ottenberg, Bookseller**
POB 15509
Wedgwood Station
Seattle WA 98115
+1-206-322 5398
Antiquarian only, especially African art, history, ethnography, travel. Catalogues issued.

708 **Red Sea Press, Inc**
11 Princess Road, Suite D
Lawrenceville NJ 08648
+1-609-844 9583
Fax: +1-609-844 0198
Subsidiary of Africa World Press (*see* **542**). Both publishers and distributors of Third World books.

709 **Revolution Books†**
9 West 19th Street
New York NY 10011-4224
+1-212-691 3345
Strong on books on Marxism-Leninism and Black liberation/ Women's oppression and liberation; also international periodicals.

710 **Gerald Rilling**
720 Colonial Drive
Rockford IL 61115-3716
+1-815-654 0389
Antiquarian, especially East African.

711 **Smithsonian Institution
Museum Shops**
Capitol Gallery Building
Suite no. 298B
600 Maryland Avenue
Washington DC 20560
+1-703-603 6041
Fax: +1-202-287 3080
Stocks mainly on African art and culture, including books for young readers; also

records, CDs, and cassettes of African music, and jewellery and craft items.

712 **Women Ink**
777 UN Plaza 3rd floor
New York NY 10017
+1-212-687 8633
Fax: +1-212-661 2704
Email: wink@igc.apc.org
Distributes resources on women and development from 70 publishers worldwide, including African-published material. Catalogues issued.

713 **Worldwide Antiquarian**
POB 391
Cambridge MA 02141
+1-617-876 6220
Antiquarian only. Specialists in books on travel concerning the Middle East, Africa and Asia. Catalogues issued.

Some UK & US distributors and dealers of non-print materials

United Kingdom

714 **The African Video Centre Ltd**
7 Balls Pond Road
Dalston
London N1 4AX
+44(0)171-923 4224
Fax: +44(0)171-275 0112
Email: 100675,3321@compuserve.com
Website: http://ourworld.compuserve.com/homepages/African Video Centre
Specializes in the wholesale and retail of videos by, for, and about the African community. Lists issued for sale by mail order. Also rental service.

715 **Concord Video and Film
     Council**
     201 Felixstowe Road
     Ipswich IP3 9BJ
     +44(0)1473-715754/76012
     A major distributor in the UK of films and
     videos about Africa.

716 **Stern's**
     74-75 Warren Street
     London W1P 5PA
     Shop at:
     293 Euston Road
     London NW1 3AD
     +44(0)171-387 5550
     Fax: +44(1)-388 2756
     London's major specialist and stockist
     of African music, contemporary and
     traditional (CDs, cassettes, as
     well as videos). Vast stocks, also
     including Latin American and other
     world music. Mail order service.

United States

717 **African Diaspora Images**
     POB 3517
     Brooklyn NY 11202
     +1-718-852 8353

718 **African Family Films**
     903 Pacific Avenue
     Suite 307A
     Santa Cruz CA 95060
     +1-408-426 3133
     Fax: +1-408-457 1333
     Email: africa@webcom.com
     Website: http://www.webcom.com/africa/
     Major media production company
     distributing films and videotapes about
     Africa.

719 **African Record Center
     Distributors†**
     1194 Nostrand Avenue
     Brooklyn NY 11225

+1-212-493 4500
Extensive selection of African records,
both traditional and contemporary.

720 **California Newsreel/Library of
     African Cinema**
     149 Ninth Street Suite 420
     San Francisco CA 94102
     +1-415-621 6196
     Fax: +1-415-621 6522
     Email: newsreel@ix.netcom.com
     Non-profit educational organization
     producing and distributing films on Africa.

721 **First Run/Icarus Films**
     153 Waverly Place 6th floor
     New York NY 10014
     +1-212-727 1711
     Fax: +1-212-989 7649
     Email: frif@echonyc.com
     Website: http://www.echonyc.com/frif/

722 **Multicultural Media**
     RR3, Box 6655
     Granger Road
     Barre VT 05641
     +1-802-223 1294
     Fax: +1-802-229 1834
     Videos, audio, CD-ROMs and books
     on music and dance from around
     the world, including Africa.

723 **Mypheduh Films, Inc**
     POB 10035
     Washington DC 20018-0035
     +1-202-289 6677
     Fax: +1-202-289 4477

724 **New Yorker Films**
     16 West 61st Street
     New York NY 10023
     +1-212-247 6110
     Fax: +1-212-307 7855

AFRICA

Listed below are a select number of booksellers and distributors *in* Africa who may be willing to handle mail orders from overseas for locally published material. (In most cases this will require pre-payment).

For a more comprehensive and fully annotated (though now somewhat dated) listing of some 400 booksellers throughout Africa, consult the appropriate sections in *The African Book World & Press: A Directory/ Répertoire du livre et de la presse en Afrique (see* **63**).

Angola

725 **Instituto Nacional do Livro e do Disco**
Rua Cirilo de Conceição
Silva no. 7-3°
CP 1248
Luanda
+244-31544

Botswana

726 **Botswana Book Centre**
The Mall
POB 91
Gaborone
+267-352931
Well-stocked general bookshop in
Gaborone's central shopping precinct.
Stock guides and catalogues issued.

727 **Southern African Literature Society**
PB 00149
Gaborone
+267-373025 Fax: +267-313228
Specialist supplier of Southern African
materials; catalogues issued.

Cameroon

728 **Librairie Editions CLE†**
BP 1501
Yaoundé
+237-223554

729 **Les Nouvelles Librairies Papeteries Plus**
BP 11422
Yaoundé
+237-223566 Fax: +237-223566

Côte d'Ivoire

730 **Edicom SA**
16 BP 466
Abidjan 16
+225-411193 Fax: +225-417711
(also at: Edicom's Library Service
1325 Quincy Street NW,
Washington DC 20011, USA)
Distributor of francophone African-
published materials to libraries and other
book buyers in the countries in the North.

731 **Librairie de France**
avenue Chardy
BP 228
Abidjan 01
+225-211518 Fax: +225-211278

732 **Librairie Générale Pociello†**
01 BP 1757
Abidjan 01
+225-211565

Egypt

733 **Al-Arab Bookshop†**
28 Faggalah Street
Cairo
+20-908025

734 **Anglo-Egyptian Bookshop†**
165 Sharia Mohamed Bey
Farid Cairo
+20-914337

735 **Lehnert and Landrock†**
44 Sharif Street
POB 1013
Cairo
+20-755324

Ethiopia

736 **Ethiopia Book Centre†**
King George Street
POB 1024
Addis Ababa
+251-1-554404

Gabon

737 **Librairie le Phénix**
BP 4102
Libreville
+241-740746

Ghana

738 **Epp Books Services**
POB 44 TUC
Accra
Fax: +233-21-779099

739 **Omari Bookshop**
POB 4221
Accra
+223-21-776212
Good range of African stocks.

740 **University Bookshop**
University of Ghana
University Square
POB 1 Legon
+223-21-500398
Fax: +223-21-500774
Extensive stocks of books on, or about Ghana.

Kenya

741 **Africa Book Services (EA) Ltd†**
Quran House
Mfangano Street
POB 45245
Nairobi
+254-2-23641

742 **Alliance Marketing and Media Services Ltd**
Barot House
Kijabe Street
POB 25936
Nairobi
+254-2-246431/338847
Fax: + 254-2-246430
Wholesaler, and distributor of books published in Kenya.

743 **Binti Legacy Bookshop and Distributors**
POB 68077
Nairobi
+254-2-245687 Fax: +254-2-561654
Email: binti@elci.gn.apc.org
A 'Development Bookshop' distributing books, self-help manuals, videos and tapes.

744 **Inter-Africa Book Distributors**
POB 73580
Nairobi
Fax: +254-2-213025

745 **Text Book Centre Ltd**
Kijabe Street
POB 47540
Nairobi
+254-330340/-45
Fax: +254-2-225779
Kenya's largest bookshop with extensive stocks.

Lesotho

746 **Mazenod Book Centre†**
POB 39
Mazenod 190

Madagascar

747 **Librairie de Madagascar**
36 Araben ny Fahaleovantena
BP 402
Antananarivo
+261-2-22454
Long-established bookshop with broad selection of titles about the island.

748 **Librairie Mixte†**
37 bis ave du 26 juin 1960
BP 3204
Antananarivo 101
+261-2-25130

Malawi

749 **Central Bookshop**
POB 264
Blantyre
+265-635447 Fax: +265-636863
Large bookshop in central Blantyre with good selection of stocks about the country.

Mauritius

750 **Librairie Allot Limitée†**
Les Arcades Currimjee
Curepipe
+230-61253

751 **Librairie Trèfle**
BP 183
Port Louis
+230-212 1106
Long-established book store with good selection of locally published material.

Mozambique

752 **Instituto Nacional do Livro e do Disco**
Avenida 24 de Julho 1921
CP 4030 Maputo
+258-420397 Fax: +258-429700

Namibia

753 **The Book Cellar**
Carl List Building
Peter Müller Street
POB 1074
Windhoek 9000
+264-61-231615 Fax: 264-61-236164
Well-stocked general bookshop in central Windhoek.

754 **Gamsberg Macmillan Bookshop**
19 Faraday Street
POB 22830
Windhoek
+264-61-232165 Fax: +264-61-233538

755 **Swakopmunder Buchhandlung**
Kaiser Wilhelm Street
POB 500
Swakopmund
+264-64-402613 Fax: +264-64-404183

756 **Windhoeker Buchhandlung**
POB 1327
Windhoek
+264-61-225216/225036
Fax: +264-61-225011

Nigeria

757 **Glendora International (Nigeria) Ltd**
Shop C4
Falomo Shopping Centre
PO Box 50914
168 Awolowo Road
Ikoji
Lagos
+234-1-269 2762
Fax: +234-1-261 8083
Arguably Nigeria's leading bookshop, carrying a large selection of books and magazines. Specializes in books on African art, African literature, philosophy, history, tradition and culture.

758 **Odusote Bookstores Ltd†**
68 Lagos Bye-Pass
POB 244
Ibadan
Oyo State
+234-22-316451

759 **University of Lagos Bookshop**
University of Lagos
Akoka
Yaba
Lagos State
+234-1-820279 Fax: +234-1-822644
Nowadays the best university bookshop in Nigeria.

Senegal

760 **Librairie Clairafrique**
2 place de l'Independence
BP 2005
Dakar
+221-222169 Fax: +221-218409

761 **Librairie Aux Quatre Vents**
55 rue Felix Faure
BP 1820
Dakar
+221-218083 Fax: +221-229536
Fine bookshop with a good range of titles about Senegal and West Africa.

Sierra Leone

762 **Ahmadiyya Bookshop**
Back Street
POB 1317
Freetown
+232-22-22617

South Africa

763 **Adams Booksellers & Stationers**
The Writer's Bookshop
341 West Street
PO Box 466
Durban 3200
+27-31-304 8571
Fax: +27-31-304 7308

764 **Books Etc. Trust**
2 Cheviot Place
Bonnie Doone
East London 5241
+27-431-354138
Fax: +27-431-354139
Email: 100075,2046@compuserve.com

765 **Christison Books**
POB 100245
Scotsville 3209
+27-331-66193 Fax: +27-331-68809
New and out-of-print Africana.

766 **Clarke's Bookshop**
211 Long Street
Cape Town 8001
+27-21-23 5739 Fax: +27-21-23 6441
Email: africana@clarkes.co.za
Website: http://www.antiquarian.com/
clarkes
A leading dealer of new and secondhand
books on Southern Africa. Bookshop in
central Cape Town with a large selection
of new and antiquarian books. Catalogues
are regularly issued. Search services for
out-of-print titles.

767 **Exclusive Books (Pty) Ltd**
POB 4628
Cape Town 8000
+27-21-419 0905
and at:
POB 7724
Johannesburg 2000
+27-11-789 5555
Fax: +27-11-798 6462
Chain bookstore with numerous branches
throughout South Africa. Flagship store is
at Hyde Park, Johannesburg, reputedly the
biggest general bookshop in Africa.

768 **Hargreaves Library Services**
POB 89691
Lyndhurst 2106
+27-11-882 6535
Fax: +27-11-882 3842

769 **Logan's University Bookshop
Literary Services (Pty) Ltd**
POB 171199
Congella
Durban 4013
+27-31-253221

770 **New Edition Bookshop**
10 High Street
Butterworth 4960
+27-474-610350
Fax: +27-474-610350

771 **Thorold's Africana & Legal
Booksellers**
Meischke's Building
42 Harrison Street 3rd Floor
POB 241
Johannesburg 2000
+27-11-838 5903
Email: thorolds@icon.co.za
Major library supplier for Southern
African-published materials.

772 **Phambili Books**
9 Rockey Street
Johannesburg 2194
+27-11-294944 Fax: +27-11-337 5736
Specialist supplier of African-published
material and also carries a wide range of
other stocks.

Swaziland

773 **AfricaSouth Books**
Swazi Plaza
POB A456
Mbabane
+268-45561 Fax: +268-46792
Good selection of books for, from, and
about Southern Africa.

Tanzania

774 **University of Dar es Salaam
Bookshop**
POB 35090
Dar es Salaam
+255-51-49192

Togo

775 **Nouvelles Editions Africaines Librairie**
239 boulevard du 13 janvier
BP 4862
Lomé
+228-216761

Uganda

776 **Uganda Bookshop†**
Colville Street
POB 7145
Kampala
+256-41-43756

Zaire Republic

777 **Librairie Universitaire†**
BP 1682
Kinshasa
+260-1-252576

Zambia

778 **University Bookshop**
University of Zambia
POB 32379
Lusaka
+260-1-252576

Zimbabwe

779 **Alpha Books (Pvt) Ltd**
Paget House
87 Union Avenue
POB 1056
Harare
+263-4-722553 Fax: +263-4-790160

780 **Grassroots Books**
100 Jason Moyo Avenue
POB A267
Avondale
Harare
+263-4-728191 Fax: +263-4-751202
A fine small bookshop in the centre of Harare. Specializes in development and Third World issues, African history and politics, gender issues and African literature. Issues regular export catalogues, and publishes *Grassroots Book News*.

781 **Kingstons**
34 Union Avenue
corner Leopold Takawira Street
POB 2374
Harare
+263-4-753310 Fax: +263-4-729260
Zimbabwe's largest bookshop.

782 **Mambo Press Bookshop†**
Old Mutual House
Speke Avenue
POB 66002
Harare
+263-4-705899

VII. ORGANIZATIONS

The listing that follows is a 'names & numbers' directory of (1) the major African regional organizations and, (2) some other important, active regional and international organizations in Africa and elsewhere, and which do not have an entry in other sections, i.e. section IV-Libraries, or section IX-Foundations, Donor agencies, etc. Listings are however restricted to full name and address, telephone and fax numbers, Email addresses and websites (where available), and the names of the organization's current executive officer(s).

Fuller information about most of these organizations's activities, history, structure, objectives, officers, finance, membership, publications, etc, can be found in several other sources, notably the annual *Africa South of the Sahara* (*see* **11**), the *New African Yearbook* (*see* **10**), *Africa Today* (*see* **141**), or the *International Directory of African Studies Research/ Répertoire international des études africaines* (*see* **83**), *Historical Dictionary of International Organizations in Sub-Saharan Africa (see* **74***)*, and the *Handbook of Regional Organizations in Africa (see* **76***)*.

1. The major regional African organizations

783 **African Development Bank** (ADB)
BP 1387 Abdijan 01
Côte d'Ivoire
+225-204444 Fax: +225-227839
Exec Pres: Omar Kabbaj (Morocco)
Exec Sec: Hedi Meliane

784 **Arab Bank for Economic Development in Africa/Banque arabe pour le développement économique en Afrique** (BADEA)
Sayed Abdel Rahmann
El-Mahdi Avenue
POB 2640 Khartoum
Sudan
+249-11-73646 Fax: +249-11-70600
Chair: Ahmad Abdallah Al-Akeil (Saudi Arabia)
Dir Gen: Ahmad Al-Harti Al-Ouardi (Morocco)

785 **Arab Maghreb Union** (AMU)
26-27 rue Okba Agdal
Rabat
Morocco
+212-7-772688 Fax: +212-7-772693
Sec Gen: Mohamed Amadou

786 **Conseil de l'entente/Entente Council (CE)**
Fonds d'entraide et de garantie de emprunts
BP 3734 Abidjan 01
Côte d'Ivoire
+225-33 28 35 Fax: +225-31 11 49
Admin Sec: Paul Kaya

787 **Economic Commission for Africa** (ECA)
Africa Hall
POB 3005 Addis Ababa
Ethiopia
+251-1-517200 Fax: +251-1-514416
Exec Sec: Kingsley Y. Amoako (Ghana)

788 **Economic Community of West African States** (ECOWAS)
Secretariat Building
Asokoro, Abuja
Nigeria
+234-9-523 1858
Exec Sec: Edouard E. Benjamin (Guinea)

789 **Organization of African Unity** (OAU)
POB 3243 Addis Ababa
Ethiopia
+251-1-517700 Fax: +251-1-513036
Chair: changes annually; 1995/96: Meles Zenawi (Ethiopia)
Sec Gen: Salim Ahmed Salim (Tanzania)

790 **Southern African Development Community** (SADC)
PB 0095 Gaborone
Botswana
+267-351863 Fax: +267-372848
Exec Sec: Kaire Mbuende (Namibia)

791 **Union douanière et économique de l'Afrique Centrale/ Central African Customs and Economic Union** (UDEAC)
BP 969 Bangui
Central African Republic
+236-61-610922
Fax: +236-61-612136
Sec Gen: Thomas Dakayi Kamga (Cameroon)

792 **Union économique et monétaire ouest-africaine/West African Economic and Monetary Union** (UEMOA)
rue Agostino Netoar
BP 643 Ouagadougou
Burkina Faso
+226-306187
Sec Gen: Mamadou Haidara (Mali)

2. *Some other important regional and international organizations and institutes (in Africa and elsewhere)*

793 **The Africa Centre**
38 King Street
London WC2E 9JT
UK
+44(0)171-836 1973
Fax: +44(0)171-836 1975
Website: http://www.demon.co.uk/africa/centre/docs/centre1/html
Dir: Adotey Bing

794 **Africa On-line**
1 Kendall Square
Building 200
Cambridge MA 02139
USA
+1-617-494 0125 Fax: +1-617-494 9422
Email: info@africaon-line.com
Website: http://www.africaon-line.com
or http://www.afrique.com

795 **African Association for Literacy and Adult Education** (AALAE)
Finance House, Loita Street
POB 50768
Nairobi, Kenya
+254-2-222391 Fax: +254-2-340849
Chair: Anthony Setsabi
Sec Gen: Paul Wangoola

796 **African Association for**
     Political Science/Association
     africaine de science politique
     (AAPS)
     19 Bodle Avenue, Eastlea
     POB MP1100
     Mount Pleasant, Harare
     Zimbabwe
     +263-4-730403 Fax: +263-4-730403
     Email: aapp@harare.iafrica.com
     Pres: Georges Nzongola-Ntalaja (Zaire)
     Admin Sec: Kwame Ninsin (Ghana)

797 **African Association for Public**
     Administration and
     Management (AAPAM)
     POB 48677
     Nairobi
     Kenya
     +254-2-521944 Fax: +254-2-521845
     Pres: William N. Wamalwa
     Sec Gen: A.D. Yahaya

798 **African Centre for Applied**
     Research and Training in
     Development (ACARTSOD)
     Africa Centre
     Wahda Quarter
     Zawia Road
     POB 80606
     Tripoli
     Libya
     +218-21-833640 Fax: 218-21-832357
     Exec Dir: Mohammed El-Mustapha
     Kabbaj

799 **African Council for**
     Communication Education
     (ACCE)
     POB 47495
     Nairobi
     Kenya
     +254-2-216135 Fax: +254-2-750329

800 **African Economic Research**
     Consortium (AERC)
     Mama Ngina Street
     International House 8th floor
     POB 62882
     Nairobi
     Kenya
     +254-2-225234
     Fax: +254-2-219308
     Exec Dir: Benno J. Ndulu

801 **African Institute for Economic**
     Development and Planning
     (AEIDP)/Institut africain de
     développement économique et
     planification (IDEP)
     BP 3186
     Dakar
     Senegal
     +221-231020 Fax: +221-222964
     Dir: Jeggan C. Senghor

802 **African Medical and Research**
     Foundation (AMREF)
     Wilson Airport
     POB 30125
     Nairobi
     Kenya
     +254-2-501301 Fax: +254-2-502984
     Dir Gen: Michael S. Gerber
     (also at 833 United Nations Plaza, New
     York NY 10017 +1-212-949 6421, USA;
     and at 11 Waterloo Street, Clifton, Bristol,
     UK +44(0)1272-238424)
     Exec Dir UK: Elizabeth Young

803 **African Network of Scientific**
     and Technological Institutions
     (AFSTI)
     POB 30592
     Nairobi
     Kenya
     +254-2-520600 Fax: +254-2-215991

804 **African Publishers' Network**
(APNET)
11th floor Megawatt House
44 Samora Machel Avenue
POB 3773
Harare
Zimbabwe
+263-4-706196 Fax: +263-4-705106
Email: apnet@mango.zw
Chair: Victor Nwankwo
Exec Sec: Gillian Nyambura

805 **African Regional Centre for**
Technology (ARCT)
FAHD Building 17th Floor
boulevard Djily Mbaye
BP 2435
Dakar
Senegal
+221-237712 Fax: +221-237713
Dir: B.J. Olufeagba

806 **African Social and**
Environmental Studies
Programme
POB 44777 Nairobi
Kenya
+254-2-747960 Fax: +254-2-747960
Exec Dir: Peter Muyanda Mutebi

807 **African Society of**
International and Comparative
Law (ASICL)
Kairaba Avenue
PB 52
Banjul
The Gambia
+220-224968 Fax: +220-224969
Pres: Mohammed Bedjaoui
Sec: Emile Yakpo

808 **African Training and Research**
Centre for Women (ATRCW)
United Nations Economic
Commission for Africa

POB 3001
Addis Ababa
Ethiopia
+251-447200 ext.301
Dir: Mary Tadesse

809 **African Wildlife Foundation**
(AWS)
1717 Massachussetts Avenue
NW
Washington DC 20026
USA
+1-202-265 8394
Fax: +1-202-265 23361
Exec Pres: Paul Schindler
Admin Dir: Elizabeth McCorkle
Field Dir Africa: Mark S. Price
(also at POB 48117, Nairobi, Kenya)

810 **Afro-Asian Peoples Solidarity**
Organization/Organisation de
la solidarité des peuples afro-
asiatiques (AAPSO)
89 Abdel Aziz Al Saoud
Manial, el Roda
Cairo 11559-61
Egypt
+20-2-363 6081 Fax: +20-2-363 7361
Sec Gen: Nouri Abdul Razzak

811 **All Africa Conference of**
Churches/ Conférence des
églises de toute l'Afrique
(AACC)
Waiyaki Way, Westlands
POB 14205
Nairobi
Kenya
+254-2-441483 Fax: +254-2-443241
Pres: Most Rev Desmond Tutu
Sec Gen: Rev José Belo Chipenda

812 **American Association for the Advancement of Science, Sub-Saharan Africa Program** (AAAS)
1200 New York Avenue NW
Washington DC 20005
USA
+1-202-326 6730
Fax: +1-202-289 4958/371 0970
Email: africa@aaas.org
Dir: Peter Schmidt

813 **Association des universités partiellement ou entièrement de langue française** (AUPELF-UREF)
Bureau Amérique du Nord
BP 400 Succ. Côte des Neiges
Montréal
Quebec
Canada H3S 2S7
+1-514-343 7232
Fax: +1-514-343 2107
Email: gilles.teasdale@refer.qc.ca
Sec: (Chef de projet, Service des banques de données) Gilles Teasdale

814 **Association of African Universities/ Association des universités africaines** (AAU)
POB 5744
Accra North
Ghana
+233-21-774495
Fax: +233-21-774821
Pres: George Benneh (Ghana)
Sec Gen: Donald E.U. Ekong (Nigeria)

815 **Association of African Women for Research and Development** (AAWORD)
BP 3304 Dakar
Senegal
+221-259822 Fax: +221-241289
Exec Sec: Veronica Mullei

816 **Centre africain de formation et de recherches administratives pour le développement/African Training and Research Centre in Training for Development** (CAFRAD)
avenue Mohamed V
BP 310
Tanger
Morocco
+212-9-942632 Fax: 212-9-41415
Pres: Aziz Hasbi
Dir Gen: Mamadou Thiam

817 **Centre for Black and African Arts and Civilisation**
PMB 12794
National Theatre
Lagos
Nigeria
+234-1831734
Dir: Zaccheus Simday Ali

818 **Centre international des civilisations Bantu** (CICIBA)
BP 770
Libreville
Gabon
+241-739650 Fax: +241-739717
Dir: Vatomene Kukanda

819 **European Union-The Lomé Convention/African, Caribbean and Pacific Countries** (ACP)
ACP Secretariat: ACP House
451 ave Georges Henri
B-1200 Brussels
Belgium
+32-2-733 9600 Fax: +32-2-735 5573
Sec Gen: Carl Greenidge (acting)

820 Institut africain pour le
développement économique et
social/African Institute for
Economic and Social
Development (INADES)
15 rue Jean Marmoz
08 BP 8 Abidjan 08
Côte d'Ivoire
+225-441594 Fax: +225-448438
Dir: René Roi

821 **Institut culturel africain/**
African Cultural Institute
(ICA)
13 avenue du Président
Bourguiba
BP 02
Dakar
Senegal
+221-24 78 82
Dir Gen: Messanvi Kokou Kekeh

822 **Institut fondamental d'Afrique**
noire - Cheikh Anta Diop
(IFAN)
Campus Universitaire
Corniche Ouest
BP 206
Dakar
Senegal
+221-250090
Dir: Abdoulaye Bara Diop

823 **Institut français de recherche**
scientifique pour le
développement en coopération
(ORSTOM)
213 rue La Fayette
F-75480 Paris Cedex 10
France
+33-1-48 03 77 77
Fax: +33-1-48 03 08 29
Website: http://www.orstom.fr
Pres: Hubert Fournier
Dir Gen: Jean Nemo

824 **Institute for African**
Alternatives
4th floor Sable Centre
41 de Korte Street
Braamfontein
2001 South Africa
+27-11-339 6752
Fax: +27-11-339 1127
Email: ifaanet@wn.apc.org
Dir: Ben Turok
(also offices in other countries of Africa)

825 **International African Institute/**
Institut africain international
(IAI)
School of Oriental and
African Studies
Thornhaugh Street
Russell Square
London WC1H 0XG
+44(0)171-323 6035/6180
Fax: +44(0)171-323 6118
Email: iai@soas.ac.uk
Chair: George C. Bond
Hon Dir: Paul Spencer
Chair Publ Committee: Elizabeth Dunstan

826 **International Centre for Insect**
Physiology and Ecology
(ICIPE)
POB 30772
Nairobi
Kenya
+254-2-802501 Fax: +254-2-803360
Email: icipe@cgnet.com
Dir: Thomas R. Odhiambo

827 **International Centre for**
Research in Agroforestry
(ICRAF)
United Nations Avenue
Gigiru, Limiru Road
POB 30677
Nairobi
Kenya
+254-2-521450 Fax: +254-2-521001

Email: icraf@cgnet.com
Dir: Pedro A. Sanchez

828 **International Congress of
    African Studies** (ICAS)
    c/o Prof. Yusuf Fadhil Hassan
    Vice-Chancellor
    University of Khartoum
    POB 321
    Khartoum
    Sudan
    +249-11-75100
    Sec Gen: Sayyid H. Hurreiz

829 **International Fund for
    Agricultural Development**
    (IFAD)
    via del Serafico 107
    I-00142 Rome
    Italy
    +39-6-54591
    Fax: +39-6-504 3463
    Pres: Fawzi Hamad Al-Sultan

830 **International Institute of
    Tropical Agriculture** (IITA)
    Oyo Road
    PMB 5320
    Ibadan
    Oyo State
    Nigeria
    +234-22-400300
    Fax: +234-22-177 2276
    Email: iita@cgnet.com
    Dir Gen: Lukas Brader

831 **International Laboratory for
    Research on Animal Diseases**
    (ILRAD)
    POB 30709
    Nairobi
    Kenya
    +254-2-632311 Fax: +254-2-631499
    Dir: A.R. Gray

832 **International Livestock
    Research Institute** (ILRI)
    POB 5689
    Addis Ababa
    Ethiopia
    +251-1-513215 Fax: +251-1-811892
    Email: ilri@cgnet.com
    Dir Gen: Hank Fitzhugh

833 **Nigerian Institute of
    International Affairs** (NIIA)
    11 Kofo Abayomi Road
    Victoria Island
    GPOB 1727
    Lagos
    Nigeria
    +234-1-615606
    Dir: George Obiozor

834 **Organisation de coopération et
    de développement
    économiques/OECD
    Development Centre**
    2 rue André Pascal
    F-75775 Paris Cedex 16
    France
    (OECD Development Centre at 94 rue
    Chardon Lagache, 75016 Paris)
    +33-1-45 24 82 00 Fax: +33-1-49 1- 42 76

835 **Pan-African Development
    Information Systems** (PADIS)
    UN Economic Commission
    for Africa
    Africa Hall
    POB 3001
    Addis Ababa
    Ethiopia
    +251-1-517200 Fax: +251-1-514416
    Email: padis@padis.gn.apc.org
    Dir: Nancy Hafkin (Officer in charge)

836 **Pan-African Institute for Development/Institut panafricain pour le développement** (PAID)
BP 4078
Douala
Cameroon
+237-421061 Fax: +237-424335
and at:
POB 133 Buea
South West Province
Cameroon
+237-322182 Fax: +237-322343
Dir: Stephen N. Mbandi
Sec Gen: N. Laban Kirya

837 **Pan African News Agency/ Agence de presse panafricaine** (PANA)
BP 4056
Dakar
Senegal
+221-241295 Fax: +221-24-241690
Email: baam@pana.pana.sn
Website: http://www.afnews.org/ans/pana/feed/panafeed.html

838 **Pan-African Union of Science and Technology** (PAUST)
BP 2339
Brazzaville
Congo
+242-832265 Fax: +242-832185
Pres: Edward Ayensu (Ghana)
Sec Gen: Lévy Makany

839 **Pan-African Writers Association** (PAWA)
PAWA House
Roman Bridge
POB C356 Cantonments
Accra Ghana
+233-21-773062
Fax: +233-21-773593
Sec Gen: Atukwei Okai

840 **Réseau culturel africain/African Cultural Network**
BP 10486
Dakar
Senegal
+221-223062 Fax: +261-217515
Dir: Falilou Diallo

841 **Society of African Culture/ Société africaine de culture**
18 rue des Ecoles
F-75005 Paris
France
+33-1-43 54 13 74
Fax: +33-1-43 25 96 67
Sec: Christiane Diop
(also at 19 rue Vincens, Dakar, Senegal)

842 **Unesco Regional Office for Education in Africa/ Bureau régional de l'Unesco pour l'éducation en Afrique** (BREDA)
12 avenue Roume
BP 3311
Dakar
Senegal
+221-235082 Fax: +221-238393
Dir: Pius A.I. Obanya

843 **Unesco Regional Office for Science and Technology in Africa/ Bureau régional de l'Unesco pour la science et la technologie en Afrique** (ROSTA)
POB 30592
Nairobi
Kenya
+254-2-621234 Fax: +254-2-215991
Dir: Paul B. Vitta

844 **United Nations Development**
Programme (UNDP)
One United Nations Plaza
New York NY 10017
USA
+1-212-906 5000
Fax: +1-212-826 2057
Email: [personalid]@undp.org
Website: http://www.undp.org
Pres: Zbigniew Maria Wlosowicz
Administrator: James G. Speth (USA)

845 **United Nations Sudano-**
Sahelian Office (UNSO)
14 ave Dimdolobsom
BP 366 Ouagadougou
Burkina Faso
+226-306355 Fax: +226-310581
Dir: Peter Branner

846 **United States Agency for**
International Development
(USAID)
2201 C Street NW
Washington DC 20523
USA
+1-202-647 2996
Fax: +1202-647 3364
Email: [personalid]@usaid.org
Website: http://www.info.usaid.gov/
regions/afr
Administrator: J. Brian Atwood
Acting Assistant Administrator for Africa:
Carol A. Peasley

847 **The World Bank, Technical**
Department, Africa Region
1818 H Street NW
Washington DC 20433
USA
+1-202-477 1234
Fax: +1-202-477 6391
Email: books@worldbank.org
Website: http://www.worldbank.org
European office: 66 avenue d'Iéna
F-75116 Paris, France

+33-1-40 69 30 00
Fax: +33-1- 40 69 30 66

848 **World Council of Churches,**
The (WCC)
150 route de Ferney
1211 Geneva 2
Switzerland
+41-22-791 6111
Fax: +41-22-791 0361
Gen Sec: Rev Konrad Raiser (Germany)

VIII. AFRICAN STUDIES ASSOCIATIONS AND SOCIETIES

Information for this section was collected through mailings of computer printouts from our database, and questionnaires were sent to a number of new entries. Associations and societies which did not respond, despite repeated attempts to obtain details about their activities, are marked with symbols as set out below. Some of those may no longer be active, or may currently be dormant.

Abbreviations and symbols used:

†	- repeat entry from 1st ed. (1989); information not verified; entry updated as far as possible, from secondary sources
Φ	- provisional new entry, but questionnaire has not been completed; unverified information drawn from secondary sources

corp	- corporate [subscriptions]
Exec Sec	- Executive Secretary/Director [with current term of office where provided]
Found	- year founded
indiv	- individual [subscriptions]
inst	- institutional [subscriptions]
Obj	- objectives
ord	- ordinary [subscriptions]
Pres	- President
Sec	- Secretary
stud	- student [subscriptions]
Publs	- publications issued

849 **African Literature Association**
(ALA)
Africana Studies and Research Center, Cornell University
310 Triphammer Road
Ithaca NY 14850-2559
USA
+1-607-255 0415

Fax: +1-607-255 0784
Email: ava2@cornell.edu
Website: http://h-net.msu.edu/~aflitweb/
Found: 1974
Obj: The African Literature Association is an independent non-profit professional society open to scholars, teachers and

writers from every country. It exists primarily to facilitate the attempts of a world-wide audience to appreciate the efforts of African writers and artists. The organization welcomes the participation of all who produce the object of our study and hopes for a constructive interaction between scholars and artists. The ALA as an organization affirms the primacy of the African peoples in shaping the future of African literature and actively supports the African peoples in their struggle for liberation.
Pres: Arthur D. Dayton (1996-97)
University of Kansas
Dir: Anne V. Adams
Membership dues: $15.00-40.00 depending on annual income; $50.00 institutional $80.00 sponsor $5.00 African stud in Africa
Membership privileges: all members receive the *ALA Bulletin*
Meetings: annual meetings; one meeting in Africa every five years.
Publs: *ALA Bulletin* (*see* **182***);* membership directory is printed in the summer issue of the *ALA Bulletin*; up-to-date bibliography of African Literature is a regular *ALA Bulletin* feature.

850 **African Studies Association of Australasia and the Pacific (AFSAAP)**
c/o African Research Institute
La Trobe University
Bundoora
Victoria 3083
Australia
+61-9-299 7418
Fax: +61-9-351 3166
Email: gertzel@spectrum.edu.au
Found: 1978
Obj: to promote further understanding of Africa in Australia; to provide a forum for discussion of African affairs; to provide a journal where members may publish a range of material, academic and non-academic, on African issues and Africa-

Australia relations.
Pres: Paul Nursey-Bray (1996-97), University of Adelaide
Sec: David Lucas & Christine McMurray c/o Africa Research Institute, La Trobe University
Membership dues: A$20.00 A$25.00 outside Australasia A$5.00 stud
Membership privileges: receive *Review and Newsletter*, published 2Yr
Meetings: annual African Studies Conference; small groups meetings, informally, in a number of universities.
Publ: *AFSAAP Review and Newsletter (see* **178***), Directory of Africanists in Australia, New Zealand and Papua New Guinea*

851 **African Studies Association (ASA)**
Emory University*
Credit Union Building
Atlanta GA 30322
USA
+1-404-329 6410
Fax: +1-404-329 6433
Email: africa@emory.edu
Website: http://www.sas.upenn.edu/African_Studies/Home_Page/ASA_Menu.html
Found: 1957
Obj: Welcomes members with scholarly and professional interests in Africa.
Founded in 1957 as a non-profit membership corporation, the African Studies Association provides useful services to the Africanist community, hosts a national convention of African studies annually, and publishes and distributes scholarly Africanist materials.
Pres: Sandra Greene (1997)
Exec Dir: Chris Koch
Membership dues: $35-85 indiv depending on income $95 inst in US and overseas $55 African inst
Membership privileges: members receive *ASA News*, the *African Studies Review*, and *Issue: a journal of opinion*. Members may vote to elect officers of the

Association, serve on ASA committees, organize panels at annual meetings, and receive special discounts on ASA Press publications.

Meetings: meeting held annually in the autumn, in different regions of the US each year, and providing an occasion for panels, plenary sessions and discussion groups, exhibits and films.

Awards: Herskovits Award *(see* **932**), Distinguished Africanist Award *(see* **929**), Conover Porter Award *(see* **928**).

Publ: *ASA News (see* **292**), *African Studies Review (see* **290**), *Issue: a journal of opinion (see* **297**); also occasional publications, monographs, reference works, etc. published under the ASA Press imprint *(see* **544**).

*Note: the ASA will relocate to Rutgers University, New Brunswick NJ, late in 1997.

852 **African Studies Association of**
    South AfricaΦ (ASASA)
    POB 392
    University of South Africa
    Pretoria 0001
    South Africa
    +27-12-429 6430
    Fax: +27-12-328 8153 [?]
    Found: 1960
    Pres: Denis Venter 1993-95
    Sec: Pierre Hugo

853 **African Studies Association of**
    the UK (ASAUK)
    School of Oriental & African
    Studies, University of London
    Thornhaugh Street
    Russell Square
    London WC1H 0XG, UK
    +44(0)171-323 6253
    Fax: +44(0)171-436 3844
    Found: 1963
    Obj: to promote lively debate in the academic study of Africa. It is open to anyone with an interest in African studies.

Pres: J.D.Y. Peel (1996-98)
Sec: Nici Nelson
Membership dues: £25.00 ord £10.00 stud £75.00 corp
Membership privileges: members receive *African Affairs*, and may participate (at privileged rates) in conferences, seminars, and symposia. Combined membership with the Royal African Society *(see* **862**) is possible at a supplementary charge of £4.00.
Meetings: regular conferences and symposia which explore the frontiers of teaching and research in Africa; annual general meeting.
Publ: *ASAUK Newsletter (see* **246**)

854 **Africana Librarians Council**
    (ALC)
    c/o African Studies Association
    Emory University
    Credit Union Building
    Atlanta GA 30322
    USA
    +1-404-329 6410
    Fax: +1-404-329 6433
    Email: africa@emory.edu
    Found: 1957
    Obj: this is not an association, but a sponsored organization of the African Studies Association *(see* **851**). It has a broadly based membership including those whose full-time profession is Africana librarianship, as well as librarians in other areas but with interests in African studies collection development. There are two sub-committees: the Committee on Cataloging and Classification plays an important role in articulating the concerns of Africana librarians regarding the manner in which Africana materials are catalogued and classified; the Committee on Bibliography provides a clearing house for information and support of bibliographic projects;
    Pres: Joe Caruso, Columbia University (1996-97)
    Sec: Ruby Bell-Gam, UCLA (1994-96)

Meetings: Open semi-annual meetings are held in Spring and Autumn, the latter always coinciding with the annual meeting of the ASA

Awards: Conover-Porter Award *(see 928)*

Publ: *Africana Libraries Newsletter (see 291), Africana Librarians Council Directory (see 65)*

855 **Arbeitskreis der deutschen Afrika-Forschungs-und Dokumentationstellen** (ADAF) (Working Group of German Africa Research and Documentation Centres)
c/o Institut für Afrika-Kunde
Neuer Jungfernstieg 21
D-20354 Hamburg
Germany
+49-40-356 2523
Fax: +49-40-356 3511
Found: 1967
Obj: a loose network of 14 member institutions in Germany with Africa-related research and/or documentation activities and interests. Main objective is to facilitate the exchange of information about on-going activites in the field of African studies and Africanist documentation.
Pres: Rolf Hofmeier
Sec: Axel Halbach, Herbert Weiland
Membership dues: none
ADAF-Rundbrief (newsletter) ann.

856 **Asociacion Española de Africanistas** (AEA) (Association of Spanish Africanists)
c/o Ramiro de Maezetu,
s/n Colegio Mayor NS Africa
Ciudad Universitaria
28040 Madrid
Spain
+34-91-554 0104
Fax: +34-91-554 0401
Found: 1984

Obj: to encourage the study of every aspect of the African continent; to promote interest in African subjects; to collaborate with African institutes overseas; to improve focus in Spain on the sub-Saharan region as well as the Maghreb; to stimulate in Spain, the level of consciousness of the African contribution to Hispanic culture.
Pres: José U. Martinez Carreras
Sec: Belén Pozuelo Mascaraque
Membership dues: n/a
Meetings: annual courses on African history
Publ: *Estudios Africanos (see 221), Boletin de la AEA, Cuadernas Monograficos*

857 **Canadian Association of African Studies/Association canadienne des études africaines** (CCAS/ACEA)
c/o CCASLS/CCSSER
Centre d'études de l'Asie de l'Est
Université de Montréal
CP 6128 Succ A
Montréal Quebec
Canada H3C 3J7
+1-514-343 6569
Fax: +1-514-343 7716
Email: denm@ere.umontrel.ca
Found: 1970
Obj : to promote the study of Africa in Canada, the improvement in knowledge and awareness of Africa as well as problems and aspirations of its people on the part of the Canadian public. The facilitation of scholarly and scientific exchange, and the provision of a link between the Canadian and African scholarly and scientific communities.
Pres: Jane Parpart
Sec: Dickson Eyoh
Membership dues: Can$70.00 ord Can$45.00 retired Can$35.00 stud
Membership privileges: subscription to *Canadian Journal of African Studies*
Meetings: conferences, seminars; annual meeting, usually in May.

Publ: *Canadian Journal of African Studies*
(see **183***), CAAS Newsletter*

858 **Conseil européen des études**
africaines (CEEA)/ European
Council on African Studies
(ECAS)†
c/o M. J-P. Blanck
Centre de géographie appliquée
CEREG
3 rue de l'Argonne
F-67083 Strasbourg Cedex
France
+33-388 35 82 47
Found: 1985
Obj: international non-governmental
organization formed by the community of
Africanists in Europe and intended to
serve all those who, in one way or another,
are engaged in the study of African
civilizations, cultures and societies.
Membership is largely constituted of
national committees of African studies for
each European country, but is also open to
Africanist scholars residing in a European
country with no national committee or
association.
Pres: A. Coupez
Exec Sec: J-P. Blanck
Membership dues: 1.5 ECU per national
committee member
Meetings: General Assembly meets every
four years; the Standing Committee/
Executive meets once or twice a year; the
CEEA also organizes and encourages
conferences and symposia both in Europe
and in Africa.
Publ: *Bulletin du CEEA/ECAS Newsletter;*
La Documentation Africaniste en Europe
(see **4***)*
Ed note: organization currently dormant?

859 **Indian Society for Afro-Asian**
Studies (ISAAS)
297 Saraswati Kunj
Indraprastha Extension
New Delhi 110092, India

+91-11-224 8246 Fax: +91-11-242 5698/
332 9273/335 5019
Email: dp@isaas.delnet.ren.nic.in or
isaas@giasdl01.vsnl.net.in
Found: 1980
Obj: engaged in studies, seminars, surveys,
publications to increase awareness about
the peoples and countries of Africa and
Asia, and Afro-Asian perspectives and
viewpoints.
Pres: Lalit Bhasin
Sec: Dr Dharampal
Memebership dues: Rs1,000 SAARC
region $100 overseas
Membership privileges: participation in
general body meetings, eligible to vote and
be sponsored in elections to office;
concessional or free participation in
seminars.
Meetings: International Conference on
Cooperation every two years on issues
concerning this region; also seminars,
training courses, conferences-conventions.
Publ: *Newsletter* (qtly), *IRAA* (2Yr),
Proceedings of seminars/conferences,
various monographs

860 **Nihon Afurika Gakkai** (Japan
Association for African Studies)
c/o Dogura & Co
1-8 Nishihanaikecho
Koyama, Kita-ku
Kyoto 603, Japan
+81-75-451 4844
Fax: +81-75-451 0436
Found: 1964
Obj: to promote studies and field research
on nature, society, and humanities of the
continent of Africa, and its nearby islands.
Thus, it aims to enhance the standard of
African studies in Japan. In order to
pursue the above aim, it holds conferences
and seminars, publishes the *Journal of*
African Studies, promotes academic
exchanges, and conducts other activities
necessary for achieving its aim.
Pres: Hideo Oda (1996-99), Keio Gijuku
University

Sec: Koji Hayashi
Membership dues: 6,000 Yen
Membership privileges: entitled to receive the *Journal of African Studies* and attend the annual conference.
Meetings: annual conference held on the last Saturday and Sunday of May every year. Several seminars are held by four branches of the association, namely Kanto area, Kansai area, Chubu area, and Tohoku area, each year.
Publ: *Africa-Kenkyu* (Journal of African Studies 2Yr), *Nihon Africa Gakkai Kaiho* (Newsletter of the Japan Association for African Studies, ann)

861 **Nordic Association of African Studies**
c/o Department of Asian and African Languages
Uppsala University
POB 513
SE-75120 Uppsala
Sweden
+46-18-181091 Fax: +46-18-181094
Email: abdulaziz.lodhi@afro.uu.se
Found: 1991
Obj: to promote the study of Africa and its languages and cultures; to advance studies of Africa through international cooperation, especially between the Nordic countries; to act as a forum for Africanists, particularly in the humanities.
Chair: Arvi Huskainen, University of Helsinki
Sec: Abdulaziz Y. Lodhi, Uppsala University
Membership dues: SEK170 institutions, SEK140 individuals
Membership privileges: members receive two issues of *Nordic Journal of African Studies* by airmail
Meetings: general meetings, Executive Board meetings, and Editorial Board meetings held during 'Africa Days' at the Nordic/Scandinavian Institute of African Studies in Uppsala; and Nordic seminars

on African linguistics held in Trondheim, Norway.
Publ: *Nordic Journal of African Studies (see 223)*

862 **The Royal African Society**
School of Oriental & African Studies
University of London
Thornhaugh Street
Russell Square
London WC1H 0XG, UK
+44(0)171-323 6253
Fax: +44(0)171-436 3844
Found: 1901
Obj: to strengthen and encourage an interest in the continent of Africa through its influential quarterly journal *African Affairs*, a lively meetings programme and conferences.
Pres: Sir Michael Caine (1996-2001)
Sec: Lindsay Allan
Membership dues: £23 (full); £10 (student); £75 (corporate)
Membership privileges: receive the journal African Affairs and may attend speakers' meetings and conferences; members may use the library of the School of Oriental and African Studies. The Society has close links with the African Studies Association of the UK *(see 853)* and members may participate in ASAUK conferences and symposia.
Meetings: discussion meetings and conferences with distinguished politicians, diplomats, aid officials, academics and journalists; normally about 25 meetings are held each year.
Publ: *African Affairs (see 232), A Directory of Africanists in Britain* 3rd ed. *(see 81)*

863 **La Société des africanistes**
(Society of Africanists) (SDA)
Musée de l'Homme
17 Place du Trocadéro
Et 11 novembre

F-75116 Paris
France
+33-1-47 27 72 55
Fax: +33-1-47 04 63 40
Email: ferry@mnhn.fr
Found: 1930
Obj: scientific study of the African
continent and its inhabitants from
prehistoric times to the present day and the
dissemination of knowledge acquired.
Pres: Geneviève Calame-Griaule (-June
1997); M.J. Tubiana
Sec: Marie-Paule Ferry
Membership dues: FF250
Membership privileges: access to loan
system of the library of the Musée de
l'homme
Meetings: monthly conferences from
October to June, seminar in 1996 "African
women in France"
Publ: *Journal des Africanistes (see* **197***),*
Mémoires de la société des africanistes

864 **Société Suisse d'études**
 africaines/ Schweizerische
 Afrika-Gesellschaft (SAG-
 SSEA) (Swiss African Society)
 Postfach 3000 Bern 1
 Switzerland
+41-31-322 7043
Fax: +41-31-322 7001
Email: beat.sottas@bk.admin.ch
Found: 1974
Obj: promotion and coordination of
African studies research. particularly in
inter-disciplinary areas; organization of
meetings and seminars; collaboration with
other academic institutions in Switzerland
and abroad, collaboration with public and
private donor agencies, provision of
documentation and information about
Africa.
Pres: Beat Sottas
Sec: Thomas Bearth
Membership dues: Fr.75 ord Fr.25 stud
Fr.150 corp
Membership privileges: receive quarterly
Newsletter, and special offers on

occasional publications and the annual
Schweizer Afrika-Bibliographie
Meetings: regular meetings and study-
group get-togethers; annual general
meeting.
Publ: *Schweizer Afrika-Bibliographie*
(ann), *Newletter* (qtly)

865 **Standing Conference on**
 Library Materials on Africa
 (SCOLMA)
 c/o The Library, SOAS
 University of London
 Thornhaugh Street
 Russell Square
 London WC1H 0XG, UK
+44(0)171-323 6104
fax: +44(0)171-636 2834
Email: rt4@soas.ac.uk
Website: http://www.brad.ac.uk/acad/
dppc/dppclib/homepage.html
Found: 1962
Obj: to provide a forum for librarians and
others concerned with the provision of
materials for African studies in libraries in
the United Kingdom. To monitor, co-
ordinate and improve the acquisition of
library materials on Africa, especially
through its co-operative Area
Specialisation Scheme for the acquisition
of materials from Africa. Sponsors
bibliographical projects; publishes
bibliographical works and a journal.
Organizes conferences and seminars on
African bibliographical topics.
Membership is open to institutions and
libraries concerned with library materials
on Africa.
Chair: John Pinfold
Sec: Barbara Turfan
Membership dues: £18
Membership privileges: receive a copy of
African Research and Documentation.
Meetings: regular meetings and seminars;
four international conferences have been
held and the proceedings published.
Publ include: *African Research and*
Documentation (see **244***); SCOLMA*

*Directory of Libraries and Special
Collections on Africa (see* **126***); Theses on
Africa 1976-1988 (see* **158***); Writings on
African Archives (see* **120***); Images of
Africa: papers presented at the 1994
SCOLMA conference; New Directions in
African Bibliography (see* **3***); Maps and
Mapping of Africa (see* **28***);
African Population Census Reports:A
Bibliography and Checklist (see* **137***); UK
Resources for Southern African studies;
Theses on Africa 1963-1975 (see* **157***);
African Periodicals in the Library of the
British Museum (Natural History); African
Newspapers on Microfilm; Debates on
African Legislatures*

866 **Vereinigung von Afrikanisten
in Deutschland** (VAD)
(Association of Africanists in
Germany)
c/o Institut für Afrika-Kunde
Neuer Jungfernstieg 21
D-20354 Hamburg
Germany
+49-40-356 2525
Fax: +49-40-356 2511
Email: iak@hwwa.uni-hamburg.de
Found: 1968
Obj: an academic association dedicated to
the analysis of current problems of
development in Africa as well as the
historical roots thereof. It aims at
promoting interdisciplinary research and
international cooperation of scientists
concerned with African development.
Pres: Gerd Spittler 1996-98 (University of
Bayreuth)
Sec: Rolf Hofmeier
Membership dues: DM50
Meetings: multi-disciplinary conference on
development problems in Africa every two
years.
Publ: Schriften der VAD (monograph
series), *VAD Rundbrief* (ann newsletter)

867 **Werkgemeenschap Afrika**
(Netherlands African Studies
Association)
c/o Afrika-Studiecentrum
POB 9555
NL-2300 RB Leiden
Netherlands
+31-71-527 3372
Fax: +31-71-527 3344
Email: gmvuijk@worldaccess.nl
Found: 1979
Obj: aims to promote African studies in
the Netherlands; one of its main
responsibilities is to play an intermediary
role between its members and the
government, particularly in respect of
annual allocation of government research
grants to Dutch Africanists in the
Netherlands. Keeps a data-base of Dutch
Africanists.
Pres: Albert Trouwborst (1996-99)
Sec: Trudeke Vuijk (1995-98)
Membership dues: n/a
Membership privileges: participation in
the activities of the Association.
Meetings: yearly conference in the
autumn; spring workshop to assist
applicants for research grants.
Publ: *Directory of Africanists in the
Netherlands*

IX. FOUNDATIONS, DONOR AGENCIES, NETWORK ORGANIZATIONS IN AFRICAN STUDIES (or active *in* Africa)

This section identifies the major foundations, donor agencies or network organizations either supporting research in African studies, and/or active *in* Africa.

Several new organizations were added to our database for this second edition of the *African Studies Companion*. Information was collected through mailings of computer printouts from our database, and organizations listed for the first time were sent questionnaires. Several did not in fact complete our questionnaires, but merely forwarded brochures, annual reports, etc., from which we have extracted relevant information. A number of organizations did not respond at all (even after several reminders), and thus we could not verify the information currently held on file; these are marked with the symbols as set out below.

Some donor organizations, foundations, or other grant-making bodies are, understandably, reluctant to be included in reference works such as this, as they fear that inclusion of their organization may generate a large number of applications from scholars, or others, which they would have to turn down, and thus leading to unnecessary administrative work for them. We hope that the information provided makes it very clear which organizations are grant-making and which are not. It should also be noted that several of them, as indicated under their entries, only support projects through NGOs or through bilateral programmes with individual African countries.

For those organizations which completed and returned questionnaires and/ or verified information, the following information is provided: full name and address; telephone and fax numbers; Email address (and Website for some); year founded; a brief description of the principal objectives of the organization and activities; source(s) of finance/ funding; name(s) of president of governing board or board of trustees; names of executive officer(s) and/or executive director; names of programme officer(s) in charge of Africa-related projects; details of activities, programmes, etc. in the African studies field, or activities *in* Africa; grants and awards made in the African studies field (including research grants, training support, workshop/conference support, publication support, etc.) *or* support of activities, projects, or relief operations, etc. *in* Africa; guidelines for applications for research support (where applicable) and/or procedures for submitting proposals; major publications issued. Details of regional offices in Africa (and names of resident directors or programme officers) are given as far as is possible, and if donor organizations provided this information.

Abbreviations and symbols used:

†	- repeat entry from 1st ed. (1989); information not verified; entry updated, as far as possible, from secondary sources
Φ	- provisional new entry, but questionnaire has not been completed; unverified information drawn from secondary sources

Act in A	- activities, project or relief operations support in Africa
Act in AS	- activities, programmes, etc. in the African studies field [or A/AS if both applicable]
Adv	- adviser
Ag	- acting [director, etc.]
Appl proc	- application procedure [guidelines for submitting proposals]
Chair	- Chairperson of Governing Board, or Board of Trustees
Dep Dir	- Deputy Director
Dir	- Director
Dir Gen	- Director General
Exec Dir	- Executive Director
Exec Off	- Executive Officer
Exec Sec	- Executive Secretary
Fin	- finance/funded by
G/Aw	- grants and awards made [if applicable]
Gen Man	- General Manager
Gen Sec	- General Secretary
MD	- Managing Director
Obj	- principal objectives and activities
Pres	- President [of Governing Board or Board of Trustees]

Prog Off	- Programme Officer(s) in charge of Africa/African studies [or other areas]
Proj Off	- Project Officer
Publ	- publications
Reg off	- regional office(s) in Africa [with full addresses if provided]
VP	- Vice-President

Austria

868 Österreichische Forschungsstiftung für Entwicklungshilfe

Berggasse 7
A-1090 Vienna
+43-1-317 4010/180
Fax: +43-1-317 4015
Email: oefse.ga@mapnes.et
Website: http://oefse.ifs.tuwien.ac.at
Found: 1967
Obj: documentation and information on development aid and developing countries with special emphasis on Austrian development aid and development policy.
Fin: Austrian Ministry of Foreign Affairs, Austrian Church organizations.
Pres : Klaus Zapotoczky (Exec Off)
Exec Off: Gerhard Bittner (Gen Sec)
Prog Off: Mag Richard Langthaler
Act.in A/AS: documentation and information on countries and regions, and special items on African development.
G/Aw: *Not* a grant-making body
Publ: *Ausgewählte neue Literatur zur Entwicklungspolitik Bibliographie* (twice yearly)
Österreichische Entwicklungspolitik (annually)

869 Wiener Institut für Entwicklungsfragen und Zusammenarbeit (Vienna Institute for Development and Cooperation) (VIDC)

Weygasse 5
A-1030 Vienna
+43-1-713 3594
Fax: +43-1-713 3594 73
Email: vidc@magnet.at
Found: 1987
Obj: the Institute is an international non-governmental organization in consultative status, category II, with the ECOSOC of the UN. Aims to foster interdisciplinary research and science in cooperation with institutions in the South; to inform on current developments in North-South relations; to organize cultural exchanges between South and North, including "culture and development" projects in the South; to advise and assist Austrian NGOs on the implementation of development projects; to organize international conferences, workshops and meetings on development issues; to implement projects for the protection of rain forests.
Fin: Federal Ministry for Foreign Affairs
Exec Off: Dolores Bauer, Michael Häupl, Peter Jankowitsch, Franz Vranitzky, Erich Andrlik (Dir Secretariat)
Act in A/AS: organizes cultural events and festivals across Austria, promotes artists from Latin America, Asia and Africa living in Austria; assists artists, solidarity groups and educational institutions on the implementation of cultural projects; supports the first cultural project of the Austrian Development Cooperation in Uganda: "Villages of Cultures".
G/Aw: *Not* a grant-making body
Publ: Report series (lectures, summaries of workshops, seminars and conferences);

publications of specific development
issues; *Echo* (VIDC bulletin)

Belgium

870 **Groupe des états d'Afrique des
Caraïbes et du Pacifique**
(Groupe ACP)Φ
451 Ave Georges Henri
B-1200 Brussels
+32-2-733 9600
Fax: +32-2-735 5573
Obj: the Lomé Convention is the principal
means of co-operation between the
Community and developing countries,
concluded by the EU and African,
Caribbean and Pacific (ACP) countries.
Commitments and support made under the
Convention includes: trade promotion;
cultural and social development; education
and training; transport and
communications; development of
production; rehabilitation. Also supports:
information and documentation; seminars;
programmes and general technical cooperation; general studies; multisectoral
programmes; delegations; administrative
and financial costs; improvements to
public buildings; project-linked
multisectoral technical co-operation.
Fin: EU-Lomé Convention
Governing Board: Committee of
Ambassadors, and Joint Assembly
Exec Off: Carl Greenridge (Ag Sec Gen)
Publ: *The Courier; Directory of ACP
Universities, Directory of ACP Technical
Institutions*

Canada

871 **Canadian International
Development Agency/Agence
canadienne de développement
international** (CIDA)†
200 Promenade du Portage
Hull
Québec K1A 0G4

+1-819-997 6100
Fax: +1-819-953 6088
Obj: to support Canadian voluntary
organizations in their development
activities by (i) encouraging and
facilitating the people-to-people
participation of Canadians in international
development through matching
contributions to those projects and
programmes of autonomous Canadian
NGOs which are compatible with
Canadian foreign and development
policies; (ii) supporting the efforts of
people in developing countries,
particularly the less advantaged, to meet
their basic needs and improve their quality
of life through a development process
which is sustainable and utilizes their own
resources to the full, in the context of their
own values.
Fin: Canadian government
Exec Off: F.L.A. Ward (Dir Gen, NGO
Divisions, Special Programs Branch)
Prog Off: Patricia Miaro (Africa & Middle
East Bureau)
G/Aw: no awards; supports the
development projects of Canadian NGOs
in Africa and elsewhere.
Applic proc: *Guide for Preparing Project
Submissions for NGO Division* contained
in *CIDA-NGO Division: Introduction and
Guide* available from the Agency.

872 **CODE**
[Canadian Organization for
Development through Education]
321 Chapel Street
Ottawa Ontario K1N 7Z2
+1-612-232 3569
Fax: +1-613-232 7435
Email: codehq@codecan.com
Website: http://www.web.net/~code
Found: 1959
Obj: an NGO which has been
collaborating, in various ways, with other
voluntary sector organizations, donor
agencies, the private sector and
government for over thirty years, to help

support a sustainable literate environment in developing countries.
Fin: Canadian public, Canadian International Development Agency, international donors
Chair: Stan Hovdebo
Exec Off: Robert Dyck (Pres)
Prog Off: Elise Tousignant (Team Leader: Ghana, Mali, Senegal, Malawi, Zambia, Zimbabwe); Michael Emblem (Team Leader: Tanzania, Kenya, Mozambique, Guyana, Belize and Ethiopia)
Act in A: library and information services to the public, promotion of reading, book donations from North America, development of information professionals, documentation centres, teacher training in use of information materials and the teaching of reading.
G/Aw: *Not* a grant-making body
Applic proc: projects submitted between April and January will be considered for funding the following fiscal year commencing April 1st. Proposals should be submitted to Team Leaders (see above). Criteria for approval of CODE projects are that the proposal be in the CODE prescribed format and that the project be consistent with CODE's mission, goals and objectives. Needs in the area of intervention are effectively researched and assessed. Issues related to economic, environment, political, social and cultural sustainability, gender and development and human rights should be addressed.
Reg off: CODE Mali, quartier de l'Hippodrome, rue 234, Porte 696, BP 2770, Bamako Mali; tel: +223-223178; CODE Tanzania, Plot 344, Urambo Street, Upanga, POB 5702, Dar es Salaam, Tanzania; tel: +255-51-39854
Publ: Ann Thompson, *The World Bank and Cooperation with NGOs*, 1992; Colin Ray, *Running a School Library: A Handbook for Teacher Librarians*, 1990; *Paper Users Manual/ Manuel d'utilisation du papier*, 1993
Note: see also CODE Europe, entry **901**

873 **International Development Research Centre** (IDRC)/ **Centre de recherches pour le développement international** (CRDI)
CP 8500 Ottawa
Ontario K1G 3H9
+1-613-236 6163
Fax: +1-613-236 7230
Email: info@idrc.ca
Website: http://www.idrc.ca
Found: 1970
Obj: supports scientific and technical research projects conceived and carried out by Third World researchers. IDRC's research activities are structured under the following themes: food security, equity in natural resource use, biodiversity conservation, sustainable employment, strategies and policies for healthy societies, and information and communication. Through the research it supports IDRC helps its partners in the developing world to identify long term practical solutions to their pressing development problems. Projects are designed to use local materials and to strengthen resident human resources and institutions.
Fin: Parliament of Canada
Pres: Keith A. Bezanson
Exec Off: Pauline Dole (Spec Projects & Info Off, Public Affairs); Raymond Audet (VP Resources Branch); Pierre Beemans (VP Corp Serv Branch); Caroline Pestiau (VP Corp Serv Branch)
Act in A: IDRC has supported over 6,000 research projects since its creation in 1970; of these over 1,700 have been in Africa. Currently 487 active IDRC research projects in Africa.
G/Aw: yes, details as above
Applic proc: (i) pre-proposal letter should be sent to the closest Regional Office; (ii) pre-proposal letter should include information of the following nature: community research priorities; objectives of the research; scientific methodology;

resources available and required; expected results; rough budget; timetable.
Reg off: IDRC Regional Office for Eastern and Southern Africa, POB 62084, Nairobi, Kenya (Reg Dir: Dr. Eva Rathgeber) tel: +254-2-713160/713161; fax: +254-2-711063
IDRC Regional Office for West and Central Africa, BP 11007, CD Annexe, Dakar, Senegal (Reg Dir: Gerald Bourrier) tel: +221-244231/240920; fax: +221-253255
IDRC Regional Office for Southern Africa, POB 477, Wits 2050, South Africa (Reg Dir: Marc Van Amerigen) tel: +27-11-403 3952; fax: +27-11-403 1417
Publ: extensive; publications catalogue available on request. IDRC Books publishes research results and scholarly studies on global and regional issues related to sustainable and equitable development.

Denmark

874 **Danish International
    Development Authority
    (DANIDA)**
    Ministry of Foreign Affairs
    Department of International
    Development Cooperation
    2 Asiatisk Plads
    DK-1448 Copenhagen K
    +45-33-920000
    Fax: +45-31-540533
Obj: Denmark's development assistance is based on the policy guidelines contained in an extensive strategy paper "Strategy for Danish Development Policy Towards the Year 2000". This paper states the fundamental policy framework for Danish development assistance: to assist developing countries in their efforts to achieve sustainable development based on the improvement of living conditions through socially balanced economic growth, and to promote equal and free opportunities for the individual. Besides

supporting the reduction of poverty through the promotion of economic growth and social development, the Strategy supports three themes which are pursued at all levels in the Danish assistance programme: women in development, environment, and democratization and human rights. Bilateral development co-operation concentrates on activities in a limited number of sectors in 20 programme countries.
Fin: Government of Denmark
Exec Off Africa-related projects: Soren Dyssegaard (Dir Dept of Info)
Act in AS: programme countries in Africa which are supported through bilateral development corporation are: Benin, Burkina Faso, Egypt, Eritrea, Ghana, Kenya, Malawi, Mozambique, Nigeria, Tanzania, Uganda, Zambia, Zimbabwe.
G/Aw: the implementation of bilateral development assistance is supported by personnel assistance. This involves posting advisers and volunteers and granting scholarships to personnel from programme countries. The scholarship programme has developed steadily especially in the area of local scholarships granted for studies in a student's own country or region.
Applic proc: n/a
Publ: *Denmark's Development Assistance 1994-1995; Danish Development Assistance. The Plan for 1996-2000.*

Finland

875 **Finland, Ministry for Foreign
    Affairs**
    Department for International
    Development Cooperation
    POB 127 Katajanokanlaituri 3
    FIN-00160 Helsinki
    +358-9-1341 6435
    Fax: +358-9-1341 6428
Obj: plans, manages and administers Finland's programmes of bilateral

development cooperation with developing countries.
Fin: Government of Finland
Exec Off: Heikki Kokkala (Education Adv)
G/Aw: does *not* provide support, grants, etc. outside bilateral programmes.
Reg off: attached to Finnish Embassies

France

876 **Agence de coopération culturelle et technique** (ACCT)Φ
13 quai André Citroën
F-75015 Paris
+33-1-44 37 33 00
Fax: +33-1-45 79 14 98
Found: 1970
Obj: intergovernmental organization of French-speaking countries for co-operation in the fields of education, culture, science, technology, and other ways which may bring the peoples of those countries closer together.
Exec Off: Jean-Louis Roy (Gen Sec)

877 **United Nations Educational, Scientific, and Cultural Organization** (UNESCO)Φ
Programme générale d'information
7 place de Fontenoy
Bâtiment III (240)
F-75352 07-SP Paris
+33-1-45 68 10 00
Fax: +33-1-43 06 16 40/ 42 73 04 01
Found: 1946
Obj: UNESCO was established in 1946 "for the purpose of advancing, through the educational, scientific and cultural relations of the peoples of the world, the objectives of international peace and the common welfare of mankind". UNESCO assists the interchange of experience, knowledge and ideas through a world network of specialists. Apart from the

work of its professional staff, UNESCO co-operates regularly with the national associations and international federations of scientists, artists, writers and educators, some of which it helped to establish.
UNESCO has established missions which advise governments, particularly in the developing member countries, on planning projects; and appoints experts to assist in carrying them out. Projects are concerned with teaching functional literacy to workers in development undertakings; teacher training; establishing libraries and documentation centres; providing training for journalists, radio, television and film workers; improving scientific and technical education; training planners in cultural development; international exchange of persons and information.
Fin: regular budget provided by member states and also through other sources, particularly UNDP
Dir Gen: Federico Mayor
Exec Off: Solomon Hailu (Dir Exec Office)
Act in A/AS: UNESCO convenes conferences and meetings, and co-ordinates international scientific efforts; helps to standardize procedures of documentation and provides clearing house services; offers fellowships; publishes a wide range of specialized works, including source books and works of reference. Activities centre around six principal areas: education; natural sciences and technology; social and human sciences; culture; copyright and communication; information and information dissemination.
G/Aw: study fellowships
Reg off: UNESCO has field offices in many African countries.
Publ: *UNESCO Courier* (mon), *UNESCO Sources* (mon), *Museum* (qtly), *Impact of Science on Society* (qtly), *International Social Science Journal* (qtly).
Note: questionnaires not completed, source: *Africa South of the Sahara, 1996*

Germany

878 Heinrich Böll Stiftung e.V
(Heinrich Böll Foundation)
Brückenstrasse 5-11
D-50667 Cologne
+49-221-207110
Fax: +49-221-207 1151/1129
Email: hbs-koeln@oln.comlink.apc.org
Found: 1987
Obj: among the principal objectives of the
Heinrich Böll Foundation are: to help
improve and realize human, civil and
minority rights within Germany and
world-wide, in co-operation with German
and non-German citizens; to overcome
party-political and social barriers and to
develop a culture of tolerance, mutual
understanding and cultural enrichment; to
further the notion and concepts of
ecologically sound and socially just
societies and to counter profit and
affluence with a philosophy and practice
of sharing; to create the conditions which
allow a free cultural and artistic
development of the individual, and to
sponsor male and female artists, especially
in the South and the East; to examine in a
trialogue between the West, East and
South, the causes and effects of conformity
with, and opposition to, dictatorship and
democracy.
Fin: Ministry of Economic Cooperation,
Ministry of Internal Affairs, Ministry of
External Relations, membership fees.
Board: Willi Hoss, Regine Walch,
Christoph Meertens
Exec Off: Frieder Wolf
Prog Off: Ulrike Hössle
Act in A: funding of projects in the area of
ecological issues, democratization (civil
society), women related issues, art and
culture.
G/Aw: supports workshop, conferences
and (occasionally) publications. In the
field of arts and literature it awards grants
to writers and artists, supports writers and
artists suffering from political persecution

and promotes innovative arts primarily in
the South.
Applic proc: proposal should be sent by an
African NGO.
Reg off: Addis Ababa - contact Asgedech
Ghirmasion

879 Deutsche Stiftung für internationale Entwicklung
(DSE) (German Foundation for
International Development)
Zentralstelle für Erziehung
Wissenschaft und
Dokumentation
Hans-Böckler-Strasse 5
D-53225 Bonn 3
+49-228-40010
Fax: +49-228-4001 111
Found: 1960
Obj: provides a forum for development
policy dialogue and advanced training of
specialists and executive personnel from
developing and transitional countries. In
addition, it supports German experts in
preparing themselves for their assignments
in developing countries and maintains the
Federal Republic of Germany's largest
centre for documentation and information
on development cooperation issues.
Conferences, meetings, seminars and
training courses support projects which
serve economic and social development,
thus contributing to an effective,
sustainable and wide-ranging development
process. The DSE cooperates with partners
at home and abroad. A considerable
number of the programmes take place in
developing countries.
Fin: mainly Federal Ministry for Economic
Cooperation and Development (BMZ)
Pres: Hans Bühler
Exec Off: Udo Bude (Head, Basic
Education), Ingrid Jüng, Wolfgang Gmelin
(Educational Systems), Lütz Hüttemann
Act in A/AS: supports educational reforms
in developing countries via an exchange of
experience among experts and political
decision makers, and by advanced training

of specialists and executive personnel in governmental and non-governmental educational institutions. The majority of DSE programmes are jointly prepared and conducted with partner organizations in developing countries.
G/Aw: *Not* a grant-making body. Supports conferences, seminars, training programmes, study tours, and provides congress travel support.
Publ: annual publications catalogue.

880 **Deutsches Welthungerhilfe/ Deutsches Zentralinstitut für soziale Fragen** (DZI) (German Agro Action)
Adenauerallee 134
D-53113 Bonn
+49-228-22880
Fax: +49-228-220710
Email: 100073,432@compuserve.com
Found: 1962
Obj: non-governmental organization engaged in worldwide development cooperation; orients its work on the guiding principle of self-help to enable people to achieve food security through their own efforts; to protect the interests of the rural population, in particular in the Third World; to improve the food situation and rural living conditions in the Third World; support for self-help programmes; emergency aid; information compilation and dissemination.
Fin: private donations, government subsidies, subsidies from the EC.
Deputy Chair: Hermann Kalinna
Exec Off: Dr Volker Hausmann (Sec Gen)
Act in A: central aim of development cooperation is in the agriculture and rural development sector. Approximately 50 per cent of the funding is devoted to improving living conditions and income of small farmers, thus ensuring an existence with human dignity.
G/Aw: *Not* a grant-making body
Publ: *Annual Report*, DW shop catalogue and brochures

881 **Goethe Institut**
Helene-Weber-Allee
Postfach 190419
D-80604 Munich
+49-89-159210
Fax: +49-89-15921 450
Email: zentralverwaltung@goethe.de
Website: http://www.goethe.de
Found: 1952
Obj: to promote a wider knowledge abroad of the German language and to foster cultural cooperation with other countries.
Fin: a registered society; finances its locations in Germany through language course fees. Institutes abroad are subsidized in part by the Federal Foreign Office; each Institute receives an amount which varies proportionately according to its intake from other sources. Current subsidies total about 300 million DM.
Pres: Hilmar Hoffmann
Exec Off: Joachim Sartorius (Sec Gen)
G/Aw: n/a
Reg off: offices throughout Africa; full list available from the Goethe Institut.
Publ: *Jahrbuch, Spracharbeit, GI Aktuell*

880 **Friedrich Naumann Stiftung†**
Margaretenhof
D-5330 Königswinter 41
+49-2223-7010
Fax: +49-2223-70188
Found: 1958
Obj: seeks to promote political liberalism by developing citizens capable of informed and responsible decision-making in their social contexts. The Foundation's work in developing countries is in five areas: civic education, training for the media, legal services and human rights, self-help initiatives and small scale industries, and political dialogue on North-South and transatlantic issues.
Fin: Federal Government (95%), private donations (5%)
Pres: Wolfgang Mischnick (Board of Directors), Walter Scheel (Board of Trustees)

Exec Off: Fritz Fliszar (Exec Dir)
Prog Off: Mr Fournier (West and Central
African states), Mr El-Ghannam (North
African states), Ms Köhler (Southern
African states).
Act in A/AS: include civic education
projects in South Africa and Benin;
regional self-help initiatives in Burkina
Faso and Côte d'Ivoire; media projects in
Egypt and Congo; a self-help scheme for
small businesses in Kenya; journalism
training in Rwanda, the Sudan, Tunisia,
Zambia and Zimbabwe.
G/Aw: most financial aid support for
development projects is jointly carried out
with like-minded liberal partners abroad.
Applic proc: (i) either through the
Foundation's scholarship programme for
study at a German university for which
application forms can be obtained from the
Foundation's Berlin office (Im Dol 2-6,
1000 Berlin 33); (ii) by submitting project
proposals to the programme officers above
for projects to be carried out in Africa in
the context of local partnerships.
Publ: extensive; catalogue on request.

Italy

883 Caritas Internationalis†

Piazza San Calisto 16
I-00513 Roma
+39-6-6988 7197
Fax: +39-6-6988 7237
Found: 1950
Obj: provides emergency aid and activities
in disaster stricken areas in all parts of the
world. Caritas is an international
confederation of 120 autonomous national
member organizations directed by its
statues 'to spread charity and social justice
in the world'.
Fin: member organizations
Pres: His Eminence Cardinal Alexandre do
Nascimiento
Exec Off: Gerhard Meier (Sec Gen)
Prog Off: Gaspard Gasana (Africa liaison)

Act in A: in line with four-year work plan
decided by each CI General Assembly held
every 4 years. Focus areas include: human
rights and peace, social services,
development, refugees and displaced
persons, collaboration within and outside
the Church. Regional work programmes in
Africa, including workshops and seminars
in areas linked to Confederation activities,
on-site training in leadership and
management, etc.
G/Aw: n/a
Applic proc: CI will consider only projects
or programmes which have first been
studied or evaluated by local national
organizations.
Publ: *Intercaritas Bulletin, International
Presence Newsletter*; monthly information
flyer; occasional dossiers, reports and CI
emergency manuals.

Netherlands

884 ACP-EU Technical Centre for Agricultural and Rural Cooperation (CTA)

Postbus 380
NL-6700 AJ Wageningen
+31-317-467100
Fax: +31-317-460067
Email: [name]@cta.nl
Website: http://www.cta.nl
Found: 1983
Obj: established in 1983 in the framework
of the Lomé Convention, a cooperation
agreement between the European Union
member states and African, Caribbean and
Pacific States. CTA's tasks are: to develop
and provide services which improve access
to information for agricultural and rural
development; to strengthen the capacity of
ACP countries to produce, acquire,
exchange and utilize information in these
areas. CTA's partners and beneficiaries
include agricultural and rural development
agencies - both government and non-
government - planners and policy-makers,
research scientists and technicians,

extension workers, trainers, farmer's cooperatives and associations.

Fin: European Development Fund (EU) Chair of ACP-EU Committee of Ambassadors

Exec Off: R.D. Cooke (Dir)

Act in A/AS: CTA programmes are organized around three principal themes: strengthening facilities at information centres including training support; promoting contact and exchange of experience among CTA's partners in rural development; providing information on demand.

G/Aw: limited programme to support training activities in the field of information management, but CTA is not a training organization. Substantial support for workshops and conferences by supporting the attendance of some 200 ACP nationals per year. Very substantial co-publications programme (financing of translations, printing costs, distribution and buy-back, etc.)

Applic proc: write to Director, CTA, submitting full details including costs; for joint activities, the contributions of all other partners should be indicated.

Publ: *Spore* (6Yr in English & French); *Esporo* (6Yr in Portuguese), *Annual report*, Proceedings of CTA seminars, CTA studies and co-publications (currently some 600 titles in catalogue which is available on request).

885 Humanist Institute for Cooperation with Developing Countries (HIVOS)
Raamweg 16
NL-2596 The Hague
+31-70-363 6907
Fax: +31-70-361 7447
Email: hivos@tool.nl

Obj: seeks to improve opportunities and scope for development for people in the South, especially in respect to human rights, pluralism and democratization. Local NGOs and social organizations play a key role by giving disadvantaged and marginalized groups a voice and place their interests on the social reform agenda. As an independent funding agency HIVOS prefers to support such organizations. Support is concentrated in a geographically limited number of regions and countries. Gives priority to the following five policy areas: economic self-reliance; the arts and culture; gender; the environment; human rights; AIDS. Aims to support organizations that enable people to assert their rights and improve access to decision-making.

Fin: Dutch public and Dutch government and EU.

Pres: n/a (22 member governing body and a management and executive committee)

Prog Off: Karel Chambille (Head Bureau Africa)

Act in A/AS: does not implement projects or programmes, nor does it send development workers to the South. Provides financial support and advice to local NGOs.

G/Aw: yes, but no details provided

Applic proc: procedures and working methods for the processing of applications and the maintenance of relations with contacts are determined in part by HIVOS' specific organizational structure. Financing takes various forms: grants are provided in the form of project, programme or partner financing (institutional support); there are also guarantees, participation and loans in the case of economic activities. The Head Office and Regional Offices also have at their disposal a micro-fund for new and experimental projects.

Reg off: 20 Phillips Avenue, Belgravia POB 2227, Harare, Zimbabwe; tel: +263-4-706704/727197; fax: +263-4-791981; email: hivos@zwe.toolnet.org

886 **Netherlands Ministry of**
     Foreign AffairsΦ
     Special Programs Section
     NGO Private Sector & Int
     Education Dept
     Bezuidenhoutsweg 67
     POB 20061
     NL-2500 EB The Hague
     +31-70-348 6720
     Fax: +31-70-348 6436
     Exec Off: Willem Veenstra (Head Culture
     & Communication Section (DCO/CO)

887 **Netherlands Organisation for**
     International Cooperation in
     Higher Education (NUFFIC)
     POB 29777
     Korternaerkade 11
     NL-2502 LT The Hague
     +31-70-4260 260
     Fax: +31-70-4260 399
     Website: http://www.nufficcs.ml
     Found: 1952
     Obj: plays a central role in international
     cooperation in higher education;
     coordinates Dutch participation in
     international student exchange
     programmes; coordinates cooperative links
     between Dutch institutions and their
     counterpart academic institutions in
     Africa, Asia and Latin America.
     Fin: Dutch Government, Commission of
     the European Union, UN organizations
     Chair: W. Dechman
     Exec Off: P.J.C. van Dijk
     Act in A/AS: MHO programme with
     projects between seven African
     universities and Dutch institutions for
     higher education, as well as a number of
     Dutch and international fellowship
     programmes.
     G/Aw: NUFFIC grants fellowships for
     training support either for regular or tailor-
     made courses/training programmes. From
     the European Development Fund (EDF),
     the European Commission offers
     scholarships for students from the 'ACP

countries'. These are the countries of
Africa, the Caribbean and the Pacific with
which the European Union has a special
relationship, as defined in the Lomé
Convention. For more information, apply
to the EU representative in your own
country. For students from South Africa
there is the EU-South Africa Fellowships
Programme. The British Council offices in
Johannesburg and Cape Town can provide
information. More than 20 South African
students and staff members will be able to
study or conduct research at a Dutch
institution as a result of CENESA
(Cooperation in Education between the
Netherlands and South Africa). The aim is
to strengthen higher education in South
Africa. The South African government
decides on the disciplines. These
programmes are coordinated and
administered by NUFFIC.
Applic proc: for more information apply to
NUFFIC or to Netherlands embassies
overseas.

888 **Technologie Overdracht**
     Ontwikkelingslanden (TOOL)
     Sarphatistraat 650
     NL-1018 AV Amsterdam
     +31-20-626 4409
     Fax: +31-20-627 7489
     email: tool.tis@tool.nl
     Website: http://www.tool.nl/
     Found: 1974
     Obj: the TOOL Foundation is active in the
     field of technology. TOOL has a
     specialized documentation centre and an
     information counter. In cooperation with
     specialists, technological advice about
     development projects is given. In addition,
     TOOL can monitor and implement
     projects. TOOL is an international clearing
     house for technology transfer and
     information services.
     Fin: Directorate General of International
     Cooperation of the Dutch Ministry of
     Foreign Affairs as well as Dutch

Cofinancing Organizations and income from projects and products.
Pres: Y. de Wit
Exec Off: M.P.C. Tiepel
Prog Off: W. Parmentier
Act in A/AS: receives over 700 enquiries each year, most from organizations and individuals working in Africa. Organizes training services for development-aid workers who are posted abroad to the Third World or who come from developing countries to the Netherlands. Transfer of technology and intercultural communication.
G/Aw: *Not* a grant-making body
Publ: various publications (catalogue available on request); also maintains mail order book shop.

Norway

889 Norwegian Agency for Development Cooperation
(NORAD)
Cultural Cooperation
PO Box 8034 DEP
N-0030 Oslo 1
+47-22-314400/314453
Fax: +47-22-314401/314473
email: firmapost@norad.telemax.no
Website: http://www.norad.no
Found: 1981
Obj: an operational organization responsible for the implementation of Norway's bilateral development cooperation, which is concentrated in three regions - Southern and Eastern Africa, Central America, and a number of countries in Asia. It is also involved in multilateral cooperation administered by the Ministry of Foreign Affairs. NORAD's ultimate goal is to contribute to lasting changes in the economic, social and political conditions of the population in developing countries. Its priority areas are as follows: cooperation for sustainable development; democracy and human rights; productive activities and employment; environment; population; gender issues; institutional development; cultural cooperation. As far as cultural development is concerned, NORAD perceives it as one of the main parts of development itself. Aims to raise the awareness of developing countries regarding their own cultural heritage, as well as to stimulate important developmental and democratization processes in these countries. This form of cooperation is also intended to contribute towards increased involvement in, and mutual respect and understanding between, the varied environments in developing countries and Norway.
Fin: Norwegian government
Pres: Tove Strand Gerhardsen (Dir Gen)
Exec Off: Thore Hem (Head of KULI Div, Cultural & Institutional Cooperation)
Prog Off: Thore Hem, Hilde R. Johansen & Lena Plau
Act in A/AS: supports cultural activities and exchange more than academic studies.
G/Aw: does not grant support in African studies field as such; supports cultural activities/exchange and government institutions and NGOs in partner countries. Contact the local embassy for more information.
Applic proc: see above
Reg off: NORAD can be contacted through Royal Norwegian embassies in African countries.

Portugal

890 Calouste Gulbenkian Foundation
Rua Dr. Nicolau de Bettencourt
P-1050 Lisboa
+351-1-793 5131
Fax: +351-1-795 5206
Found: 1984
Obj: a private Portuguese institution set up in 1956 bequeathed by its founder, Calouste Sarkis Gulbenkian, of British nationality and Armenian origin, a pioneer

of the oil industry in the Middle East who died in Lisbon in 1955 at the age of 86. The headquarters of the Foundation are in Lisbon, there is a branch in London and a Portuguese Cultural Centre in Paris which has been operating in the former residence of the founder since 1965. The Foundation is involved in a wide range of activities in Portugal and abroad, which fall within its statutory charitable aims: health and welfare, art, education and science. Also has an orchestra, a choir, and a ballet company; holds individual and/or collective exhibitions of Portuguese and foreign artists, courses, meetings, film and theatre series throughout the whole year in Lisbon as well as in other parts of the country, and abroad.
Fin: Calouste Gulbenkian Foundation
Pres: A. Ferrer Correia
Exec Off: Yvette Centeno (Dir)
Prog Off: Domingos Morais (Assessor to Dir)
Act in AS: annually awards a large number of subsidies and doctorates in Portugal and abroad; also supports programmes in scientific research and artistic creativity. The Foundation collaborates with Portuguese and foreign universities, and with international organizations. Cooperation with the new Portuguese-speaking African states is also an area in which the Foundation is involved; now includes more than 50 countries on the five continents.
G/Aw: *Not* a grant-making body
Publ: *Colóquio Artes*, *Colóquio Letres*, *Colóquio Ciências*, *Colóquio Educacao e Sociedade*; cultural bulletin; a register of University manuals and of Portuguese Culture; many books and catalogues published every year in the Foundation's publications catalogue which is available on request.

Senegal

891 **Council for the Development of Social Science Research in Africa/Conseil pour le développement de la recherche en sciences sociales en Afrique (CODESRIA)**
ave Cheikh Anta Diop
BP 3304
Dakar
+221-259822/23
Fax: +221-241289
Email: codesria@sonatel.senet.net
Found: 1973
Obj: CODESRIA is a Pan-African non-governmental organization which was set up in 1973. Deals with African research universities as well as professional organizations. Principal objectives are to facilitate research, promote research-based publishing and to create multiple fora geared towards the exchange of views and information among African researchers. It challenges the fragmentation of research by creating thematic research networks that cut across linguistic and regional boundaries. Research results are disseminated through a range of publications. Every year, between June and August, CODESRIA organizes two seminars in Dakar on "Democratic Governance in Africa" and on "Gender". Each seminar brings together about fifteen researchers.
Fin: donations from African governments, bilateral aid agencies, private foundations, membership fees and revenues from sales of publications.
Pres: Akilakpa Sawyerr
Exec Off: Achille Mbembe (Exec Sec), Tade Akin Aina (Dep Exec Sec Publications), Moriba Toure (Dep Exec Sec Grants & Training)
Act in A/AS: coordinates, supports and encourages social science research throughout Africa; supports comparative interdisciplinary research both at the

continental and national level; publishes research findings of CODESRIA sponsored research projects and the findings of African researchers sponsored by other institutions; supports training of African social scientists; collaborates with and supports other African non-governmental social science organizations. G/Aw: facilitates various kinds of research programmes aimed at covering three different levels: regional, national and individual. 1. Main organization of research has been through Multinational Working groups; 2. provides support to a number of National Working Groups; 3. Non-Programmed activities; 4. support to individual researchers especially young researchers through research grants. The programme is open to senior researchers who can work in English, who live in Africa, have completed both their university and vocational training, and have proved their research capacity by publishing on development issues.

Applic proc: more details about CODESRIA Institute etc., and its 'Small Grants Programme for Thesis Writing' are available on request.

Publ: *CODESRIA Bulletin, Africa Development* (*see* **321**); *Afrika Zamani* (*see* **322**); extensive range of monographs; catalogue available on request

Sweden

892 Dag Hammarskjöld Foundation

Ovre Slottsgatan 2
SE-75310 Uppsala
+46-18-127272
Fax: +46-18-122072
Found: 1962
Obj: the purpose of the Foundation is to organize seminars, conferences and courses on the political, social, economic, legal and cultural issues facing the Third World. Activities have developed from training courses in the strict sense into more comprehensive seminar projects with built-in research components. The Foundation concentrates on the sectoral aspects of the alternative development strategies proposed in the 1975 Dag Hammarskjöld Report, extensively elaborated in seminars on education, rural development, science and technology (especially plant genetic resources and biotechnology), health, international monetary policy, information and communication, and participation. Works closely with national aid agencies, UN agencies, inter-governmental organizations and with a great number NGOs and popular organizations.

Fin: Swedish government and private foundations
Pres: Martin Holmdahl
Exec Off: Sven Hamrell (Senior Adviser), Olle Nordberg (Exec Dir), Niclas Hällström (Assistant Dir)
Act in A/AS: Seminar on the Development of Autonomous Capacity in Publishing in Africa, 1984; Seminars on The State and the Crisis in Africa: in search of a second liberation, 1986 and 1990; Expert Consultation on the Role of Independent Funds as Intermediaries in Channelling Money for Social and Economic Development in Africa, 1995; Seminar on Education with Production in South Africa, 1995; Seminar on the Future of Indigenous Publishing in Africa, 1996. Further seminars, conferences and course details available.
G/Aw: *Not* a grant-making body
Publ: *Development Dialogue. A Journal of International Development Cooperation* (*see* **222**) (2Yr); *The State and Crisis in Africa: In Search of a Second Liberation*, Uppsala, 1992 (also available in French); *Autonomous Development Funds in Africa, Report from an Expert Consultation in Kampala, Uganda, 4-6 April, 1995* (also available in French). Catalogue available.

893 **International Foundation for
Science** (IFS)
Grev Turegatan 19
SE-114 38 Stockholm
+46-8-5458 1800
Fax: +46-8-5458 1801
Email: info@ifs.se
Found: 1972
Obj: IFAS is a non-governmental
organization with a membership of 95
scientific academies and research councils
in 77 countries, of which three quarters
are in developing countries and one
quarter in industrial countries. It aims to
develop scientific manpower in the Third
World; research grants are given to
scientists for the purchase of scientific
equipment, supplies, literature, etc.
Exec Sec: Ingrid Millquist (Int Sec)
Act in A: supports young scientists of
merit from developing countries. Their
research must fall within the areas of
aquatic resources, animal production, crop
science, forestry/agroforestry, food science
or natural products. Besides being from a
developing country, the researcher must
also implement the research in a
developing country.
G/Aw: IFS will consider applications for
projects dealing with research on most
aspects of its research areas. Projects
should be research-oriented and not a
transfer of technology. Support of routine
work at the applicant's institution will not
be considered. Applicants must consider
how the project will fit into the local
ecological and socio-economic
environment and where it will be
implemented, if and when such
considerations are relevant.
Applic proc: applicants must be: native to,
and carry out the research in, a developing
country; under 40; at the beginning of
their research career; must have an
academic degree equivalent to an MSc; be
employed at a university or non-profit
making research institution in a
developing country. The applicant's
institution is expected to provide salaries
and basic research facilities. Research
grant applications are submitted directly to
the IFS Secretariat, which relies on a
worldwide network of senior scientists to
evaluate the proposed research project.
Applications must be made on the IFS
application form (in English or French)
available from the IFS Secretariat.

894 **Swedish International
Development Cooperation
Agency** (SIDA)
Department for Research
Cooperation, SAREC
Sveavägen 20
SE-105 25 Stockholm
+46-8-698 5000/5313
Fax: +46-8-698 5656
Email: [firstname.surname]@sida.se
Website: http://www.sida.se
Found: 1965
Obj: the former agency SAREC was, on
July 1 1995, combined with the other
Swedish development assistance
authorities into a new agency Sida. The
Department for Research Cooperation,
SAREC, continues to provide research
cooperation support within the new
agency. The aims remain unchanged , i.e.
to strengthen indigenous research capacity
in developing countries and promoting
research that can produce results of
importance to the development of Third
World countries. Funds are allocated for
bilateral cooperation, regional and
international research programmes and
development research in Sweden.
   The new Sida is organized under five
regional departments. The Democracy and
Social Development Sector department
supports education, culture and media,
health, human rights, public administration
and management. Another department,
Cooperation with Non-Governmental
Organizations and Disaster Relief,
coordinates aid via popular movements
and NGOs. Sida also provides extensive
support for educational materials

programmes in a number of countries, mainly in Africa, to help to create the necessary conditions for the supply of relevant, affordable textbooks for basic education. In addition to assistance given in the context of education agreements, support is also provided for culture and media programmes with the intention of strengthening the wider literate environment. Support to libraries is given both by the division for Culture and Media and by the division for General Education under the sector department Democracy and Social Development.

Fin: Swedish government
Chair: Mårten Carlsson
Exec Off: Rolf Carlman (Dir Dept for Research Cooperation); Anita Theorell (Head, Dept Media & Culture); Ingemar Gustavsson (Head, Dept Education); Göran Hedebro (Head, Div for Thematic Programmes); Berit Olsson (Head, Div for University Support and National Research Development)
Act in A: two-thirds of the main recipient countries are in Africa, mainly in the southern and eastern parts.
G/Aw: Dept of Research Corporation projects supported are bilateral research programmes with individual African countries given governmental priority. Regional and international research bodies can also receive support. SAREC does not provide funding for individuals, except for the Swedish development research programme available for students at Swedish universities. The principal aim of bilateral research cooperation is to strengthen the research capacity of developing countries through support for research projects, research training, university libraries, and laboratories. At present it covers Botswana, Tanzania, Mozambique, Ethiopia, Eritrea, Zimbabwe, Sri Lanka, Vietnam and Nicaragua.
Applic proc: 1. SAREC/Dept for Research Corporation: requests should contain an identification of the research component

and a governmental priority. Funds are not normally intended for local costs, equipment or consultancy services, and are not tied to the Swedish market. Money can be used for specific projects, as a budget support to a research institution and for promotion of cooperation between research institutions in the recipient country and another country. No specific application forms are used.
2. Sida: apply to Sida for application procedures.
Publ: research surveys; conference reports; evaluations; publications catalogue available on request. Project catalogue, reports and popular booklets. SAREC report series (research and survey reports), gratis from SAREC

Switzerland

895 **Aga Khan Foundation**
Avenue de la Paix 1-3
POB 2369
CH-1211 Geneva 2
+41-22-909 7200
Fax: +41-22-909 7291
Found: 1967
Obj: to promote social development in certain low-income countries of Asia and Africa by funding programmes in health, education, rural development, and NGO enhancement.
Fin: donations and endowment income
Pres: His Highness the Aga Khan, Prince Amyn Aga Khan, Maître André Ardoin, Guillaume de Spoelberch,
Exec Off: Robert D'Arcy Shaw (Gen Man)
Prog Off: Mirza Jahani (Chief Exec Off, AKF Kenya); Rupen Chande (Ag CEO, AKF Tanzania); Shirin Chatur (Admin, AKF Uganda)
Act in A: selectively supports action-oriented social and development programmes in Kenya, Uganda and Tanzania.
G/Aw: a highly selective and limited number of scholarships are awarded

annually for post-graduate degree courses to students in Kenya, Tanzania and Uganda, at internationally recognized institutions of higher education. Candidates are required to have excellent academic records, be in genuine need of assistance and have admission to an internationally recognized institution of higher education.
Applic proc: scholarship application forms may be requested from the AKF branches: AKF (Kenya), POB 40898, Nairobi, Kenya, tel: +254-2-227369/223951-2/244093; fax: +254-2-337562; AKF (Tanzania), POB 125, 3512 Toure Drive, Dar es Salaam, Tanzania, tel: +255-51-68651/67923; fax: +255-51-68527; AKF (Uganda), POB 5522, Kampala, Uganda, tel: +256-41-255884/256165; fax: +256-41-255885
Publ: *International Strategy*; *Annual Report*; programme interests brochure

896 Helvetas. Swiss Cooperation for Development/ Coopération Suisse au Développement
St Moritzstrasse 15
POB 181
CH-8042 Zurich
+41-1-368 6500
Fax: +41-1-3686 5800
Email: 100540,567@compuserve.com
Found: 1955
Obj: politically independent and non-denominational private association of 30,000 members from all parts of Switzerland. Assists with development cooperation by providing technical advice and assistance and financial and material support of projects.
Fin: subsidies from Swiss Government, donations and fund-raising.
Pres: Rudolf M. Högger
Exec Off: E. Werner Külling (Sec Gen)
Prog Off: G. Nicolay, A. Bürgi
Act in A: supports original local development efforts and self-help schemes, particularly appropriate rural infrastructure schemes and appropriate programmes in sustainable management of natural resources, education, training and culture. Helvetas contributes technical help and personnel, or financial or material support.
G/Aw: *Not* a grant-making body

897 Innovations et Réseaux pour le Développement (IRED)
Case 116, 3 rue de Varembé
CH-1211 Geneva 20
+41-22-734 1716
Fax: +41-22-740 0011
Found: 1980
Obj: to strengthen Third World partners (associations, federations and popular networks) so that they may respond to the needs of their members and to those of local populations and be empowered to take the decisions concerning them at every level. Main programmes of activity includes South-South exchange of experience; institution building including the development of available resources; and information/ documentation/ communication.
Fin: governments, private foundations
Pres: (Mrs) Sithembiso Nyoni
Exec Off: Boukary Younoussi (Sec Gen, BP 13457, Niamey, Niger)
Prog Off: Rudo Chitiga (Reg Dir East & Southern Africa); Issaka Doulaye Maïga (Reg Dir West & Central Africa)
G/Aw: *Not* a grant-making body
Reg off: East & Southern Africa, Regional Development Support Service of IRED, POB CY3, Causeway, Harare, Zimbabwe; tel: +263-4-796853; fax: +263-4-722421; West & Central Africa, Service régional d'échanges et d'appui à la gestion (SEAG), BP 12675, Niamey, Niger; tel: +227-733527; fax: +227-723204
Publ: *IRED-FORUM* (available in English and French)

898 Swisscontact. Swiss Foundation for Technical Cooperation
Döltschiweg 39
CH-8055 Zurich
+41-1-463 9411
Fax: +41-1-462 3365
Found: 1959
Obj: vocational and technician training, promotion of micro-enterprises and agricultural mechanization in Asia, Africa and Latin America.
Fin: Swiss private enterprises, Swiss Government, communities and cantons.
Pres: Thomas E. Bechtler
Exec Off: Urs Egger (Sec Gen)
Prog Off: Margrit Tappolet
Act in A: vocational training in Mali, promotion of micro-enterprises in Mali, Tanzania, Uganda, South Africa and Kenya.
G/Aw: *Not* a grant-making body
Publ: *Annual Report.*

United Kingdom

899 Arts Council of Great Britain
14 Great Peter Street
London SW1P 3NQ
+44(0)171-333 0100
Fax: +44(0)171-973 6590
Email: info.literature.ace@artsfb.org.uk
Website: http://www.artscouncil.org.uk
Found: 1946
Obj: operates under a Royal Charter granted in 1994 with these objectives: to develop and improve knowledge, understanding and practice of the arts; to increase accessibility of the arts to the public; to advise and co-operate with departments of government, local authorities, the Arts Councils for Scotland, Wales and Northern Ireland and other bodies.
Fin: Department of National Heritage
Pres: The Rt Hon. the Earl of Gowrie, P.C.
Prog Off: Alastair Niven (Dir Literature); Gary McKeone (Lit Off); Jilly Paver (Lit Off)

Act in AS: occasional project funding or support for touring in England of African writers; also encourages translation of literary texts from African languages into English.
G/Aw: no special fund for African studies but cultural diversity is a priority area.
Applic proc: letter to the Director of Literature or to a named literature officer, accompanied by a description of the project and a budget. Applicants will then be advised of how to proceed. Most recommendations on funding are referred to the Literature Advisory Panel or to one of its sub-committees.
Publ: *Annual Report* and miscellaneous publications.

900 British Council
10 Spring Gardens
London SW1A 2BN
+44(0)171-930 8466
Fax: +44(0)171-839 6347
Website: http://www.britcoun.org/
Found: 1934
Obj: to promote a wider knowledge of the United Kingdom and the English language; to encourage cultural, scientific, ethnological, and educational co-operation between the United Kingdom and other countries. It pursues this purpose through cultural relations and the provision of development assistance.
Fin: 34% from government grants; 31% from agencies; 35% earned income
Chair: Sir Martin Jacomb
Exec Off: Sir John Hanson (Dir Gen)
Act in AS: awards chiefly short-term for Africans to study in Britain. Contributes to training for development of the arts in Africa.
G/Aw: as above
Applic proc: Africans who want to use British resources for the advancement of African studies and African arts should write a brief statement of need to the British Council Representative in their country and ask for an interview.

Reg off: all Anglophone countries, plus Maghreb region, Senegal, Egypt, Sudan, Eritrea and Ethiopia.

901 **CODE Europe**
The Jam Factory
27 Park End Street
Oxford OX1 1HU
+44(0)1865-202438
Fax: +44(0)1865-202439
Email: 100660,2023@compuserve.com
Website: http://www.oneworld.org/code_europe
Found: 1993
Obj: supports two vital elements of the book chain in developing countries: the strengthening of library resources in rural areas; and the development of publishing in developing countries. Concentrates on Africa and the Caribbean.
Fin: UK and European development agencies
Pres: Martin Pick
Exec & Prog Off: Kelvin Smith (Dir)
Act in AS: partners in African publishing programme
G/Aw: *Not* a grant-making body
Reg off: Elieshi Lema, CODE Tanzania, POB 5702, Dar es Salaam, Tanzania; Idrissa Samaké, CODE Mali, POB 2770, Bamako, Mali
Publ: *Partners in African Publishing Newsletter* (qtly); *Tailor-made Textbooks: A Practical Guide for the Authors of Schoolbooks in Developing Countries*
Note: see also CODE (Canada), entry **872**

902 **Comic Relief/Charity Projects**
74 New Oxford Street
London WC1A 1EF
+44(0)171-436 1122
Fax: +44(0)171-436 1541
Email: charity.projects@solo.pipex.com
Found: 1985
Obj: set up in 1985 to help disadvantaged people in UK and Africa to realize their aspirations and potential through raising and allocating funds for the issues they

support. The major project so far is Comic Relief which, with the help of five Red Nose Days, has raised over £100 million. All fund-raising costs are sponsored in cash or in kind so that every penny raised from the public is distributed to projects throughout the UK and Africa.
Fin: Red Nose Day
Pres: Paul Jackson
Exec Off: Jerry Marsden (MD) Maggie Baxter (Grants Dir)
Prog Off: Richard Graham (Africa Grants Man) Liz Marsh (Africa Grants Off) Titise Make (Africa Grants Off)
Act in A: the Africa grant-making programme supports the work of organizations who are fighting poverty and promoting social justice. Grants are made to UK registered charities whose main aim is development and who work with African organizations. Applications are considered under the five grants programmes see below.
G/Aw: Women's Grants Programme, People Affected by Conflict Grants Programme, Pastoralists Grants Programme, Disabled People Grants Programme, People Living in Towns and Cities Grants Programme
Applic proc: UK registered charities may contact the Africa Team after March 1997 for a copy of Africa Grants Programme priorities for 1997-99.
Publ: education packs: *Altogether Better Resource Pack* (aimed at teachers and school governors explaining inclusive education); *Teacher Relief 1* (Keystages 2 & 3); *Teacher Relief 2* (Keystages 3 & above)

903 **Commonwealth Foundation**
Marlborough House, Pall Mall
London SW1Y 5HY
+44(0)171-930 3783
Fax: +44(0)171-839 8157
Email: comfound@mailbox.ulcc.ac.uk
Website: http://www.oneworld.org/com-fnd/
Found: 1966

Obj: founded by Commonwealth heads of government to promote closer professional cooperation within the Commonwealth; promotes better understanding of the work carried out by non-governmental organizations and encourages the strengthening of information links among NGOs through its programmes and travel grants.
Fin: Commonwealth member governments. Target income is £2.2m., of which some £1.75m. was available for grant-making in 1995.
Dir: Humayun Khan
Exec Off: Don Clarke (Dep Dir)
Prog Off: Diana Bailey (Proj Off)
Act in A/AS: areas of interest include agriculture, education, health, rural and community development, planning, management, the media and culture.
G/Aw: travel grants for participation in small conferences and workshops, for study visits and training attachments within the Commonwealth; provides financial support to Commonwealth professional associations; funds short-term fellowship schemes in cooperation with other organizations; makes grants to facilitate the flow of professional and development information through the distribution of publications; does not fund students, research or activities limited to one country.
Applic proc: applications for grants and bursaries may be submitted to the Foundation directly. Application forms are not required. Any Commonwealth citizen with the relevant qualifications, or skills acquired through practical experience, may apply for any ad hoc award. A leaflet outlining guidance for conference organizers seeking support, is available from the Foundation.
Publ: *Non-governmental Organisations: Guidelines for Good Policy and Practice*

904 **Commonwealth Secretariat**
Marlborough House, Pall Mall
London SW1Y 5HX
+44(0)171-839 3411/747 6535
Fax: +44(0)171-930 0827/839 9081
Found: 1965
Obj: set up to organize consultations between member government of the Commonwealth and to run programmes of cooperation.
Fin: member governments
Exec Off: Chief Emeka Anyaoku (Sec Gen)
Prog Off: Mohan Kaul (Dir Management & Training Serv Div)
Act in A/AS: responds to requests for assistance or expertise from all its member countries in five continents.
G/Aw: *Not* a grant-making body. The Management and Training Services Division is aimed at increasing the Commonwealth developing countries' pool of skilled manpower in areas of importance to national development. Most recipients are middle-level technologists, managers or officials, and there is a priority for schemes which have a multiplier effect (training of trainers) or which concentrate on training for women. The Commonwealth Industrial Training and Experience Programme (CITEP) provides practical training and experience in industry, usually for six months, in developing and industrialized countries. Academic exchange awards are also made. The Management and Training Services Division provides fellowships for African students in the following two-year programmes at Africa University in Zimbabwe: Masters in Business Administration, Masters in Environmental Science, Masters in Computer Science and Masters in Policy Studies.
Applic proc: in Commonwealth countries, advice and application forms from Ministry of Education or Commonwealth High Commission; in non-Commonwealth countries, advice may be sought from the Embassies of Commonwealth countries; or

full particulars from: The Director, Management and Training Services Division, at the above address. Publ: catalogue on request. Reports, analysis and information about Commonwealth cooperation and Commonwealth and world problems, resource directories, statistical and economic bulletins, reports of Commonwealth meetings and programmes, periodical, and general information.

905 **International Institute for African Research** (IIAR)
34-36 Crown Street
Reading, Berks RG1 2SE
+44(0)118-939 1010
Fax: +44(0)118-959 4442
Email: 101743,301@compuserve.com
Found: 1991
Obj: an African-centred research institute committed to working locally, nationally and internationally with peoples of African descent to support their independence and full participation in those areas that affect their lives. Its philosophy is to develop people's capacity for growth and development. It is committed to fundamental change in the use of the skills and talents of the African world population for the development of their communities. Activities include research, publishing and higher education.
Fin: self-funded
Pres: Helen Obiazo
Exec Off: Femi Nzegwu, Herbert Ekwe-Ekwe, Beverley Joseph
Prog Off: Herbert Ekwe-Ekwe
Act in AS: postgraduate diploma in African world studies; African-centred access course to British universities; undergraduate diploma in African world studies; 6 week summer programme in African world studies; publishers (books and triannual academic journal, *African Peoples Review see* **243***)*

Publ: *Africa 2001,* 1993; *Black People and Health Care in Contemporary Britain,* 1993; *Operationalising Afrocentrism,* 1994; *African & Asian Peoples in British Probation Service,* 1995; *African Literature in Defence of History,* 1997

906 **Leverhulme Trust, The**
15-19 New Fetter Lane,
London EC4A 1NR
+44(0)171-822 6938
Fax: +44(0)171-822 5084
Found: 1925
Obj: provision of funds for academic research.
Fin: investments.
Chair: Sir Kenneth Durham
Exec Off: B.E. Supple
Act in AS: grants for research
G/Aw: mainly to UK institutions for research on African topics, but universities in developing countries also eligible.
Applic proc: policies and procedures booklet available on request.
Publ: Annual report on grants made

907 **Overseas Development Administration** (ODA)Φ
Education Division
94 Victoria Street
London SW1E 5JL
+44(0)171-917 7000
Fax: +44(0)171-917 0019

908 **Overseas Development Institute** (ODI)
Portland House, Stag Place
London SW1E 5DP
+44(0)171-393 1600
Fax: +44(0)171-393 1699
Email: odi@odi.org.uk
Website: http://www.oneworld.org/odi/
Found: 1960
Obj: an independent non-governmental centre for development research and a forum for discussion of the problems facing developing countries. The research

programme is oriented towards improving policies and their implementation both within developing countries and in the British, European Union and international spheres. Over 20 Research Fellows are currently employed at ODI.

Fin: grants and donations from public and private sources

Pres: Earl Cairns

Exec Off: John Howell (Dir)

Prog Off: Susan Amoaten (ODI Fellowship Scheme)

Act A/AS: various research projects, particularly focusing on sub-Saharan Africa

G/Aw: under the ODI Fellowship Scheme, young post-graduate economists are recruited to work for two years in the public sectors of developing countries in Africa, the Caribbean, and the Pacific. In 1995, 21 Fellowships were awarded.

Applic proc: a booklet giving full details of the scheme may be obtained from the Fellowship Programme Officer at ODI.

Publ: 'Briefing papers'; 'Natural resource perspectives papers'; 'Working papers'; 'Special reports'; 'Research studies'; 'Development policy studies'; *Development Policy Review (see* **255**) (qtly); *Disasters* (qtly); *Development Research Insights* (qtly)

909 OXFAM
274 Banbury Road
Oxford OX2 7DZ
+44(0)1865-311311
Fax: +44(0)1865-313770
Website: http://www.oneworld.org/oxfam/
Found: 1942

Obj: main priority is long-term development world-wide, helping small groups and organizations to create and sustain their own opportunities for change and improvement in their living conditions. Different traditions and cultures are taken into account. Primarily non-operational, Oxfam invests in local people. In emergencies, where local skills are inadequate to meet the immediate needs, specialists are recruited for short-term assignments.

Fin: fund-raising activities by volunteers and 800 shops in UK; some funds are given for specific projects on a joint funding basis by the ODA, the EC and other agencies including sister organizations overseas; contributions from ODA and others for disaster funds.

Chair: Chris Barber

Exec Off: David Bryer (Dir)

Act in A: activities arising from objectives above; the main work is in the provision of funds and advice for small-scale community-based development projects in agriculture, health, social development and income-generation; also helps in disasters although its work is essentially preventive.

G/Aw: grants are used as catalysts to generate other local initiatives whenever possible, always aiming to advance the cause of the poor and to work for greater justice and the fulfilment of all humankind.

Applic proc: project application summary form is available from the Overseas Dept.

Publ: catalogue of Oxfam Books available on request.

910 Plunkett Foundation for Cooperative Studies†
23 Hanborough Business Park
Long Hanborough
Oxford OX7 2LH
+44(0)1993-883636
Fax: +44(0)1993-883576
Found: 1919

Obj: to promote and develop cooperative enterprises throughout the world by providing services to individuals, cooperatives, national and international organizations; work comprises training, consultancy and research in the UK and overseas; library and information services; organization of study tours in the UK; publications and distribution of books; and provision of cooperative specialists and contacts worldwide.

Fin: independent charitable trust founded by Sir Horace Curzon Plunkett
Chair: P.Dodds
Exec Off: Edgar Parnell (Dir)
Prog Off: Liz Cobbald (Manager, Overseas Services)
Act in A: work described above in Egypt and Botswana.
G/Aw: *Not* a grant-making body
Applic proc: contact Liz Cobbald in first instance with details of specific enquiry.
Publ: extensive. Catalogue available on request; UK distributor for own titles and for titles on cooperatives from other imprints.

911 **World Association for Christian Communication (WACC)**
357 Kennington Lane
London SE11 5QY
+44(0)171-582 9139
Fax: +44(0)171-735 0340
Email: wacc@gn.apc.org
Found: 1968
Obj: international non-profit-making organization registered as UK charity, seeking to apply human values of equality and justice by means of communication. Priority given to less developed countries. Main activities include funding of Third World communication projects, training assistance, and co-publication of manuals and books on communication.
Fin: mainline churches and church agencies in Europe and North America
Pres: Rev. Albert H. van den Heuvel
Exec Off: Rev. Carlos A. Valle (Gen Sec)
Prog Off: Julienne Munyaneza (Coordinator Africa Region)
Act in A/AS: various communications programmes undertaken with partners in most countries of Africa with particular emphasis on community media. WACC is a partner of such organizations as the AACC Training Centre (Nairobi), All Africa Press Service (Nairobi), EDICEAS

(Harare), ALC (Kitwe), Interchurch Media Programme (Johannesburg).
G/Aw: Training Assistance Programme to which African students of communication may apply; support of various communications activities through a general programme of project support and through a Development Initiative Programme.
Applic proc: WACC screens projects annually for possible funding in the following year. In addition, applications to the Development Initiative Programme, for projects that are usually one-off in nature and to be implemented within a year, may be made at any time for a decision within 3 months. Application forms and guidelines available.
Reg off: Rev. Emmanuel B. Bortey, Asempa Publishers, POB 919, Accra, Ghana; tel: +233-21-221706; fax: +233-21-776725
Publ: *Media Development* (qtly) *Action Newsletter*

912 **World University Services (UK)**
14 Dulterin Street
London EC1Y 8PD
+44(0)171-426 5820
Fax: +44(0)171-251 1315
Obj: an educational charity working to highlight the importance of education in development. Assists refugees and victims of repression through educational programmes.
Fin: UK government, EC, Scandinavian governments, foundations and trusts, and individuals
Chair: Alison Girdwood
Exec Off: Cardrie Nubey (Dir); Andrew Gregg (Dir)
Prog Off: Richard Brook, Sofia Garavito
Act in A: projects and research in field of education, training, employment in refugee-affected areas and areas of conflict and repression.

G/Aw: *Not* a grant-making body. WUS can only support a few, very practically focused research projects and has very limited resources.
Publ: 'Refugee Education Research Papers', titles on women, education and development, and on education at risk, Briefing papers, other resources, refugee education advisers information packs, *WUS News, Annual Report*.

United States

913 African-American Institute, The

380 Lexington Avenue
New York NY 10168
+1-212-949 5666
Fax: +1-212-682 6174
Found: 1953
Obj: to improve relationships between the US and African countries, to increase American understanding of Africa, to promote economic and human resource development in Africa, and to support equality and justice, particularly in southern Africa.
Fin: foundation grants, AID and USIA training and visitor contracts, individual and corporate gifts
Pres: Mora McLean Chair: Roger Wilkins
Exec Off: Steve McDonald (Exec VP)
Carl Schieren (VP) Dolly Desselle Adams (Corp Sec)
Prog Off: Heather Monroe (Chief of party, ATLAS)
Act in A/AS: undergraduate, graduate and short-term training; visitor programmes; conferences and seminars; placement of African students in educational institutions in US and Africa; policy studies US-African issues.
G/Aw: *Not* a grant-making body. Achievement awards given at Annual Awards Dinner to outstanding Americans and Africans for their contribution in improving relations between the US and African countries.

Reg off: AAI programme representatives in 21 African countries. For complete list of names and addresses, telephone and fax, etc., apply to the AAI.
Publ: Conference reports

914 Carnegie Corporation of New York

437 Madison Avenue
New York NY 10022
+1-212-371 3200
Fax: +1-212-754 4073
Website: http://www.carnegie.org
Found: 1911
Obj: A philanthropic foundation created by Andrew Carnegie to promote the advancement and dissemination of knowledge and understanding. It awards grants in four main programme areas: education and healthy development of children and youth; preventing deadly conflict; strengthening human resources in developing countries; and special projects.
Fin: the Corporation capital fund, originally donated at a value of about $135 million
Pres: David A. Hamburg, Pres; Newton N. Minow (Chair)
Exec Off: Barbara D. Finberg (Exec VP and Program Chair, Special Projects)
Act in A: strengthening human resources in developing countries. This programme seeks to enhance local capacity for sustaining social and economic development in the context of transitions to democratic governance. Currently, grants are concentrated in Commonwealth sub-Saharan African countries with limited emphasis on activities in Commonwealth Caribbean countries and Mexico.
A guiding principle is the need to strengthen local capacity and generate local support for changes and actions that can sustain development. It supports work in the following categories: science and technology for development; women's health and development; transitions to democracy in Africa.

G/Aw: primarily to academic institutions and to national and regional non-profit organizations for projects that have potential for national or international impact, not for activities that are too local in scope. No grants for basic operating expenses, endowments, or facilities of individual schools or school districts, colleges, universities, or human service organizations. It does not make programme-related investments. The Corporation does not generally make grants to individuals.

Applic proc: no application forms. Grant seekers are asked to present a statement containing a description of the project's aims, amount of support required, duration, methods, personnel, and budget. Officers review the proposal in light of their knowledge of the field and in relation to the current programme priorities. If they wish to pursue matters further, they may request a more developed proposal. Additional materials may be required, including a formal request from the head of the organization and a more precise budget. There are no deadlines. The Corporation reviews requests at all times of the year. The staff tries to respond within four months of the receipt of the proposal.

Publ: *Carnegie Quarterly*, 'Carnegie special reports', 'Carnegie meeting papers', *Carnegie Newsline*, Carnegie occasional papers, and miscellaneous reports

915 **Council for International Exchange of Scholars†**
3400 International Drive NW
Suite M-500
Washington DC 20008-3097
+1-202-686 6230
Fax: +1-202-362 3442
Found: 1947
Obj: helps to administer the Fulbright Exchange Program for Scholars. The principal objectives in sub-Saharan Africa

are to increase mutual understanding between the people of various African countries and the people of the US and Africa, and to meet the needs of African universities.

Fin: United States Information Agency, through an annual appropriation of the US Congress

Chair: Jeswald W. Salacuse

Exec Off: Cassandra A. Pyle (Exec Dir)

Prog Off: Linda Rhoad (Area Chief), Ellen M. Kornegay (Prog Off)

Act in AS: grants for teaching and/or research at the university level.

G/Aw: for American scholars: i) 20-25 research awards open to most fields, including African studies, tenable 3-9 months in African countries with which the US has diplomatic relations; ii) 7 Scholar-in-Residence Awards for African lecturers who will enhance African studies programmes in the US or assist US institutions in adding international content to programmes.

Applic proc: for American scholars: eligibility requirements include US citizenship, doctorate, and university teaching experience. Applications should be submitted by September 13 for awards one year hence. Applications re details etc. are available in early April each year. For African scholars: eligibility requirements include citizenship or permanent residence in home country, doctorate, and university teaching experience. Applications must be obtained from US Embassy and submitted to a Public or Cultural Affairs Officer in August or September of each year for awards that begin a year hence. For Scholars-in-Residence, US institutions, rather than African scholars, must submit proposals by November 1 of each year for positions that begin during the following academic year. The institution names the person it wishes to host.

916 Ford Foundation, The
320 East 43rd Street
New York NY 10017
+1-212-573 5000
Fax: +1-212-599 4584
Found: 1936
Obj: the Ford Foundation is a private philanthropic institution chartered to serve public welfare. Under the policy guidance of a Board of Trustees, the Foundation works mainly by granting and loaning funds for educational, developmental, research, and experimental efforts designed to produce significant advances in solving problems of worldwide importance.
Fin: when the Foundation became a national organization in 1950, its assets consisted almost entirely of 93 million shares of Ford Motor Company stock bequeathed to it by the estates of Henry and Edsel Ford. In 1956, the Foundation began disposing of its Ford Motor Company stock and no longer holds shares in the company.
Chair: Henry B. Schacht
Exec Off: Susan V. Berresford (Pres)
Act in A/AS: grants are made primarily within six broad categories: urban poverty; rural poverty and resources; human rights and social justice; governance and public policy; education and culture; international affairs. Programme activities in individual countries are determined by local needs and priorities within these subject areas.
G/Aw: supports training research and dissemination of findings through grants primarily to African institutions working in the fields mentioned above. Supports affirmative action goals in its grant-making and internal policies. The opportunities that prospective grantee organizations provide for minorities and women are considered in evaluating grant proposals. Activities must be charitable, educational or scientific, as defined under the appropriate provisions of the US Internal Revenue Code and Treasury Regulations. Support is directed to activities within the Foundation's current interests which are likely to have a wide effect. US grants are not normally made for routine operating costs of institutions; programmes for which substantial support from government or other sources is readily available; religious activities as such; or, except in rare cases, the construction or maintenance of buildings.
Applic proc: send a brief letter to determine whether the Foundation's present interests and funds permit consideration of a proposal. No application form. Proposals should set forth: objectives; the proposed programme for pursuing objectives; qualifications of persons engaged in the work; a detailed budget; present means of support and status of applications to other funding sources; legal and tax status. Applications are considered throughout the year. Grant requests in the US should be sent to the Secretary, Ford Foundation at the above address. Requests in foreign countries should be directed to the nearest Foundation office.
Reg off: West Africa: The Ford Foundation, 29 Marina POB 2368, Lagos, Nigeria; tel: +234-630141
East Africa: POB 41081, Silopark House, Nairobi, Kenya; tel. +254-338123/4
Southern Africa: POB 30953, Braamfontein, 2017 South Africa; tel: +27-11-403 5912/13/14
North Africa and the Middle East: POB 2344, Cairo, Arab Republic of Egypt; tel: +20-2-355 2121
Publ: *Annual Report, The Ford Foundation Report*

917 Institute of International Education (IIE)†
890 United Nations Plaza
New York NY 10017
+1-212-883 8200
Fax: +1-212 984 5452
Found: 1919
Obj: design and administration of international educational exchange and

human resource development projects involving education and training in the United States and Third World Countries, as well as technical assistance, research publication, and information services. Fin: programmes are funded by US and foreign governments, international organizations, universities, foundations, and corporations.

Chair: Charles H. Percy

Exec Off: Richard M. Krasno (Pres)

Prog Off: Sheila Avrin McLean (VP Education & the Arts - overseas African projects)

Act in A/AS: Fulbright and Humphrey Programs, International Visitor Program, Energy Training Program, UNESCO Fellowships, Guinea Scholarship Program, South African Education Program, Zimbabwe Manpower Development Project, Malawi Human Resources Development Project, etc. IIE and Africa paper available on request gives full listing.

G/AW: *Not* a grant-making institution. IIE administers scholarship and training programmes for sponsoring agencies and organizations in sub-Saharan Africa. The principal sponsor of these programmes is the US government through the US Information Agency (USIA) and the US Agency for International Development (USAID); also assists other organizations both public and private.

Applic proc: foreign nationals desiring to study in the US under IIE-administered programmes usually apply through agencies in their home country (Fulbright Commission or USIS posts). IIE will, however, respond to individual enquiries as helpfully as possible.

Publ: publications under the headings of *IIE Study Abroad*, *IIE Foreign National*, 'IIE research reports', 'IIE educational associates', Seminar papers, *Educational Associate Information and South Africa Information Exchange*. Videotape on "The Fulbright Experience" also available.

918 National Endowment for the Humanities

Division of Research and Education, Room 318
1100 Pennsylvania Avenue NW
Washington DC 20506
+1-202-606 8200
Fax: +1-202-606 8204
Email: research@neh.fed.us
Website: http://www.neh.fed.us

Found: 1965

Obj: supports exemplary work to advance and disseminate knowledge in all the disciplines of the humanities. Endowment support is intended to complement and assist private and local efforts. In the most general terms, NEH-supported projects aid scholarship and research in the humanities, help improve humanities education, and foster in the American people a greater curiosity about and understanding of the humanities. Welcomes applications from individuals, and non-profit associations, institutions, and organizations. Individuals eligible for endowment assistance include US citizens and foreign nationals who have been legal residents in the United States for a period of at least three years immediately preceding the submission of the application.

Chair: Sheldon Hackney

Exec Off: James Herbert (Dir)

Prog Off: Janet Edwards (Education Development & Demonstration); Jane Rosenberg (Fellowships & Stipends); Daniel Jones (Collaborative Research); Thomas Adams (Seminars & Institutes)

Act in A/AS: through grants to educational institutions, fellowships to scholars and teachers, and through the support of significant research, the Research and Education division is designed to strengthen sustained, thoughtful study of the humanities at all levels of education and promote original research in the humanities.

G/Aw: research grants, seminars, institutes, and technology awards given to

both individuals and groups in all areas of the humanities.
Applic proc: application forms required. Deadlines vary by programme. Information and application forms are available by telephoning the Division of Research and Education at +1-202-606 8200 or by visiting the NEH Web Site at http://www.neh.fed.us

919 Robert S. McNamara Fellowships Program
Room M-4010
World Bank Headquarters
1818 H Street NW
Washington DC 20433
+1-202-458 7021
Fax: +1-202-676 0962
Found: 1982
Obj: The Robert S. McNamara Fellowships Program was established in 1982 to honour the former President of the World Bank. Every year since then, the Program has awarded approximately ten Fellowships to support innovative and imaginative post-graduate research in areas of economic development. This Program does *not* provide financial support for an advanced degree (this includes field work for a PhD).

Fellowships are open to applicants who are nationals of, or residents in, countries which are currently eligible to borrow from the World Bank. The research must be carried out in the applicant's own country, or country of residence at the time of applying.
Chair: Vinod Thomas (Dir)
Exec Off: Shobha Kumar (Administrator)
Prog Off: Ok Pannenborg (Div Chief, Western Africa Dept)
Act in A/AS: as above
G/Aw: *Length of fellowship*: fellowships are awarded for a period of 12 months, and must be commenced within six months of the award being made. They cannot be extended or renewed.

Amount of award: the amount of the award is $7,500. This is a standard amount, intended to cover research costs only, and is not negotiable. No other costs will be considered.
Research topics: proposals for the 1997 cycle should be one of the following topics: 1. Role of NGOs in development, or 2. Land reform.
No other topics will be considered.
Output: fellows are required to produce a report at the end of the Fellowship period, and include a 1,500 word abstract.
Applic proc: all applications must be submitted with the required documentation on the correct application forms. Forms for the 1997 cycle are available from all World Bank Resident Missions and from the McNamara Fellowships Program office at World Bank Headquarters in Washington, DC. All requests for application forms should quote our reference: RSM/97/1. For details about application procedures for 1998 or 1999 fellowship contact the Program.
Publ: information sheet available on request.

920 Rockefeller Foundation, The
420 Fifth Avenue
New York NY 10018-2702
+1-212-869 8500 ext.301
Fax: +1-212-764 3468/398 1858
Found: 1913
Obj: a philanthropic organization endowed by John D. Rockefeller and chartered in 1913 for the well-being of people throughout the world. It is one of America's oldest private foundations and one of the few with strong international interests. Whilst concentrating its efforts on specific programmes with well-defined goals, the Foundation adjusts its course to reflect needs as they arise. Its work lies in three principal areas: the arts and humanities, equal opportunity and school reform; international science-based development encompassing agricultural, health, population sciences, and global

environment; and several special African initiatives, including female education.

The balance of the Foundation's grant and fellowship programmes supports work in international security, international philanthropy, and other special interests and initiatives. The Foundation maintains the Bellagio Study and Conference Center in northern Italy for conferences of international scope and for residencies for artists, scholars and policy-makers, and other professionals from around the world.
Fin: private foundation
Pres: Peter C. Goldmark jr, Alice Stone Ilchman (Chair)
Exec Off: Robert W. Herdt (Ag VP) Angela G. Blackwell (VP) Lynda Mullen (Corp Sec)
Prog Off African Initiatives: Joyce L. Moock (Ass VP) David Court (Found Rep - Kenya) Micky Shepherd (Dir, Arts & Humanities) Clifford Chanin (Ass Dir, Arts & Humanities) Janet G. Marcantonio (African Dissertation Coordinator) Heather A. Bent Tamir (Sen Prog Ass)
Act in AS: in 1995; a sum of $5,814,980 was allocated for African initiatives, covering grants, appropriations and fellowships. Under the auspices of the multi-donor Association for the Development of African Education (DAE), the African Initiatives Strategy leads a working group on female education whose objective is to close the gender gap in enrolment and performance, especially at primary and secondary school levels. Through the African Academy of Sciences, nine DAE agencies support Africa's first competitive region-wide research-grants programme designed to document gender disparities in education and identify effective interventions. Forty-three major projects are now under way, and 55 researchers have received assistance to develop concept papers into full proposals.

The Foundation also supports the Forum for African Women Educationalists (FAWE), an international NGO based in Nairobi which seeks to eliminate gender bias in African education, and to that end mobilizes local and international resource to improve the quality of education on the continent. The Foundation buttresses its core programme on female education with the work of the African Forum for Children's Literacy in Science and Technology, which supports innovative programmes both in and out of school that build on popular culture in the teaching of science.

At the higher end of the education spectrum, the Foundation supports the African Economic Research Consortium (AERC), which offers economists research and training opportunities that universities in Africa are currently unable to offer. African Initiatives also supports the African Science-Based Development Professional Preparation Program. Its objective is to enhance the home-based relevance, quality and utilization of doctoral training for African students enrolled in North American universities, particularly in science and technology.

The Foundation also provides social science research fellowships in agriculture which are designed to expand the number of social scientists who have interdisciplinary research experience in international development. It is open to persons who hold a doctoral-level degree in a social science discipline and who are citizens of the United States, Canada, or a sub-Saharan African country. Fellows are placed at international agricultural research institutes based in developing countries. Appointments are for two years and carry a stipend approximately equivalent to the salary of a beginning assistant professor.
G/Aw: the Sub-Saharan Dissertation Internship Awards is a programme of competitive awards to enable African doctoral students enrolled in universities in the United States and Canada to undertake supervised dissertation research in Africa. The programme is open to

citizens of sub-Saharan African nations enrolled in doctoral programmes at universities in the United States and Canada. US permanent residents and Canadian landed immigrants are not eligible. Priority will be given to research on economic development in the areas of agriculture, environment, education, health, the humanities, life sciences, and population studies. Awards are intended to cover the costs of conducting research in the field and might include: international travel, living expenses in Africa, local transportation costs related to research, and analysis. The maximum award is US$20,000.

Applic proc: deadlines for applications for the African Internship Awards are October 1 and March 1 each year. Candidates are strongly urged to submit their applications well in advance of the date on which field work is expected to begin. Preliminary inquiries as to the relevance of the research topic and the proposed institutional setting in Africa are encouraged. The selection committee will consider only complete applications which must be prepared according to *Instructions for Preparing the Application Package* provided by the Foundation.

Grants (general): among the factors considered in evaluating grant proposals are the project's relevance to Foundation programmes and strategies, the applicant's qualifications, record of achievement, and ability to secure additional funding from other sources.

Fellowships: are awarded to individuals for training or to help further their research (More details about the applications procedure, etc. available from the Foundation).

Bellagio Study and Conference Center: residents, conferees and teams work at the Center in an international setting. The three types of opportunities at Bellagio - independent, individual residencies (one-month); team residencies, and week-long international conferences - enable the Foundation to explore a variety of topics. Special application forms are available from the Foundation.

921 Social Science Research Council (SSRC)
810 Seventh Avenue
New York NY 10019
+1-212-377 2700
Fax: +1-212-377 2700
Website: http://www.ssrc.org
Found: 1923
Obj: the SSRC is an autonomous, non-governmental, non-profit organization composed of social scientists from all over the world. The Council's primary purpose is to advance the quality, value and effectiveness of social science research. It seeks to encourage scholars in separate disciplines - e.g. anthropologists, economists, historians, political scientists, psychologists, sociologists, statisticians, and others - to work together on important topical, conceptual, and methodological issues that can benefit from interdisciplinary collaboration. Natural scientists, geographers, linguists, and scholars in the humanities also participate in many of the Council's activities. The Council's work is carried out through a wide variety of workshops and conferences, fellowships and grants, summer training institutes, research consortia, scholarly exchanges, and publications.
Fin: Ford Foundation (*see* **916**), Mellon Foundation, MacArthur Foundation, United States Information Agency, National Endowment for the Humanities, and others.
Chair: Paul Baltes
Exec Off: Kenneth Prewitt (Pres)
Prog Off: Ron Kassimir (Prog Dir)
Act in A/AS: sponsors workshops, conferences, and research development activities. Supports training and capacity-building initiatives for the social sciences on, and in, Africa.

G/Aw: International Doctoral Research Fellowships; post-doctoral research. Applic proc: competitions are cross-regional, with Africanists eligible to apply. Fellowships restricted to graduate students and advanced scholars based at US institutions. Publ: sponsors volumes based on conference/workshop papers. Sponsors a series entitled 'New directions in African studies' and works published in *African Studies Review (see* **290**) and *Cahiers d'études africaines (see* **193***)*.

922 **Wenner-Gren Foundation for Anthropological Research, Inc**
220 Fifth Avenue
New York NY 10001-7708
+1-212-683 5000
Fax: +1-212-683 9151
Found: 1941
Obj: non-profit making, privately operated foundation. Its sphere of interest is the support of research in all branches of anthropology, ethnology, biological/physical anthropology, archaeology, and anthropological linguistics, and in closely related disciplines concerned with human origins, development, and variation.
Fin: endowed in 1941 as the Viking Fund, Inc, by Axel Leonard Wenner-Gren.
Chair: Hiram F. Moody jr
Pres: Sydel Silverman
Act in AS: Developing Countries Training Fellowships are intended for scholars and advanced students from developing countries seeking additional training in anthropology, to enhance their skills or to expand or develop their areas of expertise. Candidates may pursue either a course of study leading to a doctoral degree or a specific postdoctoral non-degree plan for obtaining advanced training, in any qualified institution in the world where appropriate training is available. Awards are made for amounts up to $12,500 per year, for periods from six months to three years.

G/Aw: Small Grants: for amounts up to $15,000 are available for research in all branches of anthropology.
Regular Grants: awarded to individual scholars holding a doctorate or equivalent qualification in anthropology or a related discipline. Predoctoral Grants: awarded to individuals to aid doctoral dissertation or thesis research. applicants must be enrolled for a doctoral degree. A limited number of Richard Carley Hunt Memorial Postdoctoral Fellowships nonrenewable awards with a maximum of $10,000 is available to scholars within five years of the receipt of the doctorate, to aid the write-up of research results for publication. Developing Countries Training Fellowships: historical archives; the objective of this programme is to encourage the preservation of unpublished records and other materials of value for research on the history of anthropology. small grants (max. $15,000) are offered. International Collaborative Research Grants: for amounts up to $25,000 available to assist anthropological research projects undertaken jointly by two (or more) investigators from different countries.
Applic proc: application and budgetary guidelines can be obtained from the Foundation.
Publ: 'Biennial reports'; *Current Anthropology* (Foundation sponsored journal)

923 **World Education**
44 Farnsworth Street
Boston MA 02210-1211
+1-617-482 9495
Fax: +1-617-482 0617
Email: wei@worlded.org or swinter@jsi
Website: http://www/worlded.org
Found: 1951
Obj: a private, non-profit organization, dedicated to improving the lives of the poor through economic and social development programmes. Training and technical assistance in non-formal

education for adults, with special emphasis on community development, small enterprise promotion, food production, literacy and health education. Works in partnership with indigenous organizations, both NGOs and government institutions.

Fin: foundation grants, private contributions, USAID, Department of State

Chair: Jane Covey

Exec Off: Joel Lamstein (Pres)

Prog Off: Jill Harmsworth (Sen Off for Africa)

Act in A: Rural Enterprise Program in Kenya; training in Income Generation for Rural Women's Groups, in partnership with Tototo Home Industries of Mombasa, Kenya; support for non-governmental organizations in Mali and Senegal.

G/Aw: *Not* a grant-making body. Does *not* provide funds to individuals and organizations. Supports training in small enterprise promotion for women's groups with the Home Economics Officers of the Ministry of Agriculture and Cooperatives in Swaziland; training in the production of participatory learning materials with the Association for the Renaissance of Pulaar in Senegal; training for village workers in rural Mali; training in organizational planning and project planning for NGO members of the CCA-ONG in Mali; training and institutional support for OMAES - a Malian NGO. Also supports: strengthening parent organizations in Benin; micro-enterprise and urban revitalization in Mali; READ project in Namibia; training for women in South Africa.

Applic proc: World Education works in partnership with indigenous institutions that request a collaborative relationship, and seeks funding to do this from other sources.

Publ: *World Education Reports*, magazine for development workers; *Focus on Basics*, magazine for adult educator in the US, *Tested Participatory Activities for Trainers*, *A Study of the Structure of Opportunity on the Kenya Coast* (Women's Group Enterprises); *Jumudi/Credit Officer Training Manual* (with KREP); *Faidika/Business Training for Women's Groups* (with Tototo Home Industries)

Reg off: World Education/Namibia, Erf 7018, Khomasdal, Windhoek; World Education/Mali, BP 2137, Bamako; World Education/Senegal, BP 5270, Dakar-Fann; World Education/Benin, BP 811, Parakou; World Education/South Africa, Mansion House 8th Floor, 132 Market Street, Johannesburg.

X. AWARDS AND PRIZES

This section provides details of annual or biennial international awards, and book and literary prizes in the African studies field (and also covering some Commonwealth prizes). 'Closed' prizes, awarded to nationals of a particular country, are not included; neither are prizes linked to particular universities which are only open to students or faculty of these institutions.

Information given includes full name and contact address, details about the founder/sponsors of the award and year founded/first awarded, the aims and objectives of each award, amount of prize/award money, conditions of entry and closing date for submitting entries/nominations, and details of past (or recent) winners of these awards.

Abbreviations and symbols used:

†   - repeat entry from 1st ed. (1989); information not verified; entry updated, as far as possible, from secondary sources

Φ   - provisional new entry, but questionnaire has not been completed; unverified information drawn from secondary sources

Admin by - administration of the Award
Cl date   - closing date [for submissions]
Cond   - conditions [of entry/competition]
Found   - year founded
Obj   - objectives [of prize/award]

*Note: re book prizes sponsored by the African Studies Association, entries 924, 928, 929, and 932: please note that the ASA will be relocating to Rutgers University, New Brunswick, NJ late in 1997.

924   **African Studies Association Children's Book Award**
African Studies Association*
Emory University
Credit Union Building
Atlanta, GA 30322
USA

+1-404-329 6410
Fax: +1-404-3296 6433
Email: africa@emory.edu
Website: http://www.sas.upenn.edu/African_Studies/Home_Page/ASA_Menu.html
Admin by: African Studies Association
Found: 1994[?]

Sponsors: ASA Outreach Council
Contact: Chris Koch, Emory University, Atlanta GA 30322 or Brenda Randolph, Africa Access, 2204 Quinton Road, Silver Spring MD 20910
Obj: offered annually to the author (and illustrator, if any) of the best children's book on Africa published in the previous year. The award is designed to highlight the importance of the production of high-quality children's materials about Africa.
Cond: open to all persons and institutions interested in African affairs, with nominations made by directly by the publisher.
Cl date: end of August
Past winners:
1993: David Wisniewski *Sundiata the Lion King* (Clarion Books)
1994: no award made
1995: younger readers: Jane Cowen-Fletcher *It Takes a Village* (Scholastic Inc.); older readers: Joyce Hansen *The Captive* (Scholastic Inc.)
1996: younger readers: Doreen Rappaport *The New King* (Dial Books); older readers: Tom Feelings *The Middle Passage* (Dial Books)

925 African Young Writers Annual Award

African Young Writers Annual Award
34-36 Crown Street
Reading RG1 2SE
UK
+44(0)118-939 1010
Fax: +44(0)118-959 4442
Email: 01743,301@compuserve.com
Admin by: International Institute for African Research
Found: 1996 1st prize: essay published in *African People's Review* plus £100; 2nd prize: essay published in *African People's Review* plus £75; 3rd prize: essay published in *African People's Review* plus £50

Sponsors: International Institute for African Research
Contact: Beverley Joseph
Obj: to encourage young people to contribute through their ideas, to the development of their societies.
Cond: any youth of African descent resident anywhere in the world aged 15-18 can apply directly to the Institute. Additionally, schools are invited to put forward candidates.
Cl date: 31 March annually

926 All-Africa Okigbo Prize for Poetry†

Guardian Newspapers Ltd.
PMB 1217 Oshodi
Lagos
Nigeria
+234-1-524080/524111
Admin by: Association of Nigerian Authors
Found: 1987 US$1,500
Sponsor: Wole Soyinka
Obj: endowed by Wole Soyinka and in honour of Christopher Okigbo, the Nigerian poet who died fighting on the Biafran side during the Nigerian civil war. Aims to give recognition to the best African poetry, and to encourage a continent-wide poetic sensibility.
Cond: open to African authors for a book published in any language spoken in Africa. Published works only are eligible for entry, and may be submitted by individual poets or their publishers.
Cl date: 31 July each year

927 Commonwealth Writers Prize

Commonwealth Writers Prize
Administrator
Book Trust, Book House
45 East Hill
London SW18 2QZ
UK
+44(0)181-870 9055
Fax: +44(0)181-874 4790

Admin by: Book Trust
Found: 1987 £21,000; £10,000 for best book; £3,000 for best first published book; eight £1,000 prizes, one for best book and one for best first published book in each Commonwealth region
Sponsors: Commonwealth Foundation in association with the Royal Overseas League and the Book Trust
Contact: African region chair: Francis D. Imbuga, Literature Dept, Kenyatta University, POB 43844, Nairobi, Kenya
Obj: annual prize for the best novel, full-length play, collection of short stories or one-act plays by a Commonwealth citizen. In addition to the first prize there are runner-up prizes and four regional prizes for Africa; the Caribbean and Canada; South East Asia and the South Pacific; and Eurasia. Preliminary heats take place in these four regional centres.
Cond: works must be written in English and must have been published before each year's closing date.
Cl date: 31 December each year
Past winners: complete list available from the Administrators of the Prize.

928 Conover-Porter Award

c/o African Studies Association*
Credit Union Building
Emory University
Atlanta GA 30322
USA
+1-404-329 6410 Fax: +1-404-329 6433
Email: africa@emory.edu
Admin by: ASA Africana Librarians Council
Found: 1980 US$300
Sponsors: African Studies Association
Contact: changes annually
Obj: presented biennially to the author of the most outstanding achievement in Africana bibliography and reference works, published during the previous two years. The Award is named after two pioneers in the field of African studies

librarianship and bibliography, Helen F. Conover and Dorothy B. Porter.
Cond: open to any Africa-related reference work, bibliography or bibliographic essay published separately or as part of a larger work. Books may be nominated by individuals or by publishers.
Cl date: 31 December in alternate years
Past winners: 1980: Julian Witherell *The United States and Africa: Guide to US Official Documents and Government-Sponsored Publications on Africa, 1785-1975* (Library of Congress)
1982: Roger Hilbert and Christian Oehlmann *Foreign Direct Investments and Multinational Corporations in Sub-Saharan Africa: A Bibliography* (Campus Verlag)
1984: Hans M. Zell, Caroline Bundy, and Virginia Coulon *A New Reader's Guide to African Literature* (Heinemann/Africana Publishing Corp)
1986: Tore Linne Eriksen *The Political Economy of Namibia: An Annotated Critical Bibliography* (Scandinavian Institute of African Studies)
1988: Jean E. Meeh Gosebrink *African Studies Information Resources Directory* (Hans Zell Publishers) and Daniel P. Biebuyck *The Arts of Central Africa: An Annotated Bibliography* (G.K. Hall)
1990: Yvette Scheven *Bibliographies for African Studies, 1970-1986* (Hans Zell Publishers)
1992: Carol Sicherman *Ngugi wa Thiong'o: The Making of a Rebel:A Source Book in Kenyan Literature and Resistance*; and Carol Sicherman *Ngugi wa Thiong'o: A Bibliography of Primary and Secondary Sources, 1957-1987* (both Hans Zell Publishers)
1994: Thomas George Barton *Sexuality and Health in Sub-Saharan Africa: An Annotated Bibliography* (AMREF); and Hans M. Zell, editor *African Books in Print* (Hans Zell Publishers)
1996: Bernth Lindfors *Black African Literature in English, 1987-1991* (Hans Zell Publishers); and Nancy J. Schmidt

Sub-Saharan African Films and Filmmakers, 1987-1992: An Annotated bibliography (Hans Zell Publishers)

929 **Distinguished Africanist Award**
African Studies Association*
Emory University
Credit Union Building
Atlanta GA 30322
USA
+1-404-329 6410 Fax: +1-404-329 6433
Email: africa@emory.edu
Website:http://www.sas.upenn.edu/African
_Studies/Home_Page/ASA_Menu.html
Admin by: African Studies Association
Found: 1984 Not a cash award; award
consists of a Certificate of Lifetime
Membership of the African Studies
Association
Sponsors: African Studies Association
Admin: Chris Koch, Executive Director
Obj: offered in recognition of a lifetime's
distinguished contribution to African
studies. Criteria for the Award are the
distinction of, or contribution to,
Africanist scholarship, as measured by a
lifetime of accomplishment and service in
the field of African studies.
Cond: any member of the ASA is eligible
to propose a candidate. The nomination
must include a curriculum vitae of the
nominee, a detailed letter of nomination
justifying the candidature in terms of the
criteria of the Award, and three similar
letters from ASA members seconding the
nomination. At least two of the latter must
be affiliated with institutions other than
that of the nominee. The complete dossier
of the candidate must be submitted to the
ASA secretariat.
Cl date: 15 March each year, for
consideration for the following year.
Past winners:
1984: Gwendolyn M. Carter
1985: Elliot Skinner
1986: Jan Vansina
1987: Joseph Greenberg
1988: Elizabeth Colson

1989: Roland Oliver
1990: M. Crawford Young
1992: Philip D. Curtin
1993: J. Ade Ajayi
1995: Ali A. Mazrui
1996: not awarded

930 **Edgar Graham Book Prize †**
Thornhaugh Street
Russell Square
London WC1H 0XG
UK
+44(0)171-637 2388
Fax: +44(0)171-323 6605
Admin by: Centre for Development
Studies, School of Oriental and African
Studies
Found: 1986 £1,500
Sponsor: SOAS
Contact: The Administrator
Obj: awarded every 2 years for a published
work of original scholarship on
agricultural and/or industrial development
in Asia and/or Africa.
Cond: Works must have been published
during the preceding 2 years.
Cl date: 31 December in alternate years
Past winners:
1988: Paul Collier, Samir Radwan and
Samuel Wangwe *Labour and Poverty in
Rural Tanzania: Ujamaa and Rural
Development in the United Republic of
Tanzania* (Oxford University Press)

931 **Grand Prix Littéraire de
l'Afrique Noire**
14 rue Broussais
75014 Paris
France
+33-1-43 21 95 99
Fax: +33-1-43 20 12 22
Admin: Association des écrivains de
langue française (ADELF)
Found: 1961 FF2,000
Contact: L'Administrateur
Obj: awarded annually for a work by an
African author making an original
contribution in the French language. All

literary forms are eligible: novels, short
stories, tales, history, biography, poetry,
etc.
Cond: works published in the year of the
Award, and the preceding year, are
eligible. 8 copies of each title submitted
must be forwarded to the Award's
administrators.
Cl date: 15 June each year
Past winners:
1984: Modibo Sounkalo Keita *L'Archer
bassari* (Editions Karthala)
1985: Jean-Pierre Makouta Mboukou
*Introduction à l'étude du roman négro-
africain de langue française* and *Les
Grands traits de la poésie négro-africaine*
(Nouvelles Editions Africaines)
1986: Bola Beanga *Cannibale* (Ed P.M.
Favre); and Thierno Monemembo *Les
Ecailles du ciel* (Editions du Seuil)
1987: Jean-Baptiste Tati-Loutard *Le Récit
de la mort* (Présence Africaine)
1988: Emmanuel Dongala *Le Feu des
origines* (Albin Michel)
1989: Victor Bouadjio *Demain est encore
loin* (Balland)
1990: Ahmadou Kourouma Monnè
Outrages et défis (Seuil)
1991: awarded posthumously to Amadou-
Hampâté Bâ *Amkoullel, l 'enfant peul*
(Actes-Sud) for his life's work; and Kama
Kamanda *La Nuit des griots* (Antoine
Degrive/ Ed. l'Harmattan)
1992: Patrick G. Ilboudo *Le Héraut têtu*
(Ed. INC à Ouagadougou)
1993: Maurice Bandaman *Le Fils de la
femme mâle* (Ed. L'Harmattan)
1994: Calixthe Belaya *Maman à un
amant* (Ed. Albin Michel)
1995: awarded posthumously to Sylvain
Ntari-Bemba for his life's work
1996: Abdourahman Waberi *Cahier
nomade* (Ed. Le Serpent à plumes) and, as
a special award for his life's work, Léopold
Sédar Sengor

932 Melville J. Herskovits Award
African Studies Association*
Emory University
Credit Union Building
Atlanta GA 30322
USA
+1-404-329 6410 Fax: +1-404-329 6433
Email: africa@emory.edu
Website:
http://www.sas.upenn.edu/African_Studies
/Home_Page/ASA_Menu.html
Admin by: African Studies Association
Found: 1965 US$500
Sponsors: African Studies Association
Contact: Chris Koch, Executive Director
Obj: offered annually to the author of the
outstanding scholarly work published on
Africa during the previous year. The
Award is named in honour of Melville J.
Herskovits, one of the original founders of
the ASA (*see* **851**) and the man who is
considered to be the father of modern
African studies.
Cond: nominations must be original non-
fiction scholarly works published in
English and distributed in the United
States. The subject matter must deal with
Africa and/or related areas. Edited
collections and compilations,
bibliographies and dictionaries are not
eligible. Books may be nominated by
publishers; 4 copies of each title
nominated must be sent to members of the
Award Committee.
Cl date: usually 1 May each year
Past winners:
1965: Ruth Schachter Morgenthau
*Political Parties in French-speaking West
Africa* (Oxford University Press)
1966: Leo Kuper *An African Bourgeoisie*
(Yale University Press)
1967: Jan Vansina *Kingdoms of the
Savanna* (University of Wisconsin Press)
1968: Herbert Weiss *Political Protest in
the Congo* (Princeton University Press)
1969: Paul and Laura Bohannan *Tiv
Economy* (Northwestern University Press)

1970: Stanlake Samkange *Origins of Rhodesia* (Praeger Publishers)
1971: René Lemarchand *Rwanda and Burundi* (Praeger Publishers)
1972: Francis Deng *Tradition and Modernization* (Yale University Press)
1973: Allen F. Isaacman *Mozambique - the Africanization of a European Institution: the Zambezi Prazos, 1750-1902* (University of Wisconsin Press)
1974: John N. Paden *Religion and Political Culture in Kano* (University of California Press)
1975: Lansine Kaba *Wahhabiyya: Islamic Reform and Politics in French West Africa* (Northwestern University Press)
1976: Ivor Wilks *Asante in the Nineteenth Century* (Cambridge University Press)
1977: M. Crawford Young *The Politics of Cultural Pluralism* (University of Wisconsin Press)
1978: William Y. Adams *Nubia: Corridor to Africa* (Princeton University Press)
1979: Hoyt Alverson *Mind in the Heart of Darkness: Value and Self-Identity Among the Tswana of Southern Africa* (Yale University Press)
1980: Richard B. Lee *The !Kung San* (Cambridge University Press)
1981: Gavin Kitching *Class and Economic Change in Kenya: The Making of an African Petite Bourgeoisie, 1905-1970* (Yale University Press)
1982: Frederick Cooper *From Slaves to Squatters: Plantation Labor and Agriculture in Zanzibar and Coastal Kenya, 1890-1925* (Yale University Press); and Sylvia Scribner and Michael Cole *The Psychology of Literacy* (Harvard University Press)
1983: James W. Fernandez *Bwitti: An Ethnography of the Religious Imagination in Africa* (Princeton University Press)
1984: Paulin Hontoundji *African Philosophy* (Indiana University Press); and J.D.Y. Peel *Ijeshas and Nigerians: the Incorporation of a Yoruba Kingdom* (Cambridge University Press)

1985: Claire Robertson *Sharing the Same Bowl* (Indiana University Press)
1986: Sara Berry *Fathers Work for their Sons: Accumulation, Mobility, and Class Formation in an Extended Yoruba Community* (University of California Press)
1987: Paul M. Lubeck *Islam and Urban Labor in Northern Nigeria: The Making of a Muslim Working Class* (Cambridge University Press) and T.O. Beidelman *Moral Imagination in Kaguru Modes of Thought*
1988: John Iliffe *The African Poor: A History* (Cambridge University Press)
1989: Joseph C. Miller *Way of Death: Merchant Capitalism and the Angolan Slave Trade, 1730-1830* (University of Wisconsin Press); and V.S. Mudimbe *The Invention of Africa: Gnosis, Philosophy and the Order of Knowledge* (Indiana University Press)
1990: Edwin Wilmsen *Land Filled with Flies: A Political Economy of the Kalahari* (University of Chicago Press)
1991: Johannes Fabian *Power and Performance: Ethnographic Exploration through Proverbial Wisdom and Theater in Sahba, Zaire* (University of Wisconsin Press); and Luise White *The Comforts of Home: Prostitution in Colonial Nairobi* (University of Chicago Press)
1992: Myron Echenberg *Colonial Conscripts: The Tirailleurs Sénégalais in French West Africa* (Heinemann Educational Books)
1993: Kwame Anthony Appiah *In My Father's House: Africa in the Philosophy of Culture* (Oxford University Press)
1994: Keleso Atkins *The Moon is Dead! Give Us Our Money! The Cultural Origins of an African Work Ethic, Natal, South Africa, 1843-1900* (Heinemann)
1995: Henrietta L. Moore and Megan Vaughn *Cutting Down Trees: Gender, Nutrition, and Agricultural Change in the Northern Province of Zambia, 1890-1990* (Heinemann/James Currey/University of Zambia Press)

1996: Jonathon Glassman *Feasts and Riot: Revelry, Rebellions and Popular Consciousness on the Swahili Coast, 1856-1888* (Heinemann/James Currey)

933 Noma Award for Publishing in Africa, The
POB 128
Witney OX8 5XU
UK
+44(0)1993-775235
Fax: +44(0)1993-709265
Found: 1979 US$10,000
Sponsor: Shoichi Noma (deceased)
Contact: Mary Jay, Administrator
Obj: this annual book prize is available to African writers and scholars whose work is published in Africa. It is one of the aims of the Award to encourage the publication of works by African writers and scholars in Africa, instead of abroad as is too often the case at present. The Award is given for an outstanding new book in any of three categories: scholarly or academic, children's books, creative writing.
Cond: open to any author who is indigenous to Africa, but entries must be submitted through publishers. Each work must have been published by a publisher domiciled on the African continent or its offshore islands. Only published works qualify. Any work written in any indigenous or official languages of Africa is eligible. Three copies must be submitted to the Award's administrators.
Cl date: 31 March each year
Past winners:
1980: Mariama Bâ *Une si longue lettre* (Nouvelles Editions Africaines)
1981: Felix C. Adi *Health Education for the Community* (Nwamife Publishers)
1982: Meshack Asare *The Brassman's Secret* (Educational Press & Manufacturers Ltd)
1983: A.N.E. Amissah *Criminal Procedure in Ghana* (Sedco Publishing Ltd)

1984: Gakaara wa Wanjau *Mwandiki wa Mau Mau ithaamirio-ini* (Heinemann Educational Books East Africa Ltd); and Njabulo Simakhale Ndebele *Fools and Other Stories* (Ravan Press)
1985: Bernard Nanga *La Trahison de Marianne* (Nouvelles Editions Africaines)
1986: Antònio Jacinto *Sobreviver em Tarrafal de Santiago* (Instituto Nacional do Livro e do Disco)
1987: Pierre Kipré *Villes de Côte d'Ivoire, 1893-1940* (Nouvelles Editions Africaines)
1988: Luli Callinicos *Working Life. Factories, Townships, and Popular Culture on the Rand, 1886-1940* (Ravan Press)
1989: Chenjerai Hove *Bones. A Novel* (Baobab Books)
1990: Francis Wilson & Mamphela Ramphele *Uprooting Poverty: The South African Challenge* (David Philip)
1991: Niyi Osundare *Waiting Laughters. A Long Song in Many Voices* (Malthouse Press)
1992: Souad Khodja *A comme Algériennes* (Entreprise Nationale du Livre); and Charles Mungoshi *One Day, Long Ago. More Stories from a Shona Childhood* (Baobab Books)
1993: Mongane Wally Serote *Third World Express* (David Philip)
1994: Paul Tiyambe Zeleza *A Modern Economic History of Africa. Volume 1: The Nineteenth Century* (CODESRIA)
1995: Marlene van Niekerk *Triomf* (Queillerie Publishers)
1996: Kitia Touré *Destins parallèles* (Nouvelles Editions Ivoiriennes)
Note: a complete listing of titles which have been singled out for 'Honourable Mention' or 'Special Commendation' is available from the Noma Award Secretariat.

934 **Amaury Talbot Prize for African Anthropology, The**
c/o Barclays Bank Trust Company Ltd
POB 15 Osborne Court
Gadbrook Park
Rudheath
Northwich CW9 7UR
UK
+44(0)1606-313194
Fax: +44(0)1606-313005/6
Admin by: Barclays Bank Trust Company Limited, Executorship & Trustee Service
Found: 1960, approx. £500
Sponsor: Mrs M.W.F. Talbot (deceased)
Contact: (Ms) K.A. Yearsley
Obj: awarded to the author/s of the most valuable work of African anthropology submitted. Only works published during the preceding calendar year are eligible. Works relating to any region of Africa are accepted, however preference will be accorded first to Nigeria, then to other parts of West Africa. The academic administration of the prize is undertaken by the Royal Anthropological Institute on behalf of the trustees, Barclays Bank Trust Company Ltd.
Cond: 2 copies of each entry to: Amaury Talbot Prize Coordinator, Royal Anthropological Institute, 50 Fitzroy Street, London W1P 5HS. Entries are not returned to candidates.
Cl date: 31 January
Past winners:
1988: Marc R Scholl *The Hatchet's Blood*
1989: Michael Jackson *Path Towards a Clearing. Radical Empiricism and Ethnographic Enquiry*
1991: Karin Barber *I Could Speak Until Tomorrow: Oriki Women and the Past in Yoruba Towns* and Richard Werbner *Peers of Death*
1992: Robert Launay *Beyond the Stream*
1993: Christopher B Stiner *African Art in Transit*
1994: Geoffrey A Fadiman *When We Began they Were Witchmen: An Oral History from Mount Kenya* and Douglas H Johnson *Nuer Prophets*
1995: Liisa Malkki *Purity and Exile*

935 **Trevor Reese Memorial Prize†**
University of London
27-28 Russell Square
London WC1B 5DS
UK
+44(0)171-580 5876
Admin by: Institute of Commonwealth Studies
Found: 1987 £500
Obj: awarded every 2 years for an outstanding work of scholarship in the field of imperial and Commonwealth history in the preceding two years. Given in honour of Trevor Reese, formerly Reader in Commonwealth Studies at the Institute of Commonwealth Studies and scholar of imperial history, who died in 1976.
Cond:3 Works must have been published in the preceding two years.
Cl date: 31 December in alternate years
Past winners:
1988: James Belich *The New Zealand Wards and the Victorian Interpretation of Racial Conflict* (Auckland University Press)

XI. ABBREVIATIONS AND ACRONYMS IN AFRICAN STUDIES

The abbreviations and acronyms listed below include all the organizations listed in the book, plus those of a number of other bodies. Also included are a number of acronyms commonly used in African studies. Acronyms for on-line databases and electronic information services are excluded.

For a more complete listing consult David Hall's *African Acronyms and Abbreviations: A Handbook (see **148**).

AAAS	American Association for the Advancement of Science
AACC	All Africa Conference of Churches
AALAE	African Association for Literacy and Adult Education
AAPAM	African Association for Public Administration and Management
AAPSO	Afro-Asian Peoples Solidarity Organization
AAU	Association of African Universities
AAWORD	Association of African Women for Research and Development
ABC	African Books Collective Ltd.
ABIP	*African Books in Print*
ABPR	*The African Book Publishing Record*
ACARTSOD	African Centre for Applied Research and Training in Development
ACCE	African Council for Communication Education
ACCT	Agence de coopération culturelle et technique
ACP	African, Caribbean and Pacific Countries/ European Union - The Lomé Convention
ADAF	Arbeitskreis der deutschen Afrika-Forschungs- und Dokumentationsstellen
ADB	African Development Bank
AEA	Asociacion Española de Africanistas
AERC	African Economic Research Consortium
AFESD	Arab Fund for Economic and Social Development
AFSAAP	African Studies Association of Australasia and the Pacific

AFSTI	African Network of Scientific and Technological Institutions
AID	Agency for International Development
AIEDP	African Institute for Economic Development and Planning
ALA	African Literature Association
ALC	Africana Librarians Council
AMREF	African Medical and Research Foundation
AMU	Arab Maghreb Union
APNET	African Publishers' Network
ARD	*African Research and Documentation*
ASA	African Studies Association (US)
ASAUK	African Studies Association of the United Kingdom
ASICL	African Society of International and Comparative Law
ATRCW	African Training and Research Centre for Women
AUPELF	Association des universités partiellement ou entièrement de langue française
AWF	African Wildlife Foundation
BAB	Basler Afrika Bibliographien
BADEA	Banque Arabe pour le développement économique en Afrique
BCEAO	Banque centrale des états de l'Afrique de l'Ouest
BLDS	British Library for Development Studies (University of Sussex)
BREDA	Bureau régional de l'UNESCO pour l'éducation en Afrique
CAFRAD	Centre africain de formation et de recherches administratives pour le développement
CAMP	Cooperative Africana Microform Project
CBAA	*Current Bibliography on African Affairs*
CEEA	Conseil européen des études africaines
CFA	Communauté financière africaine
CICIBA	Centre international des civilisations bantu
CIDA	Canadian International Development Agency
CMEA	Council for Mutual Economic Assistance
CODE	Canadian Organization for Development through Education

CODESRIA	Conseil pour le développement de la recherche économique et sociale en Afrique/ Council for the Development of Social Science Research in Africa
CRDI	Centre de recherches pour le développement international
CTA	Centre technique de coopération agricole et rurale
DANIDA	Danish International Development Assistance
DSE	Deutsche Stiftung für Internationale Entwicklung
EAC	East African Community
EC	European Community
ECA	Economic Commission for Africa
ECAS	European Council on African Studies
ECOWAS	Economic Community of West African States
EDF	European Development Fund
EIU	Economist Intelligence Unit
EU	European Union
FAO	Food and Agriculture Organization of the United Nations
GATT	General Agreement on Tariffs and Trade
GDP	Gross Domestic Product
GNP	Gross National Product
HABITAT	United Nations Centre for Human Settlements
HIVOS	Humanist Institute for Cooperation with Developing Countries
IAB	*International African Bibliography*
IAI	International African Institute
IBRD	International Bank for Reconstruction and Development (World Bank)
ICA	Institut culturel africain
ICAS	International Congress of African Studies
ICIPE	International Centre for Insect Physiology and Ecology
ICRAF	International Council for Research in Agroforestry
ICS	Institute of Commonwealth Studies (University of London)

IDA	International Development Association (World Bank)
IDC	International Development Centre (University of Oxford)
IDEP	Institut africain pour le développement économique et de planification
IDRC	International Development Research Centre
IDS	Institute for Development Studies (University of Sussex)
IFAD	International Fund for Agricultural Development
IFAN	Institut fondamental de l'Afrique noire
IFS	International Foundation for Science
IIAR	International Institute for African Research
IIE	Institute of International Education
IITA	International Institute for Tropical Agriculture
ILO	International Labour Office
ILRAD	International Laboratory for Research on Animal Diseases
ILRI	International Livestock Research Institute
IMF	International Monetary Fund
INADES	Institut africain pour le développement économique et social
IRED	Innovations et réseaux pour le développement
ISAAS	Indian Society for Afro-Asian Studies
ISIC	International Standard Industrial Classification
JALA	Joint Acquisitions List of Africana
JASPA	Jobs and Skills Programme for Africa (ILO)
KIT	Koninklijk Instituut voor de Tropen
LC	Library of Congress
LDC	Less Developed Country
NEH	National Endowment for the Humanities
NIEO	New International Economic Order
NIIA	Nigerian Institute of International Affairs
NORAD	Norwegian Agency for Development Cooperation
NOVIP	Netherlands Organization for International Development Cooperation

NUFFIC	Netherlands Organization for International Cooperation in Higher Education
OAU	Organization of African Unity
OCAM	Organisation commune africaine et mauricienne
ODA	Overseas Development Administration
ODI	Overseas Development Institute
OECD	Organisation européen de coopération et développement économiques
OIC	Organization of the Islamic Conference
OPEC	Organisation of Petroleum Exporting Countries
ORSTOM	Office de la recherche scientifique et technique d'outre-mer
OXFAM	Oxford Committee for Famine Relief
PADIS	Pan African Documentation and Information System
PAID	Pan African Institute for Development
PANA	Pan African News Agency
PAWA	Pan African Writers Association
PRO	Public Record Office (UK)
PTA	Preferential Trade Area for East and Southern Africa
RSM	Robert S. McNamara Fellowship Program
ROSTA	Bureau régional de l'UNESCO pour la science et la technologie en Afrique
SADC	Southern African Development Community
SAG	Schweizerische Afrika-Gesellschaft
SAREC	Swedish Agency for Research Cooperation with Developing Countries (now part of SIDA)
SCOLMA	Standing Conference on Library Materials on Africa
SDA	Société des africanistes
SIDA	Swedish International Development Cooperation Agency
SOAS	School of Oriental and African Studies (University of London)
SSEA	Société Suisse d'études africaines
SSRC	Social Science Research Council
STIC	Standard International Trade Classification

TOOL	Technologie Overdracht Ontwikkelings Landen
UDEAC	Union douanière et économique de l'Afrique Centrale
UEMOA	Union économique et monétaire ouest-africaine
UN	United Nations
UNCTAD	United Nations Conference on Trade and Development
UNDP	United Nations Development Programme
UNEP	United Nations Environment Programme
UNESCO	United Nations Educational, Scientific and Cultural Organization
UNFPA	United Nations Population Fund
UNHCR	United Nations High Commissioner for Refugees
UNICEF	United Nations Children's Fund
UNIDO	United Nations Industrial Development Organization
UNSO	United Nations Sudano-Sahelian Office
USAID	United States Agency for International Development
VAD	Vereinigung von Afrikanisten in Deutschland
VIDC	Vienna Institute of Development
WACC	World Association for Christian Communication
WB	World Bank
WCC	World Council of Churches
WHO	World Health Organization
WIPO	World Intellectual Property Organization
WTO	World Trade Organization
ZIBF	Zimbabwe International Book Fair

INDEX

This index comprises authors/editors (personal and corporate) and titles of books (in section I), titles of journals and continuing sources, names of journal editors (but not book review editors), names of publishers, libraries/institutions, dealers and distributors, organizations, associations, foundations and donor agencies, and names of awards and prizes. Names of personnel (other than journal editors) are *not* indexed. Similarly not indexed are names of special collections in libraries, or references to publications issued by libraries and donor agencies, etc. unless they also appear as a main entry.

For this edition, and to provide additional means of access to the various listings, we have introduced a number of more general index entries which guide users to a *range* of entries and for which entry numbers appear in **bold**. As an extra feature we have also indexed the names of African publishers who are distributed in the UK or elsewhere although they may not have a main entry of their own and the index entry refers to the distributor. (Where they do have their own entry, *two* references appear in the index, one to the main entry and the other to the distributor.)

Unless otherwise indicated all references are to entry numbers. Book titles and journals appear in *italics*. A number of *see* cross-references direct attention to an alternative heading under which the required references will be found.